SOCIAL CAPITAL

SOCIAL CAPITAL

David Halpern

polity

First published in 2005 by Polity Press

Polity Press
65 Bridge Street
Cambridge CB2 1UR, UK.

Published in the United States and Canada by
Polity Press
350 Main Street
Malden, MA 02148, USA

ISBN: 0-7456-2547-9
ISBN: 0-7456-2548-7 (paperback)

A catalogue record for this book is available from the British Library and has been
applied for from the Library of Congress.

Typeset in 10 on 12 pt Palatino
by SNP Best-set Typesetter Ltd., Hong Kong
Printed and bound in Great Britain by MPG Books Ltd, Bodmin, Cornwall

For further information on Polity, visit our website: www.polity.co.uk

Contents

Preface

Fifteen years ago, as a young and naïve PhD student, I found myself trooping around some of Britain's most notorious housing estates, or projects, trying to establish whether there was a causal link between the physical environment and the residents' mental health. It wasn't a very fashionable subject, either academically or politically, and effects weren't expected to be large.

One of these studies involved looking at the mental health of residents before and after a series of physical improvements to their estate. The mental health of residents was pretty dire, with over half the adult women suffering from clinical anxiety or depression. One resident sticks in my mind, so anxious that it took many visits before she was prepared to open her door to be interviewed. She clearly hated living on the estate, and she spoke of how she would have nothing to do with her neighbours, who she felt sure would seek to steal her video if they saw it. Two years later, and she was a different woman. She was relaxed and happy, and now she spoke of her neighbours warmly as friends. There is nothing remarkable in her case, except that it was replicated across the entire street. Rates of depression and anxiety had more than halved, and the atmosphere of distrust had been replaced by one of friendly and supportive neighbouring relationships.[1]

It wasn't that the building works had gone particularly well either. The first two contractors had to be thrown off the job for gross incompetence, and a fire had caused major damage to one of the houses. But

the changes – including the shared complaints about the works themselves – had brought the residents together, and enabled them to
discover the benefits of the traditional community that fashionable
sociologists had long since condemned to the history books.

In the years that followed, even though I did not consider myself a
'social capital' researcher, such mysterious results kept appearing, like
reports of a living fossil. Work on ethnic minority mental health
revealed that, contrary to expectations, disadvantaged ethnic minority
group members often showed better mental health when clustered
together in deprived conditions than when living alone in affluent
neighbourhoods.[2] Work on the relative success of young professionals
showed the powerful impacts of having the right family contacts,
despite claims for the existence of the classless society.[3] Work on well-
being stubbornly refused to show strong associations between income
and happiness, but personal and community relationships had reliably
strong effects.[4] And a big cross-national academic inquiry into the rise
in youth crime and disorder since World War II – an inquiry that did
not look at the changing social fabric – failed to find an explanation.[5]

So here was the paradox. Traditional, locally embedded communities were seen as having declined dramatically, if not having van-
ished altogether. And, apart from a few die-hard conservatives, most
did not really mourn their passing – myself included. Going back to a
world of 'twitching curtains', as the commentator Matthew Parris once
put it in a debate we were in together, was not something that appealed
either to most academics or to policymakers. On the other hand, all the
evidence was gently hinting that there was something about the social
fabric that was very important even in a cosmopolitan, liberal modern
world. As most people seemed to know intuitively, with the possible
exception of Margaret Thatcher, there *was* such a thing as society; it
mattered greatly; and it amounted to much more than formal institutions. An all-party Commission on Citizenship in which I was heavily
involved as a graduate student got halfway there, but in 1990 there
were not the data, the conceptual framework or the political interest to
drive the issue forward.[6] Both politically and academically, it was not
the time.

And what's so important about bowling anyway . . . ?

I first met Bob Putnam in the summer of 1997, when I was at Harvard
on a visiting professorship. It is much more of a testament to his
patience than to my knowledge that we got to meet again. In my
defence, I was mainly focused on other issues at the time, such as how

the state should divide responsibility with the individual, the Third Way, and so on. And it would have been an insightful soul who made the connection from these issues to Italian regional governance or the TV-watching habits of Americans.[7]

I've since come to know Bob and his work rather better, and respect him greatly. We agree on quite a lot, but such is his prominence in this field that it may be useful to the reader if I draw out some of the points on which our views differ.

First, I am attracted to a somewhat broader definition of social capital than Bob. For me, the social capital concept extends well beyond the meso-level of traditional communities and personally known social networks into the generalized 'habits of life', or national and regional culture, that make it possible for people to get along. To say the unthinkable (to some social capitalists), I'd be pretty much as happy with the term 'social fabric' as with 'social capital'. Hence for me, the everyday habit of walking on the left in the London underground is a form of social capital, but for many social capitalists this would not be (see chapter 1 for a fuller discussion). Similarly, for me informal sanctions are an integral part of the story and concept – for reasons that I hope will become clear (see, for example, chapter 4) – while for Bob sanctions would lie outside the core concept.

Second, my perspective and interest are based on a more inter-national, or at least cross-national, perspective (see, for example, chapters 2, 4, 5 or 7). America is a pretty big and varied nation. Nonetheless, looking cross-nationally does give a different viewpoint. This differing viewpoint arises partly just because the world looks subtly different from this side of the Atlantic, but also because cross-national compar-isons give rise to methodological opportunities to test other kinds of contrast and variables. For example, the causal role of television looks very different from a cross-national perspective compared with from within the USA (see chapter 8).

Third, these differences in viewpoint and definition lead to some subtly different key conclusions. Prominent among these are whether the headline story of social capital is one of 'decline' (Putnam) or 'trans-formation' (Halpern). To me, even the US case can to some extent be read as a story of transformation rather than simple decline, as more generalized social norms come to replace the informal understandings of traditional communities (chapter 7). That is not to say, of course, that the transformation is without consequence or negative impacts in some domains, such as psychological health (chapter 3), and this poses dif-ficult questions both for individuals and for society.

Fourth, we have significant differences of view about what the policy implications of the social capital literature are. In particular, I tend to place far greater emphasis on the potentially positive role of the state; the positive role of the mass media; and the negative role of economic inequality (chapter 9). Of course, many of these differences in policy conclusions relate to the political contexts within which we work and are engaged. Bo Rothstein, writing in Sweden, would doubtless reach still different policy conclusions.

And thanks to a lot of people . . .

One of the best things about working on social capital has been the people I have met. Maybe it's just that the field attracts pathological optimists, but those I have met, and who have led the development of social capital research, almost all seem to be highly trusting and trustworthy; socially and civically engaged; open, welcoming and – of course – highly socially interconnected. It's now a much bigger field than it was in the late 1990s, and this will inevitably strain and probably change the character of working in this area, but I hope that something of that original ethos remains.

Now to thanks. I am sure that I have forgotten and will mortally offend a few people, but doubtless you know who you are and will extract a suitable apology. Thanks go to the many intellectual friends and companions who have intermittently challenged, taught and stimulated me in our social capital debates. These include: Bob Putnam, of course, but also Tom Healy, Mike Woolcock, Tom Sander, Richard Wilkinson, Peter Hall, Simon Szreter, John Helliwell, Sylvain Cote, Peter John, Perry 6, and Stephen Aldridge. The two Toms on this list merit especial thanks for their careful and detailed comments on earlier drafts. Many others have in some significant way or other prompted, influenced or helped with the rather extended intellectual journey that has characterized my interest in social capital and the practical task of completing this book, including: Lisa Berkman, David Blunkett, Brendan Burchell, David Good, Roz Harper, Tyrill Harris, David Held, Erika Jacobs, Louise Kennedy, Julian Le Grand, Sue Leigh, Joni Lovenduski, Vivian Lowndes, Zoe Morris, Geoff Mulgen, Avner Offer, Bo Rothstein, Jennifer Rubin, David Saunders, Robert Sampson, Fiona Sewell, David Smith, Danielle Stolle, Nir Tsuk, Jan Van Deth, Paul Whiteley and Stewart Wood. Special thanks, of course, must go to my partner Jennifer, and our two great kids whose football, palaeontology and toy-crashing skills I look forward to catching up with.

Today, though I maintain links to Cambridge University, I have spent much of the last three years in the Prime Minister's Strategy Unit as a senior policy adviser. I owe many thanks to my colleagues both in the Faculty of Social and Political Sciences and in the Strategy Unit for the support and flexibility that enabled me to balance various roles and complete this book. Though much of our work in the Strategy Unit does not directly concern social capital, its relevance is such that it often appears on the agenda in one way or another. Changes in social capital are one of a number of key challenges that face contemporary societies. As we shall see, social capital also affects many key policy outcomes, as well as the delivery – or 'co-production' – of public services and goods. Finally, I should add that it's great to work in an administration and political climate within which such issues, and evidence more generally, are considered appropriate and welcome. But evidence is not just for elites, it's for us all to understand and shape the world that we wish to live in.

I should stress that this book represents my views and understandings of the social capital literature, and is in no way a statement of government policy or position. This is an academic book, but the social science it contains is important because it is about holding up a mirror to contemporary society, not least so that we can reflect on what our society is, and how we could make it better. It is a long time since I have been back to many of the deprived housing estates I studied so closely as a graduate, and indeed some have now been demolished. I suspect that those residents, for the most part, wouldn't really think this book 'their cup of tea', but in a kind of way it's for them. Sometimes something does come out of those curious questionnaires you fill in, even if it takes a little while.

DSH, May 2004

1

Introduction: Concepts, History and Measurement

Features of social life – networks, norms, and trust – that enable participants to act together more effectively to pursue shared objectives . . .
Social capital, in short, refers to social connections and the attendant
norms and trust.

Putnam, 1995, pp. 664–5

Social capital has become a buzzword among political and academic
elites, though the term remains relatively unfamiliar to the general
public. Even among the politicians and scholars who use the term,
there is often confusion about what 'social capital' is, or how it should
be measured. A glance at how the term is used tells you that it has
something to do with 'community', 'civil society' and the 'social fabric'
– it's about how people are connected with one another. But such a
loose definition sounds like everything and nothing. It is thus unsurprising that to some, social capital is simply the latest fad – an intellectual sound bite largely devoid of meaning. But to others, among
them some of the most outstanding scholars in the world today, social
capital is the most important and exciting concept to emerge out of the
social sciences in fifty years.

The interest in the social capital concept comes from two directions.
First, for many policymakers, the term captures the political Zeitgeist
of our time: it has a hard-nosed economic feel while restating the
importance of the social. It implicitly counters the crude economic

political fashion of the 1980s and early 1990s especially characteristic of the USA, UK and New Zealand, as captured in Margaret Thatcher's famous pronouncement that 'there is no such thing as society'. Social capital gives a name to something that many came to feel was missing in this simplified economic worldview. The use of the term echoes the political revival of centre-left parties during the mid-1990s across the western world. It also hints at why the application of crude models of the market in many parts of the world, and especially in the ex-communist nations, appears to have run into trouble. Social capital was the missing variable that economists had overlooked.

The second direction from which interest in social capital has been driven is recent academic research. A spate of articles and research studies has emerged documenting a relationship between the form and quality of people's social networks and a range of important outcomes, including economic growth, health, crime, educational performance, and even the efficacy of governments. In many cases, researchers in different disciplines have discovered these relationships independently of one another, and often using differing definitions of social capital. It is only recently that such researchers have started to come together in the realization that there is something in common at the core of their work.

So what is 'social capital'?

Perhaps the simplest way to understand social capital is to consider a few examples. Most people are embedded in a series of different social networks and associations. We have friends. We go to work and mix with colleagues. We may belong to a union or professional association that keeps us in touch with similar professionals outside of our own work context. In our leisure time, we may play a sport with a particular group or club, and we may belong to other interest-based groups, whether this interest is knitting, model railways or astro-physics. We may also belong to a political party, or more frequently, to a pressure group working to save whales, the environment, or the right to carry weapons. And in our home life, we are part of a family, a neighbourhood, and probably a religious or ethnic community too. These everyday networks, including many of the social customs and bonds that define them and keep them together, are what we mean when we talk about social capital.

The existence of this social fabric has many benefits for the individuals and communities within it. This can be seen in the classic example offered by James Coleman, in a seminal paper, of the New York wholesale diamond market (Coleman, 1988). Coleman describes how, in this market, merchants frequently hand over bags of diamonds, often worth many thousands of dollars, to other merchants to examine at their leisure. This is done without insurance or formal agreement. To an outsider this might seem extremely risky and unwise, as there appears nothing to stop another merchant taking advantage and pocketing the diamonds. Yet the market is extremely successful and efficient. Inside the network of traders, information flows freely and exchanges can be made without the need for elaborate and expensive contracts or insurance.

This market can only work because of the closeness, high degree of trust and trustworthiness among the community of diamond merchants. To any individual trader, having access to this network of similar traders with shared understandings of how to behave honourably is an immense asset that greatly facilitates their ability to trade efficiently and profitably. Yet this facilitating community or network cannot be described as financial, physical or even human capital, even though it pays handsome returns to those with access to it. The network is instead best described as a form of 'social' capital (see table 1.1).

As we shall see, there has been considerable discussion – and disagreement – about what should be counted as social capital and what should be excluded from the concept. Sorting out the boundaries and detailed content of the social capital concept is the prime objective of this chapter. But the essence of the concept is simple enough – and readers less interested in conceptual debates may wish to skip directly to later chapters. Societies are not composed of atomized individuals. People are connected with one another through intermediate social structures – webs of association and shared understandings of how to behave. This social fabric greatly affects with whom, and how, we interact and co-operate. It is this everyday fabric of connection and tacit co-operation that the concept of social capital is intended to capture.

History of the concept

There is a familiar ritual in contemporary academic life. Bright young scholars proclaim their ground-breaking discoveries, only to be told by their older peers that they have heard it all before. Social capital research is no exception. Theoretical precursors can clearly be found in the works of many of the founding fathers of the contemporary social sciences, such as Adam Smith, de Tocqueville and Durkheim; and arguably even in the writings of some of the earliest scholars, such as Aristotle. Indeed, in so far as the social capital concept simply highlights the important role that community plays in individual well-

Introduction

Table 1.1 *Forms of capital*

Type	Definition
Capital (general use)	'1. Any form of material wealth used, or available for use, in the production of more wealth; 2. The remaining assets of a business or person after all liabilities have been deducted; net worth; 3. Any asset or advantage; . . . from the Latin *capitalis*, "of the head", important, chief' (abridged from *Heritage Dictionary*, International Edition).
Financial	Money and paper assets; for example, a sum of money in a bank. It does not directly produce goods and services, though it can be used to purchase factors of production which can produce goods and services.
Physical	Stock of produced goods that contribute to the production of other goods and services; for example, the machinery, equipment and buildings used in production.
Other tangible assets	Factors of production that nature supplies; for example, land. They are distinguished from physical capital in that the latter is produced.
Human	Stock of expertise accumulated by a worker – knowing how to do something; for example, a professional training. It is valued for its income-earning potential in future.[a]
Social	Social networks and the norms and sanctions that govern their character. It is valued for its potential to facilitate individual and community action, especially through the solution of collective action problems.

[a] There is some controversy whether human capital should include attributes other than expertise that contribute to earning potential, such as physical strength, intelligence, attractiveness etc. One concern is that such a definition may become tautological – human capital consists of individual attributes that contribute to earning potential, and vice versa.

being, it can be recognized in some of the most ancient known texts (see, for example, the I-Ching; L. Sun and Jiang, 2000).

Current interest in the role that associational life plays in society was foreshadowed over a hundred and fifty years ago in the American context in the observations of Alexis de Tocqueville. He drew attention to what he saw as the foundation stone of vibrant American democracy: 'Nothing, in my view, more deserves attention than the intellectual and moral associations in America. American political and industrial associations easily catch our eyes, but the others tend not to be noticed' (de Tocqueville, [1840] 1969, p. 517). De Tocqueville argued that 'an association unites the energies of divergent minds and vigorously directs them toward a clearly indicated goal' (ibid., p. 190). This greatly facilitated social collaboration or, in the language of contemporary social science, facilitated the solution of collective action problems. Such associational life also acted as a counterbalance to the dangers of individualism that might otherwise eventually degenerate into an 'exaggerated love of self which leads a man to think of all things in terms of himself and prefer himself to all'. Tocqueville argued that through associational life, 'feelings and ideas are renewed, the heart enlarged, and the understanding developed only by the reciprocal action of men upon one another' (ibid., p. 515).

While it is de Tocqueville who is most often quoted by political scientists, many parallels to today's social capital research can be found in the work of another nineteenth-century scholar, Emile Durkheim: 'A nation can be maintained only if, between the state and the individual, there is interposed a whole series of secondary groups near enough to the individuals to attract them strongly in their sphere of action and drag them, in this way, into the general torrent of social life' (Durkheim, [1893] 1964, p. 28). Durkheim observed that, even for the most individualistic of acts, the behaviour of individuals could not be understood in isolation from the characteristics of the community and the relationships in which they were embedded. Most famously, he illustrated his thesis with an empirical analysis of suicide. He found that although suicide was thought of as a purely individualistic act, the suicide rate was best explained by social forces external to the individual. In particular, Durkheim showed that suicide was far more common in societies and groups characterized by social dislocation and loose social bonds. In contrast, societies characterized by high levels of social cohesion and solidarity seemed able to protect their individual members from suicide through 'mutual moral support, which instead of throwing the individual on his own resources, leads him to share in the collective energy and supports his own when exhausted' (Durkheim, 1897, p. 210; quoted in Berkman and Kawachi, 2000, p. 175).

Economists can claim, with some justification, that precursors to the concept of social capital can be found in their discipline as far back as the work of Adam Smith in the eighteenth century (though other disciplines might claim Smith as their own too!). Well known for his early advocacy of the merits of markets, Smith also drew attention to the importance of mutual sympathy, networks and values in the sustaining of such markets (Bruni and Sugden, 2000). His examples were not always positive, such as when he highlighted the ways in which merchants meetings' were used by them to conspire against the public for greater private profit (A. Smith, [1776] 1979). However, despite this promising start, economists have generally not shown a great interest in the role of social networks and norms in economic life. Of course, exceptions can be identified, such as Irving Fisher's early attempt to broaden the definition of capital to include 'social organisational forms' (I. Fisher, 1906), Couse's work on the nature of the firm (Couse, 1937), or Loury's work on racial income differences (Loury, 1977). But most economists have been little concerned with this domain until relatively recently (Piazza-Giorgi, 2002).

The earliest specific use of the term 'social capital', identified by Putnam (pers. comm., and noted in Woolcock, 1998), seems to have been by Hanifan (1916, p. 130; 1920, p. 16). He used the term to refer to 'those tangible assets [that] count for most in the daily lives of people: namely good will, fellowship, sympathy, and social intercourse among the individuals and families who make up a social unit' (1920, p. 78). Two points are noteworthy about Hanifan's use of the term. First, the definition bears considerable resemblance to definitions that are current today, reinforcing the sense of continuity between past and present thinking. Second, Hanifan chose the term in order to facilitate discussions with hard-nosed businessmen who he felt would be more impressed by economic language than by 'softer' references to the importance of community. His strategy is paralleled precisely in the decision to use the term by many contemporary social scientists in their attempts to explain the importance of the phenomenon to money-minded policymakers today.

Though many researchers continued to work on related areas to Hanifan's, such as the importance of place-based relationships (Young and Willmott, 1957; Jacobs, 1961; Gans, 1962) or 'community competence' (Cottrell, 1976), the term 'social capital' was not generally used. When it did appear, it was mostly in unconnected and specialist literatures (for example, in Jane Jacob's 1961 work; in a paper by Lee Martin in the *Journal of Farm Economics*, 1963; and in Servadio's history of the Mafia, 1976).

The birth of mainstream academic interest in the concept can be dated to the late 1980s, when attention was drawn to the concept by eminent sociologists in both Europe and the USA. In Europe, Pierre Bourdieu noted that economists, whose worldview so dominated much contemporary thinking in both policy and the social sciences, had neglected the importance of huge areas of social and economic life (Bourdieu, 1986). He argued that economic orthodoxy was artificially limiting itself to the study of a narrow band of 'practices' that were socially recognized as 'economic', and in so doing was missing the fact that 'capital presents itself under three fundamental species (each with its own subtypes), namely economic capital, cultural capital, and social capital' (Bourdieu and Wacquant, 1992, p. 119). He offered the following definition of social capital:

> Social capital is the sum of the resources, actual or virtual, that accrue to an individual or a group by virtue of possessing a durable network of more or less institutionalised relationships of mutual acquaintance and recognition. Acknowledging that capital can take a variety of forms is indispensable to explain the structure and dynamics of differentiated societies. (Bourdieu and Wacquant, 1992, p. 119)

Approximately in parallel with Bourdieu, the American sociologist James Coleman published a paper that for many was the inspiration for their interest in the area. Indeed, it is clear that Bourdieu and Coleman to some extent worked together. Like Bourdieu, Coleman offered a very broad conception of social capital that was not grounded in a narrow area of study:

> Social capital is defined by its function. It is not a single entity but a variety of different entities, with two elements in common: they all consist of some aspect of social structures, and they facilitate certain actions of actors – whether persons or corporate actors – within that structure. Like other forms of capital, social capital is productive, making possible the achievement of certain ends that in its absence would not be possible. (Coleman, 1988, p. 96)

In the academic world today, one name has become almost synonymous with social capital, though, as he himself points out, he did not invent the term. He is, of course, Harvard professor Robert Putnam. His definition of social capital is widely quoted, including at the start of this chapter.

The research that put Putnam so decisively on the map was a ground-breaking study called *Making Democracy Work* (Putnam, 1993). The study compared different regions of Italy in an attempt to explain what made some regional governments more effective than others (see chapter 6 for more detail). Putnam found that the differential effectiveness of the regional governments – their speed of action, the efficiency with which they worked and their perception by the public

– could not be put down to the size of their budgets or policy frameworks. Putnam's remarkable conclusion, based on a detailed compilation of evidence, was that the critical factor in the effectiveness of the
regional governments was the vibrancy of the associational life and the
level of trust between strangers inside their regions.

Putnam's argument was essentially that the differential success of
the regional governments resulted from stable differences in social
capital between the regions. The most successful regional governments
were generally in the north. These areas had high levels of social capital
as measured by participation in 'horizontal' associational organizations, such as choral societies, and high levels of reported social trust
between strangers (see further below). The roots of this high social
capital were argued by Putnam to lie in cultural and political practices
stretching back nearly a thousand years. Regional governments that
were less effective – typically in the south – were characterized by high
levels of distrust between strangers, with people instead turned almost
entirely inwards to their families for trust and support. In such regions,
membership in horizontal voluntary associations was very much
lower, and the predominant social organization was instead 'vertical'
or hierarchical in nature, with relationships based on power and
patronage. Again, the route of such social patterns appeared to lie deep
in the past, history's hand invisibly shaping the institutions and lives
of the present.

Fukuyama was another important figure to give relatively early
prominence to the concept of social capital (Fukuyama, 1995a,b). Like
Bourdieu, though from a rather different angle, Fukuyama argued that
economists had grossly underestimated the importance of social capital
in general, and trust in particular. Fukuyama argued that the conventional characterization of political economy, which juxtaposed
the North American liberal model at one extreme with the Asian
interventionist model at the other, was grossly misleading because it
missed the similarities in their social capital. He argued that in terms
of social capital, the USA and Japan were at the *same* extreme, with both
characterized by high levels of trust between strangers. This, he argued,
was the common root of both countries' outstanding economic performances. In contrast, he argued that the economic underperformance
of nations such as Russia and those of much of Africa was rooted
in lack of trust between their own people (see chapter 2 for further
detail).

The years since 1995 have seen an explosion in the use of the term
'social capital' (see figure 1.1). Almost certainly, the controversial article
written by Bob Putnam in 1995, arguing that the USA was witnessing
a dramatic decline in its social capital, was a major spark to the literature that followed (Putnam, 1995; see chapter 7 of this book). With this

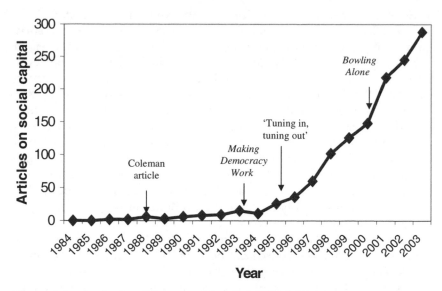

Figure 1.1 *Academic articles on social capital, 1984–2003*
Source: Figures for 1984–93 based on a combined search of Econlit, Psychlit, Crimlit and Medline; those for 1994–2003 based on Web of Science; that for 2003 projected from part-year total, assuming *pro rata* articles for remainder of year.

explosion have come waves of new empirical research, much of which is reviewed in the chapters that follow. Over recent years, a number of studies have been published providing powerful new insights into the wide-ranging effects of social capital. Much of this research has come out of the USA, often prompted by Putnam's paper. The USA has proved a particularly fruitful target of study because of the comparable data available across US states and the fact that social capital appears to vary greatly across the USA. In addition, the social sciences in the USA have an empirical and quantitative orientation well suited to this type of research. However, social capital research today is very much an international affair.

There have also been a number of attempts to refine and tighten our theoretical understanding of social capital, and it is to these developments that we now turn.

The three basic components of social capital

It is clear that much confusion has been thrown up in the social capital literature through the use of different definitions, and a number of critics have argued for a clearer distinction between the subcomponents of social capital (Portes, 1998; Anheier and Kendall, 2002; Nuissl, 2002). The brief history above shows that, even among its early proponents, significant differences exist in the form and emphasis of the definitions offered. Hanifan, probably the first to use the term, seemed to have in mind everyday habits of friendship and common civility – the informal and comforting social norms of everyday life. Bourdieu shifted the emphasis onto the material benefits to individuals of their social networks. Putnam initially included both norms and networks, though in later work he has tended to favour a slightly narrower definition focused more on social networks. He has also tended to frame the concept in terms of its public good aspects, explicitly including reference to the facilitation of co-operation, a definition that is sometimes sharply contrasted with Bourdieu's colder, more privatized definition.

So what is social capital composed of? Most forms, be they kinship, work-based or interest-based, can be seen to have three basic components. They consist of a *network*; a cluster of *norms, values and expectancies* that are shared by group members; and *sanctions* – punishments and rewards – that help to maintain the norms and network.

These three components should be recognizable in almost any form of social association, but let us illustrate them with reference to one of the most familiar and ubiquitous forms of social capital – the traditional, locally embedded community, or 'neighbourhood'. The first component is the social network. Most of us know at least some of our neighbours. These relationships may vary from simple recognition by sight, perhaps with an occasional greeting exchanged as we pass by, to deep friendships involving frequent visits to each other's homes and the exchange of both emotional and material support. Such relationships are not always experienced as positive, and can be characterized by rivalry and dislike. In some cases the community, and the network that partly comprises it, may be defined geographically or formally, such as a small rural village. In other cases, its boundaries may be ill defined. The network can further be characterized by its *density* (the proportion of people who know each other) and *closure* (the preponderance of intra- versus inter-community links).

The second component is the social norms. These are the rules, values and expectancies that characterize the community (or network) members. Living in a neighbourhood, and our relationships with our neighbours, are characterized by certain rules or 'social norms'. Many of these rules – if not all of them – are unwritten. Some of these norms have a behavioural component (requiring us to do certain things) and others may be more affective in nature (concerning how we feel about the community or group). In the modern neighbourhood, these norms might include: helping our neighbours where possible; being courteous and considerate – avoiding making loud noise at night; keeping our property and garden in a good state; sweeping leaves and snow from paths in front of our property so that people will not slip; and feeling positive and supportive towards our neighbourhood. These norms may also include more specific habits of reciprocity – keeping an eye on one another's property when we are away; looking out for each other's children; and lending each other equipment, food and even money. Of course, some of the shared norms may not be unique to this community, but may also be found in other contexts too.

The third component is sanctions. Sanctions are not just formal – such as punishments for breaking the law. Most are very informal, but are nonetheless effective in maintaining social norms (Luzzati, 2000). Neighbourhood living is associated with certain kinds of sanctions on good and bad behaviour. These often appear very mild in form but are still very effective. Neighbours find ways of communicating their disapproval of acts that violate the unwritten codes of the neighbourhood, be this the holding of frequent loud parties, selling drugs from your home, or putting a twenty-foot Christmas tree with lights on your roof. The sanction may be through someone being told directly, such as through a disapproving glance, an angry exchange of words or even the threat of action. More commonly, however, the sanction is indirect and subtle, such as through gossip and reputation. The sanction can also be positive, such as praise for a helpful act or on how good new paintwork or a garden looks.

The three components can be used to analyse any kind of community or network (see table 1.2). If I think about my work context as an academic, I could fairly easily identify who is in my department, as well as the clusters inside it (network). Much of the department's work rests on common understandings about what everyone's up to, as well as a reasonable amount of goodwill concerning matters such as the sharing of the administrative and teaching load (shared norms). From time to time, individual department members do things that don't accord with these shared understandings, and their reputation may suffer accordingly. They may also get spoken to by other members of the department, or even our head of department, and in an extreme case might even get asked to leave the department (sanctions).

Similarly, the unit I currently work in has a well-defined membership – indeed I can call up an organogram which will tell me who's in which bit and what their telephone extensions are (network). There is a pretty clear ethos and shared sense of vision – there's even an attempt at a written version for new staff, and it's periodically discussed at away-days – and there's a generally helpful and collegiate atmosphere

Table 1.2 *The three components of social capital*

Examples	Network	Norms	Sanctions
	Network members	Rules and understandings	Rewards and punishments for complying with/ breaking network norms
Traditional communities	Neighbours (lending, caring and protection – and sometimes rivalry and dislike)	Reciprocity, due care of property, challenging strangers	Recognition and honouring vs. gossip, social exclusion
New York diamond wholesale market	Other dealers (providing access to diamonds and deals)	Trustworthy exchange, without payment, of uncut diamonds for examination	Approval, disapproval and exclusion
The Highway Code (?)	Other road users	Language of signs and co-operation; when to go, stop etc.	Anger of strangers (road rage), informal 'thanks' gesture, police action

(?) = Disputed example.

(norms). And there is a never-ending stream of gossip, feedback and reflection that builds – or undermines – reputations and careers (sanctions).

Networks, norms and sanctions can have both formal (explicit, institutionally codified) and informal (implicit, tacit) aspects. A neighbourhood may be formally defined in terms of statutes and administrative units, or it may be an informally understood 'social representation' (K. Lynch, 1960). Community norms are mostly informal and tacit, but are sometimes codified into neighbourhood codes or contracts, and are occasionally even written into the deeds or leases of properties. Similarly, neighbourhood sanctions are normally informal, but may be formal, especially when the norms that they relate to are also formal.

Some researchers tend to assume that social capital refers only to informal social customs and processes, but in practice, it is often very difficult to draw the line between the two.

One can argue that the same basic three components can be made out in contexts ranging from the very intimate, such as in the family, through to super-communities, such as the nation state. Indeed, one can argue that it is these components that largely define such social structures. The question then arises of how widely the social capital concept should be drawn.

Levels of analysis: from nation to family

There is an underlying controversy over the range of phenomena that should be included in the social capital concept, much as there are for other forms of capital (OECD, 2001a). This controversy is reflected in widespread differences in the phenomena and range of networks that are referred to as social capital. Examples include: national differences in social trust; the social networks that enable some immigrant and ethnic groups to succeed where others have failed; the practices and habits of low-crime communities; the networks of parents that help schools and students succeed; voluntary associations of almost any kind; sports and special interest clubs; the social networks of friends; and the structure and character of families, from the presence of two parents in the home to the frequency with which families eat together as a whole. In short, the term has been used to refer not only to community and voluntary associations, but also to large-scale 'cultural' phenomena on the one hand, and to very small-scale, micro-level, intra-family phenomena on the other.

This diversity has led some to argue the social capital concept now risks being drained of all meaning (Portes, 1998) and is conceptually weak (Durlauf, 2002). Ben Fine, perhaps the most vocal critic of social capital, goes further, dismissing it as 'a totally chaotic, ambiguous, and general category that can be used as a notional umbrella for almost any purpose' (Fine, 2001, p. 155). Fine's criticisms are a little overblown, but it is certainly true that in many research and policy papers, the issue of what counts as social capital is implicit and often confused. Many empirically oriented researchers in various fields have begun to apply the term 'social capital' to their own work, while failing to note that the particular networks, norms or sanctions that they refer to are of a totally different type to those referred to by others (see box 1.1).

Almost all researchers would agree that non-family social networks in which people mostly know each other, such as a traditional, locally

---

Box 1.1   *Examples of overstretching the social capital concept?*

As the term 'social capital' has come to be used more and more widely, it is sometimes being picked up and used in very different contexts and with a very different meaning. For example, a recent paper on 'Social capital from carbon property: creating equity for indigenous people' discusses how the trade in 'carbon credits' can be structured to ensure that they become a form of 'social capital' for indigenous people, as opposed to another tool for capitalists to exploit indigenous people with (Saunders, Hanbury-Tenison and Swingland, 2002). In our terms, these authors are talking more about making a set of tangible assets into a public good that benefits the local inhabitants than about social capital as meant by social scientists.

Another example, drawn from the social sciences, is a paper on '"If you're light you're alright": light skin color as social capital for women of color' (Hunter, 2002). The paper analyses how skin colour hierarchies were established and maintained, such that lighter skin colour even within the African American community is associated with higher status and earnings. It is an interesting question as to how the 'value' associated with light skin colour should be handled, but it doesn't seem to fit the conception of 'social capital' espoused here. Some might see it as a form of human capital, rather like physical strength, but this would be controversial too.

A more difficult call is whether all of the wide variety of social norms and habits that characterize a community count as social capital. For example, most of the Scots like to drink whisky, while the French prefer wine, but do these shared social norms constitute social capital? In my view, there is a line to be drawn between social norms that govern essentially private forms of consumption (e.g., our preferred drink), and social norms that shape the character of our social interactions with others (e.g., a norm of reciprocity). The former is an example of 'cultural capital' while the latter is a form of social capital. But others might disagree.

---

based community or Coleman's example of diamond merchants, are clear examples of social capital. More controversial are examples that either involve a very intimate network, such as the family, or at the other extreme, involve a 'network' of total strangers.

The argument for social capital as a macro-level concept

There is real disagreement between researchers as to whether the character and form of relationships between relative strangers is to be considered a form of social capital. When visiting different nations, one cannot help but be struck by the differences in how people commonly behave – the habits and customs of everyday life. Southern Europeans think the British habit of queuing very odd, even baffling, while the British get very angry with overseas visitors who seem to be trying to jump the queue. Visitors to Germany may be stunned to find themselves told off for walking across a clear road when the pedestrian signal indicates stop, while visitors to India may be equally stunned, even terrified, by the apparent death-defying chaos on India's busy roads. Foreign visitors to America may find themselves unsure how to respond to shop assistants saying 'have a nice day', while cut-throat American businesspeople bemoan the difficulty of doing business in 'less trustworthy' parts of the world. Are these merely quaint 'cultural' differences, or are they important aspects of social capital?

The answer to this question depends partly on one's theoretical viewpoint. What is certainly true is that the sharing of these cultural habits often greatly facilitates the ability of a nation's population to get along together, and of individuals to achieve their aims with minimal conflict with others. In this sense, many aspects of national and regional culture fit the loose definition of social capital in table 1.1.

To illustrate this point, let us consider the everyday example of the rules of the road. Whenever we go somewhere by car, bike or bus, instead of taking the financial risks of the New York diamond merchant, we risk our lives. Yet, at least in most of the modern industrialized nations, we do so casually. This is only possible because we all share and, for the most part, rigorously abide by a common set of rules about how to behave on our roads. It is a remarkable thing, when you reflect on it, that this largely informal system works so well. For example, in the UK, a nation with a particularly low rate of deaths on the road, the Highway Code was not even a legal document until relatively recently.

The opportunity and temptation to break the rules – such as driving through a red light when the junction appears clear – is frequent. Indeed, in many parts of the world, such 'rules' are routinely broken, and are sometimes hard to discern at all. But in those nations where sticking to the rules of the road is the norm – even though on occasion individuals would benefit from breaking them – people generally end up getting to their destinations faster and more safely than they otherwise would have done.

How does this example relate to the three components of social capital that we saw in the previous section? The rules, or social norms can clearly be made out – some kind of common understanding of how to behave that ends up facilitating everyone's actions. The sanctions are also fairly easy to see – these may include formal punishment and fines, but also informal sanctions, such as when drivers swear, hoot and gesticulate at someone who has broken a rule of the road. The network is more difficult to make out. The members of a nation state can hardly be said to know each other. But they are bound to interact with one another on a day-to-day basis (and with those of their own nation, not of others). They also normally share some form of loose identity and, most importantly, they can be said to share a common understanding of how to behave in relation to one another.

In terms of theory, it is noteworthy that Coleman's influential definition can comfortably encompass macro-level cultural norms in the envelope of social capital – assuming that these norms in some way facilitate co-operative action. But against this, Coleman's functional definition has been subject to criticism precisely because it can include such a variety of very different phenomena under its broad conceptual umbrella.

A strong argument for the inclusion of macro-level phenomena in the social capital definition has come from those working on regional (and national) differences in trust between strangers, and the relationship between these differences and various empirical outcomes. Prominent among these advocates have been Kimberly Lochner, Ichiro Kawachi and their co-researchers, and economists such as Steve Knack (Lochner, Kawachi and Kennedy, 1999; Knack and Keefer, 1997; see also chapters 2, 3 and 4).

If we decide that macro-level aspects of society, such as cultural and social habits, are to be included in the social capital concept, then this immediately raises the question of whether to include the more formal dimensions along which communities, regions and nations differ. In particular, we have to consider whether institutional structures should be considered as part of social capital. Coleman's definition would certainly seem able to encompass the formal political, legal and economic institutions of a community or nation.

High-profile support for this 'big tent' definition has come from the World Bank. The bank, which has been highly active both in terms of research and in attempts to operationalize the concept, offers a definition of social capital that clearly and explicitly includes institutions:

> Social capital refers to the institutions, relationships, and norms that shape the quality and quantity of a society's social interactions. Increasing evidence shows that social cohesion is critical for societies to prosper economically and for development to be sustainable. Social capital is not just the sum of the institutions [that] underpin a society – it is the glue that holds them together. (World Bank, 1999)

For many researchers (including Putnam) and practitioners (including the OECD), the World Bank's 'big tent' definition of social capital is a step too far. Interestingly, the main argument against the big tent definition is as much practical as conceptual. The fear is that the inclusion of political, legal and institutional structures in the definition makes the concept more difficult to grasp and tends to direct attention away from the area of greatest neglect – the importance of informal networks and norms.

The argument for social capital as a micro-level concept

While Kawachi et al. have made a strong case for the social capital concept to include the macro-level, they have also been among those expressing unease at the stretching of the concept. Working mainly on the relationship between social capital and health, Kawachi has expressed concern about how social capital has been used to refer both to the new generation of work on the macro-, or ecological, level and to an older continuing literature on the individual or micro-level effects of social networks.

This conceptual tussle is reminiscent of a couple trying to share a blanket that they feel is only big enough for one. For Kawachi, it is the meso- and macro-levels that are central to the concept and that he wants to see covered – and he would be happy to see the micro-level left out: 'Social cohesion and social capital are both collective, or ecological, dimensions of society, to be distinguished from the concepts of social networks and social support, which are characteristically measured at the level of the individual' (Kawachi and Berkman, 2000, p. 175). Kawachi et al.'s suggestion that the social capital concept be reserved *exclusively* to refer to ecological and macro-level phenomena is clearly at variance with most of the earlier, broader definitions of the concept, including those of Coleman and Bourdieu. In contrast, there are some researchers who have used the concept to refer solely to intimate networks of the type that Kawachi et al. are seeking to exclude from the definition. Examples of such work include research on the effects of having one or two parents, or on the support received from close friends and relatives (e.g. Furstenburg and Hughes, 1995; Teachman et al., 1996).

At the more theoretical end, there has been more than one prominent meta-review of the social capital literature that has expressed doubt about the inclusion of relatively macro-level phenomenon in the definition of social capital (notably Portes, 1998; Edwards and Foley, 1998). Portes, discussing whether social capital can be seen 'as a feature of communities and nations', concludes 'I believe that the greatest theoretical promise of social capital lies at the individual level'. He continues by saying that while 'there is nothing intrinsically wrong with redefining it as a structural property of large aggregates, [t]his conceptual departure requires ... more care and theoretical refinement than displayed so far' (1998, p. 21). Though using a rather different line of argument, Edwards and Foley (1998) end up with a similar conclusion: 'We would argue that for purposes of empirical research, social capital should be divested of any social-psychological value added and treated as a more restricted social-relational concept appropriate to social networks and organisation' (Edwards and Foley, 1998, p. 136). Hence it is clear that, contrary to the suggestion of Kawachi et al. and the broader definition of the World Bank, there is a strong counterlobby trying to take the social capital definition in precisely the opposite direction; in other words, towards a more micro-level and grounded approach.

Social capital as a multi-level concept

Both diffuse weak networks and norms at the national, macro-level and strong dense networks and norms at the intimate, family or micro-level fit within broader definitions of social capital. Although the nature of the networks, norms and sanctions we see at each of these levels of analysis differs, they remain recognizable.

Nonetheless, the juxtaposition between the arguments of those who wish to restrict the concept is quite striking. To use another metaphor, the concept of social capital acts like an intellectual Rorschach test. Different researchers and reviewers, depending on their own preoccupations, see in its conceptual blotches a definition that includes their own interests, but often excludes those of others.

Should we try to 'award' the term to one group or other, or somehow split the difference? Or should we look for a concept that encompasses both poles of the macro–micro division? I find the suggestion by Kawachi et al. that we reserve the term 'social capital' only to refer to a subset of macro-level effects difficult to sustain, as well as sitting uncomfortably with the definitions employed by those originating the term. Ecological effects are clearly to be found in small groups (even families), while macro-level ecological effects still require micro-level explanatory accounts. But similarly, I find moves by Portes, Edwards and Foley et al. to exclude the macro-level phenomena mistaken. The empirical results that researchers such as Kawachi et al. have been discovering in recent years, such as the close relationship between average levels of trust between strangers and health outcomes at the state or national level, are very difficult to account for without reference to a social capital concept operationalized at the macro-level. So if we don't use the term in that context, then we'll have to invent another one that means much the same.

Furthermore, as we shall see in later chapters, there is an important story that can be told about how different and evolving societies appear to substitute social capital at one level for that at another. This suggests some functional equivalence between the different levels, and is strong evidence for a conceptual envelope that can encompass these different levels. That said, by the same account, we should be attentive to these different levels of analysis and ready to distinguish between them. In this sense, we need to have our conceptual cake and eat it. We need to make the conceptual distinction between these levels, layers or 'species' of networks in society, yet also need to recognize that in some important sense they are part of the same 'sociological genus'.

Functional sub-types of social capital: bonding and bridging

Recent theoretical work has sought to break the notion of social capital down into different sub-types. Perhaps the most important of these distinctions is between 'bonding' and 'bridging' social capital:

> Some forms of capital are, by choice or necessity, inward looking and tend to reinforce exclusive identities and homogeneous groups. Examples of *bonding* social capital include ethnic fraternal organisations, church-based women's reading groups, and fashionable country clubs. Other networks are outward looking and encompass people across diverse social cleavages. Examples of *bridging* social capital include the civil rights movement, many youth service groups, and ecumenical religious organisations. . . . Bonding social capital provides a kind of sociological superglue whereas bridging social capital provides a sociological WD-40. (Putnam, 2000, pp. 22–3, italics added)

Putnam credits the coining of the bonding–bridging distinction to Gittell and Vidal (1998). What is certainly clear is that this distinction has attracted widespread use in a very short time-span, not least because it captures an important characteristic of networks and the social identities that lie within them. In terms of networks, it loosely echoes the earlier distinction made by Mark Granovetter between the role played by 'weak' ties and 'strong' ties (M. S. Granovetter, 1973, 1985). Weak ties, he noted, such as with acquaintances and various 'contacts', were extremely useful to people in terms of getting information, opportunities and jobs. Strong ties, such as with family and close friends, provided a more intense, multi-stranded form of support, and as such might be expected to play a greater role in emotional well-being.[1] In short, different forms of social network, characterized by different forms of personal ties, seem to have different advantages and benefits (Six, 1997a; de Souza Briggs, 1998; see also later chapters).

While Granovetter's empirical work anticipates the bonding–bridging distinction in terms of networks, the more philosophical work of Hegel can be said to anticipate the distinction in terms of norms. Hegel contrasted the strong bonds of reciprocity and care that are found inside families and small communities (what we might call normative bonding social capital) with the self-interested norms that tend to predominate between relative strangers. Given this tendency towards a lack of co-operation between strangers, Hegel highlights the importance to societies of establishing norms of 'impersonal altruism', notably through state action, through which relative strangers can co-operate successfully (what we might call 'normative bridging' social capital).[2]

In an important paper, published in parallel to Gittell and Vidal's work, Michael Woolcock attempted to develop a theoretical framework to explain how different societies could be characterized by the relative prevalence of different kinds of social capital in them (Woolcock, 1998). In retrospect, some confusion was created with the use of different terms for similar conceptual distinctions. For example, Woolcock echoed the bonding–bridging distinction by contrasting intra-community ties, which he called 'integration' (i.e. bonding), with extra-community networks, which he called 'linkage' (i.e. bridging). He suggested how different combinations of these ties in a community or nation characterize different types of society (see figure 1.2).

The theoretical distinctions made by Gittell and Vidal (1998) and Woolcock (1998) will doubtless soon be joined by many others. Woolcock has subsequently shown particular interest in the idea of *linking* social capital (see below). Fedderke, De Kadt and Luiz (1999) have suggested a cross-cutting distinction between two functions of social capital: 'transparency' and 'rationalization'. *Transparency* refers to the extent to which a community's social capital facilitates the flow of information and generally reduces 'transaction costs' (see chapter 2 on the economy for more on this). Hence a society with more bridging social capital would be seen as having more transparency, as information would flow rapidly between communities and groups. *Rationalization* refers to the extent to which 'social capital moves from rules and norms that assume substantive content, to rules and norms that are

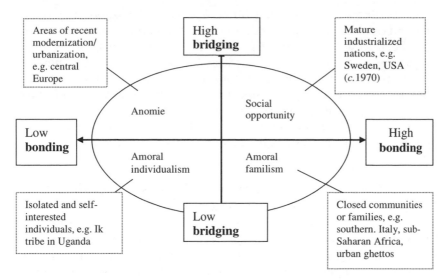

Figure 1.2 *How different mixes of bonding and bridging social capital make different types of society*
Source: Loosely adapted from work by Woolcock (1998), revised to employ the bonding–bridging terminology of Gittell and Vidal (1998).

procedural in character' (Fedderke et al., 1999). Hence a community with social behaviour governed by rigid traditional rules would be regarded as having less rationalization than one with behaviour that is more situationally flexible and driven by outcome-oriented rules.

Which of these many distinctions, dimensions and rival conceptions of social capital ultimately 'wins' depends less on the elegance of the theory than on the extent to which they prove useful heuristics to research and policy, and on their ability to explain the empirical regularities currently being documented. For example, one recent finding has been that – at least within the USA – there is a fairly high, positive correlation between bonding and bridging social capital at the individual level (Putnam, pers. comm.). In other words, contrary to what many had expected, those individuals and areas with many connections to other similar individuals in those areas also tend to have high levels of connections to distant and different others. This suggests that while the bonding–bridging distinction may be important in some cases, maybe we don't need to worry quite so much about always measuring both bonding and bridging social capital – if an individual or community is rich in one, then they will probably be rich in the other too. On the other hand, other recent research has shown that bridging and bonding social capital has different empirical qualities, reinforcing the importance of the distinction. For example, bridging social capital has been found to decay at a much faster rate than bonding social capital. A study on the social networks of bankers found that nine out of ten bridging relationships in one year are gone in the next, even though they are highly valuable and associated with both more positive peer reputations and higher pay (Burt, 2002).

In sum, the bonding–bridging distinction is becoming widely used, but most other distinctions have yet to achieve a wider currency.

Power and the concept of 'linking' social capital: is social capital a public good?

A frequently made point about social capital is that, unlike other forms of capital, it is a public good that benefits a group and is not the sole property of single individuals. As such it is vulnerable to free-riding. If you are part of a social network, or live in a community in which a norm of co-operation and helpfulness is widespread, you can derive benefits from that network or norm even if you do little or nothing to maintain it.

However, it has come to be recognized that, in practice, many forms of networks are not fully public goods in that they are not equally accessible to anyone. In this sense, social capital may often be only a 'semi-public' or 'club' good. Indeed, in some cases, it may exist in forms that the wider group would regard as bad or pathological, such as the Mafia.

Some researchers have tried to draw up a definition of social capital that somehow excludes these darker aspects, or potentials, of social capital. This is more characteristic of popular than academic presentations of the concept. Putnam has sometimes been interpreted as in this camp and as giving an overly positive and selective spin to the concept (Edwards and Foley, 1998). But a careful reading of his work shows that he is well aware of the negative examples of social capital. Indeed, he dedicates an entire chapter to the 'Dark side of social capital' in his most comprehensive work on the subject (Putnam, 2000, ch. 22).[3] As he and others point out, like other forms of capital, social capital may be used to achieve objectives that some may regard as 'bad'. Social capital facilitates co-operative action, but there is nothing to say whether that action will be for the general good or bad, just as physical and human capital may be used for good or bad, to make medicines or weapons.

Nonetheless, the review by Edwards and Foley (1998) correctly draws attention to the overly positive tenor and emphasis on the public good of some of the social capital literature. They suggest that researchers should return to Bourdieu's more realistic definition with its emphasis on social networks more as personal assets than public goods. Interestingly, this re-emphasis brings the social capital concept closer to how we normally think of other forms of capital that are typically privately owned and consumed. The position can be forcefully backed up by the long-established sociological literature documenting class differences in the extent and character of individual networks (e.g. Goldthorpe, Llewellyn and Payne, 1987; Hall, 1997, 1999). Middle-class and professional individuals tend to have significantly larger and more varied networks than working-class or less affluent individuals. In the terminology introduced above, the middle classes have far more bridging social capital (weak ties) and this is a major personal advantage in terms of work and professional self-advancement.

Edwards and Foley explore this issue in some detail. Their point is that it is not sufficient simply to describe the size and density of a person's network. We must also look at the resources that the network connects the individuals to. Imagine if you compare your social networks with those of a prominent billionaire (or if you are a billionaire, you might compare your network to those of one of your middle managers). If you are a fairly well-connected middle-class person, it might be that the numerical size of your network might not be all that different from that of Bill Gates, Richard Branson, Prince Al Waleed bin Talal or whoever (though it is probably a little smaller). Indeed, your network might have *more* bridging across social classes than theirs, given that your average billionaire is unlikely to have too much contact with large sections of the population. But if we instead look at the resources that the billionaire's network provides access to compared to our own, we would see a world of difference. The billionaire's social network is sure to include the top politicians of their country – and probably of a few other countries too; top bankers; leaders of industry and so on. An assessment of the resources in a person's social network provides a rude awakening to those who would view social capital in purely public good terms.

Psychologists and sociologists studying social networks have long been aware of this issue. For example, in the literature on 'social support' – which stretches back more than forty years – researchers have estimated the levels and types of resource that individuals receive from their social networks, documenting marked differences in the material and emotional benefits support available across social classes (see also chapter 3).

However, an awareness of the private good aspects of social capital does not require us to abandon the term. Rather it obliges us to build a consideration of power and resources into the concept, and to recognize its 'club good' aspects (Szreter, 2002). An attempt to do the former can be seen in Woolcock's work, at least in relation to the power of the state and the elites that control it. Woolcock argues that an important characteristic of state–society relations is how closely tied, or embedded, the state is to or in the society over which it presides. He calls this 'synergy'. He also highlights a cross-cutting dimension concerning the state's institutional coherence, competence and capacity. He calls this 'organizational integrity'. In a similar way to how a particular combination of bonding and bridging at the micro-level characterizes particular societies (see above), Woolcock argues that particular combinations of synergy and organizational integrity at the macro-level characterize distinct forms of state–society relations (see figure 1.3).

Woolcock creates a cross-cutting matrix of his four dimensions to form a typology of sixteen different types of nation, though he does not attempt to fill in these cells with particular nations. (Of course, if you employed a finer distinction than 'high' or 'low' on each dimension then you would end up with a typology of even more types.) He does

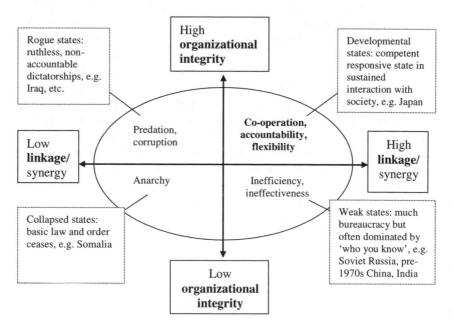

Figure 1.3 *How particular combinations of synergy and organizational integrity at the macro-level characterize distinct forms of state*
Source: Loosely adapted from Woolcock (1998).

not specify exactly what the relationship is between the dimensions. For example, he does not specify if a particular combination of synergy and organizational integrity will tend to foster a particular combination of bonding and bridging social capital at the micro-level (or vice versa).

The issue of how societies deal with asymmetrical power relationships is not limited to the state–society relationship. It arises whenever we consider the relationship between two individuals, communities or institutions where the parties have very unequal resources. Woolcock, Szreter and others have started using the concept of 'linking' social capital to describe the extent to which an individual's, or community's, networks are characterized by linkage between those with very unequal power and resources. Given the inherent asymmetry of such bonds, linking social capital may necessarily involve norms of mutual respect or moral equality that counterbalance the narrow, rational self-interest of the resource rich ('normative linking' social capital). Hence linking social capital may be provisionally viewed as a special form of bridging social capital that specifically concerns power – it is a vertical bridge across asymmetrical power and resources.[4]

It should be noted that the introduction of the concept of linking social capital only partly deals with the concerns raised by Edwards and Foley. To some extent, the issue is once again the level of analysis. We can either view a society's social capital from the macro-level, or we can zoom in and view it at the micro-level. If that society is characterized by high levels of bridging and linking social capital, then when we zoom in we should get a reasonably similar picture wherever we happen to have focused. This is because high levels of bridging and linking indicate a society that is highly interconnected, thereby sharing power and resources through a never-ending and evenly spun web of connections. On the other hand, if the society is characterized by low levels of bridging and linking then, depending on its underlying level of inequality, we will get a very varied picture of its social capital at the micro- or individual level. This is because the society is fragmented into relatively disconnected personal networks or strata. In such a society, we will see power and resources heavily clustered into segregated (and protected) club goods, cliques and 'protected enclaves'.

In so far as even the most nearly ideal society has only a limited amount of linking social capital, one should be cautious about inferring the experience of particular individuals or classes in society from average or macro-level measures. We shall return to the issue of the darker potentials of social capital, particularly of certain forms, in later chapters. For now we shall move on in an attempt to draw together the conceptual strands outlined so far.

Pulling the conceptual strands together

When we stand back from the conceptual arguments above, we should be able to see something useful and interesting – namely a conceptual map of the field. Each argument serves to articulate a different dimension of social capital, and for the most part, the dimensions seem perpendicular to one another. In short, we see three major cross-cutting dimensions:

1 components – networks, norms, sanctions;
2 levels or domain of analysis – individual, group, community, nation etc.;
3 character or function – bonding, bridging, linking.

This is shown in stylized form in figure 1.4. The complexity of this figure shows that we should be wary about making snap global judgements about whether a society or community is high or low in social capital, because it might be high in one type but low in another.

Consider what this framework implies in practice. Suppose I am interested in an individual's social capital (or at least that of their context). I may start by asking about their bonding social capital – whom they have close relationships with (family networks etc.), the norms that operate in those relationships (confiding, caring and support etc.) – and perhaps also about the sanctions that operate when the norms are broken (withdrawal of affection etc.). I will also need to ask about the more extended aspects of the individuals' networks – whom they are connected to – covering their friends and acquaintances outside of their immediate network (bridging social capital), and about how they are connected to those with more or less power and resources (linking).

This individual-level analysis will tell us a lot about this person's social capital, but it won't be the whole story. Ideally we will also want to know about how this person's social network connects with those of others in that community and society – the ecological level. Is the person a 'sociometric star' – highly connected and sociable – in a desert of otherwise disconnected individuals, or is everyone in the neighbourhood or community equally interconnected? In short, we will need to look at the extent to which bonding, bridging and linking are widespread across the community (the meso-level). And, depending how 'big tent' a definition we accept, we will want to know the extent of bonding, bridging and linking networks, norms and sanctions at the regional or national level.

In sum, we can draw from current theoretical debates a rich map or typology that we can use in later chapters to guide us through the wide-ranging social capital literature.

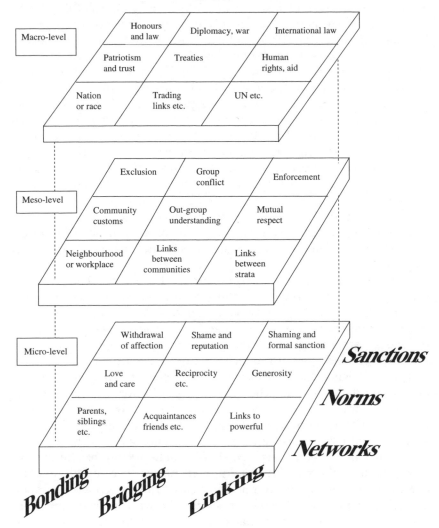

Figure 1.4 *A conceptual map of social capital (with examples)*

Is 'social capital' the right term?

We are now in a position to reconsider briefly the critique that the social capital concept bundles too much together, and that we should forget the term and simply concentrate on its components.

The issue ultimately rests on whether social capital is more than the sum of its components. The three components of social capital clearly have a systematic interrelationship with one another. Networks are partly defined, and help form, group norms (Tajfel, 1970, 1981). Group norms are partly held in place by the existence of sanctions (Posner and Rasmusen, 1999). In turn, effective sanctions rest critically on the existence of shared norms and network structure, such as a degree of closure (Coleman, 1988). Similarly, it seems very likely that the micro-, meso- and macro-levels of social capital have some kind of empirical, causal relationship to one another. The case for describing the character and trade-offs between different functions of social capital – bonding, bridging and linking – also seems very strong. They are complementary functions by definition. Hence there is a strong argument for viewing these different components, levels and characteristics together under the same heading – what we have called 'social capital' – because we believe that they have an intimate causal relationship with one another. They are part of a joined-up system or fabric. A big part of the puzzle is to understand the functioning of this greater whole, not just to measure the components.

There is a second strong argument in defence of keeping these components together under the same conceptual heading, and that is the supposition that the components can, to some extent at least, substitute or compensate for one another. In other words, we put the components together in one big family or genus because we believe that they have some degree of functional equivalence. It is the recognition of this equivalence that was one of Coleman's outstanding insights and that really lit the fuse for the current explosion of interest in social capital. Norms, networks and sanctions can partly compensate for one another (for example, see Katz, 2000). Hence a highly closed, or dense, network might be able to function effectively with very few explicit norms, while a very low-density network might still exhibit high trust and effective functioning if its norms were highly explicit and its sanctions severe. Similarly, highly generalized norms, such as civility or formalized codes of conduct between relative strangers within whole nations, may be able to substitute for some of the functions that were performed by more intimate micro-level norms and networks in traditional communities in societies at earlier stages of development (cf. Hawthorn, 1988; see also chapters 7 and 8). The degree of substitutability across bonding, bridging and linking social capital is less obvious. But it is definitely the case that individuals and even societies sometimes appear to forgo one such form of social capital (e.g. bonding) for another (e.g. bridging), such as when migrants to urban areas leave behind the bonding social capital of their village for the opportunities offered by the rich bridging social capital of the city.

Is it really 'capital'?

Before leaving current theoretical debates, we should at least mention the concern among some that social capital really isn't 'capital'. This viewpoint has been strongly stated by some economists, notably by Arrow and Solow (see Dasgupta and Serageldin, 2000). An alternative, for example, is to regard it as a factor that reduces 'transaction costs' – making it easier for people to work together – but without describing it as a form of capital *per se* (Paldam and Svendsen, 2000).

The concern tends to focus on 'fungibility'; that is, capital can be transformed from one form to another, common accounting can be agreed to compare the value or equivalence of different forms, and capital may be traded or sold. I can sell my gold krugerrands in a market place and buy some shares instead, but can the same be said of social capital? Some researchers have argued that the term causes a 'metaphorical confusion' between social 'capital' as a substantive quantity and as a process of embedded, goal-directed relationships (Bankston and Zhou, 2002).

This raises an interesting empirical question that we will need to address: can we substitute, differentially invest in or even trade our social capital? It was suggested in the previous section that we might be able to do this, at least to an extent. As individuals or a society, we do have some choices about the extent to which we invest in social capital, and even the type that we invest in. People, companies and communities regularly make decisions to 'invest' in their social networks by holding parties, dinners and other forms of socializing. Some people diligently send Christmas cards to all their friends and associates, keeping in touch with changes of address and changes in circumstances; others don't bother. And there are clearly opportunity-costs in such investments.

Recent empirical research suggests that people do indeed shrewdly 'invest' in their social capital just as theory predicts (Glaeser, Laibson and Sacerdote, 2002). For example, individual-level social capital rises, and then falls, with age, reflecting its advantages in the labour market (see chapter 2); rises in occupations with greater returns to social networks and skills; and falls with expected mobility, suggesting a rational disinvestment in advance of a move. Some have argued that even the most fundamental human decisions of whether to enter a long-term relationship, and how many children, if any, to have, are best understood as explicit investments in social capital (Astone et al., 1999).

Similarly, individuals, companies and communities have real choices between investing in social versus other forms of capital, though they may not see it in this way. Corporate managers can choose between buying new machines (physical capital), sending individuals on training courses (human capital), or sending a whole group of employees and associates on an adventure weekend that builds networks and trust between them (social capital).

On the other hand, it is also true that we can't phone up our broker and ask him to sell one chunk of our social network or norms and buy another. Partly this is because social capital is, to an extent, a public or club good and is therefore not entirely under our personal control (or ownership), but it is also because social capital is slow to form and change. Even when some decisions concerning our social capital appear partly under our control, such as the decision to end a marriage or exit a community, the 'transaction' may be painful, extended and irreversible. However, we might note that such limitations apply to other forms of capital too. For example, roads, rail networks and other forms of physical infrastructure may be safely termed as capital despite being partly public goods. Similarly, human capital is slow to change, and cannot literally be sold in terms of clean ownership transfer as might be demanded by certain classical conceptions of capital. Even the value and fungibility of forms of financial capital are not perfect. As Putnam points out, 'an eggbeater and an aircraft carrier both appear as physical capital in our national accounts, but the eggbeater is not much use for national defence, and the carrier would not be much help with your morning omelette' (Putnam, 2000, p. 21).

There are also concerns about the idea that when social capital is used, rather than being used up like other forms of capital, it generates more of itself – the more you socialize, the larger your networks get. However, this argument may have been overstated. It has been found that the overuse of social capital can lead to its depletion. For example, a study of investment in a transition economy found that communities that completed an early social fund project were less likely than comparison groups to complete other local infrastructure projects, 'suggesting that social capital was expended in these early projects' (Chase, 2002, p. 219). Similarly, individuals who draw heavily on their social networks without putting much back in tend to find themselves increasingly isolated and alone (see chapter 3 on the effects of depression).

Of course, some economists aren't too happy with the notion of human and some other forms of capital either, in the same way as some accountants aren't too happy about the idea of 'intellectual property' (Miller, 1996; Helliwell, pers. comm.). But if we get too enslaved by narrow definitions, we'll soon find that there is nothing of interest, or even of much economic value, left in the 'capital' concept at all. An economic model that ignores social capital, human capital and investment in public goods would be a pretty poor model.

In fact, many economists are warming to the idea of social capital (Temple, 1998; Piazza-Giorgi, 2002; also see chapter 2 on economic growth). The OECD's interest in the area has also added considerable credibility to the concept, and particularly the publication of its report for finance ministers, *The Well-Being of Nations: The Role of Human and Social Capital* (OECD, 2001a). There is a good chance that by 2010 the term will be at least no more controversial than 'human capital' is today.

Ironically, there is evidence of some backlash against the term by social scientists who feel uncomfortable with the 'economics-ization' of the social realm. Most prominent among these critics has been Ben Fine, who accuses social capital theorists of being 'fundamentally complicit with mainstream economics' (Fine, 2001, p. 193). But Fine has not been alone in this view. Others have argued that social capital 'blurs crucial analytic distinctions', with 'important ideological consequences' (S. S. Smith and Kulynych, 2002, p. 149); is a neo-liberal 'trojan horse' (Spies-Butcher, 2002); and obfuscates the idea of poverty as a focus of concern (Adams, 2002). Hence we see a curious dance between a group of economists worrying about the contamination of economics by 'soft' sociology, while a corresponding group of sociologists worry about the contamination of sociology by a 'hard' but narrow rational-choice worldview of economics. Perhaps we should see this mutual suspicion as a good sign, indicating that these rival disciplines that have too long been held apart are being forced back onto a more realistic common ground.

The practical problem of measuring social capital

One of the reasons why some economists and others don't like the concept of social capital is that it appears very difficult to measure. This is aggravated further by the use of very different measures of social capital by different researchers (Schuller, Baron and Field, 2000).

The issue of measurement inconsistency is partly resolved by the conceptual discussion above in which we identify the wide range of social networks and norms that can all be legitimately described as social capital. But this still leaves a formidable measurement task for any researcher or government brave enough to attempt a 'social capital audit'. Box 1.2 addresses aspects of this concern.

Box 1.2   What makes a good measure?

Reliability refers to whether a measure can be trusted to give the same result if repeated. For example, if we ask a hundred people whether they think that their neighbours can be trusted, then ask the same people the same question a week later, the correlation between the two measures is referred to as test-retest reliability. If the neighbourhoods have not changed much in the intervening week, we would expect this correlation to be high. Reliability is generally viewed as a necessary but not sufficient condition for a measure to be valid.

Surface, or 'face', validity refers to whether a measure 'looks right' – in other words, it intuitively seems that it captures the concept that we are trying to measure. It is an obvious starting point for judging a measure, but is not the most important test. For example, response rates to surveys and 'giving the finger' to other drivers have both proven to be reliable measures of communities' social capital, even though neither of them seems an obvious indicator at first.

Criterion-related validity refers to whether a measure relates to other 'gold-standard', independent indicators of the same entity. For example, we could judge the validity of people's self-report of organizational membership by comparing their answers to the records of the organizations themselves.

Predictive validity refers to whether the measure accurately predicts other outcomes or variables that are of particular interest. It is arguably the most important form of validity. For example, we may ultimately care less about whether a measure of social trust relates to organizational membership than about whether this measure predicts other important outcomes such as economic growth, health, crime and so on.

A rough-and-ready measure: 'social trust'

The standard measure of social capital is often taken to be the number or density of voluntary organizations in an area (e.g. Paldam and Svendsen, 2000). The principal justification for this measure is that it appears as a pivotal measure in Putnam's classic Italian study (Putnam, 1993). However, despite its popularity, three serious weaknesses of this as a measure can be identified. First, it only appears to tap a narrow, meso-level, network-based definition of social capital. If one is at all persuaded by the discussion above, then this is a perilously slim base to measure the concept from. Second, it has proven a surprisingly difficult and controversial measure in practice, in that the composition and nature of groups can be ambiguous and can change over time. Hence any particular list of organizations is apt to be challenged as incomplete, biased, or not comparable across countries (Rich, 1999; Lowndes, 2000; de Ulzurrun, 2002). Furthermore, a numerical measure of density may fail to capture important qualitative differences across organization types. Third, studies conducted since Putnam's Italian case study have sometimes failed to replicate the patterns of association between the density of organizations and the predicted outcome variables (e.g. Knack and Keefer, 1997). This indicates poor 'predictive validity', which may itself reflect the narrowness and unreliability of association-based measures.[5]

However, many studies have been successfully conducted using a very simple measure of social capital, namely the extent to which most people in a given community, region or nation trust each other. This is normally tapped by asking the question:

'Generally speaking, would you say that most people can be trusted or that you can't be too careful in dealing with people?'

1 Most people can be trusted
2 Can't be too careful
9 Don't know

(World Values Survey, 1981–3, 1990–2, 1995–7)

'Surface validity' of the social trust measure follows from the theoretical discussion above (see box 1.2). The net result of people being connected up in social networks with shared norms that facilitate co-operative action should be the emergence of trust. It may be argued that the underlying issue is not trust *per se*, but trustworthiness. After all, if I put my trust in people who in reality cannot be trusted, then the resultant 'co-operation' will be one-sided and short-lived. That said, it is reasonable to assume that people's answer to the question reflects their experiences in reality. Furthermore, it is reasonable to argue that widespread trust and trustworthiness are themselves an important part of the normative dimension of social capital (cf. Coleman, 1988).

The proportions of people agreeing that 'most people can be trusted' turns out to vary greatly from nation to nation, as well as from region to region (see chapter 2, figure 2.1). The data for 2001–4 show the proportion saying that most people can be trusted varies from around two-thirds in Scandinavian countries such as Norway, down to less than one in twenty in South American countries such as Brazil. The data indicate that this measure is remarkably stable over time – at least over the 1980s and 1990s, for which we have data – indicating that it is reliable as a measure (see chapter 7 for more detail on trends). This measure of social trust has been used as a 'rough-and-ready' indicator of social capital at the national level by a number of researchers, and this success in predicting important outcomes is evidence of arguably the most important form of predictive validity (e.g. Knack and Keefer, 1997; Whiteley, 1997; Halpern, 2001).

A check on criterion-related validity can be made by comparing the social trust measure with other more elaborate measures of social

---

Box 1.3 Case study: identifying the 'civicly disengaged'

The British General Household Survey ran a 'social capital' module in 2000, which included a range of questions covering civic engagement, neighbourliness, social networks and social support. Within each of these areas, many questions were asked, but often tended to correlate with each other. Items that correlated highly were combined into indexes within each of these areas. For example, the civicly disengaged were defined as people who:

- had not been involved in a local organization,
- had not taken an action to solve a local problem,
- did not feel well informed,
- and did not feel that they could influence decisions that affect the neighbourhood, alone or working with others.

Around 16 per cent of people fell into this category, ranging from 7 per cent in the most affluent areas to 22 per cent in the most deprived areas. The civicly disengaged were most likely to be:

- young (older age groups tend to be progressively more engaged),
- women,
- ethnic minorities,
- more poorly educated,
- with dependent children,
- private or social renters (as opposed to owner occupiers),
- and having recently moved house.

For further information, see Coulthard, Walker and Morgan (2002).

capital. Recent detailed work on the USA, which shows substantial regional variation in levels of expressed social trust, offers such an opportunity. Putnam (2000) constructed an elaborate index to measure the differences in social capital across the US states. From a variety of sources, fourteen state-level measures were combined, including measures of home entertaining and socializing with friends, group membership and attendance, voluntary and community service of various kinds, attendance at public meetings, electoral turnout, and social trust. It turns out that the strongest single correlate with the overall index was the percentage of people agreeing that most people can be trusted, the correlation being .92 with the overall index. This means that 85 per cent of the variability captured by the index was captured by the simple measure of social trust.

In sum, questionnaire items tapping social trust, averaged at the community, regional or national level, appear to be simple, reliable and valid indicators of social capital at the aggregate level.

More elaborate measures of social capital: towards a 'Vitamin model'

The theoretical discussion has outlined a number of different dimensions of social capital, such as bonding, bridging and linking, and ideally we should measure all these. This implies the need for a battery of measures. 'Quick and dirty' measures are always useful to have available – not least when fighting for valuable space in national surveys – but most serious researchers also want to understand exactly which aspects of social capital have which consequences, and how they relate to each other (Boix and Posner, 1995; Rothstein, 2001; Nuissl, 2002; Pattie, Seyd and Whiteley, 2004).

The metaphor that is used in a number of places in this book is that of a vitamin model (cf. Warr's vitamin model of employment; Warr, 1987). A healthy and effective community needs a blend of different types of social capital, just as a person needs a blend of different vitamins in their diet to be physically healthy. In principle, then, we need measures of each of these forms of social capital, or vitamins.

If we take the example of bonding social capital at the individual level, we can look to the large psychological literature on social support for clues about measures. Psychologists have now spent several decades developing and refining measures aimed at tapping the supportive qualities of people's social networks, including the extent to which they feel belonging, and receive emotional and practical support (see, for example, Berkman and Kawachi, 2000). Interestingly, it turns out that, rather as with the general social trust question above, the answer to a simple question can go a long way to capture the quality of an individual's supportive network. The typical formulation of this question is: 'If you have a problem, or something is worrying you, do you have someone who you can turn to?'

However, in many areas we do not have a long-established literature to guide us towards the simplest, shortest question that will capture each type of social capital. Researchers across the world are therefore working to develop such measures.[6] Several nations are in the process of developing or conducting what might be termed national 'audits of social capital', using short questionnaires ranging from a few minutes to over an hour, and with sample sizes ranging from a few thousand to twenty thousand plus. Because of the disagreements and differences in emphasis that we have seen in the review above, it is inevitable that the measures contained in these various surveys will differ substantially, though a common core module has been agreed by researchers across several nations.

It is difficult to shortcut this process of measurement development, though some are certainly trying. One group has experimented with the use of neural network models to help identify key distinguishing variables (Veiga et al., 2000). As noted above, a number of early studies used the absolute number of associations and their membership numbers as a measure of (meso-level) social capital. However, many of these were subsequently criticized for drawing the net of what counts as an association too narrowly, missing the emergence of new forms of association or other informal patterns of association (Rich, 1999). There has also been criticism that the list of recognized associations tends to be male biased, neglecting more female forms of association such as those over childcare arrangements (Lowndes, 2000). Ideally the researcher is looking for a compromise between a measure that is reasonably comprehensive, and therefore valid and reliable, and one that is short enough to be used in practice. Unfortunately, it can sometimes take years to reach such a compromise.

The measurement problem is made significantly more difficult when we consider the issue of cultural differences in the expression of social capital. There are undoubtedly national and regional differences in forms of social capital. Clearly, most organizations have a regional base and therefore the actual organizations that are found will vary from place to place. For example, there is no equivalent of the (American) National Rifle Association in Britain, and similarly no equivalent of the (British) National Trust in the USA. More difficult still, forms of co-operative norms and organizational structures may vary from place to place. Hence, the British and North American habit of queuing is not shared by all nations, while certain eastern norms concerned with putting the community before self-interest are not necessarily shared by certain western nations.

This measurement problem is not necessarily solved by the standard practice of constructing indexes. A premise for two items being put into the same index is normally that they are reasonably correlated with one another. But given functional equivalence, when one indicator is prevalent in one area or country and a different one in another area or country, then the two indicators may be uncorrelated (i.e. not statistically associated). Yet despite this, they may indicate the same thing. In other words, they may be functionally equivalent forms of the same underlying type of co-operation or social structure, despite their different (culturally bound) forms.

The indications that social capital may be manifested, at least partly, in different ways in different cultures make cross-national measurement a complex process. These differences are not merely measurement error – communities and nations can have qualitatively and quantitatively different forms of social capital. These differences may also lead to some variations in the causal relationships between social capital and outcome variables. For example, Americans are far more hostile and resistant to using the state as a solution to collective problems than are the populations of most European nations. This is associated with a different pattern of social capital in the USA and Europe and, almost certainly, leads to different causal relationships between the variables (see chapters 8 and 9).

This complexity has led some to argue that social capital can only be understood in its local context (Edwards and Foley, 1998). However, as we shall see in the literature presented in later chapters, many common consequences and causal patterns can be seen of social capital across a variety of contexts. In other words, while we may see a huge variety of forms of social capital, the underlying functions and causal outcomes are often remarkably similar.

In summary, we need to move towards a multi-faceted model of social capital, and considerable progress has been made in this direction, as we see in part II (especially chapter 9). However, the process of developing cross-culturally valid forms of measurement is not straightforward and is likely to be a source of continued debate and focus for many years to come.

Where to from here?

We are witnessing a maturing and broadening of the social capital agenda. Data are now starting to become available in several countries from bespoke social capital surveys, in contrast with many of the previous data, which were typically drawn from a few items buried within general purpose surveys. These surveys are creating benchmarks that can be used to track changes over time, and should also help researchers fill out the social capital concept empirically. Within countries, numerous agencies and government departments are also looking at the concept of social capital, including at how it may affect their own area of concern and how it may be measured. For example, the Bush administration has moved to ensure that both volunteering and social capital data are gathered to run alongside their flagship domestic policy programmes of expanded volunteering and civic engagement.[7]

International bodies have also become very interested in social capital. As mentioned above, a relatively early entry into the field was the World Bank, which had assembled a powerful team of researchers to look at the role played by social capital in development by late 1998. It also set up a useful website of material related to social capital, sought to develop a common measure that could be used across a wide range of countries, and even hosted an electronic discussion bulletin ('Let's Talk') to enable experts across the world to exchange information and ideas. Similarly, the OECD has followed up its interest in social capital on the back of its 2001 report, including an international meeting on the subject of measurement. This OECD–Office of National Statistics joint conference, hosted in London in September 2002, brought together experts and the statistical agencies of more than twenty countries to discuss and co-ordinate social capital measurement. Social capital was also the main theme of the UN's Sienna group meeting in 2002.

One final aspect of the current research on social capital that is worth noting is the sheer range of disciplines that it involves. It would be misleading to call this research truly cross-disciplinary, as much of it remains locked away in the rigid divides that characterize much of contemporary academic activity. Nonetheless, it is a rare concept indeed that excites simultaneous interest across political science, economics, sociology, criminology, psychology, education and so on. It is this remarkable emerging body of research that this book draws together, and that has made this book possible at all.

Summary and conclusion

Social capital as a term has been used sporadically since the early twentieth century, but only came into wider and more consistent usage following the work of Coleman, Bourdieu and Putnam in the late 1980s and early 1990s. The term refers to the social networks, norms and sanctions that facilitate co-operative action among individuals and communities. From 1995, there has been an explosion in research on the topic across a wide range of academic disciplines. This expansion shows no sign of slowing, with national and even international policymakers and institutions showing increased interest in the concept and its apparent consequences.

While differing definitions and usage can be found between researchers, an overall typology of social capital can identified. This typology incorporates three different dimensions of social capital: its main components (networks, norms and sanctions); the level of analysis employed (individual-, meso- and macro-levels); and its character or function (bonding, bridging and linking).

There is some disagreement about how far the social capital concept or 'tent' should be stretched. There is a strong logical case for extending the definition to include institutions and formalized norms. But there is also a strong practical case for keeping the definition 'lean and mean' in order to focus research and policy on the important and neglected role of informal social networks. There is also some disagreement about whether social capital is really 'capital', but a fairly robust defence of the term can be presented – at least as robust as that for the term 'human capital'.

Controversy still surrounds the measurement of social capital, but a rough-and-ready measure with reasonable reliability and validity seems to be 'social trust', that is, the extent to which people in a given community or region feel that others can generally be trusted. Work is currently under way in a number of countries on national 'audits' of social capital, and these should lead to more detailed information on the different types of social capital and their consequences. However, the development of cross-nationally accepted and comparable measures of all the different dimensions of social capital may be some way off, because of cultural differences and the problem of establishing functional equivalence.

Further reading

For an early and influential grappling with the *social capital concept*, Coleman's classic 1988 paper remains very readable, mixing clear examples with a powerful theoretical analysis. Michael Woolcock's work is also recommended for the more academically inclined – look out not only for his lengthy 1998 paper, but for his forthcoming (at the time of writing) edited work exploring the application of the social capital concept in a wide range of developing national contexts.

For more *critical academic reviews* of the social capital concept, the papers by Portes (1998) and Edwards and Foley (1998) are recommended. Ben Fine has also published a series of critical reviews and a bitingly critical, though partial book (2001).

There is also now a lot being done by *government and official bodies*. The World Bank website is a fantastic resource for both academics and policymakers, and includes useful summaries of large numbers of research papers. Look out too for their ongoing work to develop an off-the-shelf social capital measurement tool designed to be applicable to a wide range of national contexts, and especially to the developing nations. See www.worldbank.org/poverty/scapital/. The OECD (2001a) report is worth a look, particularly for its exploration of the parallels between social and human capital, and the interrelationships between them. And for a useful data-bank of all the questions ever used to measure social capital, see the UK Office of National Statistics website at www.statistics.gov.uk/socialcapital.

Part I

Why is Social Capital Important?

2

⟨⟨⟨⟩⟩⟩

Economic Performance

Tony Restell read Economics and Management Studies at St John's College [Cambridge], graduating in 1996. Here he shares with us the tremendous difference that being a Johnian has made in the launch of his internet venture.

> ... thumbing through my address book I found countless Johnians willing and able to help. And so it is that tasks that might have taken many man-weeks have been condensed into man-days. Cold-calling exercises have been transformed into pleasant introductions.
> ... interpersonal networks are critical in setting up an internet venture – the more you can draw on a strong network of people and contacts, the more productive and successful you will be.

Johnian News, Issue 7, Lent term 2000

There are strong theoretical reasons to expect social capital to affect economic performance. The efficient functioning of markets requires a good flow of information to connect buyers and sellers, and the ability to enforce contracts or other negotiated arrangements easily and cheaply. Economies with such features should be conducive to innovation and entrepreneurialism, risk-taking and investment, effective competition and the efficient allocation of resources.

Information flows should be strongly affected by the size and character of social networks. At the extreme, an atomized population of isolated hunter-gathers virtually precludes the possibility of a market. But information flow, while necessary, is not a sufficient condition for an efficient market. Whether a given sale, exchange or purchase proceeds also depends on a range of 'transaction costs' – such as the commission to be paid, the legal costs, and the risks involved. These transaction costs also prove to be heavily affected by social capital, and especially by prevalent norms and sanctions. Social capital reduces transaction costs by altering the terms of trade; eliminating, or greatly reducing, the need for expensive contractual arrangements; generating decision flexibility; and saving time (P. N. Wilson, 2000). In short, trust, reputation and informal sanctions can strongly supplement formal contracts, the legal system and formal sanctions.

In this, and subsequent chapters, the evidence is reviewed and organized by level of analysis: individual or micro-level; community or meso-level; and regional, national or macro-level (see chapter 1 for a fuller discussion of the distinctions between these levels).

Micro-level economic effects

Evidence for the economic effects of social capital at the micro-level can be summarized in the phrase 'it's not *what* you know, but *who* you know that counts'. The college graduate and internet entrepreneur quoted at the start of this chapter is not the first to have noticed that his address book is one of his most valuable assets.

One key channel through which social capital can affect an individual's economic outcomes is through its effects on educational attainment and school drop-out. Having a family who support and encourage you while young can have a substantial impact on your educational attainment and subsequent earnings (see chapter 5). But it has been found that even when educational attainment, IQ and parental resources have been statistically controlled for, indicators of more limited or less supportive social capital in childhood – such as growing up in a single-parent family or with family conflict – significantly predict the risk of unemployment in adulthood (Caspi et al., 1998). It would seem that social capital starts to affect labour market outcomes even in early childhood (see also chapters 4 and 8).

Labour market functioning

Studies of long- and short-term unemployment, over many years, have found that the probability of leaving unemployment is strongly affected by the individual's social network. This is because a very large proportion of jobs are filled by applicants who heard about them 'along the grapevine' – that is, through word of mouth and personal contacts (M. S. Granovetter, 1973; White, 1991; Montgomery, 1991; Six, 1997a; Hannan, 1999). Similarly, following migration or relocation, those using personal networks tend to find jobs that are better quality (Eby, 2001) and longer-lasting (Aguilera, 2003).

Estimates of the proportions of jobs filled by word of mouth vary, but are almost universally high. For example, one recent study of low-paid labour markets found that 60 per cent of vacancies were filled using recommendations from existing employees (D. Brown et al., 2001). The phenomenon is not restricted to the low-paid: studies of top managers have similarly found that they largely find their jobs through informal channels (Boxman, de Graaf and Flap, 1991). Another recent study, examining all 35,000 job applicants in the recruitment process of a mid-sized US high-tech organization between 1985 and 1994, found that 80 per cent of white employees used personal networks to find out about employment opportunities there – though only 5 per cent of black employees did so (T. Petersen, Saporta and Seidel, 2000; see further below).

Unemployed individuals whose friends are outside of the labour market are at a serious disadvantage, in that they will not hear about job opportunities since they are disconnected from those who would know about such opportunities (W. J. Wilson, 1987). This helps to explain the strong positive association that is found between the size of an individual's friendship network and their labour force participation (Aguilera, 2002). But as Granovetter's work famously showed, it is most often 'weak ties' – connections through loose associates, distant relatives and friends – that are of most benefit in the labour market. It is through these connections – that is, bridging network social capital – that individuals are exposed to a much wider range of information and opportunities (M. S. Granovetter, 1973, 1985).

Individual earnings

It is not only the unemployed who benefit from more extensive bridging social capital. A series of studies of the employed has shown that those who progress furthest and fastest tend to be those with the most extensive contacts (Podolny and Baron, 1997). It is noteworthy that even in the toughest and most competitive financial centres of the world, much business continues to be conducted largely on the basis of trust relations and successful traders work hard to maintain this trust (Burrough and Helyar, 1991).

There is considerable evidence that those with more extensive networks tend to get paid more – though the causal direction needs to be carefully considered. Professionals and managers tend to have considerably larger and more varied social networks than working-class individuals, and this pattern has been found across nations (Goldthorpe, Llewellyn and Payne, 1987; Aldridge, 2001).

Controlling for other factors, those with more extensive social networks – from farmers to top businesspeople – tend to come out financially ahead. For example, in Boxman et al.'s study of 1,359 top managers in the Netherlands' larger companies, managers' incomes were found to be substantially related to their social capital (measured as external work contacts and memberships), even having controlled for their education, experience and seniority in the organization as measured by their number of subordinates (Boxman, de Graaf and Flap, 1991). Similarly, a world away in Madagascar, the sales and value-added of agricultural traders were found to be significantly related to the extensiveness of their social networks, even having controlled for both individual characteristics and physical inputs (Fafchamps and Minten, 2002).

On the face of it, from an economic point of view, it's really worth having a large social network – especially if it includes the wealthy and powerful – and those who broker information between groups and individuals can derive considerable benefits from their position in the social network (Burt, 1999). This works even for the wealthy. For example, it has been shown that firms get a better deal from their bank if their directors go to the trouble of getting to know their bank manager, all other things being equal (Uzzi, 1999). Similarly, a life history study of technology-based firms found that those with founders that had more direct and indirect relationships with venture investors were significantly more likely to obtain funding and to succeed (Shane and Stuart, 2002).

In short, social networks are strongly implicated as a factor that helps explain individual differences in earnings, as well as many other outcomes (see also chapters 4 and 5, on crime and education). More extensive social networks provide information about a wider range of job opportunities to choose between and, once in a job, provide access to valued customers, other traders and co-workers, and to sources of finance (Fafchamps and Minten, 2002; Shane and Stuart, 2002; R. A. Baron and Markman, 2003).

But there is a sting in the tail. While our social networks are generally a powerful and positive resource – at least for those with such networks – they can sometimes work against us. If somebody in our social network takes against us, they can be a powerful foe, blocking our career advancement and poisoning our social network against us (Moerbeek and Need, 2003). This is an important point to note: as we shall see repeatedly throughout this book, our social capital is not always good for us.

Ethnic, social and gender differences: does social capital contribute to disadvantage?

We have already seen that those with more extensive social networks tend to be at an economic advantage, that the middle classes have more extensive and diverse social networks than the working class, and that this differential helps to sustain the disadvantage of the less privileged in society. Social capital may help to explain the robust finding in the social mobility literature that upward mobility has been far more common than downward mobility over recent decades – in this case, what goes up doesn't seem to come down (Aldridge, 2001). The rich social contacts of middle-class families help to ensure that even their less able children find good jobs, whereas less well-connected working-class children must rely on their abilities to mark them out (see also chapter 5).

Much the same appears to apply to many ethnic differentials. For example, as noted above, Petersen et al. (2000) found that black US employees were far less likely to have found out about employment opportunities via personal networks than were white employees (5 per cent compared with 80 per cent). It was found that once account was taken of the method of finding out about job opportunities, race had no further effect on the outcome of the hiring process. Petersen et al. therefore concluded that access to and effective utilization of social networks largely explain black–white differences in labour market progress.

This observation was made early on by Loury (1987, 1992). He argued that even if the financial and human capital advantages of white Americans were somehow removed, black Americans would still be at a disadvantage because of their weaker connections to mainstream institutions.

Similarly, research conducted for a UK government report on ethnic minorities found that one of the barriers to their labour market advancement was a lack of social connections. Black and minority ethnic professionals in particular felt that they lacked the networks to enable them to advance their careers. They also felt at a disadvantage because access to professional social connections was not intrinsic in their upbringing (Cabinet Office Strategy Unit, 2002). This echoes previous research that has found that having a parent or relative already involved in a profession makes it significantly easier for individuals to get key professional positions and placements (Halpern, 1992).

On the other hand, the strong ties within many immigrant ethnic communities provide an invaluable stepping stone for the economic survival and advancement of group members. Studies have repeatedly demonstrated that successful first-generation immigrant communities, often excluded from mainstream financial and civic institutions, succeed by forming enclaves with a range of indigenous social institutions for support (Waldinger, Aldrich and Ward, 1990; Massey and Espinosa, 1999; Sanders, Nee and Sernau, 2002). This, together with chain-migration (family and friends gradually joining migrants over time), largely explains why labour markets tend to become ethnically segmented, with certain occupations becoming dominated by particular ethnic groups (Portes and Zhou, 1992; Oigenblick and Kirschenbaum, 2002; Wang and Hsiao, 2002).[1] Interestingly, this strong bonding social capital can ultimately hold back the economic progress of entrepreneurial immigrants as waves of subsequent immigrants make further demands on their resources. This helps to explain why many immigrants subsequently break away from the security of the enclave, often changing their names in the process to make their ethnic origins less obvious, so as not to find their hard-earned assets being drained by later generations of newcomers.

Similar arguments have been made to help explain the relative disadvantage of women, and possibly gender segregation, in the labour market. This is a large and well-established literature, though it has only very recently started to employ the language of social capital (Metz and Tharenou, 2001; Scantlebury, 2002). In essence, women's lack of access to the 'old boys' network' (literally) can put them at a disadvantage, particularly in the higher echelons of the labour market, where the 'glass ceiling' appears to operate.

So – will investing in social capital make you rich and successful?

The short answer to this question is 'maybe' – such an investment should make individual success a little more likely, especially if it involves bridging and linking social capital to the 'right' circles. But before we throw ourselves headlong into an endless series of cocktail parties and social events in search of economic advancement, there are a few points that should be considered about this micro-level literature.

First, there are some concerns about the robustness of some of the findings. In particular, even with the best methodological controls, there is a residual concern about the direction of causality between individuals' social networks and their economic advancement. Many of the studies are essentially cross-sectional – they measure the association between variables at one point in time. It may be that more extensive social networks might themselves arise from successful employment or reflect job role, performance or wealth, rather than the network determining the employment or earnings. At least some of the associations between social networks and success arise as a result of underlying individual differences such as social intelligence or competence. However, the evidence is that social intelligence and social capital have some independent effects on financial success over and above each other. For example, a recent study of the financial success of entrepreneurs in the high-tech and cosmetics industries found that social capital (having an extensive social network etc.) assisted entrepreneurs in gaining access to persons important for their success. But once such access was attained, it was the entrepreneurs' social competence that influenced the outcomes they experienced (R. A. Baron and Markman, 2003). Similarly, individuals differ in their ability to mobilize the social capital available to them, and sometimes the financial advantages that flow from new skills and experiences are partly mediated by the skill to mobilize this social, as well as human, capital more effectively (Ma, 2002).

Discussion of causal direction will be a recurrent theme in this book. In this particular literature, most experts are fairly confident that in relation to the labour market effects, a large part of the causality does run from the network to the outcome. For example, longitudinal studies that track movements in and out of employment, such as after mass redundancies, suggest pretty convincingly that those with more extensive social networks – especially to those still in employment – are significantly more likely to gain new employment (White, 1991; Six, 1997a). In contrast, the evidence is less conclusive about the causal relationship between individuals' social networks and earnings. The initial indications are that more extensive social networks give you a headstart, but that you also need to have the skills to follow this advantage through.

Second, while most studies emphasize the benefits of extensive social networks for individual personal advancement, and particularly of bridging social capital or weak ties, we should note that there may be some downsides too. For example, one study found that although having large, sparse networks of informal ties did indeed have a positive effect on career advancement, those with the largest 'buy-in' networks also had the lowest job satisfaction (Podolny and Baron, 1997). Similarly the strategy of successful immigrants or the upwardly mobile working class – trading the security of strong bonding social capital for the wider economic advantages of social bridging capital – sometimes comes at a price, notably in terms of health and well-being (see chapter 3).

Finally, micro-level evidence raises the issue of whether the apparent advantages of an extended social network are a 'zero-sum game'. If a given individual gains an advantage through having a more extensive personal network, is this simply at the corresponding cost of those without such a social network? As DeFilippis (2001, p. 793) argues:

> if there is one job, and everyone is connected to the same networks and realise the same benefits of social capital, then you cease to have the kinds of networks that Putnam and Coleman are talking about . . . If everyone is connected then everyone . . . would lose the benefits of those connections because they would no longer gain capital from them (in this case, the job) . . . yuppies network precisely to get ahead of everyone else.

There is a powerful counter to De Filippis's argument. If information flows more freely through more extensive social networks, then even if these networks are evenly spread, the labour market should function more effectively because of increases in allocative efficiency. The network should ensure that the right people get into the right jobs and at low cost, hence implying more than a zero-sum game. However, this important issue cannot be resolved empirically at the individual level. Instead, it requires an ecological-level analysis at the meso- or macro-level, and it is to this that we now turn.

Meso-level economic effects: communities as markets

The New York diamond market, as described in Coleman's classic study, is a clear example of the potential economic benefits of social capital at the meso- or community level (Coleman, 1988; see chapter 1). The high shared understandings and trustworthiness that exist inside the community of diamond merchants greatly lower the costs associated with showing diamonds to one another and pursuing mutually beneficial deals. Most individual traders gain from these arrangements – it is not a simple zero-sum game, as the whole community of traders benefit within this network of mutual interdependence.

The New York diamond market might be argued as being too atypical to tell us much about the operation of most markets, for it rests on an underlying, pre-existing, orthodox Jewish community with its pre-existing strong ties and shared moral code. However, less dramatic but essentially similar examples can be seen in other business contexts. Relationships between business parties are often based on informal contracts and implicit agreements (Burrough and Helyar, 1991). Indeed, one of the earliest applications of the social capital concept was to the understanding of commercial activity, such as studies of the character of Japanese industry (Lorcher, 1982).

Even in this high-tech world of e-based world markets, it remains the case that most business continues to be channelled not just by price signals but by social networks (Urry, 2002). People tend to buy from and do deals with those that they know, be they farmers or city financiers, and the business lunch remains as ubiquitous today as ever. Today's market is high-tech, but still 'high touch'.

Neighbourhood and community effects

The key evidence for neighbourhood or community effects should be a visible impact on economic attainment at the neighbourhood level even after individual-level characteristics have been controlled for. For example, Buck (2001) shows that for any given level of individual disadvantage, as the level of unemployment in the area increases, so the chances of that individual escaping poverty fall. As the level of unemployment in the area exceeds around one in four, the chances of escaping poverty drop dramatically.

This story of double disadvantage is a familiar one to policymakers and sociologists the world over. It was this phenomenon that Wilson was talking about in his classic text, *The Truly Disadvantaged* (W. J. Wilson, 1987). Wilson's work concerned the poor black communities of Chicago, but similar stories can be told for pockets of disadvantage in many large cities. In London, for example, at the same time as many employers, such as those in the hotel industry, complain that they cannot fill basic vacancies, pockets of high unemployment persist. Qualitative work shows that young people in such areas often appear largely unaware of the job opportunities only a few miles away. Even when they are aware of the jobs, they somehow do not believe that they will be able to secure them, or the fact that the job is some ten miles away in an area that they and their friends are unfamiliar with means that they do not apply.

These findings indicate how social networks and norms, and particularly the paucity of connections to advantaged individuals in mainstream employment, become self-reinforcing at the neighbourhood level. The neighbourhood and its social capital collapse in on themselves, like a shrinking star turning into an inescapable black hole. The poverty and paucity of neighbours' and friends' networks reinforce each other, leaving a bleak and often seemingly intractable problem. In contrast, when members of a poor community reach out, seeking work and opportunities more widely – such as through temporary economic migrations – they can act as a powerful bridge to new sources of affluence (Potot, 2002).

To some extent the absence or presence of valuable social capital within an area acquires a monetary value in the form of house price differentials. These differentials are partly an expression of other neighbourhood characteristics, such as low crime and high-performing schools (themselves also affected by social capital; see later chapters). But this monetarization helps cement neighbourhood social capital differentials, with the affluent and well-connected buying themselves access to a more valuable social network, while leaving others locked into pockets of network poverty.

A ray of hope comes from those areas and neighbourhoods that have managed to turn themselves around. Often at the heart of such stories lie the efforts of an exceptional individual or group of residents who galvanize the community, stimulating co-operation and encouraging a more confident, outward-looking and high-aspiration orientation among the residents.

One inspiring and well-documented example is that of Tupelo, Mississippi, which turned itself around from one of the poorest counties within the US in the early 1940s into a highly successful model of community and economic development (Grisham, 1999). This was despite lacking natural resources, transport connections to other areas, and a university; having been ravaged by a terrible tornado; and losing its only significant factory in the late 1930s. Its turnaround has been largely credited to the exceptional leadership of a local newspaper proprietor. He persuaded local business leaders and farmers to pool their money to buy a siring bull – a decision that led to the creation of a lucrative dairy industry. The local Chamber of Commerce was disbanded and a Community Development Foundation, open to everyone, was created instead. A major cultural change was achieved, with a less hierarchical and more co-operative, self-help style that improved schools, created an educational centre and a medical centre, and drove clean-up campaigns.

Another example is the city of Curobato in Brazil, which was turned around by an ex-architect mayor. In the absence of cash or resources, community credit schemes were set up which rewarded children from the slums for recycling materials, leading to a cleaner and healthier

environment. Other schemes followed, such as a system of environmental credits that encouraged development and the creation of public
parks at the same time. The net result was not just a changed environment, but a changed culture – and a city economic growth rate that
consistently outstripped that of other Brazilian cities.

Similar arguments have been made in other areas. For example,
socially and ethnically based affiliations – particularly those associated
with consultative norms – have been shown to be an important influence on the spread and adoption of new, more productive technologies
among African farming communities (Isham, 2002). Similarly, the productivity of academic departments is affected not only by the cohesiveness of the department but also by its links and affiliations with
others outside the faculty (Bjarnason and Sigfusdottir, 2002; Del Favero,
2003).

The firm as a form of social capital

It can be argued – rather convincingly – that one of the most common
and important forms of social capital is the firm or company. The
attempt by many corporations to 'outsource' almost every activity one
can think of, leaving only the brand name and core management inside
the company, raises the puzzle of why we need companies at all. This
fascinating question was raised over sixty years ago by Couse, who
asked why firms were necessary given that individuals can simply buy,
and sell, labour and products directly (Couse, 1937). The answer, of
course, is that there are major economic advantages to bringing
together a group of individuals with complementary skills into a
closely co-ordinated network, with shared understandings and mutual
commitments that facilitate co-operative action for maximum productivity. The existence of the firm means that the individuals inside it can
rely on one another to be there when they need each other, to share
information, and to perform tasks without elaborate contracts and bar-
gains having to be negotiated for each separate act (Szreter, 1999; Donalson and Dunfee, 1999; Spangnolo, 1999). Relying on firm-based social
capital instead of a system of formal pricing should be particularly
attractive when the transaction costs might be high, the good is inex-
pensive, demand is inelastic, the group continues to interact over time,
and the time between interactions is short (Borcherding and Filson,
2002; Annen, 2003).

In short, the firm can be viewed as a form of social capital – and
perhaps primarily as 'bonding' social capital. Individual economic
agents club together into a relatively dense network (a workforce).

They develop shared norms and objectives (a corporate culture, an understanding of roles and appropriate behaviour, and a shared understanding of the product or company purpose). And the firm incorporates sanctions to maintain these norms and internal networks (peer and management pressure, economic rewards and advancement, and formal and informal punishments for underperformance or defection).

Between-firm social capital and economic clusters

However important the internal bonds that define the firm are, the links between the firm and its trading partners are also important. This is analogous to the importance of 'weak bonds' to the individual economic agent. Strong and cohesive bonds inside the firm may prove of limited use if the firm lacks a suitable network of suppliers or links to potential consumers of its products.

Strategic alliances between firms can offer significant competitive advantages by providing access to valuable information, finance and the opportunity to develop joint products (Ireland, Hitt and Vaidyanath, 2002; Shane and Cable, 2002; Koba and Prescott, 2002). For example, many successful high-tech engineering firms, be they in the USA, Europe or Asia, now run compatible design and ordering software and share much commercially sensitive information. This close sharing of software and information enables them to meet tighter deadlines and maintain optimum efficiency. Such high-risk strategies are only possible in a context of a network of suppliers who trust one another and share common understandings (Lane and Bachman, 1995, 1998).

A similar story can be told for many successful traditional firms too. The retailing firm of Marks and Spencer built up a world-wide reputation for the quality of its products, but in fact manufactured nothing itself. Its success rested on culturing strong relationships with its suppliers – building long-term relationships in which product quality was delivered in exchange for loyalty and commitment on the part of the retailer. Successful car manufacturers and various other retailing groups are seen as doing much the same.

In recent years, there has been great interest in why companies working in the same sector often cluster closely together, even though they are often competitors (e.g., Leadbeater, 1999). The most famous example of this is perhaps Silicon Valley in California. Other examples include the optics industry around Rochester, New York; crafts and fashion clothing in north-central Italy; and the motor racing industry in the south of England. Examples of the economic advantages of clustering can also be found in developing economies, such as in Indonesia (Weijland, 1999).

One reason that this clustering occurs is because the companies may build on the back of an existing network of expertise, such as a university with particular strength in that area (e.g. the successful science park that has developed around Cambridge, England). In other cases, such as the motor racing industry, the cluster grew out of informal groups of enthusiasts – a series of post-war motor racing clubs and a network of enthusiasts, in the case of formula one racing (M. Jenkins, 2001). Once formed, the cluster itself becomes the backbone of the network. Essentially, the close proximity of the firms lowers transaction costs, making it easier for people to connect with one another outside the confines of their own firm to trade information, products, ideas and even people. Similarly, firms find that employees recruited through referral and 'connections' are usually of higher average quality (Montgomery, 1991; see also previous section). Firms within industrial clusters benefit from fine-grained and tacit knowledge exchanges, and subtle local 'spill-over' effects. Innovations and reductions in costs spill over to reduce both the firm's own costs and those of its local rivals, setting up the conditions for a creative mix of local co-operation and competition known as 'co-opetition' (Soubeyran and Weber, 2002).

But close proximity is not enough, as many failed attempts to replicate Silicon Valley have shown. Successful business networks are typically as much 'social' as 'business' in character, such that, as one Canadian study found, dividing between the two can be difficult (Araujo, Bowey and Eastern, 1998). For example, Route 128 in Boston, despite its clustering of high-tech firms, has failed to achieve the innovative vibrancy of its Californian cousin. This is thought to be precisely because Route 128 firms failed to let go of their traditional norms of corporate hierarchy, secrecy, self-sufficiency and territoriality (Saxenian, 1994; Putnam, 2000).

The potential benefits of inter-firm co-operation and social capital can be substantial. One recent study looking at Denmark, Ireland and the UK found that government programmes to promote collaboration and networking among small and medium enterprises (SMEs) were associated with enhanced business, knowledge and innovation performance (Cooke and Wills, 1999). Many firms involved in one of the programmes, having discovered the benefits of enhanced social capital, planned to continue to develop it in future even if they had to fund it privately. Similarly, Fountain has argued that the US federal government should invest directly in social capital formation in the science and technology sector, and not just directly in science and technology, in order to maximize innovation and economic returns (Fountain, 1997).

All these examples may be viewed as illustrating the role played by bridging social capital at the meso-level – how firms network with other firms, trade and develop shared informal understandings for mutual benefit.

These relationships also have a 'linking' component, in that they may involve connections between firms and communities with very uneven economic power. Most successful firms have long since learnt the value of upward links, such as those to the political elite. Making sure that your corporation's point of view is heard when policymakers are deciding on the regulatory and tax environment in which you operate may be one of the best investments that a firm can make. On the other hand, regional and local policymakers have learnt that it makes sense to link up with local businesses. Such links can be invaluable when bidding for central or federal government funding; can help foster regeneration and growth, such as through 'guardian angel' schemes, where established businesses support new ones; and can strengthen community-level outcomes, such as through school–business links and employer–community forums.

Firms are also learning that it can be in their own long-term interest to build links down into the communities in which they are based (Pike, 2000). Partly this is because, in a world of better-informed consumers, reputation matters. Such investment can improve employee loyalty, thereby strengthening the firm's bonding social capital and improving the quality of people it can attract. Also, in the very long term, it is to the advantage of the firm and those within it that the community in which it is based flourishes. It is interesting to note that some firms, admittedly a tiny minority at present, have even started to take on the language of social capital literature.

But the literature also contains an important warning. Many – perhaps all – industrial clusters eventually fail. The same shared tacit knowledge that gives the cluster its advantage, if not challenged and renewed, can become a barrier to more radical innovation and change. Consider, for example, how the once powerful British steel industry, clustered around Sheffield, or the British motor industry came to be overtaken by more innovative and outward-looking European, Asian and American competitors. A key factor behind the long-term survival of an economic cluster is not only its internal patterns of co-operation, but the extent to which it also develops forms of social capital and institutions that plug structural holes and provide links to knowledge and trends outside of the cluster (Molina-Morales, Lopez-Navarro and Guia-Julve, 2002).

Optimizing a firm's social capital

There are different forms of social capital, and these have somewhat different roles even within the innovation process (Landry, Amara and Lamari, 2002). Firms and clusters can become over- or underinvested in one form of social capital or another (see also chapter 9). Firms frequently refashion their network social capital by rearranging their internal organization – merging or separating divisions, and so on. It can be more difficult to change the normative aspects of a firm's social capital, and especially the social norms of the firm usually referred to as 'corporate culture'. This culture may become maladaptive. Typically, this is because some of these unspoken norms can become inappropriate as a result of changing market conditions. These shared assumptions and norms can then become a barrier to change (e.g. Clausen and Olsen, 2000).

If a firm is too tightly bonded, it may neglect its bridging social capital – its relationships to the world outside. This risks leaving it out of touch with its markets, suppliers and competitors. Ethnographic studies of entrepreneurial firms confirm that there may be an optimum level of bonding, or embeddedness, beyond which further bonding becomes counterproductive by insulating the firm from information beyond its own internal networks (Uzzi, 1997). This can be a particular problem for large corporations, especially if they have operated as effective monopolies for much of their corporate history. One way of overcoming this problem is by overturning the traditional business theory of internalizing R&D, and instead externalizing research through corporate venturing. This strategy has been pursued by some of the most successful high-tech companies, such as Cisco Systems, Intel and Sun (Ferrary, 2003).

A fascinating current example of a company trying to move to this new model from the traditional strategy is the UK telecom giant British Telecom. It had a huge but inward-looking research base that, despite its size, was felt to be underperforming and stifling employee creativity and entrepreneurship. This research operation employed around 6,000 people concentrated on an ex-military base, with high security fences and an atmosphere of great secrecy. This is now being transformed. The fences have come down, other firms are being invited onto the site, and employees are being encouraged to set up their own firms. It is a dramatic example of a firm trying to reinvest its resources from bonding to bridging social capital. In essence, BT is trying to turn itself and the firms working with it from a 'Route 128' model into a 'Silicon Valley' model.

On the other hand, a firm that only invests in its bridging social capital and neglects to build a strong social network and culture within itself is vulnerable to fragmentation and a loss of identity. Outsourcing of research can only go so far – firms still need to maintain sufficient technical knowledge within them in order to be able to understand and judge the value of research done outside (so-called 'absorptive capacity': Anand, Glick and Manz, 2002).[2] And excessive bridging and linking may also provide opportunities for corruption, especially when connected to the political arena, and thereby lower overall economic performance (e.g. Hillman and Ursprung, 2000).

Anglo-Saxon business opinion throughout the 1980s and 1990s appeared to lean strongly towards the 'hire-and-fire' view and away from the more traditional corporate welfare and commitment model. Some commentators – among them Granovetter, pioneer of the 'strength of weak ties' model – believe that this move was often mistaken, as corporate welfare programmes, such as those seen in Japanese firms, can bring substantial economic advantages to firms (M. Granovetter, 1990). Small, dense and stable interpersonal networks can have significant advantages, such as providing consistent role expectations that in turn contribute to job satisfaction and reduce turnover (Podolny and Baron, 1997). Indeed, social capital in the workplace appears to be a better predictor of quality of life at work and job satisfaction than are any of the traditional indicators of the characteristics of the worker, the company or the work environment (Requena, 2003). And people-oriented, trust- and reciprocity-based management styles can encourage higher employee morale and productivity (Donkin and Lewis, 1998).

As always, it appears to be a matter of balance, and the optimum level of this balance is likely to vary across sectors. There is now a burgeoning literature offering advice to managers on how to build up whatever form of social capital their firm maybe lacking. Increasingly the argument is being made that it is entirely possible for managers to develop and manage networks systematically. For example, management experts Cross and Prusak argue that senior executives should use network analysis to identify four key role-players in their organizations: central connectors, boundary spanners, information brokers and peripheral specialists (Cross and Prusak, 2002). Once managers know who these people are, they can use this knowledge to get things done, and if the network lacks these people, these roles can be actively developed. Other recent papers, to mention but a few, include advice on lessons from game-playing (Orbanes, 2002); promoting flexibility and human resource management to enable workers to accumulate and acquire social capital (Ferrary, 2002); investing in trust-building, communication and employee focus (Watson and Papamarcos, 2002); organizational citizenship (Bolino, Turnley and Bloodgood, 2002); design of incentives (Rob and Zemsky, 2002); and overhauling the entire network of interactions between workers (Gant, Ichniowski and Shaw, 2002).

In summary, social capital can be seen to play a central role in the success or failure of firms, and functions as both 'glue' and 'lubricant' to get things done (Anderson and Jack, 2002). Indeed, the firm itself can be seen as an important form of social capital. Successful firms and regional economies show a balance of investment between bonding social capital (within-firm), bridging social capital (between-firm) and linking social capital (for example, between firms and their regulators), and avoid an overinvestment in only one form.

Macro-level effects: social capital and economic performance at the regional and national level

The evidence above suggests that having a rich and varied base of social capital should be associated with higher levels of economic growth at the macro-, or aggregate, level. An early and prominent advocate of this position was the social commentator Fukuyama. He argued that key differences in political economics across the world reflect differences in their underlying social capital (Fukuyama, 1995a,b). He pointed out that the orthodox categorization of the USA and Japan as polar opposites in terms of their political economies was paradoxical given that they both led the world in terms of their economic performance. However, this paradox could be resolved once it was recognized that the two nations had the common characteristic of high social capital, and high trust between strangers in particular.

Social capital and national economic performance

A series of empirical studies have supported Fukuyama's basic proposition. Nations with high social capital (as measured by social trust between strangers in the World Values Survey; see figure 2.1) tend strongly to be wealthier nations (as measured by GDP per capita). Relationships have been found between social capital and rates of growth both inside nations (e.g. in Italy; Putnam, 1993) and between nations (Whiteley, 1997; Knack and Keefer, 1997; La Porta et al., 1997).

Whiteley used a measure of social capital that was based on a combination of responses to survey questions on trusting people in general, trusting family members, and trusting your own nationals (a factor

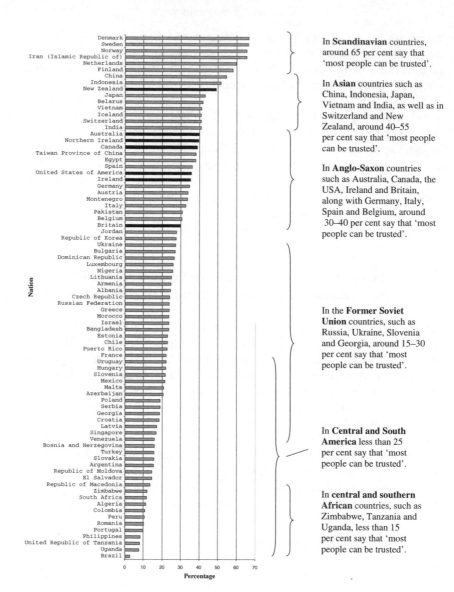

Figure 2.1 *National differences in social trust: percentage agreeing that 'most people can be trusted*
Source: Data from the fourth World Values Surveys, 2001–4.
(Anglo-Saxon nations marked in bold.)

score). He compared various models' ability to predict the log of mean economic growth from 1970 to 1992. Whiteley found that social capital significantly predicted the growth rate even having controlled for real GDP per capita in 1970, investment, primary school enrolment, population growth, government share of GDP, the openness of the economy, and the nature of the state (Confucian, social corporatist or communist). He also found that the effect of social capital was robust, remaining a significant predictor in bootstrap and subset regression – in other words, it wasn't just due to one or two outlying nations.

One weakness of both Whiteley's and La Porta et al.'s papers is that they use social trust as measured in the WVS 1990–3 to predict growth in the period 1970–93. If the hypothesis is that social capital leads to higher growth in the future, what we really want to see is the reverse in terms of time frame; in other words, the association between national social trust around 1990 and economic growth from 1990 to 2000. Clearly, we are limited in this respect by the data that are currently available. However, there are two pieces of evidence that should give us greater confidence that the relationship is causal. A comparison of the 1981–3 and 1990–3 WVS data on social trust show little change over the period, supporting the hypothesis that at the national level, social capital tends to be fairly stable over time (therefore 'exogenous' over modest time runs; see also chapter 7). Second, Whiteley ran an analysis using the WVS 1981–3 data alone instead of the 1990–3 data, and showed a similar pattern which remained significant despite the smaller sample of countries.

Whiteley's most parsimonious model – with all the non-significant variables deleted – indicates that social capital is more important to economic growth than is human capital, one of the main focuses of endogenous growth theory. It also has about the same impact on economic growth as the 'catch-up' variable (countries that start behind tend to catch up), though somewhat less importance than investment in physical capital. Whiteley concluded:

> It is clear that social capital is an important factor in explaining cross-national variations in economic growth. When the variable is incorporated into a modified neo-classical model, it is a highly significant predictor of growth in a diverse set of countries, and in the presence of various control variables . . . and cannot be ignored in any adequate model of economic growth. (Whiteley, 1997, p. 18)[3]

Knack and Keefer (1997) reached very similar conclusions in parallel to Whiteley, finding that trust and civic norms were strongly associated with economic growth in a sample of twenty-nine market economies.

They found that trust's relationship to growth is especially large in poorer countries. In contrast, they found that associational activity, such as levels of volunteering and membership of clubs, was unrelated to economic growth rates.

The Knack and Keefer paper is interesting in that they try to identify what factors might account for these important underlying national differences in social trust. Given the weak relationship between associational life and either economic growth or trust, they are sceptical about the 'bottom-up' model of Putnam (1993), which suggests that social trust is born out of associational life. Instead they point to the positive role played by formal institutions that effectively protect property and contract rights, and which thereby underwrite the social trust so important to economic exchange. Kentworthy reaches a similar conclusion, arguing that institutional arrangements play a more important role in fostering economic co-operation, and thereby development, than does civic activism (Kentworthy, 1997). Knack and Keefer also identify a negative role played by polarizations along lines of class or ethnicity.[4] Such polarization may reduce social trust between groups, and especially bridging social capital across them, leading to less information flow and higher transaction costs.

The conclusion that social capital, be it normative or network, matters to economic growth at the macro-level is strongly supported by a growing tide of national case studies. Low or inappropriate social capital has been implicated in the poor economic performance of Africa (Collier and Gunning, 1999; Azam, Fosu and Ndung'u, 2002); of the transition economies of central Europe (Neace, 1999; Geib and Pfaff, 2000); and of Mexico, despite the existence of the North American Free Trade Agreement (Robey, 1999). Similarly, studies of individual countries have suggested that social, economic and ethnic polarization tend to undermine local economic growth. To take one of many examples, a study of Fiji concludes that the fractures between Indo-Fijian family business networks and the Fijian business and political elite 'limit, if not preclude, the creation of the local social capital that might foster self-sustaining local economic growth' (M. Taylor, 2002, p. 302).

In contrast, social capital, in the form of networking and honouring network obligations, has long been thought to have played a major role in the relative success of Asian tiger economies (Barnes and Crawford, 1986). Similarly, the effectiveness of development finance schemes in emerging markets (by multilateral and bilateral institutions) has been found to be significantly explained by differential endowments of social capital (Tufarelli and Fagotto, 1999). And illustrating the benefits that follow from a less polarized, more tolerant society, an analysis of the European low countries identifies a widespread humanist norm of mutual respect for other cultures as a key element in their long-standing economic success (Krug, 1999). The argument goes that a trading nation is more likely to be successful – short of sheer military might – if its traders approach other nationals with respect and acceptance.

Finally, Knack and Keefer's observation that social trust has a particularly strong relationship with economic growth in poor countries, presumably due to the relative absence of alternative formal mechanisms of enforcing contracts, is supported by detailed case studies. Studies of business development inside the former eastern bloc, including interviews with successful entrepreneurs, strongly emphasize the role played by reciprocity and trust. Social capital enables entrepreneurs to obtain financial capital and other needed assets in a context that otherwise often lacks effective institutions to enforce contracts (Kolankiewicz, 1996; Neace, 1999). However, in contrast with Knack and Keefer's general observation, within the eastern bloc countries it seems to be participation in civic organizations rather than social trust that best predicts growth (Raiser et al., 2002). Similarly, a study of business networks in Tanzania found that trust within the social networks of businesspeople played a key role in innovation, but that the weakness of formal institutions discouraged manufacturers from extending their social relations beyond core networks (Murphy, 2002). In short, informal social networks and trust matter in all countries, but in countries without alternative and effective formal methods of enforcing contracts they are absolutely critical.

Within-nation regional effects

Similar relationships have been found between regional economic performance within countries and social capital. Putnam's original study of Italy documented how the high social capital regions, mainly in the north, were the most economically productive (Putnam, 1993). Across US counties, social capital has been found to have a positive effect on growth rates (Rupasingha, Goetz and Freshwater, 2002). And across the regions of Britain, there is a strong association between levels of civic engagement and economic productivity (Casey, 2003).

Simple associations do not prove a causal relationship between social capital and economic performance. It could be argued, once again, that the economic prosperity of a region in some way stimulates social capital. For example, increased wealth might lead to more leisure time, or to less distrust as people do not have to compete over scarce resources.

One regional study that did involve a longitudinal component was a follow-up analysis of the Italian case by the Canadian economist John Helliwell. He found that in the years following the creation of the new regional tier of government in Italy, the high social capital regions achieved a faster economic growth rate than the low social capital regions (Helliwell and Putnam, 1995; see also chapter 6). This study provides much more powerful evidence of a causal relationship running from the regions' social capital to economic growth.

A detailed challenge has recently been made to the hypothesis that high social capital within a region is good for growth by Richard Florida and his colleagues (Florida, Cushing and Gates, 2002). Using data from across 206 regions of the USA, Florida et al. argue that the most innovative regions are those that have low social capital but that readily welcome outsiders and provide a challenge for their ideas, such as San Francisco, Seattle and Washington DC. Florida et al.'s key evidence is that there is a strong association between a region's innovative activity and measures of social tolerance and diversity, specifically the 'gay index' (an area's proportion of gay couples) and the 'bohemian index' (the proportion of musicians, designers, writers, actors, photographers and dancers in the labour force). Florida et al. go on to argue that the same lesson applies for individual companies, which should foster diversity and openness internally in order to succeed, even if this is at the cost of some internal cohesiveness.

Richard Florida presents his work as a direct refutation of the social capital approach, and of Putnam in particular.[5] In fact, viewed through the lens of a more realistic and multi-faceted notion of social capital, his work turns out to be a useful confirmation at the regional level of our earlier conclusion (at the individual and meso-level) that an excess of any one form of social capital – typically bonding – can hinder economic prosperity. The causal relationship between social capital, diversity and economic growth is clearly very complex. Economic growth within a city tends to act as a magnet for immigration, leading for a more diverse population over the short to medium term. This diversity and high residual mobility tends to put a strain on social trust and social networks. However, once we control for factors such as diversity and mobility, we find that social trust remains robustly associated with economic performance. This requres a sophisticated, multivariate level of modelling, not claims staked on any single or simple bivariate associations.

If we consider diversity and social capital at the same time, we find that both matter. For example, Rupasingha et al. found that ethnic diversity, income equality and social capital all contributed to regional variations in convergence in economic growth rates across US counties (Rupasingha, Goetz and Freshwater, 2002). The ideal environment for economic productivity is one that is cohesive and trusting, but *also* confident, open and diverse – in our terms, has both bonding *and* bridging social capital.

It is clear that more work needs to be done to establish the causal direction at the level of the region, and to understand exactly which aspects of social capital – or even which combinations of social capital – maximize growth rates, and under what conditions.

The relationship to government, institutions and culture

Whether one regards institutional arrangements, such as the strength and coherence of the legal system, as part of a nation's stock of social capital depends on how broad a definition of social capital you choose to employ (it is not counted as such in this book; see chapter 1). High social trust may boost economic growth partly through its positive effects on the formal structures of government and the state. High social capital is strongly associated with: lower rates of government corruption; higher bureaucratic quality; higher compliance with paying taxes; better infrastructure quality; and the greater efficiency and integrity of the legal environment (La Porta et al., 1997; see also chapter 6). The types of policies (social and public good investment) and political legitimacy associated with the governments of high social trust countries may further help to create the conditions for economic growth and prosperity (Szreter, 2002; Azam, Fosu and Ndung'u, 2002). The creation of a good public infrastructure and a healthy and well-trained population clearly can facilitate economic growth. There are also ecological effects in play – a given individual can be more productive when surrounded by others who are skilled and able (Currie, 1996). In addition, political administrations that are seen as legitimate create conditions of political and economic calm that reduce conflict, including industrial conflict. High political legitimacy, comparing across nations, is associated with lower rates of strikes and industrial conflicts (Bornschier, 1989).

These data, when combined, point to the existence of a long-term virtuous circle within which social trust, high-integrity government and economic growth reinforce one another (see chapter 8). These effects on growth may be conditional, in that they interact with other factors such as the opportunity for trade. If there are very few opportunities for transactions to occur, such as in a given historical period, then levels of social capital and trust will be largely irrelevant to economic performance.

It is also likely that there are direct effects on economic growth of 'culturally based' differences in social norms and their expectancies. For example, tolerance of self-interested acts, such as keeping money that you have found, is much lower in Scandinavian countries than in southern European countries (Halpern, 1995b). And there is a strong negative correlation at the national level between average levels of social trust and levels of self-interested values (Halpern, 2001). If it is culturally acceptable to be highly self-interested – to cheat if you get a chance – then economic transactions will need to rely more heavily on formal contracts, insurance and severe sanctions. In short, the cultural normative base will strongly and directly affect the level of transaction costs (Autiero, 2000; van-de-Klundert, 1999). A high social capital culture is one within which people tend to conform to Couse's models, in which 'people never pass up an opportunity to co-operate for mutually advantageous exchanges', as opposed to Machiavellian models in which 'no one will pass up an opportunity to gain a one-sided advantage by exploiting another party' (Hirshleifer, 1994).

The importance of culture: evidence from game theory experiments

The importance of the cultural or normative base is illustrated by experiments rooted in game theory. These have shown that the positions that people take are strongly affected by social norms (Guttman, 2000). Generally speaking, people (in the industrialized west) are found to be co-operative even when this is not strictly rational. For example, in the 'ultimatum game', where one person divides a pot of money but both parties must agree to accept the arrangement to receive the money, individuals co-operate more than is narrowly rational (Camerer and Thaler, 1995). It is also noteworthy that if the proportion offered to the non-dividing party is below a certain level (around a quarter) then it will be refused even though that means that nothing will be received.

A related finding is that people will often accept a lower payment in such games if this prevents risk being assumed by someone for whom they have sympathetic feelings. This web of sentiment was, of course, seen as central to the effective functioning of the economic and social world by the 'father of economics', Adam Smith (Smith, [1776] 1979). The widespread existence of such sentiments reduces tendencies to free-ride and default for personal advantage, and should therefore lead to substantial benefits at the macro-level even if these are not secured by any one particular individual. In this sense, having a conscience makes economic sense, at least at the macro-level (R. H. Frank, 1987).

An interesting twist to this story is the finding that those who study economics – and are therefore especially exposed to the classical self-interest model – show less co-operative behaviour than those studying other disciplines (R. Frank, Gilovich and Regan, 1993). For example, the defection rate in a prisoner's dilemma experiment was 60 per cent among economics majors compared with only 39 per cent among non-economics majors. Similarly, economics professors are less likely to give to charity than their colleagues. This appears to be the result of learning, not constitution. While non-economics majors show a trend towards greater co-operation in prisoner's dilemma experiments as they move towards graduation, economics majors show no such trend. In short, economists appear to end up believing their own self-interested models and therefore make the assumption that others will cheat on them if they have the chance. This lowers levels of co-operation, implying that the community of economists may be less productive than they would otherwise be.

The form of national economies and social capital

Fukuyama also argued that the *form* of social capital affects the *type* of economy that a nation develops. Nations with high social capital in the form of trust between relative strangers are much better able to support large corporations and the types of economic activities associated with them, such as car production or heavy industry. In contrast, nations with social capital predominantly in the form of trust within families (noting that some theorists might not count this as social capital; see chapter 1) will have economies based on small family firms. Such firms may have an advantage in certain fast-moving commercial sectors, but will tend to fail in areas requiring larger scales of production or organization. In such countries, if heavy industry is to exist it will have to be run by the state (e.g. France).

In essence, Fukuyama argued that a society's prevalent form of social capital might give it an advantage in some sectors but not others. Hence the USA, with high trust between strangers, had a tendency to build corporations, and was therefore good at the kind of things that corporations do well, like building cars or planes. Italy, in contrast, with high trust inside families, had a tendency to build small family firms and was therefore better at the kind of things that small firms do well, like fashion clothing.

Note that in the analyses conducted by Whiteley, no differentiation was made between types of social trust, which were instead lumped together in a single index on the basis that they significantly co-vary. However, Fukuyama's theory can be said to have received strong systematic support in La Porta et al.'s analysis of the WVS data (La Porta et al., 1997). Having controlled for economic growth, a strong association was found between social capital, as measured by trust between strangers, and the ratio of sales generated by the top twenty publicly traded firms to GDP (data from WorldScope Global 1996). In contrast, strong family ties were found to be bad for the development of large firms, the association between the relative share of the top twenty firms and family trust being strongly negative.

The finding that different forms of trust are associated with different forms of economic organization does not imply that one form or other will necessarily be associated with higher economic growth. This may depend on market conditions.

Meanwhile, certain forms of social capital may actually be damaging to economic performance at the national or regional level. Adam Smith's famous example of how traders can conspire together within private trade organizations to drive up prices to their own private advantage is a classic illustration. This specific hypothesis was confirmed in the study of regional economic performance in the UK. While it was found that most forms of social capital were associated with better regional economic performance, higher levels of membership in local Chambers of Commerce were actually associated with poorer economic performance (Casey, 2003). Similarly, the turning around of Tupelo, Mississippi, was partly attributed to the disbanding of the exclusive Chamber of Commerce and its replacement with a Community Foundation open to all (Grisham, 1999; see above).[6]

Fukuyama predicts that differences in social capital between nations will become even more important in the future. For example, he argues that China will ultimately be held back by its low level of public trust relative to family trust, as this implies that it will either have an unbalanced economy lacking heavy and large industry or will have inefficient industries run by the state.[7] There is certainly a widespread belief that the 'new economy' – based more on knowledge and weightless trading, as opposed to the traditional economy based on the production and shipping of heavy goods – will prosper best in contexts with diffuse, flexible and high-trust social networks. Nations and regions with such social networks and norms should be better placed in such an economy than those with denser and more fragmented social capital.

Social capital at the global level

There is a question about how much economic growth is boosted at a *global* level by the extent of generalized social capital. In the same way as we can argue that within a nation state shared social norms and interlinked social networks facilitate co-operative economic action, we can argue that global social capital should facilitate global growth.

A simple illustration of this beneficial effect is the extent to which cultural links, shared norms and mutual respect make trading between nations easier. Krug's identification of the important role played by a humanist norm of mutual respect in the trading success of the Low Countries is an elegant example (Krug, 1999). The positive role played by migrants inside the US economy might be considered another example, noting that benefits typically flow to both the donor and recipient nation (Laws, 1997). Similarly, studies of expatriates working inside multinational corporations have found that they play a key role in bringing local expertise and constructive diversity to corporations – and indeed the more boundary-spanning activities that these expatriates engaged in, the more power they had in their companies (Au and Fukuda, 2002).

It is a fascinating issue whether the international development of shared normative frameworks such as the bill of human rights, which is generally characterized as an instrument of social or moral development, will in fact prove to be a key driver of global economic development. If we buy the argument that shared normative frameworks at the national level facilitate economic activity by oiling the works of everyday transactions between citizens, then we should expect that the spread of an increasingly common normative framework across the world will similarly raise global economic performance.

A key piece of evidence suggests that even in a more globalized world, social networks continue to matter greatly. Economists have noted that capital movements and other forms of trade drop off dramatically across national borders (Feldstein and Horioka, 1980; Helliwell and McKitrick, 1999; Keller, 2002). For example, one study has estimated that the US–Canadian border leads to a drop-off in trade equal to a distance of nearly 10,000 miles within those countries (McCallum, 1995). These massive drop-offs are clearly not explained by distance or transport costs, or by tariffs or non-tariff trade barriers (Grossman, 1997; N. Chen, 2004). Instead the evidence increasingly suggests that this puzzling effect reflects the structure of people's social networks. This hypothesis is strongly supported by patterns of telephone traffic and migration (Mackay, 1958; Obstfeld and Rogoff, 2000; Helliwell, 2003). Further confirming evidence comes from the finding that, as of yet, the euro has not led to an increase in trade intensity among the EU nations using the currency compared with that between euro- and non-euro-using nations (N. Chen, 2004; Helliwell, 2003). Ironically perhaps, while between-nation differences in economic growth rates seem to be most heavily affected by differences in social trust and other social norms, when it comes to global trade, social networks still dominate. After all our global trade agreements, we still like to trade with people that we know.

Summary: how and why does social capital affect economic growth?

At the individual level, having more extensive social networks – especially networks that reach widely (bridging network social capital) – and feeling that you can trust others (normative social capital) is associated with lower unemployment and higher earnings. These individual-level variations certainly help shape how the economic cake is divided up, but they do not, by themselves, show that social capital affects overall economic growth. Indeed, variations in social capital are implicated in perpetuating social class and ethnic differences in economic attainment, with the poor and disadvantaged being held back by their relative lack of access to the helping hands of well-connected friends and acquaintances.

Nonetheless, meso-level evidence clearly supports the theory that social capital generally contributes to economic productivity and growth. Neighbourhoods with concentrated unemployment perform disproportionately worse than would be expected on the basis of the disadvantage of the individuals within them, and this can be attributed to the lack of social connections to the employed and economically advantaged. The firm itself can be viewed as an important and widespread form of social capital – a network of individuals with shared norms and understandings that facilitate their ability to co-operate economically for mutual advantage. The literature is full of examples of how both bonding inside firms and bridging between firms and the world outside generally facilitates economic growth. The economic advantages of industrial districts and clusters also illustrate the potentially positive effects of social capital at the meso-level.

This said, the literature indicates that it is possible to overinvest in certain forms of social capital, such as when a firm or district becomes overly internally bonded, cutting itself off from the markets and ideas beyond its internal corporate community. In such cases, an excess of a particular form of social capital can be as economically damaging as a deficit is in others. This evidence fits the 'vitamin' model proposed in chapter 1. Firms and communities need a range of different types of social capital in order to succeed economically, with both too much and too little of a given form of social capital being potentially toxic. Similarly, some forms of social capital, such as cartels, while benefiting those involved, can actually inhibit aggregate economic performance.

The macro-level data, as they currently exist, strongly support the view that social capital generally facilitates economic growth. Social trust between strangers, in particular, has been shown to be strongly associated with national rates of economic growth. While these macro-level studies do not prove causality, the wealth of laboratory studies and meso-level and within-nation evidence all serves to buttress a causal account. A normative value-base that predisposes individuals to act in a trustworthy manner, even when there are short-term incentives to cheat, oils the workings of the economy from top to bottom (see figure 2.2). That said, when it comes to global trade and explaining the dramatic drop-off of trade across borders, the humble structuring of our social networks again looms large.

Of course, social capital is by no means the only factor that affects economic growth. This is directly illustrated by examples of regions with apparently similar social capital but with divergent growth rates (Engstrand and Stam, 2002). But in general, micro-, meso- and macro-

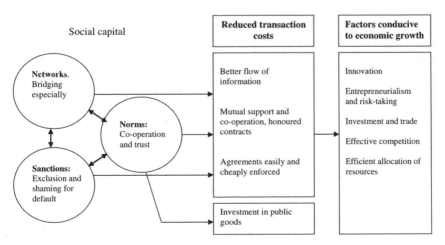

Figure 2.2 *The causal relationship between social capital and economic growth*

level data all point to the role that social capital plays in improving the flow of information through an economy and generally lowering transaction costs. In addition, social capital may have indirect positive effects on the economy, such as by encouraging the development of a legal and public policy environment that further reinforces trust and is conducive to long-term human and physical investment.

Further reading

For readers looking to retrace economists' use or the history of the term 'social capital', Glenn Loury (1987) is often credited as being a key early proponent and independent inventor of the term in his work on the causes of racial inequality.

In terms of theory, Fukuyama's work is very readable and has been very influential, and readers can choose between his lengthy book on *Trust* (1995a), or shorter articles on the same topic (1995b). If you want to look at just one good empirical article, try the paper by Knack and Keefer (1997). For a fuller and fascinating exposition of the role of social networks in explaining cross-national trade, look at the work of John Helliwell (e.g. 2002b).

For a strong counter-view, at least in rhetoric if not in detail, try Florida, Cushing and Gates (2002).

3

Health and Well-Being

Of all the domains in which I have traced the consequences of social capital, in none is the importance of social connectedness so well established as in the case of health and well-being.

Putnam, 2000, p. 326

The study of the relationship between social capital and health goes back over a century to Durkheim's seminal study on suicide (Durkheim, 1897). Durkheim observed that, despite the intensely personal character of suicide, the total number of suicides in a society was generally very stable, though it differed markedly between societies and regions. Through a careful examination of many statistics that would put much present-day research to shame, he found much lower rates of suicide among the married than the widowed or divorced; in the winter months than the summer; and in Catholic nations and regions than Protestant. He argued:

all these manifestations, however independent of one another they seem, must surely actually result from a single cause or single group of causes, which dominate individuals. Otherwise how could we explain that all these individual wills, ignorant of one another's existence, annually achieve the same end in the same numbers? At least for the most part they have no effect upon one another; they are in no way conjoined; yet everything takes place as if they were obeying a single order. There must then be some force in their common environment inclining them all in the same direction, whose greater or lesser strength causes the greater or less number of individual suicides. Now the effects revealing this force vary not according to organic and cosmic environments but solely according to the state of the social environment. (Durkheim, [1897] 1951, pp. 304–5).

Durkheim discusses various 'types' of suicide. 'Egoistic' suicide, on which he spends most time, is evidenced in the higher rates of suicide among Protestants than among the more closely integrated Catholics and Jews; among the unmarried and widowed; in areas with smaller family sizes (indicating households were breaking into smaller units); and in urban areas. In each case, higher rates of suicide appeared to be associated with higher levels of 'excessive individualism'. In this respect, Durkheim noted that the suicide rate tended to drop during times of war, reflecting the increased bonding of a nation when threatened by a common enemy. His conclusion was that 'suicide varies inversely with the degree of integration of the social groups of which the individual forms a part' (ibid., p. 209).

Durkheim's work was remarkable for its early use of statistics blended with sophisticated theory, and for its recognition of what we now call ecological effects. It was not until the 1960s that psychologists took up the baton with an emerging interest in the role that 'social support' may have in relation to health, and especially mental health, and the role played by the individual's social network in buffering them from life's adversities. More recently, medical researchers have also entered the field, broadening attention to the impact of people's social networks on physical health.

Most of this psychological and medical literature is focused on the individual, examining the links between individuals' personal relationships and their health (a micro-level analysis). Despite Durkheim's early influence, there is rather less research available documenting meso- and macro-level effects, though there has been some recent resurgence of interest in this level of analysis (see, for example, Berkman and Kawachi, 2000). Some sociological work on health differentials is also relevant to our enquiry for insights into how social capital may impact on health at the macro-level (see, for example, Wilkinson, 1996).

In the sections below, evidence of the impact of social capital on both mental and physical health is considered at the individual, community and macro-level.

The micro-level: all you need is love?

Over the last several decades, psychologists have noticed that individuals with poor health, and particularly mental health, generally have significantly smaller social networks. In short, those suffering from chronic illnesses appear to have fewer intimate relationships and friends. People suffering illnesses also tend to report a lower *quality* of support, regardless of the number of persons in their social network (Sarason, Sarason and Pierce, 1990).

Large numbers of cross-sectional studies have reported this strong association between the size and quality of people's social networks and their health, with people who are less socially isolated and more involved in social and civic activities tending to have better health (e.g. F. E. Baum et al., 2000; Veenstra, 2000). However, this result is subject to alternative interpretations. First, it may be that the reported association arises because of respondent bias (Halpern, 1995a). This is a particularly serious problem in relation to mental health. An individual suffering from depression, for example, is likely to report more symptoms and perceive any given level of support as lower than someone not suffering from depression. Similarly, some individuals are more positive in their general outlook on life, and therefore report their relationships and health as better than those of others even if they are objectively identical. Such bias can lead to misleading positive associations in cross-sectional data, especially when they rely on self-reports of health and relationships.

Second, the direction of causality is often unclear. It could be that people end up more isolated *because* of their illness, rather than the other way around. Do personal relationships protect your health, or does your health affect your relationships? For example, early retirement, and the associated loss of social contact with work colleagues, is often associated with poor health. But early retirement is often the result of existing illnesses, rather than the other way around. Similarly, depression has been found to cause serious marital and other relationship problems, with less positive communication, more conflict, and the depressed partner or friend often being experienced as a 'burden' (Bothwell and Weissman, 1977; Hokanson et al., 1989; Gotlib and Macabe, 1990).

In addition, there is evidence that personality variables can sometimes help explain the covariance between positive relationships and good health at the individual level. For example, some people appear to have a 'hardy' personality: an internal locus of control (a sense of control over your own fate); a tendency to see adversity as a challenge not a crisis; and a general sense of commitment to whatever they do. This 'hardiness' makes them both perceive and experience less ill-health (Kobassa, 1979; Blaney and Ganellen, 1990).

These methodological issues present a considerable challenge to any researcher attempting to understand the causal relationships between social capital and health.

Mental health

As noted above, response bias is a major problem when trying to disentangle the relationship between mental health and social capital or support. Depressed people can be expected to complain about their relationships, whatever the reality.

One way to overcome this problem is to use objective ratings by third parties. This was the method employed by the classic, landmark study of depression in a sample of women in London (G. Brown and Harris, 1978). Following very detailed interviews, the circumstances of respondents' lives, as well as their level of depression, were rated by independent observers. Brown and Harris found that those women who had suffered major life events, such as a major loss or chronic illness, were significantly more likely to suffer from a major depressive episode. Even so, many women who suffered from a major life event did not develop depression. The researchers found that the existence of a close, confiding relationship seemed to reduce greatly the likelihood of depression. In the year following a major life event, a woman without a husband or boyfriend to confide in was *four times* more likely to develop depression than one with such a relationship (41 per cent versus 10 per cent developed depression). Intimate, confiding relationships other than with partners – such as with a parent, sibling or friend – offered some protection from depression, but not as great as having a partner to confide in (26 per cent developed depression). Interestingly, the absence of such relationships was not a significant risk factor in itself – in the absence of a life event, depression was very rare whatever relationships existed.

Brown and Harris's work has now been widely replicated, and it is generally accepted that intimate, confiding relationships act as a 'buffer' to protect individuals from the adversities of life. It is a robust finding that people who are isolated and lack intimate social support are more likely to suffer from depression when under stress, and to remain depressed for longer, than those who have such support (Sherbourne, Hayes and Wells, 1995).

Intervention studies have provided further evidence for the causal role of supportive relationships in protecting against depression (Kawachi and Berkman, 2001). Harris et al. have shown, in a randomized trial on a sample similar to that covered in their original classic study, that volunteer befriending led to a significant reduction in depressive symptoms a year on compared with matched controls (T. Harris, Brown and Robinson, 1999). Similarly, Mittleman et al. found that sessions of family and individual counselling, and access to a support group, significantly reduced the risk of depression among spouse caregivers of patients with Alzheimer's disease (Mittleman et al., 1995).

Another factor identified by Brown and Harris as a powerful risk factor was having suffered the loss or death of one's mother before the age of 11 (G. Brown and Harris, 1978). This finding, that the presence of emotional support – warmth and affection – during childhood is an important protective factor against later depression, has been supported by prospective longitudinal studies and studies of children raised within institutions. A key mediator is the impact on the person's feelings of self-worth and self-esteem. It has been clearly shown that children whose parents were less affectionate, less involved and more hostile towards them during childhood are very much more likely to become depressed as adults (Crook, Raskin and Elliot, 1981; Lefkowitz and Tesiny, 1984).

More generally, social integration – the extent to which people have a good range and frequency of social contacts – tends to play out as a 'main effect'. In other words, regardless of how much stress an individual is under, people with a higher level of social contacts tend to report better mental health (A. W. Williams, Ware and Donald, 1981; see Cohen and Wills, 1985, for a detailed discussion of buffering versus main effects in mental health). This is not just a western phenomenon. For example, a study of Russia found that almost 10 per cent of variance in 'emotional health' was explained by measures of social integration (R. Rose, 2000).

Similarly, being in work, as opposed to unemployed, appears to have a positive impact on mental health and well-being (Warr, 1987). Of course, there are lots of reasons why work has this positive impact. Most obviously, work brings in money, and protects individuals from economic hardship – its 'manifest' function. Work also brings with it a social network, and a sense of identity and meaning (Jahoda, 1972, 1982, 1995). The substantial impact of unemployment on well-being certainly exceeds the loss of well-being that can be attributed to the lost earnings *per se* (Clark and Oswald, 2002; Helliwell, 2002a; Donovan and Halpern, 2003). Longitudinal research also clearly implicates the social contact and support that work brings (Holohan and Moos, 1981).

By way of balance, it should be noted that not every personal relationship will have a universally positive impact on mental health. Close relationships with abusive, depressed or disturbed individuals can often have damaging impacts on mental health. Similarly, when support shades into dependence, it can bring with it feelings of helplessness and resentment (G. R. Lee, 1985; Kawachi and Berkman, 2001).

Interestingly, it has also been argued that the much higher rates of depression among women could partly be explained by the higher reliance among women on personal, confiding relationships and the obligations that such relationships bring. Women may therefore be more vulnerable to the loss of such support, and more heavily affected by the adversities that affect others in their social network (Belle, 1987; Busfield, 1996). For example, a study of effects of social support from the extended family in a southern US black community found that this support was beneficial for the mental health of young men but unhelpful for women. This negative effect was attributed to the heavy obligations that were incurred by young women (Dressler and Badger, 1985).

The protective effect of relationships extends beyond depression to many other mental disorders. For example, people with few supportive relationships are particularly vulnerable to post-traumatic stress disorder following a traumatic event (Perry et al., 1992). A lack of support at the time of trauma predicts the severity of the stress disorder up to six years afterwards, regardless of initial symptom levels (Dalgleish et al., 1996). Similarly, several longitudinal studies have shown that social networks and social participation appear to act as a protective factor against dementia or cognitive decline over the age of 65 (Fabrigoule et al., 1995; Bassuk, Glass and Berkman, 1999; Fratiglioni et al., 2000).

An issue of great historical controversy within the mental health literature is the relationship between close personal ties and schizophrenia. Schizophrenia affects around 1 in 100 people at some point in their lives, and is often a highly debilitating lifetime condition. Typically involving auditory hallucinations and inappropriate affect, it is most people's image of being 'mad'.[1] Early work and some psychoanalytic writing suggested that intimate relationships might be the cause of such severe psychotic disorders (Laing and Esterson, [1964] 1970). One popular hypothesis was that some intimate relationships, far from acting as a protective factor, consisted of pathological patterns of interaction that trapped the individual in 'double binds' with no way out. For example, a critical parent might say to a child, 'Why don't you ever bring your friends back?' But if the child did bring her friends back, she would be criticized for having such 'bad' friends.

These early double-bind hypotheses were not borne out by later research, not least because it was found that the so-called pathological patterns proved to be common in families without psychotic members. Nonetheless, it has been found that relapse rates tend to be significantly higher when patients suffering from schizophrenia are released back into the care of their own families, and in particular where the family is characterized by high levels of 'expressed emotion' – frequent negative, critical comments. For example, one study found that relapse rates of patients suffering from schizophrenia, even when on medication, were more than four times higher when patients were released into high- rather than low-expressed-emotion families (Vaughn and Leff, 1976). The causality was strongly supported by the finding in the same study that reducing face-to-face contact with the high-expressed-emotion relatives could substantially reduce the relapse rate, leading to the common recommendation by psychiatrists that schizophrenic patients seek to reduce their face-to-face contact with members of their own family. Intervention studies aimed at reducing levels of expressed emotion in the family, through a combination of education about the disorder and family therapy, have also been shown to reduce relapse rates dramatically, again increasing confidence about the causal impact of high expressed emotion on at-risk individuals (Hogarty et al., 1991).

Such results lead to the headline view that, in general, close personal ties tend to protect against depression but may aggravate schizophrenia. But a more accurate interpretation is that relationship *quality* matters, particularly for individuals at risk of schizophrenia. Hence one can argue that – be it for everyday psychopathology, depression or even schizophrenia – strong, positive, confiding personal relationships tend to protect the individual from mental ill-health. But at the same time, we need to recognize that while most close personal relationships are positive, supportive and confiding, this is not true for all relationships, and that this positivity can be strained to breaking point by severe mental illness in a family member.

Happiness

As one might have guessed, the factors affecting positive, subjective well-being are pretty much a mirror image of those driving everyday psychopathology. In this respect, it is no surprise to find that happiness, or life satisfaction, is strongly affected by personal relationships. With the possible exception of genetic factors – some people appear to be genetically programmed to be happier than others – satisfaction with family life fairly consistently tops the polls of factors that predict individual happiness. The married are very substantially happier than the unmarried; those living together are happier than those living alone; and the separated are particularly unhappy (Donovan and Halpern, 2003).

Friendship is also a good predictor of well-being, if slightly weaker than marriage. Other measures of social connection also have signifi-

cant effects, like going to church or being a member of some other voluntary association (Argyle, 1987; Helliwell, 2002a).

It is instructive to compare the relative importance of income on happiness with that of personal relationships. Being richer is associated
with being happier, though the relationship is non-linear and not very
strong. There seem to be diminishing returns to income, with the very
rich hardly any happier than the comfortably well-off – though this gra-
dient of happiness is more marked outside of the generally wealthy
OECD nations. Similarly, lottery winners, while certainly very happy
in the short term after winning, don't seem to be much happier in the
long term than the average person. In contrast, the positive effects of
strong personal ties seem extremely robust. As Putnam puts it, using
data from a massive rolling American survey, 'in round numbers,
getting married is the "happiness equivalent" of quadrupling your
annual income' (Putnam, 2000, p. 333; DDB Needham Life Survey
data). Similarly, the economist Oswald has estimated that getting
married appears roughly equivalent in happiness terms to US$100,000
per annum extra on your salary (Donovan and Halpern, 2003).[2]

Putnam argues that 'these findings will hardly surprise most Americans' (ibid., p. 332), though I am not so sure. When surveys have
been conducted asking (Americans) to rate directly the importance of
different aspects on life satisfaction, financial situation comes out top,
and certainly much higher than ratings of marriage or family life
(Campbell, Converse and Rodgers, 1976). Hence people *think* that
income matters more than personal relationships to their life satisfaction, although the data clearly indicate the reverse.

Physical health

One might feel that it's no big surprise that mental health, and especially depression, is affected by relationships – most of us would expect
that – but what about physical illnesses?

It turns out that all kinds of physical illness are predicted by a lack
of supportive relationships. Documented effects range from the substantially elevated death rates of spouses in the two years following
the death of their own partner, to the frequency of physical complications in childbirth, to the probability of dying in a heatwave. To take
the latter for example, an analysis of a recent Chicago heatwave found
that those who died were disproportionately likely to have been
socially isolated (Klinenberg, 2002).[3] Supportive relationships even
offer a buffer against the common cold – indeed are one of the
only really effective protective factors known. Sheldon Cohen, who has
been conducting carefully controlled experiments that deliberately

expose subjects to either doses of the common cold or harmless saline, has found that the probability of developing a full-blown cold is dramatically influenced by the extent of the individual's supportive relationships, all other factors having been controlled for (Cohen et al., 1997).

The apparent health-protecting power of positive personal relationships was illustrated by early longitudinal studies. In the 1950s a group of randomly chosen Harvard students were asked about the warmth of the relationship with their parents. Thirty-five years later, their medical records were checked. Of those who rated their relationships with their parents as warm and close, a little under half (47 per cent) had serious diseases diagnosed in midlife, but of those who had described their relationship with their parents as strained and cold, *all* (100 per cent) had serious diseases diagnosed in midlife (Russek and Schwartz, 1997). Similarly, a fifty-year follow-up of over 1,000 male medical students at Johns Hopkins University found that those who had described their relationships with their parents as close and caring were much less likely to have suffered, or be suffering, illness (Thomas and Duszynski, 1974). Indeed, closeness of the father–son relationship earlier in life was found to be the single best predictor of who would get cancer later in life, even having controlled for a host of other behavioural and socioeconomic factors.

Supportive relationships appear to be particularly important as a buffer to the negative effects of stress. For example, researchers have found that among mothers-to-be who have experienced major life change, the rate of physical complications was three times higher among those who lacked supportive relationships (Nuckolls, Cassel and Kaplan, 1972).

As mentioned at the start of the section, there are methodological difficulties in picking apart the causal relationship between health and personal relations. However, the conducting of painstaking (and expensive) longitudinal studies has moved the debate dramatically forward. The results of these studies have convinced all but the most hard-line of sceptics that the quality of an individual's relationships has a real and substantial impact on their mental and physical health. As a recent review noted: 'Over the last 20 years 13 large prospective cohort studies across a number of countries from the United States to Scandinavian countries to Japan have been conducted that show that people who are isolated or disconnected from others are at increased risk of dying prematurely' (Berkman and Glass, 2000, pp. 158–9). Such studies are much less vulnerable to the criticisms that dog cross-sectional studies, because the individuals' social networks are assessed prior to the onset of illness. One of the authors of the quotation above, Lisa

Berkman, was herself a leading figure in one of the first of these major prospective studies, Almeda County (Berkman and Syme, 1979). At the start of this study, in 1964, social ties were measured on an index assessing marital status, contacts with friends and relatives, and church and group memberships. Respondents were then tracked for a nine-year period concluding in 1974. It was found that men and women who lacked social ties at the start of the study were 1.9 to 3.1 times more likely to die during the study period than those with more social contacts. This relationship between social ties and mortality persisted even having controlled for health behaviours such as smoking and alcohol consumption, physical activity, preventive health care, and a range of baseline health measures. Furthermore, the increased risk of death was not limited to any one cause of death. Those who lacked social ties were at increased risk of dying from ischaemic heart disease, cerebrovascular and circulatory disease, cancer, and any other cause (a residual category).

Very similar results have been found by all the prospective studies since, with the only caveat being that the increased risk of death that results from social isolation has been found less consistently for women than for men (effects were found for both sexes by Berkman and Syme, 1979; Orth-Gomer and Johnson, 1987; but mainly in men by House, Robbins and Metzner, 1982; Blazer, 1982; Schoenbach et al., 1986; Welin et al., 1985; and R. M. Kaplan et al., 1988). The perceived quality of support tends to have a greater impact on mortality than the quantity of social interaction, which is a similar result to that found in the literature on mental health (Blazer, 1982; see also above). In general, individuals who are socially isolated have between two and five times the risk of dying early from all causes compared with those who have strong social ties (Berkman and Glass, 2000).

Research on cardiovascular disease tells a similar story. A number of follow-up studies of individuals who have suffered from myocardial infarctions (MI, or heart attacks) have shown that those with intimate social ties are much more likely to survive the years following an attack than those who are socially isolated (Ruberman et al., 1984; Orth-Gomer and Johnson, 1987; Berkman et al., 1992; Case et al., 1992). Typically, the socially isolated show a risk of mortality around three times higher in the years following an MI than those with close social ties. Research has been less definitive about the role that social ties play in the incidence, or first occurrence, of MIs. Some studies have found associations (e.g. Orth-Gomer et al., 1993) while others have not (Kawachi et al., 1996). This may partly reflect the methodological problem of having sufficient numbers in a prospective sample to find a statistically significant effect.[4] Meanwhile, laboratory work has shown that animals who are socially isolated develop considerably more atherosclerosis, or clogging of the blood vessels, than do less isolated animals – atherosclerosis being the central process of cardiovascular disease (Shiverly, Clarkson and Kalpan, 1989).

The indications are that social networks have a larger impact on the risk of mortality than on the risk of developing a disease (Vogt et al., 1992; Kawachi et al., 1996). In other words, it is not so much that social networks stop you getting sick as that they help you to recover when you do get sick. This is rather like the buffering effect described by Brown and Harris for depression – social networks may not save you from the normal adversities of life, but they help you survive them intact.

The final, and remarkable, evidence comes from the results of experimental intervention studies where some individuals received a boost to their social networks while matched controls did not. For example, in one study, men who had suffered a heart attack were randomly assigned into three groups. One group received no additional support; the second received advice and information about diet, exercise and cardiovascular pathophysiology; and the third received the same advice but also participated in support groups. Five years on, it was found that those who received advice had a lower recurrence rate of heart attacks than those who did not receive the additional advice (21.2 versus 28.2 per cent). However, those who also participated in the support groups had a much lower recurrence rate of just 12.9 per cent (Friedman et al., 1986).

The Friedman et al. study can be criticized on the basis that the support groups were specifically aimed at Type A, or hostile, behaviour, and that perhaps this explained much of the positive effect rather than the support from the group *per se*. However, this criticism cannot be levelled at a similar study of women with metastatic breast cancer. These patients were assigned either to a conventional medical care group, or to an experimental group who were given the same treatment but were also encouraged to meet together for ninety minutes once a week for a year. Much to the surprise of the researchers, the survival rate of the women who met was double that of the control group (Spiegel, 1993). Similarly, a study by Fawzy et al. found that patients with malignant melanoma, or skin cancer, who were randomly assigned to a six-week support group were significantly more likely to have survived six years later (Fawzy, Fawzy, Hyun et al., 1993). As Dean Ornish, the medic who famously demonstrated the impact of diet and lifestyle change on heart disease, concluded about these results: 'if a pharmaceutical company found that drug X doubled the length of survival in women with metastatic breast cancer, almost every doctor would be prescribing it . . . Full-page ads would proclaim the benefits in medical journals and news magazines' (Ornish, 1998, pp. 56–7). If future intervention studies confirm these results, then presumably medical practice will at some point turn to social capital not just as a possible contributor to health, but as a remedy for illness too.

Understanding the causal pathways: the role of stress

An interesting puzzle is why social networks and support protects individuals' health in such a general way. A big part of the answer appears to lie in work on 'stress', including how the body deals with it and how social support may affect it. Back in the 1930s, Hans Selye noticed in his medical practice that regardless of the type of disorder being examined, patients often complained of diffuse joint and muscle pain, disturbance of the intestines, loss of appetite and weight, and other general symptoms (Selye, 1956). Selye moved from these clinical observations to laboratory-based work on rats. He found that whatever alarming or damaging agents rats were exposed to – bacterial infections, trauma, heat or cold, or other stimuli – a degree of non-specific damage was superimposed on the specific damage of any given agent.

Selye hypothesized that organisms exhibited a general, non-specific mobilizing reaction in response to such threats – the General Adaptation Syndrome. The initial response was an *alarm reaction* consisting of bodily changes triggered by the sympathetic adrenomedullary system, inhibiting digestion and speeding up metabolic activity (the 'fight-or-flight' reaction), together with increased sensitivity to changes in the stressor. If this initial stage was prolonged, the organism then moved to a phase termed *resistance*. This was driven by the hypothalamo-pituitary adrenocortical system, maintaining a higher metabolic rate and blood glucose level, while lowering levels of libido and eventually also depressing the activity of the immune system. Finally, if the organism continued to be exposed to intense stress, it eventually reached a state of *exhaustion*, where behavioural and physiological adaptive reserves are depleted, and the body becomes highly susceptible to disease (Selye, 1956, 1978; A. Baum, Singer and Baum, 1982; Kiecolt-Glaser et al., 1994, 2002).

The General Adaptation Syndrome helps to explain how widely varying stressors can lead to essentially similar outcomes. As Freeman (1986) notes, 'the phenomenon is largely non-specific in both its determinants and its consequences . . . enhancing susceptibility to disease in general rather than having a specific aetiological role' (p. 293). A simple way to think of this is that a stressed organism neglects the routine bodily maintenance that keeps it healthy, and hence it shows what appears as accelerated ageing.

It is less widely noted that Selye also observed that some 'treatments', such as rest, eating soft foods, and even blood letting, had non-specific curative effects. Are intimate social networks another such non-specific curative treatment? The answer appears to be 'yes', and there is a rapidly expanding medical literature seeking to identify the processes involved.

While sustained stress seems to drive the body to suppress its own biological self-maintenance, and particularly the functioning of the immune system, positive social relationships seem to have the reverse effect (Kiecolt-Glaser et al., 1994). Studies have now shown that vulnerability to infections ranging from the common cold to HIV is greatly reduced by the presence of more extensive supportive social networks, and that this is mediated by improved immune system functioning (Cohen et al., 1997; Therell et al., 1995).

More work needs to be done to identify the exact nature of the causal pathways between stress, social ties and health. It seems pretty clear that supportive social relationships are able to modify or counteract the stress reaction in both humans and other mammals, but the precise details are still being worked out. At least four pathways can be identified.

First, the presence of supportive relationships generally implies that the individual is likely to be exposed to less stress. Much human stress, as measured by life-event scales, concerns disruption or the absence of social networks. Indeed, arguably the most serious stressors that an individual has to cope with are inseparable from measures of social support, such as the death of a loved partner or relative (T. H. Holmes and Rahe, 1967).

Second, the presence of social support is known to modify the consequences of stress. At the simplest level, support can buffer individuals against a particular loss or threat by offering a substitute, supplement or 'instrumental' support. If you lose some money, but you have a wealthy relative who can help you out, then this is a much less serious threat to your well-being than to that of someone who lacks such support. Indeed, in a developing world context, this support can mean the difference between life and death on a day-to-day basis (Woolcock and Narayan, 2000). Survival through a famine or other natural disaster rests mainly on whether you have a family or community network who will share food, water and shelter. Similarly, even among the poorest of communities, sick individuals can still access expensive health care where supportive family and friends club together to cover the costs (Aye, Champagne and Contandriopoulos, 2002).

Support can also provide a psychological or emotional boost, changing our interpretation of stressful events or giving us the psychological strength to cope with them. This is illustrated by an experiment where individuals had to give a public talk – an event that most consider very stressful and that is associated with the classic physiological stress reaction. Those who were told that someone was available just outside the room to help them if they should need it showed a more modest stress reaction, in the form of lower blood pressure both before and during the speech, even though no help was actually given (Kamarck, Manuck and Jennings et al., 1991). This result fits with a long line of research showing that it is not just the actual stress that matters, but the perception of it, and the perception of whether it can be controlled (Glass and Singer, 1972).

Third, social support may shape people's behavioural reactions to stress. For example, whether you react to a crisis by drowning your sorrows in Scotch or by trying to find a more adaptive solution may depend on the support and guidance of those around you. It may also depend on how much you value your life, and how positively you feel about yourself (your self-esteem and self-efficacy), which in turn may depend heavily on how you feel that others see you. In this respect, it is interesting to note that unhealthy behaviours, such as smoking, drinking, physical inactivity and poor diet, are strongly associated with social isolation (Berkman and Syme, 1979; Berkman and Glass, 2000).

Fourth, and more subtly, it may be that an individual's basic reactivity to stress is affected by the quality of their supportive relationships early in life. Selye noted in his early experiments that chronic exposure to stress led to long-term physiological and behavioural adaptations. There is increasing evidence that the experience of excessive stress early in life may 'hard-wire' us to excessive reactivity for the rest of our lives (Gunnar and Nelson, 1994; Suomi, 1997). This reactivity may help to explain findings such as that of a Swedish study that family dissension in childhood was associated with more than a 50 per cent increase in mortality among men and women aged 30–75 (Lundberg, 1993).

Summary of the effects of personal networks on health

In sum, the literature documenting the positive effects on health of close, confiding personal relationships is extremely convincing. Putnam has caused some controversy by arguing that: 'Statistically

speaking, the evidence for the health consequences of social connectedness is as strong today as was the first surgeon general's report on
smoking. If the trends in social disconnection are as pervasive as I
argued [within the USA] . . . then "bowling alone" represents one of the
nation's most serious public health challenges' (Putnam, 2000, p. 327;
see chapter 7 for a discussion of trends in social capital). Questions certainly remain – such as why the protective effect on physical health
appears to be much more reliable for men than women. But the main
conclusion is clear. Close personal relationships, and intimate, confiding relationships in particular, generally have highly positive impacts
on individual mental health, happiness and physical health.

The meso-level: community and health

As mentioned in the previous section, it is not only intimate personal
relationships that impact on individual health. Having more friends,
going to church and taking part in voluntary associations – in rough
order of importance – all have some positive impact on health. Evidence for this comes from both cross-sectional and longitudinal
research.

The positive health impacts of friendship, community and work-
based social networks, as shown by individual-level survey data,
indicate the importance of community or meso-level social capital on
health. For some researchers, this is evidence enough of a meso-level
effect. However, a tougher and more appropriate test of a true meso-
level (ecological) effect is to ask whether this level explains health over
and above the effects of relationships as measured at the individual
level. It is one thing to say that individuals who have supportive friendships at work or in the neighbourhood tend to be happier and healthier. But it is another to say that some firms or neighbourhoods create
such a positive atmosphere that the average level of well-being is
increased more than could have been expected from each individual's
circumstances. One leading research group has gone as far as to say
that these individual-level effects should be referred to as social
support, and the term 'social capital' should be reserved exclusively for
higher-level 'ecological' effects – the meso- and macro-levels (Berkman
and Kawachi, 2000; see chapter 1).

Mental health and happiness

Durkheim's work on suicide, quoted at the start of this chapter, offers
a classic example of the impact of social cohesiveness on mental health.

However, the vast majority of studies on mental health that have followed it have been focused on individual rather than community effects.

Brown and Harris's classic study of depression is a typical example, excellent though it is in its own terms. These researchers concluded that it was only intimate relationships that had an impact on mental health. They felt that there was no evidence that, say, neighbours or the wider community had an impact on mental health (Harris, pers. comm.). But the problem is that there is no way they could have known this from their method. The study focused on a few hundred women in one small area of a single city. The research design did not include any significant variation in the neighbourhood or community context, so there is no way that the wider context could explain any variance within this study.

Studies that have included questions on the neighbourhood have found a significant relationship with self-reported mental health. For example, an analysis of the British Household Survey found that people who reported low levels of neighbourhood social capital were approximately twice as likely as those reporting high levels to suffer from psychiatric morbidity (measured as scores higher than 3 on the 12-item General Health Questionnaire; McCulloch, 2001). However, such studies rely on the same individuals' reports of their neighbourhood social capital, and may therefore be subject to response bias.

Cross-cultural studies have suggested that the tighter and more cohesive social networks of more traditional communities may help explain the lower rates of mental illness that are often reported within them. For example, a study of the Old Order Amish, a strict religious sect in Pennsylvania which maintains a tightly knit, closed community, largely cut off from the modern world, found that the Amish suffered from unusually low levels of depression (Egeland and Hostetter, 1983). Equally strikingly, no sex difference was found in the rate of depression, undermining the conventional wisdom that the much higher rate of depression found among women in most western populations is the result of biological factors (Watts and Morant, 2001).

One concern about such cross-cultural studies is that the findings might reflect cross-cultural differences in the expression or reporting of symptoms. To overcome this issue, one needs to turn to studies contrasting the rates of mental illness of similar types of individuals or groups living in different community contexts.

A large number of such studies have now been conducted, and have shown that otherwise similar members of the same ethnic, religious and even occupational groups tend to have significantly lower rates of mental illness when group members live close together. A very early demonstration of this effect was provided in a study of Chicago (Faris and Dunham, 1939). The researchers found that black people living in primarily black areas had lower rates of mental illness than better-off black people living in white or mixed-race areas.

This result is known as the 'group density effect', and has now been replicated for many groups and in many contexts (see Halpern, 1993, for a review). The effect is particularly striking given that ethnic minority groups tend to live in areas of concentrated disadvantage, and that such residents would generally be expected to have poorer mental and physical health. In contrast, those ethnic minority individuals who 'escape' from these areas of deprivation through economic advancement into more affluent areas would be expected, through both selection and simple causation, to have better than average mental and physical health. The result is therefore doubly surprising – it cannot be the result of social selection, and must be the result of some form of 'social causation'. The most plausible interpretation is that being embedded in a community is associated with more support from friends and relatives – bonding social capital – and with shelter from the direct discrimination of the wider group (Halpern, 1993).

The only credible alternative explanation is that somehow the findings are the result of cultural differences that exist between minority group members who live in areas of differing levels of concentration. For example, if the members of ethnic minority groups who live in areas of greater group concentration were less acculturated, then perhaps linguistic differences or different patterns of reporting might explain the group density effect. However, this explanation was tested directly in a large-scale and careful study of the mental health of different ethnic groups living in Britain. Interviews were conducted in the respondent's own favoured language, follow-up validation interviews were conducted on subjects appearing to be suffering from mental illness, and ethnically matched interviewers were used throughout. Once again, despite suffering from very high levels of deprivation, individuals from ethnic minority groups were found to have better mental health when living in areas of high group concentration than when living in areas of low group concentration, even though these were typically more affluent areas (Halpern and Nazroo, 2000). This effect was robust to statistical controls for acculturation and fluency in English.

The large potential impact of neighbourhood on well-being is indicated by the finding that residential satisfaction is affected more by getting on with your neighbours than by the physical quality of the dwelling (Halpern, 1995a). For example, the subjective quality of life of the over-65s has been found to be significantly affected by personal and neighbourhood social capital even after controls have been made for social expectations, personality and psychological characteristics (optimism–pessimism), health and wealth (Bowling et al., 2002). In contrast, socioeconomic differences contributed little.

Although the group density effect has proved to be extremely robust, the occasional exception has been noted. For example, some work has suggested a negative group density effect for Catholics in parts of Ireland and for the Pakistani community in Britain (Halpern, 1993; Halpern and Nazroo, 2000). Just as was noted at the individual level, we should be wary about presuming that all relationships and communities will be universally beneficial to mental health: the character of relationships, and the demands made within them, matter too. One example of the double-edged nature of community for mental health is that there is some evidence that people with pre-existing psychoses tend to have higher hospital readmission rates in neighbourhoods with higher levels of social capital (McKenzie, 2000; social capital measured as areas with high community safety). McKenzie postulated that this was because of low community tolerance of deviant behaviour. A similar effect was found for former psychiatric patients on a housing estate battling against demolition. When residents on the estate thought that the estate was to be demolished their medical consultations rose but those of the former patients fell, and when it appeared that the estate would be saved and community spirit rose, while the residents' medical consultations fell, those of the former patients rose (Halpern, 1995a).

The double-edged potential effects of community on mental health can also be illustrated from a classic source. Durkheim's work on suicide is repeatedly quoted as a perfect illustration of the power of social networks and social integration to protect individuals from acts of self-destruction (e.g. Putnam, 2000; Berkman and Glass, 2000). As we saw at the start of this chapter, Durkheim provides compelling evidence of the potentially protective effects of strong community bonds against the risk of suicide. Most of the data strongly support the supposition that those who are more socially isolated are at higher risk of suicide, and that more 'anomic' and individualistic cultures have much higher rates of suicide. However, Durkheim also provides a clear, but much less quoted example of the exact reverse. He observed that within the military suicide was up to ten times higher than in the civilian population. He observed:

> This fact is at first sight all the more surprising because it might be supposed that many causes would guard the army against suicide. First,

from the physical point of view, the persons composing it represent the flower of the country. Carefully selected, they have no serious organic flaws. Also, the esprit de corps and the common life should have the pro- phylactic effect here which they have elsewhere. What is the cause of so large an aggravation? (Durkheim, [1897] 1951, p. 229)

Durkheim tested whether it was the result of factors such as the higher proportion of unmarried men. But the rate of military suicide was still much higher than that of the unmarried male population within each nation. He tested whether it was to do with 'disgust' with military service among new recruits, but found that the suicide rate rose with longer service (though it was also higher in the first six months). And he tested whether the rate might be the result of the hard- ships and conditions of service, but found that the rates were consis- tently highest in the most elite units who had the best conditions of service.

Durkheim's explanation was that the tight networks and obligations of the military way of life stimulated what he called 'altruistic' or 'heroic' suicide. He argued that military codes of conduct and honour, while probably making armies more effective, also meant that indi- vidual soldiers might sometimes take their own lives over relatively trivial matters of honour or saving face. This explained the paradoxi- cal finding that while the most traditional and socially cohesive nations had the lowest overall suicide rates, their military personnel had the *highest* suicide rates. It seemed as if the same forces that bound men together in a civil context and thereby protected them from acts of self- destruction had exactly the opposite effect in the military context, a tight and highly anti-individualistic organization in the business of violence. This also explained the final puzzle that, at the time that Durkheim was writing and many traditional forces of social cohesion were starting to unravel, while suicide rates were generally increasing, military suicides were falling everywhere.

Physical health

The health literature is full of ecological effects. Imagine a deadly virus that can spread relatively easily within a human population. If a couple of people who live in isolation catch the disease, while they may die, the wider impact will be limited. If, on the other hand, these people live in the middle of a busy city, the impact could be devastating. Clearly, the impact of such a virus on humans depends on the context – there are massive 'ecological effects'.

If community- or meso-level social capital affects physical health, then we should see variations in community health that are not reducible to individual characteristics. One well-studied example is that of the small US town of Roseto, Pennsylvania. Researchers noted that this town had unusually low death rates that could not be accounted for by individual risk factors such as smoking, diet or exercise (Bruhn and Wolf, 1979; Egolf et al., 1992; Wolf and Bruhn, 1993; Wilkinson, 1996). In particular, the age-adjusted death rate for heart disease in Roseto was less than half of that of the neighbouring towns. Despite the Rosetans' unhealthy taste for high-fat home cooking, heart attacks were very rare.

> The data obtained over a span of twenty years in the Italian-American community of Roseto, when compared with those of neighbouring communities, strongly suggests that the cultural characteristics – the qualities of a social organisation – affect in some way individual susceptibility to myocardial infarction and sudden death. The implication is that an emotionally supportive social environment is protective and that, by contrast, the absence of family and community support and the lack of a well-defined role in society are risk factors. (Bruhn and Wolf, 1979, p. 134)

The researchers were struck by the closely knit and egalitarian ethos of life in Roseto. The town was largely made up of Italian Americans descended from migrants who had arrived in the 1880s, and who had developed a distinctive town culture:

> the sense of common purpose and the camaraderie among the Italians precluded ostentation or embarrassment to the less affluent, and the concern for neighbors ensured that no one was ever abandoned. This pattern of remarkable social cohesion, in which the family, as the hub and bulwark of life, provided a kind of security and insurance against any catastrophe, was associated with the striking absence of myocardial infarction and sudden death. (Bruhn and Wolf, 1979, p. 136)

Was it that Rosetans were simply lucky enough to have the right genes for healthy hearts? No. We know this because at the very time that Roseto first came to be studied by medical researchers, the tight-knit community of the town was beginning to unravel. Sure enough, by the 1970s, the materialistic habits of the rest of America had lodged themselves in the town, and the younger generations began to break away from the town's more civic habits. With these changes, the disease rates for the town rose sharply. By the 1980s MIs were actually higher than for neighbouring towns (Egolf et al., 1992; Wolf and Bruhn, 1993).

The difference in death rates between Roseto and the neighbouring towns is not unique. In Britain, for example, a recent government report noted that the death rate from coronary heart disease in people under 65 was almost three times higher in Manchester than in Kingston and Richmond, a pleasant suburb of London (74 and 25 per 100,000 respectively in 1996–8; Department of Health, 2000). Similarly, research has shown that there appears to be a significant amount of variability in heart disease that is attributable to the district rather than individual level (Hart, Ecob and Smith, 1997). However, in the past, no official statistics have been gathered on social capital variables, so it is not known to what extent these might contribute to such neighbourhood variations. It may be that non-social capital variables, such as diet, lifestyle and poverty-related stress, account for most of the variations. We simply do not know.

However, just as in the mental health literature, important evidence for community-level effects on physical health have been found by studies of the relationship between neighbourhood racial composition and health.

For example, a Chicago-based study found that the higher the percentage of black residents in the neighbourhood, the lower the rate of low birthweight black infants born there, even having controlled for individual maternal characteristics (E. Roberts, 1997). In other words, birthweights of black children, a key indicator of health not only in childhood but throughout life, were higher in the black ghettos despite the higher levels of deprivation within those areas. Similarly, a study of 166 New York neighbourhoods found that black people living in primarily black areas had significantly lower cardiovascular disease mortality and all-cause mortality than those living in white areas, having controlled for education, employment, poverty, occupation, income and birthplace (Fang et al., 1998). Most recently, a multilevel analysis of deaths from heart disease in Texas found that black people and Hispanics living in neighbourhoods with higher proportions of their own ethnic group lost fewer years of life from heart disease than their peers living in less homogeneous neighbourhoods (Franzini and Spears, forthcoming). This neighbourhood effect was robust to controls for crime, percentage of owner occupiers, house values and education levels.

The neighbourhood effects found by these studies are not huge – typically in the range of 5 to 10 per cent of the explained variability. Nonetheless, they are striking because they suggest that the support gained from living with other community members is sufficiently powerful to outweigh the negative impact of living in an area of higher deprivation – exactly as was seen for mental health (see above).

In contrast, we need to consider whether social networks might have a negative effect on health by facilitating the spread of disease. In essence, bonding social capital ought to help infections spread through a community, just as dry weather helps spread wildfire, and bridging social capital ought to help infections spread from one community to another. This supposition is supported by studies of the spread of disease. Disease transmission is strongly shaped by patterns of social networks, and can be predicted from the density and mixing of networks, commuting and other patterns of human contact (Neaigus et al., 1994; Morris, 1995; Wallace and Wallace, 1997). Hence frequency of drug use and the spread of HIV can be predicted from the density and character of social networks (Newcomb and Bentler, 1988; Latkin et al., 1995; Wallace and Wallace, 1997; Lovell, 2002; Soskolne and Shtarkshall, 2002).[5]

On the other hand, experimental work has shown that supportive networks generally offer strong protection against disease once exposure to the infectious agent has occurred (Cohen et al., 1997; see above). Furthermore, social networks – especially when characterized by high trust and mutual concern – are an important channel for the spread of 'good practice' in terms of health behaviour. As Berkman and Glass note, 'social influence which extends from the network's values and norms constitutes an important and under-appreciated pathway through which networks impact health' (2000, p. 146). This impact can be positive or negative depending on the nature of these norms and values, and on the accuracy of the knowledge being transmitted. For example, school climate has been found to be significantly associated with smoking in children, controlling for gender, ethnicity and social class (Vuille and Schenkel, 2002). Similarly, a Swedish public health survey found that there was a strong neighbourhood effect on variation in physical inactivity, but that social capital *per se* did not influence this inactivity one direction or another (M. Lindstrom, Moghaddassi and Merlo, 2003).

Data from the Almeda County study suggest that on average the impact of social capital is more positive than negative, as those with higher levels of social integration showed lower levels of high-risk health behaviour (Berkman and Glass, 2000). This may reflect psychological as well as knowledge factors. For example, the socially isolated may fail to give up smoking not because of a lack of knowledge, but because they regard it as one of their few pleasures in life (Marsh and Mackay, 1994).

Summary: the health benefits of living in a cohesive community

It should be clear from the above that we cannot assume that a strong cohesive community will always benefit the health of its members, though generally cohesive communities do tend to bring such benefits. For physical health and health-related behaviour, the effects of social capital depend heavily on the culture and habits of the community itself. If your community strongly encourages you to smoke, then this is unlikely to benefit your health.

The effect of the community over and above that of the individual factors is generally estimated to be relatively modest. The presumption must be that most of these neighbourhood effects are actually mediated by the quality of the individual's own social capital, though it is important to note that this may itself be partly ecologically determined. It is easier for an individual to build up a close and supportive social network within a community of like-minded and culturally similar individuals. For the ethnic minority and other disadvantaged groups, the avoidance of contact with hostile others and with direct discrimination may also play a role.

We have relatively few studies that are able to handle the considerable methodological difficulties that are involved in identifying community-level effects of social capital on health, not least because data are rarely gathered on social capital, and even more rarely with any clustering at the neighbourhood level. This is starting to change, not least because of the growing recognition of the potential importance of social capital variables. For example, medical epidemiologists have been speculating that the significantly higher life expectancies of the Finno-Swedish minority living in Finland (around 5 per cent of the population) may be the result of social capital factors, just as in the case of Roseto in the USA. This enhanced interest should mean that within a few years we will have a better understanding of the impact of social capital on health at the meso- or community level, and that we will have a wider range of examples to draw on.

The macro- or national level

We saw at the start of the chapter that Durkheim's explanation of suicide was that there must be 'some force in their common environment' inclining unrelated people to kill themselves. For the most part, suicide is committed so rarely that those who do it are unlikely to know each other or share immediate networks. Instead the common link must lie at a higher level of the social fabric – that is, the link is at the cultural or macro-level.

Mental health and happiness

Curiously, there are relatively few studies to date that directly examine the hypothesis that national differences in rates of mental illness might partly be explained by national variations in social capital. It may be that this largely reflects the great controversies that have raged over the comparability of mental health statistics across countries. The fact is that official mental health statistics, such as compulsory detainment by virtue of insanity, probably tell us more about legal frameworks and service provision than they do about rates of disorder. Similarly, it is only very recently that countries have started to conduct national community-based surveys of mental health, and to date these are few in number and have not been standardized to facilitate cross-national comparisons.

However, cross-national studies have been conducted on both happiness and life satisfaction. These national differences are very substantial. The Danes, for example, have consistently reported being much happier and more satisfied with life than the Italians or French. Summating data over more than 15 Eurobarometer surveys starting from the mid-1970s, we find that around 55 per cent of Danes report being 'very satisfied' with life as a whole. In contrast, only around 10 per cent of Italians or French report such satisfaction.

Until very recently, the general interpretation of these national differences was that they just reflected 'noise' in the data, and especially cultural and linguistic differences in expression. The Danes weren't really happier – they just said they were. But this sceptical interpretation gets into trouble on several counts. First, the examination of critical test cases has suggested that linguistic differences do not readily explain away the national differences. Particular attention has focused on the case of Switzerland, where French, German and Italian speakers live together. It is found that whatever language they speak, the Swiss report being significantly happier than their French, German and Italian neighbours whose languages they share (Inglehart, 1990). The same applies to Belgium, where the French speakers are about as happy as their Flemish-speaking compatriots, and much happier than the French speakers over the border in France. The critical factor appears to be nationality, not the language spoken. Second, and rather importantly, random noise should generate random patterns, but as we shall see, this is certainly not the case.

Can these differences be explained by social capital? As well as being happier, the Danes also report much higher levels of social trust than the French or Italians (see figure 2.1). If we widen the pool of nations to include not only Europe but all of the industrialized nations, we find that there is a strong positive relationship between social trust and well-being (r = .66; data from the World Values Surveys). This is an interesting finding, but far from conclusive. As we saw in chapter 2, higher-trust nations are generally much wealthier – possibly partly as a result of their high social trust and capital. If we statistically control for wealth, then the relationship between trust and happiness greatly weakens, suggesting that perhaps more trusting nations are happier because they are richer, not because they are more trusting. Also, if we introduce a wider set of nations, the strength of the relationship again weakens, not least because the nations of South America are extremely untrusting, but still pretty happy.

To have a chance of making any progress with this problem, we need a sophisticated model. We need to control for all kinds of national differences, such as income, age, education and health. Equally importantly, we really should seek to control for a whole host of individual-level variables and then see if there remain any national differences to explain. Fortunately, just such an analysis has been produced by the Canadian economist John Helliwell (Helliwell, 2002a). This analysis confirms the micro-level effects mentioned earlier: individuals who are more socially connected in terms of marriage, church and voluntary associations are significantly happier. But the elegance of Helliwell's work is that it does not stop there, but goes on to examine aggregate-level differences too.

The analysis uses data from the three waves of the World Values Surveys, totalling data from 87,806 people from 46 different countries. This data set is large enough to permit many factors to be taken into account. By way of introduction, we might note Helliwell's results in relation to income. Sure enough, Helliwell found that at the individual level, people who earned more were more satisfied, albeit with diminishing returns. He found a similar pattern at the national level, with wealthier nations being more satisfied, but with a pattern of sharply diminishing returns. However, he found that when these individual-level differences were controlled for, higher income at the aggregate level was associated with *lower* life satisfaction. In other words, as those around you get richer, your happiness goes down. This is what is called a 'negative externality'.

Turning to social capital variables, a very different pattern was seen. When individual-level differences in trust, group memberships and so on were controlled for, aggregate levels of trust and group and church memberships were still significant and were associated with *higher* levels of life satisfaction. In other words, the more that other people around you trust each other, go to church and participate in voluntary organizations, the happier you get regardless of whether you take part or not. In contrast to income, social capital appears to throw off *positive* externalities in terms of well-being. Similarly, having compatriots who are honest, as measured by intolerance for cheating with taxes, is associated with higher life satisfaction, even having controlled for the individual's own attitude to cheating with taxes.

An interesting detail of the model is that the effects of education on well-being drop out of the equation. At the simple (bivariate) level, there is a positive association between being better educated and being more satisfied with life. This model suggests that it is not education *per se* that brings happiness, but rather that more educated people are happier because they earn more, form more relationships, get more involved in their society, trust more and have better physical health.

Helliwell constructs a large and complex model, incorporating over forty variables in the final version. Nonetheless, as it uses cross-sectional data it can still be subject to the standard criticism that the causal arrow may run in any number of directions. Perhaps happy people join clubs rather than clubs make people happy? Equally worrying, perhaps there is some other variable or systematic response bias that leads to the pattern of results? In particular, it is known that some individuals are much more positive in their responses and perceptions of the world in general, and this can throw up spurious associations in cross-sectional data (Halpern, 1995b).

Helliwell employs a clever trick that at least deals with the second of these potential problems. He introduces individuals' perceptions of their own state of health as a control variable. Perceptions of health have quite a strong association with subjective well-being – as my grandmother used to say, 'as long as you've got your health . . .'. Introducing perceptions of health into the equation almost certainly introduces an element of 'partialling fallacy', artificially reducing the size of the associations between life satisfaction and the other variables in the equation.[6] In this sense it is conservative analysis. But the beauty of using it as a control variable is that this should control for optimism or positive response bias. If people are overly positive about reporting, then they will over-report how good their health is in just the same way as they over-report their life satisfaction, so controlling for either one should eliminate the effect of such bias.

Recently Helliwell has shifted his attention from happiness to suicide, returning to Durkheim's original focus (Helliwell, forthcoming). His provisional results represent a remarkable replication of Durkheim's original findings, but extended across countries and using modern statistical methods. He finds that social capital and other related variables explain more than *half* of the substantial variation in national suicide rates. For example, the model indicates that an increase in social trust of 10 percentage points – a fairly modest difference given that 2001–4 levels range from around 3 per cent in Brazil to around 65 per cent in Nordic countries – would reduce annual suicide rates by 4 per 100,000 in males and 0.5 per 100,000 in females. This is a massive difference considering that average national suicide rates are around 25 for men and 8 for women.

In sum, Helliwell concludes that national differences in social capital – from civic engagement through to co-operative social norms – contribute to both happiness and suicide, and do so over and above individual differences in social capital. Although his analyses still ultimately rely on a cross-sectional method, they are about as sophisticated as such analyses can be. Also, because of the enormous range of national variation in life satisfaction, suicide and the other variables employed, they have considerable statistical power. His work is of interest not only because of its fascinating results, but because it sets a methodological standard for other studies to follow.

Physical health

The strong evidence for social capital having an impact on health at the macro-level comes from data on the USA. Kawachi et al. found a very close relationship between the age-adjusted mortality rates of US states and various measures of social capital aggregated to state level (Kawachi et al., 1997). The age-adjusted mortality rate was significantly related to average levels of group membership ($r = -.49$), perceived lack of helpfulness ($r = .71$; measured by percentage responding 'people mostly look out for themselves') and social mistrust ($r = .79$; measured by percentage responding 'you can't be too careful in dealing with people'). Indeed, social mistrust accounted for 61 per cent of state-level variations in total mortality.

The question arises whether social mistrust is really a cause or just a symptom. States that show higher levels of mistrust are also significantly poorer as measured by the percentage of households below the federal poverty level ($r = .52$). Poverty is also associated with higher mortality ($r = .57$). Controlling for poverty did somewhat attenuate the relationship between mortality and social trust, but still left the relationship highly significant. It remained significant not only for total mortality, but also for infant mortality, deaths from malignant neoplasms (cancer) and cerebrovascular disease (Kawachi et al., 1997).

A similar but weaker pattern was seen for the relationship between group membership and mortality. Before any statistical controls, group membership levels explained 22 per cent of state-level variations in mortality. Controlling for poverty reduced this effect but it remained statistically significant for total mortality and malignant neoplasms.

Kawachi et al. have since replicated the key findings of this study using Americans' self-perceived health, and teenage births, as the outcome measure (Kawachi, Kennedy and Glass, 1999; Gold et al., 2002, respectively). Self-rated health is known to be a very good predictor of mortality and disability, despite its simple nature (Idler and Benyamini, 1997). Once again, within states with higher levels of social mistrust, a much higher proportion of the population reported having 'fair or poor' health ($r = .71$). However, the significant advance in this study was that information was also available about socioeconomic and health-related factors at the individual level.

As expected from the wider literature, strong associations were found between self-rated health and age, low income, poor education, ethnic minority status, smoking, obesity and lack of health insurance. As would have been expected from what we have already seen of social capital at the micro-level, living alone was also strongly and independently associated with poorer self-rated health (odds ratio 1.93; 95 per cent confidence interval 1.34–2.80). However, even after controlling for all these variables, individuals living in states with low social capital still tended to report poorer health (the odds ratio of describing your health as poor in low- versus high-social-trust states, other factors controlled for, was 1.41; the 95 per cent confidence interval being 1.33–1.50). As the authors conclude, 'these findings were consistent with an apparent contextual effect of state-level social capital on individual well-being, independent of the more proximal predictors of self-rated health' (Berkman and Kawachi, 2000, p. 184).

Similar conclusions were drawn from their path analysis of teenage births across thirty-nine US states (Gold et al., 2002). The teenage birthrate was affected by both poverty and income inequality, but the effect of inequality appeared to be primarily mediated through its negative impact on social capital.

Much the same result has now been replicated using data from across forty regions of Russia, and across the twenty counties of Hungary. Again using a cross-sectional, ecological analysis, significant associations were found between indicators of social capital (civic engagement in politics, quality of work relations, and so on) and both life expectancy and mortality rates (B. P. Kennedy and Kawachi, 1998).

The interpretation is that in post-Soviet Russia, people living in regions characterized by lower levels of informal support have been especially vulnerable to hardship and illness following the transition to a market economy.

The Hungarian results are quite similar. Mortality rates, calculated for those aged 45–64, were strongly associated with perceived trust, reciprocity and support received from civic and religious organizations (Skrabski, Kopp and Kawachi, 2003). Mortality rates were most strongly associated with levels of mistrust, much as found in the US data. Gender differences were also noted, with male mortality rates most affected by variations in help from civic organizations, but with female mortality most associated with perceptions of reciprocity. The authors conclude that 'psychosocial factors may indeed be important determinants of the mortality crisis' in the former Soviet Union countries, and also that 'in a relatively traditional society, middle aged men seem to be more vulnerable to rapid changes in social contexts' (p. 118). The latter conclusion curiously echoes the finding that social capital appears to have a bigger and more consistent impact on men than on women in longitudinal health surveys reported earlier, perhaps reflecting a greater variability in men's social capital or a greater sensitivity to its absence.

A public health controversy:
material versus psycho-social accounts

The debate has been raging for some years about the relative importance of material and economic factors on health versus psycho-social factors, including social capital. In particular, there is great controversy over the causes of national differences in health (R. M. Kaplan, Sallis and Patterson, 1993; F. Baum, 1999).

There is no doubt about the existence of substantial national variations in health and longevity. For example, despite having similar levels of wealth, people live on average about eight years longer in Greece than in Saudi Arabia; five years longer in Iceland than in the United Arab Emirates; four years longer in Japan than the USA; and three years longer in Sweden than in Germany. Similarly within the USA, average life expectancy differs markedly between states, including between states with similar average incomes.

However, there is no convincing published evidence to date that cross-national variations in health outcomes, unlike across-US-states variations, can be explained by social capital variables. Indeed, across Europe, there appears to be a negative relationship between social trust and mortality, at least for heart disease. In other words, high-trust northern nations such as Sweden and Denmark often have higher age-adjusted mortality rates than low-trust southern nations such as Italy and Greece.

The US data suggest a strong effect of both social capital and economic inequality. Kawachi et al. measured inequality with a 'Robin Hood Index': the aggregate household income in each state that would have to be taken from above-average-income households and given to those below average in order to achieve equality in incomes. As one might imagine, this correlates quite highly with poverty, as the more households there are below the poverty line the more one would have to transfer from the rich to achieve equality of incomes ($r = .74$). The Robin Hood Index is also strongly associated with mortality ($r = .65$) and with social mistrust ($r = .71$).

These high correlations indicate that income inequality, social mistrust and mortality are all very closely related, making it quite difficult to separate them. Kawachi et al. use a technique called path analysis to do this, and it indicates that social distrust mediates the relationship between inequality and health. Essentially, when you control for levels of mistrust, the effect of inequality on health largely disappears, whereas when you control for inequality, a significant relationship remains between social mistrust and health. The simplest interpretation of this analysis is that inequality leads to social mistrust, and social mistrust in turn leads to poorer population health. However, on its own this interpretation needs to be viewed with some caution because the variables are so compounded (strongly correlated), and, of course, the data are cross-sectional, making cause and effect difficult to separate with confidence. One possibility is that inequality stretches the social fabric, leading to a breakdown of social capital. This is the interpretation of Kawachi et al. (1997) and receives some additional support from the study of crime (see chapter 4).

However, the story is less clear when one turns to cross-national differences. In general, people living in poor nations have worse average health and lower life expectancies than those living in wealthy nations. Almost nobody disputes that among the poorest nations, lack of wealth and resources has a massive impact on health. For nations with GNPs per person of around US$1,000 or less, average life expectancies are less than 50 years. In contrast, for nations with GNPs per person of around US$5,000 – still fairly poor by the standards of the industrialized west – average life expectancies approach 70 years. However, at higher levels of wealth, increases in GNP per capita bring diminishing returns. The wealthiest nations, with GNPs per person of around US$25,000, have life expectancies approaching 80 years – a respectable 10 years more than those who earn on average a fifth less, but around half as large a longevity gain as those who earn a fifth less again (J. Lynch et al., 2000a, 2000b).[7]

This pattern of diminishing returns means that within the wealthier industrialized nations, the strength of the relationship between national wealth and health virtually disappears. If we take the world's richest nations in 1995 there is, if anything, a weak negative association between wealth and health (r = −.11; Wilkinson, 2000). Considerable national differences in health remain between these wealthy nations, but it would seem that these are better predicted by economic inequalities within countries than the economic differences between them (Wilkinson, 1996; G. A. Kaplan et al., 1996).[8] Some, notably Richard Wilkinson, have argued that social capital is part of this story.

Income shows a simple pattern of diminishing returns to health at the individual level, suggesting that countries with more inequality might be less healthy because they have disproportionately more poor, and therefore sick, people. However, studies have shown that controlling for individual-level wealth does not eliminate national differences in health, just as Kawachi et al. found for the differences between US states (Daly et al., 1998; Soobader and LeClere, 1999). A heated debate has ensued over whether this residual effect can best be explained by a 'psychosocial environment' or social capital account (Wilkinson, 1996, 2000; F. Baum, 1999) or by a 'neo-material' account (J. Lynch et al., 2000a, 2000b; Muntaner et al., 2002).

Wilkinson has argued forcibly that, within the wealthy nations, it is relative rather than absolute income that primarily impacts on health. He argues that absolute wealth or poverty determines the ability to buy goods, but that relative inequality determines your position in society.[9] In affluent societies, even the relatively poor are able to obtain the basic goods necessary for sustenance – food, water, shelter and basic health care. However, relative poverty still means low status, exposure to greater insecurity and greater stress.

Apart from mapping the strength of the relationship between inequality and health at the macro-level, Wilkinson highlights other kinds of evidence in support of his argument. He points to the large numbers of studies that have shown the close relationship between social gradients and health. Among the best known and methodologically strongest of these is that conducted by Marmot et al. In what are widely known as the Whitehall studies, Marmot et al. examined the relationship between the health and the position of British civil servants of all grades. It was found that even the smallest differences in grade – manifest by room size, desk size, carpet, and even coat-stand, as well as salary – were associated with significant and systematic differences in both physical and mental health (Marmot, 1986; Marmot et al., 1991). The higher the grade, the better the civil servants' age-adjusted physical and mental health.

Wilkinson also cites the large numbers of animal studies that have shown the powerful negative health impacts of being in the non-dominant position in a social hierarchy. He points to the idea that there are two basic forms of social organization among human and non-human primates: 'agonistic' societies based on dominance hierarchies and 'hedonic societies' based on egalitarian co-operation (Trower, Gilbert and Sherling, 1990). Essentially, Wilkinson argues that economically unequal nations are 'agonistic' societies with clear dominance hierarchies, within which power and coercion provide access to resources regardless of the needs of others. In contrast, more equal nations are characterized by more co-operative social relations within which people's needs are recognized and mediated through obligations of sharing and reciprocity. He argues that 'social relations tend to atrophy in a more hierarchical society' and that 'social affiliations and friendship networks appear highly protective of health, just as low status is linked to worse health' (Wilkinson, 2000, p. 412).

The argument against Wilkinson is that his psycho-social account neglects the importance of material conditions. Some have gone as far as to argue that social capital theory effectively 'blames the victim' for their own ill-health, while ignoring the effects of macro-level social and economic policies (Pearce and Smith, 2003). Other non-social capital interpretations certainly exist. It is likely that those sections of the population with the worst health have a disproportionate impact on public health in general. For example, if you have a group of poor and destitute individuals living in your midst, they will become a 'sink population' in which infectious diseases such as tuberculosis can gain a hold and spread. The idea that the affluent majority can protect itself from the risk of infection by turning its back on the problem and moving out to the suburbs is not supported by the evidence. Disease soon spreads from sink populations along transport and commuting links: 'Poor neighbourhoods in large central cities, suffering greatly from urban decay triggered and sustained by policy, have a disproportionate influence on the health, safety, and well-being of a huge proportion of the American population, including rich people' (Wallace and Wallace, 1997, p. 1344).

Lynch et al. (2000a) offer a metaphor of the worse health of economy airline passengers, compared with those in first class, after a long-haul flight. They point to how the worse condition of the economy passengers after the flight relates to their cramped conditions and poorer food, not to their envy as they leave the plane and see the size of the first-class seats (J. Lynch et al., 2000a). In the same way, they argue that income inequality affects health because it is related to poorer investments in health public infrastructure – education, health services, transportation, environmental controls, quality of housing and occupational health regulations – and not because of inequality or social capital *per se*.

Evidence for their case comes from the finding that across the Canadian provinces, unlike across the USA, little relationship is found across regions between inequality and health (N. A. Ross et al., 2000). They argue that this implies that the key relationship is not between inequality, the psycho-social environment and health, but between the quality of services and health – hence the generally high quality of public services in Canada eliminates the effect. Similar evidence can be drawn from the work of social historians who have shown how patterns of public investment were critical in offsetting the negative health impacts of industrial development (Szreter, 1999). Another piece of evidence, mentioned above, is that across Europe, there appears if anything a negative relationship between social trust and mortality, at least for heart disease.

The overall emphasis of Wilkinson's work is on psycho-social pathways, and this arguably gives the impression of a neglect of more traditional public health explanations. Perhaps in his concern to counter the view that economic growth *per se* is always a good thing, Wilkinson underplays the extent to which absolute wealth can generate benefits for health. Lynch et al.'s work also highlights the potentially important role of other cultural factors that may help to explain large aggregate differences (such as the Mediterranean diet), and that may not be present to the same extent in the US context. Nonetheless, their critique feels overstated on a number of points.

The Canadian example is interesting, but the Canadian provinces are also characterized by much less inequality overall (as well as being small in number), greatly limiting the ability of inequality to explain variance for straightforward statistical reasons. In fact, another more recent study did find a significant relationship between income inequality and mortality across health districts in Canada (Veenstra, 2002a). Interestingly, the same study found that social capital, measured by associational and civic participation, was associated with lower mortality – and that wealth *per se* was unrelated to mortality.

Second, while the aeroplane metaphor is clever in its simplicity, it is also a little misleading. To make it comparable to real studies, one would have to control for the individual-level characteristics – the wealth of the passengers, size of seats and so on – and then see if there was any difference between the classes. In the equivalent national (and within-USA) studies that have done this, marked differences remain, implying that in the metaphor, controlling for seat size etc. would still leave a difference between the classes to be explained. Even more critically, a key part of the argument is not just that the passengers in economy class end up with worse health than those in first class, but that the existence of the class differences has an impact over and above the individual material conditions – the size of the seats and so on. Hence the appropriate test would be between planes that had substantial class differences and those with only one class. Viewed through a social capital lens, the social relationships that build up between the 'passengers' over long periods of time – both within and between classes – are a critical part of the story.

In fact, in Lynch et al.'s most recent paper – an analysis of age- and cause-specific mortality across sixteen wealthy nations – they find that economic inequality is related to mortality rates, and particularly to birth and infant survival and non-intentional injuries (Muntaner et al., 2002). However, they find evidence for a materialist explanation in the significant association between the strength of a nation's welfare state and mortality rates. Nations with more socialist and social democratic voters, more socialist and women members of parliament, more years of social democratic government and larger welfare states had lower mortality rates. Social capital was also associated with lower age-adjusted mortality, but this relationship was weaker than that with economic inequality and the strength of the welfare state.

Ironically, the reason why the impact of social capital – and inequality – is less than clear cut at the cross-national level may be because of the action of social capital at the meso- and micro-levels. One of the most effective strategies that people have for dealing with the negative effects of inequality and status hierarchies is to seek social environments – or 'protected enclaves' – which are frequented by people who make them feel good about themselves, not who make them feel inferior, stupid or ignorant (Charlesworth, 2000; Wilkinson, 2000). The strength with which people seek to create such enclaves will logically be driven by the level of inequality at the macro-level – and to the extent that they are successful, they should neutralize the negative effects of inequality at the macro-level.

Summary: interpreting the results at the macro-level

Happiness and life satisfaction data are strongly supportive of macro-level effects of social capital on well-being. The data assembled by Kawachi et al. on physical health variations are also supportive, and appear to show powerful ecological effects across US, Russian and

Hungarian regions. However, there is an absence of work on cross-national mental health differences and social capital, and the cross-national data on physical health and life expectancy are ambiguous and clouded in controversy.

Where macro-level effects have been seen, three key pathways appear to be the most likely mediators.

First, people in high-trust states and regions may generally be 'nicer' to one another. This could mean that life in such states is generally less stressful – both friends and strangers may be more pleasant and civil to one another, making everyday life easier and less conflictual. It could also indicate that people are generally more supportive of one another, from friends and neighbours helping out in times of need through to strangers giving directions and not taking advantage. Partly this might reflect the unmeasured action of social capital at the meso- and micro-level (see above), but also might reflect a true macro-level effect – a culture of civility and respect between strangers.

Second, the effect might relate to economic inequality. Inequality might be associated with poorer health because of the disproportionately poor health of the very poor, and the spreading of this ill-health to the rest of the population. Inequality has frequently been found to be strongly associated with social capital measures at the aggregate level, and trying to unravel this relationship with respect to health is difficult. For example, Putnam noted a very strong relationship between inequality and a composite index of civic engagement in his study of Italy (r = .81; Putnam, 1993; see also chapter 8). All the rival research groups in this area have found that statistically controlling for inequality greatly attenuates the strength of the association between social capital and health, or vice versa, though they differ in their interpretation of this (Kawachi et al., 1997; Veenstra, 2002a,b; Muntaner et al., 2002). The story is complicated further by the potentially offsetting tendency of group members to bond together in the face of inequality.

A third possibility is that high social trust states have better health because they have better public services. Government investments in hospitals, welfare provision and public utilities are all thought to have a substantial impact on population health, a view supported by Lynch et al. (Muntaner et al., 2002). But once again, the case has been made that there is a strong reciprocal relationship between state-level social capital and government performance and its ability to develop and implement policy, and between economic inequality and the strength of the welfare state (see chapter 6). It is certainly the case that across US metropolitan areas, areas with high social capital report better access to health care (Hendryx et al., 2002). Across policy areas, the argument has been made that higher social capital leads to higher support and more effective lobbying for public services. In the context of health:

> Social capital could affect this capacity by, for example, affecting support for redistributive policies or for universal health-care insurance, both of which could represent core government objectives. A government operating in a jurisdiction with a low level of social capital may lack electoral support for such interventions and so could not proceed with them (at least not without significant political risk). (Lavis and Stoddart, 1999, p. 14)

As this quotation indicates, government action may also lie behind differences in levels of inequality. Indeed, social mistrust is highly negatively correlated across US states with the maximum welfare assistance as a percentage of per capita income (r = −.76; Kawachi and Berkman, 2000, p. 186). Hence, in the US context at least, we find ourselves with evidence of a triangle of reciprocal relationships between social capital, inequality and government action (see figure 3.1).

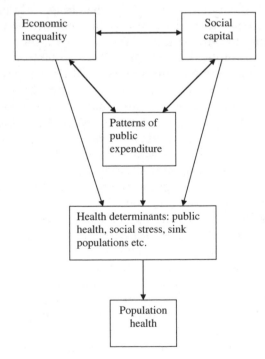

Figure 3.1 *The relationship between social capital, inequality and health at the macro-level*

In sum, the current literature suggests that at least some of the substantial macro- or large-scale aggregate differences in health and well-being may be explained by social capital and the quality of relationships. There is a strong, but not proven case that social capital differences partly mediate the impact of inequality on health, but also a strong case that inequality has other pathways to its impact, such as a direct pathway explained by the impact on public health of unhealthy 'sink' populations. State actions almost certainly have significant impacts on public health too, and government-sponsored programmes help to explain macro-level differences, though such action may itself partly rest on the social capital that characterizes the nation or region (Woolcock, 1998; Szreter, 1999; Lavis and Stoddart, 1999; see also chapter 6).

The basic triad of relationships shown in figure 3.1 stands up to scrutiny, but the weights that we should put on the different links remain to be determined conclusively and may vary. There is a particular need for studies that compare cross-national differences in both mental and physical health using standardized measures and that employ careful controls for individual-level health behaviours, such as diet. It is probably wrong to think that there is an absolute answer to the weights that can be put on each of the causal pathways, as these are themselves probably context-dependent. In Canada, for example, the role played by inequality appears much less than in the USA, partly reflecting differences in health-care systems. Similarly, it is probably the case that social capital differences play a larger role in the USA than in Europe, where differences in government actions probably explain more variance.

Summary

This chapter has explored the relationships between social capital and both mental and physical health. At the individual, or micro-, level the evidence suggests a very strong relationship indeed. In roughly descending order of importance, people who are married, have close friends, go to church or are members of clubs have significantly better health than those who do not. To a limited extent, there seems to be substitutability across different types of relationship – as long as you have someone who loves and supports you, you should experience the protective effects.

In general, a similar pattern is seen for mental and physical health. Confidence in these results is strengthened by their replication in a large number of longitudinal studies, within which social isolation at one time is strongly predictive of ill-health and age-adjusted mortality at a later date. Individuals with supportive personal relationships are generally less likely to suffer from depression; show less cognitive decline in older age; and are several times less likely to die prematurely than the socially isolated.

There are caveats to these very positive results. For physical health, the effects have been less consistently seen for women than for men. For many major illnesses, such as heart disease and stroke, the protective effects of personal relationships have been more clearly shown for survival rates after the disease has first struck than in preventing the first onset of the disease. And it has also been shown that the health effects of close personal relationships are not invariably positive. Personal relationships can be channels for infectious disease and unhealthy behaviour, and for certain disorders, such as schizophrenia, can sometimes worsen the prognosis if they bring heavy obligations or are critical in character.

Considerable work has now been done to explore the bio-psycho-social pathways that explain how personal relationships generally act to protect health. These include instrumental buffering effects (e.g. financial help in times of hardship); cognitive effects (e.g. changing perceptions and responses to stress); and physiological effects (e.g. confiding in friends improves the functioning of the immune system). These robust individual-level findings lie at the root of Putnam's strong statements about the relationship between social capital and health.

At the community, or meso, level there is also reasonable evidence of positive effects of social capital on health. The fascinating case study of the small town of Roseto in the USA appears to show how a close and egalitarian community can serve to protect its members from heart disease, even if it fails to encourage a particularly healthy diet. Similarly, the low rates of depression within highly cohesive communities, such as the Amish, suggest a similar positive effect on mental health. Ethnic and group density effects on both mental and physical health supply further key supporting evidence. Groups that cluster together seem able to benefit their community members' health, through reducing exposure to discrimination and increasing mutual support. However, these ecological results are only modest in size, at least compared with the impact of individual-level social capital on health.

At the macro-level, there is strong evidence of positive ecological effects of social capital on happiness, life satisfaction and reducing suicide rates. The evidence is more complex for physical health. There is clear evidence of social capital impacting on physical health across within-nation regions, notably the USA, over and above the impacts of income levels or individual-level health-related behaviours. Studies of cross-national differences also show substantial variations in physical health that cannot be adequately accounted for by differences in income levels. However, there has been considerable controversy over what explains these national differences. The combined evidence indicates that a triangle of reciprocal relationships between social capital, inequality and public expenditure patterns account for macro-level differences in population health – together with some other traditional explanations such as diet and lifestyle. There is little or no evidence on the relationship between mental health and social capital at the national level.

The existing evidence has already led some experts to propose that health policy should focus on social capital as an important and largely neglected lever to improve public health (Abbott, 2002; Gilbert and Walker, 2002; D. M. Petersen, 2002; Pilkington, 2002; Watt, 2002). But there has also been a significant backlash (Pearce and Smith, 2003). At this point, what is needed is proper, well-constructed clinical trials of social capital interventions, and especially at the meso-level.

In the rush to apply social capital theory to health, it is important to recognize that the causal pathways that account for the impact of social capital on health are not the same at all levels of analysis. As one review speculated:

> the processes determining the causes and consequences of social capital may be quite different at each of these levels of aggregation. For example, at the level of the local community, social capital depends much more on the day-to-day interactions between neighbours than on distal social policies. In contrast, the level of social capital at the state or country level is more likely to reflect the influence of culture, social or economic policies and other macro social forces. (Lochner, Kawachi and Kennedy, 1999, p. 11)

As we have seen, the quality of individual relationships has a big impact at the micro-level, while at the macro-level, government policies loom large. But there is overlap too. It is highly plausible that some government actions can have consequences that reach right down to affect the quality of everyday relationships; while at the same time, culturally based habits of interaction and trust may have profound impacts on government functioning and policies (see chapters 6 and 8).

Two general causal themes emerge across the levels of analysis. It is found repeatedly that the *quality* of relationships matter. Just knowing someone is not enough – the relationship needs to be supportive and positive to have beneficial impacts on health. Second, the most powerful health impacts appear to arise from the most intimate relationships – micro-level bonding social capital. While this latter point may seem obvious, it is worth noting that this is not true for all outcome variables. Economic advancement, for example, appears to rest rather more on diffuse bridging social capital (see chapter 2).

This last contrast helps to explain the striking finding that upward social mobility at the individual level is often associated with *poorer* health – even though generally higher socioeconomic occupations are associated with better health. In short, when we decide to take a fantastic new job in some distant city, and leave our humble origins behind, it may be good for our bank balance but bad for the intimate relationships that maintain our health and well-being. This potential tension is an important one to consider, and shall be returned to in later chapters.

Further reading

For an excellent recent set of reviews covering the empirical literature on social capital and (mainly physical) *health* by the leading researchers, see the edited volume by Berkman and Kawachi (2000). These authors have also produced a short but balanced review on mental health (Kawachi and Berkman, 2001). A short review on mental health and social capital can also be found in McKenzie, Whitley and Weich (2002). On both life satisfaction and suicide, look up John Helliwell's excellent articles (e.g. 2002a). For a more populist approach, try Ornish (1998).

For a thoughtful and challenging view on the relationship between social capital, *inequality* and health, look at Richard Wilkinson's book (1996). If you do look at this, you might do well to balance it with a look at some of those who take a different view, such as J. Lynch et al. (2000b) or Muntaner et al. (2002).

4

Crime

A mother of six children, who recently moved with husband and children from suburban Detroit to Jerusalem, described as one reason for doing so the greater freedom her young children had in Jerusalem. She felt safe letting her eight year old take the six year old across town to school on the city bus and felt her children to be safe in playing without supervision in a city park, neither of which she felt able to do where she lived before.

Coleman, 1988, p. 99

As criminologists frequently remind us, crime is a complex and varied phenomenon. Violent crimes such as murder don't seem to have a great deal in common with everyday offences such as property theft. Despite this, there are also some remarkably clear patterns that demand a more general explanation, such as the cross-culturally observed peak in offending in the late teenage years, or the widespread increase in recorded crime in western industrialized nations in the post-war era.

It is clear that there are many causes of crime – and just about as many theories. Popular theories abound, many of which are poorly supported by the evidence. For example, the popular belief that poverty causes crime, or is even strongly associated with it, is not generally supported by the evidence. Periods of high economic deprivation, such as the Great Depression, were not associated with unusually high crime (D. J. Smith, 1995). This evidence has led us to believe that if poverty has an effect on crime, it is conditional on other variables (Faulkner, Hough and Halpern, 1996).

The social capital concept is a relative newcomer to the crowded world of criminological theory, though the ideas it embodies will be familiar to most criminologists. By definition, social capital focuses attention on the potential influence of social relationships, co-operative norms and informal sanctions on offending behaviour. It ties together a thread of causal explanations across existing theories, and potentially bridges a long-standing division in criminology between micro- (psychological) and macro- (sociological) approaches. In addition, social capital theory has helped stimulate new and promising research, while at the same time it has provided a new focus of attention for policymakers concerned with reducing levels of crime. However, as should be expected, the relationship between social capital and crime proves complicated. In particular, the various components of social capital sometimes seem to have contradictory effects on crime.

As with the review of economic and health effects, this chapter starts with an examination of the relationship between social capital and crime at the individual or micro-level, before examining the evidence for meso- and macro-level effects. I shall then attempt to summarize the causal relationship between social capital and crime more generally.

The micro-level: the social capital of offenders and victims

Committing crime is a surprisingly popular activity among young men the world over. Typically, around a third of young men have acquired at least one conviction for a serious or indictable offence by the time they reach their thirties (D. J. Smith 1995; Home Office, 2003). If we look behind official statistics to surveys of the 'normal' population, we might safely conclude that most men briefly 'experiment' with crime when young. Most young men stop offending after one or two convictions. However, a few go on to commit a lot of crime. About 5 per cent of men seem to be responsible for about two-thirds of attributed crime, with the most serious of persistent offenders having started offending at an early age (Faulkner, Hough and Halpern, 1996; Hagell and Newburn, 1994). Offenders are normally generalists, committing a variety of crimes, not just one type (Gottfredson and Hirschi, 1990).

These robust patterns throw up basic questions for any general theory of crime. Why do so many young people offend, compared with the very young and older adults? Why do a minority persist in offending, while the majority give it up? And why men, but not women?

Let us start with the persistent relationship between age and crime. This has been one of the greatest puzzles in the criminological literature, and is a pattern that is seen across the world. Almost all offences peak in the age range from 15 to 18 in self-report data (Farrington, 1986), though this peak is a few years later in arrest data (D. J. Smith, 1995).[1] Or put another way, why is that so many young people experiment in crime, but then desist so dramatically?

The principal explanation seems to lie in the normal development of social capital and relationships over the life span, and in the informal 'social control' associated with these relationships. In normal development, children are strongly bonded to their family and parents, but these child–parent ties tend to weaken during the teenage years (Leffert and Petersen, 1995).

> there is generally a period of instability before the young person settles into a job and forms a new family . . . During the transitional period, the young person is moving away from the restraining influence of his or her parents, and has not yet invested in reciprocal adult relationships that may in future be a restraining influence. On this account, adolescents are unruly because they slip between the mechanisms of informal social control that are effective for children and for adults. . . . This field of research is currently very active, but it now seems that the formation of social bonds may turn out to be the central explanation for desistance from crime after adolescence. (D. J. Smith, 1995; pp. 428–30)

This theory is not a new one (see, for example, Trasler, 1980), but it has been given a significant boost since 1993 by the work of Sampson and Laub. They reanalysed the life-history data of a sample of 500 convicted teenage offenders and 500 non-delinquents from the 1940s and 1950s. They found that job stability, commitment to conventional education and occupational roles, and marital attachment were causally predictive of desisting from criminal offending. They concluded that 'social ties . . . create interdependent systems of obligation and restraint that impose significant costs for translating criminal propensities into action' (p. 141). These social ties offer major opportunities for achievement and satisfaction too – a carrot, not just a stick – encouraging the young person to trade in the pleasures of teenage crime for those of the adult world and mainstream society (Trasler, 1980).

The beauty of Sampson and Laub's work is that it helps to explain not only why most young men briefly experiment with crime, but also why a minority fail to give it up – another of criminology's key puzzles. It is informal social control and the internalizing of certain norms that keeps most of us from offending, and not the threat of the law or formal punishments. Hence, those who do not establish new, strong social ties as young adults are at high risk of persistent offending.

There is a rival hypothesis that we need to consider. What if social disconnection is itself simply a symptom of an antisocial or 'deviant' personality? Many personality and psychological variables have been offered as explanations of why some people are more likely to offend than others, such as low intelligence, low self-control, high impulsivity and aggression. Perhaps it is these traits that lead some individuals to avoid conventional adult relationships, and other people to avoid them, while at the same time independently increasing the likelihood of offending?

Evidence for this personality-based explanation can be seen in early risk factors such as mental disturbance, abuse of drugs and early experience of violence or abuse, and even in genetic studies. Many of the simple associations with persistent offending are causally ambiguous, such as having an unstable job record, having delinquent friends, and early failure at or exclusion from school. In each case, it is not immediately clear whether the association is caused by an underlying personality trait, or whether it is the social context that causes the offending. For example, is getting thrown out of school merely a symptom of a 'criminal personality', or is it a contributory cause of later offending – lacking qualifications, the young person turns to crime as their best option to earn a living?

The answer is that both types of causes are operating. Individual characteristics to some extent affect the environments and social networks that people become engaged in. For example, hyperactivity in childhood is associated with significantly higher levels of subsequent youthful aggression and misconduct (Brannigan et al., 2002). However, it has also clearly been shown that the young person's environment and networks then have substantial additional effects on the future offending behaviour (Sampson and Laub, 1993). Similarly, one can also argue that the individual characteristics that partly drive later choices and transitions are themselves affected by the social environment of the young person. For example, having a remote or distant father during childhood, experiencing harsh or erratic discipline or hostile parenting, or having parents with an unstable job record are all additional predictors of later offending (Farrington, 1992; Brannigan et al., 2002). Hence we see a loose mutual reinforcement between the individual's social context and their evolving character and lifestyle. But this is not a fully deterministic relationship. A chance encounter or positive relationship can change the person's life course dramatically.

A nice illustration of the potentially positive effects of a supportive social relationship is provided by Zoccolillo et al. (1992). In a longitudinal study of troubled and disadvantaged young people, they noted the familiar finding that conduct disorders in childhood were strongly predictive of antisocial personality and other problems in adulthood. But, supporting Sampson and Laub, they found that the minority of troubled children who bucked this trend almost always had a supportive non-deviant spouse or partner. Quinton et al. (1993) found similar positive effects of supportive cohabiting relationships, but also noted how young people with conduct disorders were less likely to pair off with such supportive partners, hence setting up a vicious circle of weak social bonds and further deviance.

Gender differences may be partly explained in the same terms too, though also noting the potentially powerful influence of cultural and biological factors. Girls and young women are strongly encouraged to engage in caring relationships, just as acts of aggression are more readily tolerated in young boys and men. While some gender differences in behaviour may have a partial biological basis, others do not but are culturally tolerated in one sex but not the other. For example, crying occurs with approximately the same frequency in young boys and girls, but is seen by western parents as normal in girls but evidence of a problem in boys (Simpson and Stevenson-Hinde, 1985). Whether driven by cultural or biological factors, girls are more likely to engage in caring relationships within the family and subsequently enter marriage at a younger age. In essence, girls are more closely bound into exactly the relationships that are implicated in reducing crime among young men.

The social control or social capital hypothesis is supported by empirical evidence from many countries and contexts. In the USA, analysis of the 1958 Philadelphia Birth Cohort Study, for example, shows how a person's social capital affects both preferences and earnings in the legitimate sector, and how strengthening bonds to society increase the costs of deviant behaviour to the individual and thereby make criminal acts less likely (J. Williams, 1997). Social capital, such as peer influences during youth, are key predictors of criminality over and above the young person's human capital, such as number of years of schooling (J. Williams and Sickles, 2002). In Sweden, a study of 800 15-year-old students showed how parental involvement, at both individual and aggregated school level, generated social capital that was influential in the prevention of a wide range of deviant behaviour among youths (P. Lindstrom, 1993). In Germany, a study of 500 young people showed the critical role played by parents and schools in suppressing delinquency and right-wing extremism, especially in the context of the widespread anomie in the former East Germany (Hagan, Merkens and Boehnke, 1995). In China, a study of 269 recidivists with at least one rearrest found that after controlling for the usual risk variables, reoffending was greatly reduced if the offender was married or had a job arranged after release (Liu, 1999). And in Canada, data from two studies of street youths showed how parental rejection, family disruption and negative school experiences account for decisions to take to the streets, and also how employment can redirect their lives from homelessness and crime-based lifestyles (Hagan and McCarthy, 1997). In short, the presence or absence of close, mainstream personal relationships is strongly and causally implicated in whether a given young person becomes involved in, and persists with, criminal offending.

Gangs and 'negative' social capital

The analysis presented so far tells a broadly positive story about the role played by social networks in preventing offending. Essentially, it has suggested that the socially disconnected are very much more likely to offend criminally. But this story is not complete and proves a little more complicated from a social capital point of view.

The typical persistent young offender is not just disconnected from mainstream social networks – they may also be connected to a 'rival' or deviant social network within which offending may be considered acceptable, even expected, behaviour. This is illustrated, for example, in the Hagan and McCarthy study of street youths in Toronto and Vancouver. Street youths are not only disconnected from the mainstream social fabric, but also become socially embedded in relationships that transmit skills and knowledge about street crime – what the authors call 'criminal capital' (Hagan and McCarthy, 1997). Similarly, a study on juvenile delinquency in Columbia identified 'capital social perverso' (perverted social capital) as playing a major role in the reproduction of juvenile delinquency (Rubio, 1996), and the peer influences documented in the cohort studies often encourage, rather than discourage, criminality (J. Williams and Sickles, 2002).

Reading like something out of a Dickens novel, one US government report highlighted the existence of 'schools for scoundrels' organized by con-artists to tutor other cons in the fine art of making a 'sting'. Police reported that it was not uncommon for cons to exchange 'hit lists' – the names of those they had successfully defrauded – upon leaving one region for another (US Senate Special Committee on Aging, 1993).

This is a clear example of one of the potential downsides of social capital – any particular form of social capital is not necessarily a 'good' for all concerned. The most notorious example in this area is, of course, organized crime or the Mafia (Servadio, 1976). Criminal social capital – having friends who are also involved in crime – is certainly a form of social capital in that it can make conducting crime easier. Members of a gang can take on bigger jobs, can have one person act as a lookout while others commit the crime, and can provide a web of contacts to fence stolen goods and obtain illegal items. At higher levels of society, this is manifested as corruption and the abuse of power (see, for example, Blomberg, Maier and Yeisley, 1998). This criminal capital obviously doesn't look like much of a good to the rest of society, and it illustrates the point that – like other forms of capital – social capital can be used to facilitate 'bad' as well as 'good' acts.

One researcher has coined the term 'negative social capital' to describe non-conventional, antisocial relationships such as gangs (Liu, 1999). Liu, in a study of Chinese recidivists with at least one rearrest, found that while conventional forms of social connection reduced reoffending, gang membership – or 'negative' social capital – significantly increased it (Liu, 1999). The use of the term 'negative social capital' is attractive in this example, but is problematic in a wider context as it rests on a *post hoc* judgement from a particular point of view as to what is negative (see chapter 1). For example, whether you view an underground resistance movement as positive or negative clearly depends on whose side you are on.

Semantics aside, it is clear that there are often forms of social capital with objectives that appear to be problematic for the wider society. The policy goal then becomes to break up or redirect these forms of criminal social capital and to encourage at-risk individuals to connect to more mainstream networks. Paradoxically, one of society's main tools for dealing with crime may have exactly the reverse effects of this policy goal. Putting offenders in prison tends to weaken family and mainstream community bonds, and often little effort is made to rebuild these bonds or the communities affected (D. R. Rose and Clear, 1998; Hagan and Coleman, 2001). At the same time, prison may reinforce the individual's connections to alternative or criminal forms of social capital.

Victims

This chapter has concentrated so far on the social capital of individual offenders. Interestingly, a similar review can be conducted from the

viewpoint of victims. Such a review leads to a curiously parallel conclusion – the more socially disconnected you are from mainstream
society, the more likely you are to become a victim of crime.

Drawing on data from the 1979–85 longitudinal mortality study,
Kposowa, Singh and Breault (1994) examined the effects of marital
status and social isolation on homicide in a sample of 200,000 US adult
males. They found that being unmarried and socially isolated were
both associated with significantly higher rates of homicide victimization. Controlling for age and other socioeconomic covariates, single
persons were 1.9 times more likely to be murdered than married
persons. Divorced, separated and widowed individuals were 1.7 times
more likely to be murdered than married people. Socially isolated individuals were 1.6 times more likely to be murdered than the socially
connected.

There is a positive relationship between social isolation and crime
more generally, notably among the elderly (B. Holmes, 1985; US Senate
Special Committee on Aging, 1993; Yin, 1982) and also between social
isolation and fear (Gomme, 1986). For example, the British Crime
survey shows that people who are separated or single are around four
times more likely to be the victim of a violent crime than those who are
married (8.9 and 8.7 per cent chance compared with 2.1 per cent; Povey
and Allen, 2003). These figures partly reflect age, but even the divorced,
who tend to be significantly older and therefore at less risk of violent
crime, are still more than twice as likely to be the victim of such crime
than the married (4.8 compared with 2.1 per cent). The effect of marital
status dwarfs that of factors such as household income or employment
status on victimization.

One well-documented way in which the link between isolation and
victimization can arise is when some, generally elderly, residents get
left behind following waves of migration out of inner cities, such as
occurred in the USA from the 1960s onward. Those original residents
who chose to remain, or who were unable to move, find that many of
the friends and neighbours they knew have left, leaving them socially
isolated. They may then become 'prime targets' for the young new
residents around them (Nova Institute, 1977).

To some extent, social isolation and fear also arise as a reaction to
crime (Lewis, 1981). In particular, victims often feel forced into social
isolation because they lose their sense of trust in others (Bard and
Sangrey, 1979). Unfortunately, this may set up a vicious cycle, further
reinforcing fear and potentially vulnerability too.

The criminological literature tends to focus on inner-city high-crime
areas. However, social and geographical isolation can also be a risk
factor inside affluent suburbs, at least for burglary (see also next section

on neighbourhoods and crime). The risk of an individual house or apartment being burgled varies greatly within any given area. Major risk factors include the physical isolation of the property – location in the country; fewer than five other houses in sight; and being set at a distance from the road – and the property's surveillability – not being overlooked at the front by other houses and the majority of the sides of the property not being visible from public areas (Forrester, Chatterton and Pease, 1988). The combination of such factors can influence the probability of burglary by ten-fold or more.

One of the most consistent and disturbing findings of the criminological literature is that those who were abused as children or young adults are very much more likely to experience further violence and abuse as adults. This is particularly well documented in the case of sexual abuse and violence against women (see, for example, the recent survey of 6,800 women in Australia; Coumarelos and Allen, 1996). One of the critical mediators of this effect appears to be that childhood abuse profoundly affects the individual's self-concept and the relationships that they subsequently form (Irwin, 1999). Early developmental disadvantages begun in chaotic and abusive families are perpetuated by chains of negative interactions, relationships and behaviours. Prosocial options diminish and, in more extreme cases, ties to the conventional world are broken (Whitbeck and Hoyt, 1999).

This pattern looks remarkably similar to that described for delinquency (see above). Early sexual abuse tends to lead to continuation of negative developmental trajectories. A lack of trust and paucity of connection to a trustworthy adult world create a negative spiral. A positive, trusting relationship can break this cycle, but is made less likely by the individual's personal history and circumstances. For those young adults who reach the streets, potential offenders are then close at hand, and the cycle of abuse, distrust and disconnection worsens still further (Tyler, Hoyt and Whitbeck, 2000).

Interestingly, for those who do end up on the street, one of the best ways they can protect themselves from being the victims of further violence is by forming what homeless young people call 'street families'. These fictive kin relationships have been shown to offer considerable protection to vulnerable young people who lack other more conventional forms of social capital (McCarthy, Hagan and Martin, 2002).

The meso-level: community and crime

The last point illustrates how crime often becomes contextually bound. Although to some extent we can understand crime from the individual perspective – in the personal histories of offenders and even victims – it becomes clear that crime is also a characteristic of the situation. Crime occurs in situations that bring together potential offenders with potential victims, and typically in social and environmental contexts that lack the normal inhibitors of crime (Miethe and Meier, 1994). This brings us to the issue of how social capital at the meso- or community level can affect crime.

There are very substantial variations between neighbourhoods in crime rates (Levy and Herzog, 1974; Sampson, Morenoff and Earls, 1999). Prominent in this variation is a substantial urban–rural differential. For example, robbery and personal attack tend to be more common in cities, especially those with populations greater than 250,000, than in rural areas or in cities with fewer than 250,000 inhabitants; and within cities, attacks tend to be highly concentrated in inner-city areas (Walmsley, 1988; Halpern, 1995a; Povey and Allen, 2003). However, the same urban–rural differential is not found in all parts of the world, and is not thought to have been constant over all historical periods – indeed it is thought that in much of the previous 500 years, crime was generally much higher outside of cities.

Substantial covariation is found at the neighbourhood level between crime rates and other measures of 'social pathology', such as delinquency, vagrancy and the presence of the mentally ill (Faris and Dunham, 1939; Wedmore and Freeman, 1984; Levine, Miyake and Lee, 1989). At least some of this covariation needs to be understood as the result of selection effects and social drift. Once a neighbourhood gets a bad reputation, the more affluent and economically able residents tend to leave, and this in turn can lead to further deterioration of the neighbourhood and a downward spiral sometimes known as 'tipping'.

Importantly, crime is certainly not limited to poor neighbourhoods. A detailed analysis of the British Crime Survey by neighbourhood types showed that crime was highest in two seemingly very different kind of areas – 'striving' and 'rising' neighbourhoods (Aitchison and Hodgkinson, 2003). 'Striving' areas fit with the popular image of a high-crime area, characterized by public housing estates (or projects) with elderly, lone-parent and unemployed residents, and typically multi-ethnic and low-income too. In contrast, 'rising' areas are characterized by a preponderance of well-off professional singles and couples. But what these areas tend to have in common is low social capital, and often high mobility. The burglary rate in both such area types is roughly double that of other areas (5 per cent per annum compared with 2–3 per cent in other areas). Similarly, vehicle theft in such areas is roughly two-thirds higher (15–16 per cent compared with 9–10 per cent).

A key question is whether this neighbourhood variation in crime can be adequately explained in terms of individual-level variables, such as the concentration of offenders in an area. As we have seen above, this would not preclude a social capital explanation in as much as individual-level outcomes themselves rest heavily on the social networks of the young person. But social capital theorists believe that something more is happening at the community level that can be attributed to the sum of the parts – an ecological-level effect.

One way in which neighbourhoods function as more than the sum of their parts is through the positive externalities of micro- or family-level social capital. As Putnam and other scholars have pointed out:

> the presence of lots of stable families in a neighbourhood is associated with lower levels of youthful lawbreaking, not because the adults serve as role models or supervisors, but because the adults rear well-adjusted and well-behaved kids. Thus 'good families' have a ripple effect by increasing the pool of 'good peers' that other families' kids can befriend. If we think of youthful troublemaking as a communicable disease – a sort of behavioural chicken pox that spreads through high schools and friendship groups – then stable families provide the vaccines that reduce the number of contagious kids capable of infecting others. (Putnam, 2000, p. 314)

This view is supported by evidence of the positive effects of stable families on reduced school drop-outs and delinquency (Simcha-Fagan and Schwartz, 1986; Darling and Steinberg, quoted in Putnam, 2000), and of the generally negative effects of juvenile gangs in the absence of alternative strong forms of social capital (K. Scott, 1993; Covey, Menard and Franzese, 1997). One can even find support for Putnam's contagion metaphor in that the spread of delinquency and violent crime has been successfully modelled in exactly the same way as the spread of contagious diseases such as AIDs (Wallace and Wallace, 1997).

There are other fairly straightforward ways in which neighbourhood variations can be seen to emerge. Simply put, crime can be expected to be higher where there are large numbers of potential offenders in close proximity to large numbers of victims. A useful statistic to illustrate this is that, at least in Britain, around three-quarters of burglaries are committed by people who have walked to their target (Forrester, Chatterton and Pease, 1988). Similarly, violence at night is heavily associated with drinking, and it is found that most attacks occur on the principal routes that lead from drinking establishments to late-night transport facilities (Poyner, 1983). Hence, it is unsurprising to learn that typical high-risk neighbourhoods also tend to be characterized by the presence of more major thoroughfares, a larger percentage of commercial and mixed land use, more permeable boundaries, the close proximity of poorer areas, and higher provision of public parking and vacant land (Reppetto, 1974; Bevis and Nutter, 1977; Greenberg and Rohe, 1984; Evans and Fletcher, 1998). In general, high-risk areas show a high degree of accessibility and a low degree of homogeneity of land use – they are neighbourhoods that are easy for potential offenders to get to, move around in, and be anonymous in.

But such high-crime neighbourhoods also tend to have another characteristic, as hinted above – low social cohesion. Neighbours are less likely to know or trust each other, residential turnover is higher, and generally people feel less committed to the area. The question is, how do these pieces fit together? Is social cohesion lower in such neighbourhoods as a result of crime, or does low social cohesion actually help cause the crime? More subtly, could it be that the accessibility, and perhaps social mix, of certain neighbourhoods cause both higher crime and lower social cohesion independently?

The concept of 'collective efficacy'

We should recognize that it is genuinely difficult to pick apart this kind of entangled causality. But there are a number of pieces of evidence indicating that social cohesion and social capital do play a causal role in neighbourhood crime levels.

Once again, the criminologist Robert Sampson has been ahead of the pack. In a thorough and highly competent series of papers, Sampson et al. have examined the relationship between social cohesion, informal social control and violent crime across 343 neighbourhoods of Chicago (Sampson, Raudenbush and Earls, 1997; Morenoff, Sampson and Raudenbush, 2001). The researchers measured 'informal social control' by asking residents the likelihood that their neighbours could be counted on to intervene if, say, children were skipping school and hanging about on street corners, or a fight broke out outside their house, or their local fire station was threatened with budget cuts. They also measured 'social cohesion and trust' by the level of agreement with statements such as 'this is a close knit neighbourhood' and 'people in this neighbourhood generally don't get along' (the latter reverse coded). They found that these two measures were strongly correlated across neighbourhoods ($r = .8$), and therefore combined them together into a single index of what they called 'collective efficacy'.

Utilizing the statistical technique of multi-level modelling, Sampson et al. found that collective efficacy had a strong negative association with neighbourhood violent crime. This negative association persisted even after individual-level characteristics were controlled for, such as marital status, homeownership, ethnicity, mobility, years in neighbourhood, age and socioeconomic status. However, one can still argue that the casual direction might run from crime to collective efficacy, rather than the other way around. It might be that residents living in areas that had experienced high crime might have become afraid to engage in acts of social control and have become generally less trusting of their neighbours. To test this, Sampson et al. controlled for levels of prior violence as measured by a three-year average of the homicide rate five years earlier. Sure enough, prior levels of violence *did* predict significantly lower levels of community efficacy five years later (r = −.55). Nonetheless, even when prior violence was controlled for, collective efficacy was still a significant negative predictor of crime five years on.

The latter result is of particular interest as it represents a relatively tough test of causal direction, strongly implying this is from community efficacy to crime rather than the other way around (though evidence was found of this also). The authors went on to show that the association between concentrated disadvantage and violence was largely mediated by collective efficacy, as was the relationship between residential instability and violence. In other words, a major reason why racially mixed and high turnover neighbourhoods have higher violent crime is because neighbours in such areas find it more difficult to build up trusting relationships with one another, or to build up shared understandings that give them the confidence to enforce a shared 'moral order'.

Sampson et al. argue that collective efficacy acts to reduce crime not because it makes residents more likely to intervene directly in serious crime, but because it makes them more likely to intervene in its precursors, such as discouraging the gathering of teenage gangs, drug-taking or other forms of incivility. They suggested that collective efficacy might also act to reduce crime by making the community more effective at eliciting services, support and interventions from the statutory services. As well as organizing community fetes, the cohesive and well-organized community is good at campaigning for more police on its streets.

Sampson et al. found that collective efficacy was positively related to friendship and kinship ties (r = .49), organizational participation (r = .45) and neighbourhood services (r = .21). But controlling for these network social capital measures, along with all other significant factors, still left collective efficacy as by far the largest predictor of violent crime. Sampson et al. concluded: . . . 'these results suggested that dense personal ties, organisation, and local services by themselves are not sufficient: reductions in violence appear to be more directly attributable to informal social control and cohesion among residents' (Sampson et al., 1997, p. 923)

There is some evidence of a similar story for the fear of crime. In neighbourhoods that residents describe as where 'people help each other' as opposed to where 'people go their own way', fear of crime is consistently lower (Fletcher and Allen, 2003). In the neighbourhoods where people are described as going 'their own way', concerns are higher about burglary, car theft, being attacked, rape, being insulted or pestered in a range from 33 to 83 per cent. Feeling unsafe to walk alone is roughly two-thirds higher in such areas, and feeling unsafe while at home is roughly doubled. Another study found that informal ties with neighbours reduced the fear and mistrust usually produced by neighbourhood disorder, though formal participation in neighbourhood organizations had little positive buffering effects (C. E. Ross and Jang, 2000; see also review of Neighbourhood Watch schemes below). Similarly, a study of crime in 487 buildings housing some of New York's poorest residents found that tenant pro-social norms, as well as participation in tenant associations and a building's formal organization, predicted lower crime in those buildings following the survey (Saegert, Winkel and Swartz, 2002). These observations, which will be returned to later, hint that it is the social *norms* aspects of social capital rather than the *network* aspects that explain much of the neighbourhood variation in crime and fear (see chapter 1 for a discussion of these distinctions).

Neighbourhood Watch:
a test of the community–crime hypothesis?

If a stronger sense of community and informal control can reduce crime, then efforts to build up such informal control should reduce crime. In this sense, the attempts to create 'Neighbourhood Watch' schemes in many parts of the world since the mid-1980s should provide us with a useful test of the role that community plays in preventing crime.

There are several problems with this 'test' that need to be considered. First, there are major methodological problems involved in assessing the effectiveness of Neighbourhood Watch schemes. The areas within which such schemes most commonly thrive are affluent low-crime neighbourhoods (Laycock and Tilley, 1995). For example, a study of 3,700 Neighbourhood Watch schemes in England and Wales noted that such schemes were much less likely to be initiated by residents in high-crime areas and were much more likely to fail in such areas (Husain, 1988). This generates a misleadingly positive overall correlation between such schemes and lower crime rates, and rendering conventional cross-sectional methods unhelpful.

Neighbourhood Watch schemes are also thought to increase the reporting of crime, and this throws up further methodological problems for longitudinal approaches, especially if reliant on official statistics. Substantial 'displacement effects' can also occur, meaning that it's important to track a wide range of crime measures as well as the crime rates in adjacent areas. For example, in one large-scale evaluation of a domestic burglary reduction programme, although domestic burglary rates fell by 35 per cent in the areas covered, car thefts *increased* by 82 per cent and non-domestic burglary increased by 124 per cent (J. Webb, 1996).

Second, Neighbourhood Watch schemes are typically implemented in conjunction with other types of intervention, such as target hardening (fitting additional window and door locks). For example, one of the early and most impressive interventions – the Kirkholt project – demonstrated a dramatic reduction in crime in a high-crime neighbourhood in Britain (Forrester, Chatterton and Pease, 1988). However, in the Kirkholt project, the introduction of the Neighbourhood Watch scheme happened alongside several other interventions, including target hardening and better coordination between the police and other agencies.

Third, one can argue that a Neighbourhood Watch scheme is a pretty thin sort of community. Although such schemes often have very dynamic and committed leaders, the 'members' often show a relatively limited level of commitment (Barton, 2000; V. J. Webb and Katz, 1997; Laycock and Tilley, 1995; McConville and Shepherd, 1992). Putting up a sign and occasionally looking out of your window to see if your neighbour's car is still there isn't quite the same as what most people think of as 'community'.

Nonetheless, with literally thousands of such interventions having occurred across the world, a quick examination of the results seem appropriate, with a particular focus on before-and-after evaluations.

In the USA, the data are distinctly mixed. One typical study – of 53 neighbourhoods in Cincinnati – concluded that Neighbourhood Watch schemes had no impact on crime (B. W. Smith, Novak and Hurley, 1997). Others have been somewhat more positive, such as an evaluation of experiments with community policing in Chicago which did seem to have led to some falls in crime (Skogan and Hartnett, 1997).

In the UK, a longitudinal study of 1,500 residents in two areas of Leicester found reductions in burglaries in the 12 months following the schemes' implementation, though the study noted a renewed rise after this. The authors felt that the initial reduction could not be attributed to environmental improvements since few were initiated during the project period, and that it therefore could be attributed to the Neighbourhood Watch schemes (Matthews and Trickey, 1994). Another study found marked reductions in burglary and car theft in three out of six intervention areas, but a lack of success in the remaining three areas (Husain, 1988, 1990). On the other hand, a detailed evaluation of two Neighbourhood Watch schemes in London found that, if anything, crime *increased* slightly in the programme areas in comparison to the control areas, though fear of crime decreased (Bennett, 1988). Another concluded that the overall effects were 'insubstantial', and though the launch of such schemes sometimes brought benefits for some individuals, most projects quickly become dormant (McConville and Shepherd, 1992).

Studies outside of the US and UK show similar mixed, but mildly positive, results. A study of six Neighbourhood Watch projects in the Netherlands found that crime fell considerably in three of the six areas covered, but noted that the schemes had proved very hard to get started in some areas (Lohman and van Dijk, 1988). An evaluation of Neighbourhood Watch schemes in Victoria, Australia, concluded that such programmes brought about a reduction in crime in the short term, but that the absence of reliable measurement cast doubt on their long-term benefits (Mukherjee and Wilson, 1987). And an evaluation of the impact of Neighbourhood Watch schemes in Taipei, Taiwan, concluded that drug and juvenile crimes had been reduced, but that the schemes had no impact on violent crime, minor robbery or total crime. Burglary and the number of 911 calls appeared to be increased, though this might partly have reflected increased reporting (L. J. Lee, Cheurprakobkit and Denq, 1999).

How should we interpret this literature? One clear finding is that pre-existing social capital tends to be a prerequisite for successful Neighbourhood Watch schemes, and many of the failures of such schemes – typically in high-crime areas – relate to the absence of this social capital. Participation tends to be predicted by prior involvement in a community organization and length of residence in an area (Hourihan, 1987; Yanay, 1994). Second, we can conclude that the impact of these schemes is generally modest, unreliable and typically short-lived – though occasional marked successes have occurred. One interpretation of these results is to say that perhaps the importance of neighbourhood social capital in relation to crime has been overrated – the results are surely negative enough to be cause for reflection among law enforcement agencies. A more plausible interpretation, anticipated at the start of this section, is that neighbourhood schemes are simply too 'thin' to constitute a serious test of the Sampson 'collective efficacy' or neighbourhood social capital hypothesis. In some cases these schemes have even come to be viewed as political cover for the withdrawal of community policing (Yarwood and Edwards, 1995).

Interestingly, where successes have been claimed, these often refer to the occurrence of wider changes in the character of the community. These include improvements in social cohesion and in residents' satisfaction with the area (Bennett, 1988), improved community bonds through resident interaction, and better police–community relationships (Mukherjee and Wilson, 1987). In sum, it would seem that Neighbourhood Watch schemes are a poor substitute for 'real', living communities, even in their own terms. If we believe that strong, self-confident communities, where people take an active interest in the behaviour that's occurring outside their front doors, can reduce crime – and there is good evidence to think that they can – then we'll need to look a little harder at what creates such communities and shared understandings (see chapters 8 and 9).

The macro-level:
national and regional differences in crime

Sampson et al.'s analysis suggests that rather than social networks *per se* reducing crime at the neighbourhood level, it is the shared informal norms and social habits of the community, together with a sense of mutual trust, that hold down crime. Having neighbours who intervene in minor incivilities, such as kids skipping school or spraying graffiti, seems to prevent a neighbourhood deteriorating into more serious crime. And neighbours who trust one another can more effectively work together for their collective advantage, be it for better schools or better policing. We can also square this with the idea that having a higher proportion of stable families with well-behaved kids makes it easier for neighbourhoods to achieve this atmosphere of shared understandings and trust. With more well-behaved kids and stable families around, the neighbour's intervention when a couple of kids have skipped school is far more likely to be effective.

Prevalent social norms

Norms appear to have both a direct and an indirect effect on the occurrence of crime. Even within and between similar-sized cities, in some areas residents feel happy to let their children walk to school or leave their cars unlocked, while in others they do not. An innovative illustration of this phenomenon was provided by the psychologist Philip Zimbardo, who experimented with leaving a car with the hood (bonnet) open in different locations on opposite sides of America and observing the result. An abandoned car left in New York was having pieces removed within half an hour, and was little more than a shell after twenty-four hours. An identical car left in Palo Alto remained completely untouched except for an old man walking his dog shutting the hood and mumbling something about the rain affecting the engine. Equally informative was that when the experimenters finally emerged out of their hiding places to collect the Palo Alto car after several days of boredom, someone called the police to report that something suspicious was going on! The contexts did not differ in terms of formal laws, but differed hugely in the informal accepted norms of behaviour.

The observation that it may be shared norms rather than networks that are most important for crime prevention raises the possibility that similar effects could be seen on a much wider scale than the neighbourhood. This is indeed the case.

Research in the USA comparing states has demonstrated an almost incredibly strong relationship between crime levels and social capital. Kawachi et al. found that states with lower levels of trust, as measured by standard survey questions, had significantly higher rates of homicide ($r = .82$), assault ($r = .61$), burglary ($r = .54$) and robbery or mugging ($r = .45$; Berkman and Kawachi, 2000). Once again, this is a cross-sectional result and therefore the causal direction can be contested. Perhaps trust is lower in some states because of the crime rate? Putnam has reported that the relationship between crime and social capital remains strong and highly significant even if one controls for levels of fear, as measured by people agreeing with the statement that they 'worry that my family may become a victim of a crime' (Putnam, 2000, ch. 18, n. 4). If it were the case that crime caused people to be afraid and to withdraw their trust and engagement with the community, then controlling for fear should eliminate the relationship. It does not – the partial correlation is somewhat attenuated, but remains highly significant (partial $r = -.53$ between social capital index and homicide).

A recent study has analysed the age-adjusted homicide rate across US states from 1973 to 1993 (Galea, Karpati and Kennedy, 2002). The

Box 4.1   What explains variations in fear of crime?

A puzzle for many criminologists is the very weak relationship between objective rates of crime or victimization, and levels of fear of crime. For example, across countries people tend to overestimate the probability that they will be burgled over the following year by 10- to 50-fold. Furthermore, national variations in peoples' estimates of being burgled bare virtually no relationship to actual variations in burglary rates.

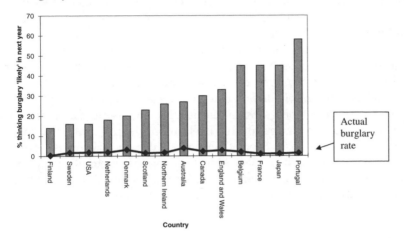

One possible explanation is that, since actual crime – in this case bur-glary – is relatively rare, people estimate its likelihood from the more general character of relations with other people, and from the media.

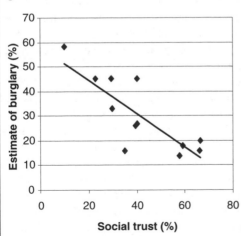

In contrast to the lack of a relationship between fear of and actual burglary, if we plot fear against gen-eralized ratings of trust in strangers, a strong relation-ship is found (r = −.82). The less we think others can be trusted, the more we think that we may be the victim of a crime. This find-ing may help to explain the frustrating experience of a number of Anglo-Saxon countries, notably Britain, where crime has fallen, yet most people think it has *increased*. Such perceptions may be driven more by wider changes in social trust than it is by the objective crime rate – and such social trust has declined in Anglo-Saxon countries over recent years (see chapter 7).

social capital measures were social trust and per capita membership in voluntary associations, using data from the General Household Surveys. Controlling for levels of income and urbanization, states with lower levels of social trust were found to have significantly higher homicide rates, replicating the results of Kawachi et al. But the time series data also enabled the authors to examine how changes in social capital and homicide were interrelated over time. They found a complex bidirectional relationship, concluding that increases in violence could reduce social trust and vice versa, leading to a non-linear and dynamic relationship between the two.

Further questions remain about this relationship. Is crime in the US southern states higher because these states happen to have a disproportionately low number of trusting neighbourhoods? It is clearly implausible that all the low social trust neighbourhoods happen to be clustered in certain regions of the USA by accident. Furthermore, a typical US state contains tens of millions of people, orders of magnitude larger than a typical social network. This regularity is a large-scale phenomenon requiring a macro-level, ecological explanation. What, for example, is the mysterious factor that makes Louisiana so untrusting and uncooperative, as well as giving it the highest murder rate in the USA?

Inequality

Kawachi et al. offer income inequality as a likely cause of lower trust. They found a strong positive relationship ($r = .74$) between violent crime and income inequality across US states. Both these variables were found to covary strongly with social trust, but less so with median income – in other words, social trust and crime are driven by economic inequality rather than poverty *per se*.

However, unlike Sampson et al., Kawachi et al. suggest that the key causal link in the relationship between violent crime, social trust and inequality is low self-esteem, dignity and social status. Their evidence for this hypothesis comes largely from the detailed work of the forensic psychiatrist Gilligan (1996). Gilligan concludes, on the basis of twenty years of work with violent offenders, that violence is almost never born of simple economic motives, but out of the issues of 'honour and shame [that] are so crucial to human social relations'. Specific incidents of violence almost invariably have their roots in minor incidents of 'disrespect' or insults to self-esteem or dignity. An individual whose self-esteem and dignity have already been eroded by low social status is particularly vulnerable to such insults. Inequality therefore has its impact by exaggerating social status differentials and undermining the relative dignity and self-esteem of the 'have-nots'.

The relationship between economic inequality and violent crime is supported in cross-national data. More economically unequal nations have significantly higher rates of violent crime (r = .55; Eisner, 2001). It would seem that economic inequality stretches the social fabric to breaking point, and this is manifested in both reduced social capital and increased violence (see also chapter 3 and 8). Other differences that sometimes make it more difficult for people to get along can also have the same effect, such as a more ethnically heterogeneous population (Putnam, 2000, p. 309, n. 4). Yet even when such social composition is statistically controlled for, social capital still remains statistically significantly related to crime, suggesting that there is still more to explain about the social capital–crime relationship at the macro-level.

Further evidence for the role of social norms

Another possibility that fits with the Sampson et al. analysis is that norms may help to explain regional and national differences in crime. A key norm that appears to underlie differences in offending behaviour is the extent to which narrowly self-serving or self-interested behaviour is considered acceptable. An analysis of the relationship between the known covariants of crime, such as urbanization, age and sex, has shown that in all cases the higher crime category is associated with the expression of higher levels of self-serving or self-interested values (Halpern, 2001). People living in larger cities, younger people and males tend to express significantly higher levels of self-interest as measured, for example, by their attitude towards keeping a lost object that they have found ('finders keepers').[2] It is also interesting to note that such expressions of self-interested values have increased significantly since the 1960s, coinciding with rises in crime. In 1969, 88 per cent of Europeans disapproved of acts of 'finders keepers', but this had fallen to 68 per cent by 1990, the fall having occurred across all nations (Halpern, 2001; see also chapter 7).

In a more direct test, national differences in levels of expressed self-interest were compared with levels of crime as measured in the International Crime Victimization Survey (Halpern, 2001). The ICVS is gathered using the same methods and questions across countries, and is therefore not subject to the problems of comparability inherent in conventional recorded crime statistics. The hypothesis was confirmed: countries with higher average levels of expressed self-interest had significantly higher levels of reported crime (r = .51), and this relationship persisted even after controls were added for wealth, inequality, urbanization, and so on.

Self-interested values were found to interact with economic inequality – economic inequality was associated with disproportionately higher crime in countries where self-interested values were prevalent. In other words, rather than economic inequality universally driving up crime, it only does so when combined with high levels of self-interested values.

This leaves us with a new question: what stimulates self-interested values or norms in the first place? To some extent more self-interested norms simply feel like an integral part of modern life. People are generally quite happy about keeping the wrong change from a large supermarket, but much less so in the context of a traditional small corner store (Johnston, 1988). Modern urban living forces us into contact with large numbers of strangers every day. In order to get through the day, we must effectively learn to ignore other people (Milgram, 1977). In one of the *Crocodile Dundee* films, Paul Hogan's hero from the outback comes to New York and goes round introducing himself to bemused strangers, who of course interpret this behaviour as a sign of insanity. Ignoring strangers is a normal part of city life, particularly in a large metropolis like New York.

Despite this, it would seem that some cities are more antisocial than others in their habits, as illustrated in the Zimbardo abandoned car experiment. National differences in self-interested values are not eliminated by controls for urbanization, though they are affected by it (Halpern, 2001). Similarly, some nations, such as Indonesia and Japan, have maintained low crime rates despite urbanization, and researchers have identified the retention of underlying culturally based 'communitarian' values as a major part of the explanation (Strang and Vernon, 1992; M. D. West, 2002).

There is an interesting final twist to this story. Countries with higher levels of social trust tend to have slightly lower crime rates. But once you control for levels of self-interested values and economic inequality, you find that higher social trust at the national level is associated with *more* crime. It may be that at a given level of inequality and population self-interest, being more trusting – leaving doors and cars unlocked – is a mistake. It is as if inequality provides the 'motive' for crime (seeing the wealth of others); social norms provide the 'means' (if it is considered more acceptable to act in a self-interested way); and social trust can sometimes provide 'opportunities' for crime (such as unlocked houses and cars). At least for cross-national differences, the *trustworthiness* of the population, as indicated by the prevalent social norms, is a better indicator of crime levels than whether people are trusting *per se*.

Summary of macro effects

It should be stressed that not all forms of crime are related to macro-level variables in the same way. For example, violent crime is particularly affected by economic inequality, while drug abuse is more affected by GDP per capita (more wealth, more drug abuse). Property crime, in contrast, is little affected by either variable, but is significantly related to the proportion of the population living in urban areas (Eisner, 2001).

This is a complicated picture, so let us try and summarize it. Large national and regional differences in crime exist, just as large neighbourhood differences exist at the smaller scale. Across US states, violent crime has a particularly close relationship with social trust and composite indicators of social capital. Cross-nationally, a more general measure of crime – and therefore one that concerns property crime more than violent crime – has been found to covary with self-interested values. These analyses do not use directly comparable measures, and our conclusions must therefore be subject to suitable health warnings. Nonetheless, the evidence so far indicates that societies subject to pressures that strain the social bonds within them, such as high levels of economic inequality or ethnic heterogeneity, suffer higher crime levels. This is mediated, particularly in the case of violent crime, by a weakening of the society's social capital – the extent to which people trust and respect each other, achieve a common consensus of accepted behaviour, and intervene to maintain this consensus. There also appear to be regional and national variations in underlying norms that affect crime. Just as in the abandoned car experiment, it simply seems to be more culturally acceptable in some regions and nations to take advantage of, and sometimes cheat, other people. But is this social capital?

Having a national culture of civic-mindedness – thinking it unacceptable to cheat other people, strangers or not – does not fit a narrow definition of social capital as exclusively networks of known individuals (see chapter 1). But it certainly does meet most definitions: 'networks, *norms*, and trust, that facilitate coordination and co-operation for mutual benefit' (Putnam, 1996; italics added).

Conclusion:
crime and social capital – the interaction between levels

The evidence indicates that social capital has a causal impact on crime at the micro- (intimate), meso- (community) and macro- (regional) levels, and this is summarized in figure 4.1. At the micro-level, we find that individuals who are less bound into intimate and trusting relationships are more likely to become both offenders and the victims of crime. Strong, consistent and trustworthy intimate relationships draw the young person into a web of commitments, values and 'mainstream' satisfactions that inhibit criminal offending. Some individuals find it more difficult than others to build up such relationships, either because of early family relationships characterized by absence, abuse or inconsistency; or because of constitution. But it remains the case that the entry into such mainstream relationships at any time of life can have a critical effect on suppressing offending behaviour. Furthermore, if conventional pro-social relationships are weak, 'negative' forms of social capital may fill the void, such as juvenile gangs, binding the individual into an alternative and competing set of norms and loyalties.

At the meso- or community level, we find these individual and family stories reinforcing one another. Peer influences can be strong, and a critical mass of deviant or pro-social young people can push the 'average' strongly one way or another, creating a distinctive culture in a school or neighbourhood that is difficult for any one individual or family to resist. At the same time, neighbourhoods differ substantially in their 'collective efficacy' – the extent to which neighbours trust one another and join together to enforce everyday norms of acceptable behaviour. High socioeconomic status, low levels of residential mobility, denser friendship and kinship ties, and higher levels of organizational participation are all associated with higher collective efficacy. Concentrated disadvantage and social and ethnic heterogeneity are associated with lower collective efficacy. However, collective efficacy is not reducible to all these factors and has an effect on crime over and above them.

Finally, we also see large-scale regional and even national differences in crime levels that appear to relate to social capital. Partly these differences appear to reflect macro-level social and economic forces, such as economic inequality, that strain the social fabric across the society, reducing trust, mutual respect, and the common ground on which social capital at the micro- and meso-levels must be built. Regional and national differences also highlight the potential role of cultural and normative differences – the informal rules of everyday life – in crime. In much the same way as neighbourhoods differ in their social norms, so too can whole nations.

In reality, the influence of these levels is entwined. Psychologists have noted the positive outcomes for children of what they call 'authoritative parenting', characterized by warmth and praise for achievements, guidance and control through clear and consistent

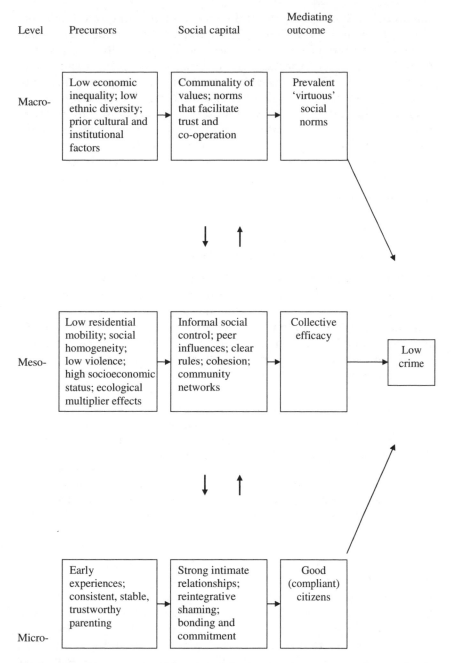

Figure 4.1 *Summary of social capital and crime at micro-, meso- and macro-levels*

standards, and yet giving the child a say and allowing some independence (Baumrind, 1973; Shaffer, 2005). In part this is a highly personal phenomenon, but it can also be understood as culturally based both in terms of the accepted practices and in terms of the implicit values that characterize the child's socialization. In other words, even the most intimate relationships may have some cultural (macro-level) determinants – such as the shift away from an emphasis on obedience to independence of thought as a quality valued by parents in children, or the changing attitudes to gender roles (Halpern, 1995b). At the same time, most macro-level effects ultimately require a micro-level explanation, or at least correspondence. Prevalent values and behaviours are generally sustained by, and rooted in, the actions of individuals and communities.

The issue of shaming

Another important example that highlights the interlinking of the different levels of analysis is the phenomenon of 'shaming'. Braithwaite has argued, very convincingly, that the ability of societies and communities to 'shame' individuals who might offend is critical in the prevention of crime (Braithwaite, 1989, 1993). More specifically, he contrasts 'reintegrative shaming' with 'stigmatisation'. Both are forms of punishment, but:

> Stigmatisation is shaming which creates outcasts, where 'criminal' becomes a master status trait that drives out all other identities, shaming where bonds of respect with the offender are not sustained. Reintegrative shaming, in contrast, is disapproval dispensed within an ongoing relationship with the offender based on respect, shaming which focuses on the evil of the deed rather than on the offender as an irremediably evil person, where degradation ceremonies are followed by ceremonies to decertify deviance, where forgiveness, apology, and repentance are culturally important. (Braithwaite, 1993, p. 1)

Although Braithwaite does not refer to the social capital literature, the parallels are striking. He points out, for example, that 'shaming affects us most when we are shamed by people who matter to us' and that 'people enmeshed in many interdependent relationships with others are exposed to more sources of effective shaming' (1993, p. 12). Similarly, both literatures lay great emphasis on both the importance of the social network and the internalized values or norms that make it work. It would seem that reintegrative shaming is only possible given the existence of social capital – it would not be an option in a highly atomized society. Such a society would instead have to rely on simple punishment, be it economic or physical. On the other hand, the mere existence of social capital does not ensure that reintegrative shaming, rather than stigmatization, is employed. The relationship may therefore be stated as follows: social capital is a necessary but not sufficient condition for reintegrative shaming.

As with parenting practices, it is difficult to reduce shaming to a single level of analysis. Shaming is something experienced by the individual, and most often meted out by a close friend or relative. But its effectiveness largely rests on the existence of a bigger network or community, and its form and character are largely culturally determined.

Finally, we might also note that shaming is itself one of the mechanisms that makes social capital work. Indeed, prevalent informal sanctions, such as shaming, are so key to the functioning and character of social networks that they were argued to be one of the three basic components of social capital at the start of this book (see chapter 1). In as much as social capital is a public good, it is always open to an individual to take advantage – to free-ride – on the social capital maintained by others. Shaming is one of the most important sanctions available to network members to act against such free-riding.

The concept of the 'behavioural setting'

Psychologists have a concept that nicely captures this coming together of the micro-, meso- and macro-levels. Ecological psychologists try to explain the phenomenon through the idea of the 'behavioural setting' (R. G. Barker, 1968).

For example, imagine an alien seeing a library for the first time. It is like a little behavioural ecosystem in which each component plays its part. The readers all follow a commonly understood programme: they get their books, they sit and read quietly and so on. Other people in the setting collect returned books, and unused books on desks, and place them back on shelves in an orderly manner. Furthermore the whole physical environment reinforces and shapes the behaviour. Bits of wood are stuck together at just the right height to enable the readers to sit down, while others are at just the right height to put books on for reading. Even if you had never been in a library before, you'd have a pretty good chance of knowing what you were supposed to do. And if you did get it wrong – you started talking loudly or eating your lunch – other people in this little behavioural universe would soon try to reshape your behaviour by staring, informing you of the rules or ultimately ejecting you from the setting.

Such a behavioural setting, just like a neighbourhood, school or family, is truly a social and behavioural ecosystem, with individual details, local rules and cultural understandings all converging to shape the result jointly. Similarly, in each case one can identify the practices of informing, enforcing and ejecting that are employed by occupants of the setting in response to ensure that the social norms are maintained. Crime too has to be understood in terms of behaviour settings, and sometimes in their breakdown. Pro-social behaviour or offending emerges not just from an individual but from a whole fabric of actions, relationships and shared understandings.

Concluding comments

Criminologists have typically considered much of the evidence in this chapter under the rubric of 'social disorganization theory'. This 'disorganization' can refer both to that within the family or micro-environment and to that within the community. It is not my intention to encourage criminologists to give up their current terminology, but it is important to recognize that the story that they tell and the social phenomena that they explore are the same as those examined by economists, health professionals, educationalists and so on, namely social capital.

Finally, there is an issue about time frames. This chapter, like so much of the literature, talks about causality but doesn't really consider in any detail what is the length of time between cause and effect. In the moment before a crime is committed, we might consider the immediately prior causes: the intentions of the offender, the pressures of the situation, the individual's attitudes, the actions of bystanders and so on. But the roots of any given situation build up over long periods of time. An individual's attitudes and attachments build up over years; the character and accepted rules of a neighbourhood may build up over decades; and the shared cultures of national norms may build up over centuries. In some cases, these different time frames mean that there may be tensions across the layers of causality that we have examined. For example, social trust within a community may be the basis for crime reduction over the long term, yet might also provide opportunities for crime for a given individual in the short term.

In sum, despite the important differences between different types of crime and the large number of other causes for crime not considered here, and however you look at it and at whatever level, social capital is heavily implicated in the causes of crime. As we see throughout this book, it is not just a simple story of 'more is better', as there are examples of certain forms of social capital actually facilitating crime. Rather, it is more about understanding the potential role that can be played by differing forms of social capital for good or bad. There is a great deal more work to be done to pick apart the precise importance of social norms versus networks versus sanctions, and of one level versus another. But on the basis of the evidence so far, we can be confident that crime and social capital – and particularly violent crime and social capital – are part of the same story.

Further reading

To get a feel for how these processes play out at the *individual level*, have a look at Sampson and Laub (1993). For an outstanding paper looking at how some of the social capital of *neighbourhoods* can affect crime, try Robert Sampson once again: Sampson, Raudenbush and Earls (1997).

Crime or victimization surveys are rich sources of information and are generally considered more trustworthy than police statistics. They are being conducted more often, with increasingly large sample sizes, and can be linked to more and more contextual and geographical data. Many countries now conduct such surveys and their reports can be downloaded free. Findings from the US National Crime and Victimization survey can be found at www.ojp.usdoj.gov/bjs/cvict.htm. The British equivalent can be found at www.homeoffice.gov.uk/rds/bcs1.html. The International Crime Victimization Survey provides useful comparisons between over fifty countries and is ripe for further research; it can be found at ruljis.leidenuniv.nl/group/jfcr/www/icvs/Index.htm.

On a more theoretical level, the work on *shaming* is fascinating: Braithwaite (1989) or in a shorter form, Braithwaite (1993).

5

~~~❧❧~~~

Education

The evidence is now beyond dispute. When schools work together with families to support learning, children tend to succeed not just in school but throughout life . . . When parents are involved in their children's education at home, their children do better in school. When parents are involved at school, their children go further in school, and the schools they go to are better.

Henderson and Berla, 1994, quoted in OECD, 2001a, p. 92[1]

A great deal of research has focused on how deficits in social capital can lead to negative outcomes, such as criminal offending and delinquency (see chapter 4). In many ways, the relationship between social capital and educational outcomes mirrors that of crime. But despite the confidence of the opening quotation above, the literature is not without controversy (Dika and Singh, 2002). This literature challenges some of the received wisdom of the educational and policy communities, especially that higher spending is the most important key to educational attainment.

Educational underachievement is a key link in the cycle of disadvantage (Goldthorpe, Llewellyn and Payne, 1987; Kiernan, 1996). A host of variables play a part in this cycle of disadvantage, ranging from parental education to cultural capital and, of course, financial resources (Quinton and Rutter, 1988; Feinstein and Symons, 1999; A. Sullivan, 2001; Desforges and Abouchaar, 2003; see also chapter 8 and figure 8.1).

Research has shown that the human and financial capital of the parents helps to predict the educational success or failure of children. But a significant amount of the remaining variance is explained by social capital, and social capital also helps explain the impact of the parents' human and financial resources.

As in previous chapters, we shall work through the layers of effects from the intimate or micro-level through the community or meso-level right up to the large-scale or macro-level. But education, unlike the other outcome variables we have examined, arguably has a special relationship with social capital in that it is also viewed by some as a key tool in the creation of social capital. Virtually all OECD nations now have explicit 'citizenship' education programmes, and those few that don't are generally in the process of introducing them (Torney-Purta et al., 2001). The issue of what creates social capital is returned to in some detail in chapter 8, but in as much as education specifically is implicated, the issues will be flagged in outline here.

The micro-level: supportive families

Many studies have now concluded that the size and quality of a child's immediate social network – principally their family – has a significant impact on the child's educational achievement. As indicated by the quotation at the start of the chapter, the importance of this impact is now widely recognized.

Studies have found that children whose parents are both physically present and attentive tend to achieve better test scores, are more likely to complete high school and are more likely to attend college (Valenzuela and Dornbusch, 1994; Furstenberg and Hughes, 1995; Parcel and Geschwender, 1995; Y. Sun, 1999; Desforges and Abouchaar, 2003). Much of this evidence comes from the USA, mostly using the National Educational Longitudinal Study (NELS) – a longitudinal study of over 20,000 children that therefore allows statistical controls for other factors such as socioeconomic status. But researchers in other countries have found similar effects. For example, Majoribanks has tracked the experiences of children in Australia and in Hong Kong, finding that family social capital – relationships between parents and children – are moderately to strongly associated with adolescents' educational attainments, especially in boys (Majoribanks, 1991; Majoribanks and Kwok, 1998). Similarly, an analysis of the UK's National Child Development Survey concluded that parental attentiveness was a key predictor of a young person's educational attainment at 16, having controlled for the child's own ability and attentiveness at age 10 (Feinstein and Symons, 1999).

In the early years of a child's development, attentive and responsive adults draw the child into the social world, reinforcing and echoing the child's own interactions – what psychologists call 'meshing' – capturing the child's interest and helping it direct its own attention (Shaffer, 2005). In short, interactions with attentive adults are the key channel through which the child develops emotional and social control, and becomes an attentive and effective self-learner.

The role of educational aspiration

A large part of the educational impact of parents on children seems to be mediated by their aspirations. Parents who are more involved with their children seem generally to encourage in the child higher educational and occupational aspirations (Majoribanks and Kwok, 1998; Desforges and Abouchaar, 2003). This in turn helps to explain why the parents' – and especially the mother's – own educational attainment is such an important predictor of their child's attainment. High levels of parent–child interactions generally increase the expectations of both child and parent (Hao and Bonstead-Bruns, 1998). And high levels of parent–child interactions help to explain the higher achievement of many immigrant groups. The effect is most marked when parent and child are in agreement – when they are in disagreement, higher interaction may actually depress expectations.

These results tie in with other, more general work showing that having higher expectancies – believing in yourself – has a very substantial positive effect on educational attainment (Weiner, 1979). It has been shown that kids given false positive feedback subsequently perform better than controls. In one famous experiment, it was shown that children whose teachers were given false test results, which indicated that the children were brighter than they actually were, were found to have shown marked educational improvements one year on (Rosenthal and Jacobson, 1968).[2] In other words, if people believe in your abilities and give you positive feedback, they increase your aspirations and encourage you to aim high and to achieve. This, of course, is exactly what happens in most parent–child interactions.

Quantity versus quality

An important question arises about 'quantity' versus 'quality' in these social relationships and networks. This question has arisen with particular urgency in relation to the issue of single-parent families, a group whose numbers have risen sharply in most countries. Psychologists have studied in detail how the quality of early parent–child interactions affects the child's development, including their intellectual and academic attainment. The poor academic performance of children in orphanages or social care can partly be attributed to disrupted social relationships with adult carers, and not least with their high turnover (Hodges and Tizard, 1989; Rutter, Quinton and Hill, 1990). Similarly, it has been found that maternal depression early in the child's life markedly disrupts the quality of mother–child interactions, and can lead to significantly lower intelligence test scores at age 11, particularly in boys (Sharp et al., 1995).

Educationalists have handled this issue by distinguishing between 'structural' and 'process' aspects of family relationships. Structural factors refer to the number of adults in the household, their formal relationship (e.g. biological or step-parent), and the number of siblings. This roughly equates to the 'network' component of social capital (see chapter 1). Process factors refer to the level and quality of interactions inside the network, regardless of its structure, and relates more to social norms and informal sanctions.

In general, both structure and process aspects of family social capital affect high school students' educational achievements (see, for example, Israel, Beaulieu and Hartless's 2001 analysis of the NELS). However, one cannot assume that *any* kind of increased contact with adults in the home environment will be associated with improved educational achievement. Indeed, it may be that some kinds of increased parent–child interaction will increase in response to educational problems (though this does not necessarily mean that they are unhelpful). Hence one analysis of the NELS found that while many aspects of increased parental involvement, such as parent–child discussion about school, were associated with higher student achievement, others were negatively associated with achievement, such as homework checking by parents (Desimone, 1997). This same study found too that the impact of parental involvement also varied by social group. In particular, parental involvement was generally a less positive influence for low-income students (see also Valadez, 2002).

But it is the issue of single-parent households and, to some extent, households where both parents work that has been the focus of most controversy. Many studies have found that, in terms of educational outcomes and not dropping out of school, two parents are generally significantly better than one – in other words, structural or network social capital (quantity) counts (McLanahan and Sandefur, 1994; Teachman, Paasch and Carver, 1996; Pong, 1998). Partly this result is explained by the fact that having two parents around, as opposed to one, implies more child–parent contact. Further support for this simple structural interpretation lies in the finding that having more brothers and sisters, or being later born in a family, is associated with marginally lower IQ and worse educational achievement (Zajonc and Markus, 1975). Essentially, having more kids in the household 'dilutes' or reduces the time that later-born children are able to spend with their parents.

However, careful analysis has shown that educational outcomes for the children of single parents are depressed for reasons other than the amount of parent–child contact. One contributory factor is lower household income, but it is by no means the only, or even dominant, factor. Single-parent families turn out to have smaller social networks and fewer social ties than two-parent families (McLanahan and Sandefur, 1994). They move home significantly more often than intact two-parent families, thus disrupting the family's social networks and changing school more often. Research has yet to demonstrate conclusively whether this lower educational achievement and higher drop-out rate are a result of disruption of the social networks of the child and parent, including with the school, or the result of the trauma of family break-up (Teachman, Paasch and Carver, 1996).

Similar factors help to explain why children with step-parents underperform educationally – for example, early school drop-out in step-parent families is more than double that in families with both bio-logical parents present (Teachman, Paasch and Carver, 1996). Despite step-parent families having much higher incomes than single parents, they still tend to move home more than two-biological-parent families and have more limited and disrupted social capital.

Further evidence against the simple 'quantity counts' hypothesis is found in the parental working literature. A simple structural model of family social capital implies that children with both parents working will also be at a disadvantage, but this has not been found to be the case. Detailed research has found both positive and negative impacts of having both parents working (or the only parent working in the case of single parents; Parcel, Nickoll and Dufur, 1996). M. O'Brien and Jones (1999), in a study of working-class mothers, found that children performed best when their mothers were in employment, particularly if this employment was part-time. Higher educational aspirations appeared to explain much of this positive effect. Similarly, Bianchi and Robinson (1997) found that children of mothers who are employed part-time watch significantly less TV and read more than the children of mothers at home full-time. What seems to happen is that working parents – at least part-time working parents – work hard to ensure that they have 'quality time' with their children, perhaps partly to compensate for their time at work. This was reflected in the striking finding that the children of part-time working mothers have been found to have more access to their mothers' time than those whose mothers were full-time homemakers (M. O'Brien and Jones, 1999). These interesting findings have led some to suggest that policies to encourage flexible part-time working arrangements will significantly benefit child cognitive development and educational outcomes (Parcel, Nickoll and Dufur, 1996).[3]

It's not just child–parent interactions that count

Individual social capital is not reducible to the immediate relationships within the family. Children, and parents, differ in their social capital in many other domains, such as whether they are engaged in community or voluntary activities or whether they have ongoing relationships with teachers or the parents of school friends.

In a small but detailed study of young at-risk parents, Furstenberg and Hughes (1995) found that the educational attainment of the child was significantly predicted by measures of the mother's social capital, not just the child–parent interactions themselves. These predictions held even after controlling for parents' human capital and the child's past attainment. Children did better at school when the mother herself received (and gave) more support from her own mother (the child's grandmother); the more of the child's friends the mother knew; the stronger the mother's help network; and if the mother saw a close friend at least weekly. The educational aspirations of friends, as well as parents, were also found to be important to some aspects of educational attainment.

Similarly, a statistically sophisticated study of rural disadvantaged girls found both within-family and community-oriented forms of social capital were significantly related to post-secondary education participation, high school graduation, and workforce participation (Doebler, 1999). This study found that participation in extra-curricular school activities had the strongest effect in each of the statistically significant models.

As we have already noted, large-scale analyses of the NELS have shown that family mobility has a negative impact on educational achievement, and this implicates the importance of the wider social network of the child and parent. It is the disruption of this social capital external to the family itself that explains much of the relationship between family structure and educational outcomes (Teachman, Paasch and Carver, 1996, 1997; see also above).

It is unsurprising to find that relationships to teachers also contribute to educational outcomes. Both parent–teacher relationships and child–teacher relationships have been found to contribute to higher educational performance and post-secondary educational trajectories (Teachman, Paasch and Carver, 1996, 1997; Jordan and Plank, 2000).

The educational attainment of ethnic minorities

The educational achievement of ethnic minority groups is a source of considerable interest and concern in many countries across the world. In Britain, for example, the educational achievements of different ethnic groups are found to vary widely, with many groups overachieving compared with the white majority, but with some substantially under-achieving (Madood et al., 1997).

Research has found that social capital plays a similar general role in the educational achievements of ethnic minority groups and of the white majority. For example, 'familism' was found to improve grades in both Mexican and Anglo adolescents in the USA (Valenzuela and Dornbusch, 1994; n = 3,168). Teachman, Paasch and Carver (1996) found that black Americans were around a quarter to a third more likely than white Americans to drop out of school, but that this poorer performance could be fully attributed to their relative lack of financial, human and social capital. Similarly, Plutzer (1998) found, in a study of black American girls and young women, that parents who provided close supervision could greatly help their children set and reach their educational goals. And Qian and Blair (1999) and Yan (1999), both using the NELS, found that parental involvement in school activities had a strong impact on the educational aspirations of African Americans and Hispanics.

Some variations in effects have been reported across groups. For example, one study reported large variations in the strength, and even direction, of the impact of parental involvement across ethnic groups (Desimone, 1997). In particular, this study found that parental involvement variables were generally less significant for Asians than for whites, blacks or Hispanics, though this might reflect lower levels of variability in this group.[4] A similar result was found for parental involvement on the take-up of mathematics – a choice known to pay significant long-term educational and earnings returns – for white compared with Latino students. Parental involvement was found to be effective for white students, but not for Latinos – and particularly ineffective for lower socioeconomic Latinos (Valadez, 2002).

More importantly, differences in levels of parent–child and parent–school social capital help to explain differences in educational achievements across ethnic groups (Qian and Blair, 1999; Yan, 1999). Hence low levels of family social capital help to explain the generally lower levels of educational achievement among black Americans. Those few black students who are successful had high levels of family social capital and parental involvement, as high as those of comparably successful white students (Yan, 1999).

Finally, it is worth noting that individuals are not blind to the strengths and weaknesses of the social capital available to them. Focus group work has clearly revealed that ethnic minority group members feel at a disadvantage because they lack the social networks of more established majority groups, especially within the prestigious professions (see also chapter 2). There is evidence that this is one of the reasons why ethnic minority and disadvantaged groups are heavy investors in education, often against the odds. While the affluent and well connected can build a successful career on their connections, those from disadvantaged, less well-connected families instead must concentrate on attaining academically (Zweigenhaft, 1993). If your family's connections don't give you the social capital you need, then an alternative option is to concentrate on building up your human capital instead. Another alternative, though not always an educationally effective one, is to join the school basketball or football team as a way of accessing alternative forms of social capital (Eitle and Eitle, 2002).

Mentoring: an experimental intervention

Experimental interventions are always interesting in that – when they work – they make us much more confident that we've got the causality right. Of course, they're also important in that they suggest that we can do something about what's going on.

When it comes to families and intimate social capital, true experiments are difficult and perhaps unethical. However, a very interesting test of the social capital hypothesis in this area is presented by attempts to boost the educational achievements of disadvantaged kids by boosting their social capital in the form of mentors. Policy interventions of this form are still in their infancy, and systematic evaluations are hard to come by.

Johnson evaluated the Sponsor-a-Scholar programme in Philadelphia (Johnson, 1999). The basic idea of the programme is simple – 'that caring and influential adults – related or not – can provide youth with a form of social capital that is invaluable for their development'. She found that the Sponsor-a-Scholar programme had a positive and significant impact on academic performance in the 10th and 11th grades, but not in the 12th grade. She also found that it had a significant positive impact on the extent of college preparation activities, and on college attendance during the first year after high school. Of equal interest, she found that disadvantaged students benefited most from the programme. This is consistent with the evidence that such students are most likely to lack social capital, as well as other forms of capital, and are therefore the most likely to benefit from the intervention.

Another, perhaps even more impressive result has been reported by Kahne and Bailey (1999). The programme they describe is an intervention at a much younger age than that of the Philadelphia programme. They evaluated two 'I have a dream' (IHAD) programmes, both focused on children in the 6th grade. Each IHAD sponsor adopts an entire 6th grade class and, together with a project coordinator, provides these students with long-term financial, academic and social support in the hope that they will graduate from high school and attend college. The researchers found that the programmes were 'enormously successful'. Graduation rates rose from 37 per cent and 34 per cent to 71 per cent and 69 per cent respectively – i.e. roughly doubled. The researchers identified enhanced social capital as critical to the success of the programme. In conclusion, they point to the large potential of such interventions as a policy tool to assist young people in inner-city contexts.

In contrast to these two very positive studies, a recent British experimental study found markedly negative results (Defty and Fitz-Gibbon, 2002). A sample of 120 'underaspiring' 15-year-old children were identified from across fifteen schools. These children were identified on the basis of their low expectation of staying on in school post-16 despite being of similar ability to their peers. Half of the 'underaspirers' were randomly assigned to an intervention group that involved identifying them for the school so that additional pastoral guidance could be provided. The control group remained unidentified to school. It was found that the children who had been identified and given additional guidance actually performed significantly worse in their subsequent GCSE exams at age 16 than the control group. Furthermore, the more counselling they received, the worse their results – though this might have reflected their greater needs.

How can we square the dramatically positive results of the 'Sponsor-a-Scholar' and 'I have a dream' programmes with the depressingly negative results of the British study? One possibility could be the quality of the intervention and the relatively mature age of the children. However, much more likely is that the naming of one child among many as likely to fail in the British experiment caused more harm than good through a process of labelling and possibly stigmatization. This result is in line with much earlier studies showing that identifying a child as less able can affect teacher expectancies and lower performance, and hence that individual interventions to prevent delinquency can actually lead to worse outcomes (Rosenthal and Jacobson, 1968; McCord, 1978; Dishion, McCord and Poulin, 1999). In contrast, the successful US studies intervene with a whole peer group at one time, rather than singling out an individual child as a failure.

These positive results strongly suggest that deficits in social capital may play a role in the educational underperformance of many disadvantaged young people. They suggest that these deficits can be at least partly compensated for by offering alternative forms of social capital. However, it appears very important that the mentoring intervention does not inadvertently label an individual child as a failure relative to their peers, and it also appears to be more effective if offered relatively early in the young person's educational career.

The meso-level: school and community effects

Coleman, in his now classic paper (Coleman, 1988), noted how educational failure in the USA was very much lower in Catholic schools than in conventional secular schools even when the financial and human capital of parents was controlled for. He noted how the drop-out rate was three times less in Catholic high schools than in public high schools. Coleman suggested that the reason for this was the strength of the networks that linked parents, children and the Catholic school together.[5] Parents, students and teachers were bound together in a network of shared values and with a high degree of 'closure'. In other words, in a typical Catholic school it was no good skipping school with one of your friends and thinking that it wouldn't get back to your parents.

Coleman's findings have been replicated by more than one research group. Bryk, Lee and Holland (1993) calculated that if an average public (state) school were able to adopt the communal character of a demographically similar Catholic school, it would leap from being average to the top 20–30 per cent on most measures. They found that small school size also helped, a result replicated in other studies (Bryk, Lee and Holland, 1993; Langbein and Bess, 2002). Smaller schools tend to have better academic results and fewer disturbances than larger schools – though it appears possible to mitigate these size effects through other forms of social capital building, notably through big interscholastic sports programmes (Langbein and Bess, 2002).[6]

Coleman's findings were also broadly confirmed in Teachman, Paasch and Carver's reanalysis of the NELS (1996, 1997). They found that children in Catholic schools were very much less likely to drop out of school before the 10th grade. Even after statistically controlling for parents' income and education, living in a rural area, living in the south, gender, ethnicity, number of siblings and sibling drop-out, the odds of dropping out of high school were reduced by about 45 per cent by attending a Catholic school. The positive effect of Catholic schools was not explained by structural family characteristics, such as having a step-parent, though these family factors were powerful independent influences on drop-out rates. Catholic schools were associated with high levels of parent–school connectivity, and this appeared to be a key driving variable. The Catholic school effect was also partly explained by lower levels of residential mobility among the families who used them.

> We have interpreted the impact of the number of school changes within the framework of social capital. We have assumed that changing schools reduces the ability of parents and children to make wise decisions about schooling. They have less information about schools, teachers and classes. They may be less able to take advantage of resources that schools and teachers can provide. Teachers may be less committed to children who have moved and, therefore, less willing to make additional investments of time and energy into children. Children may feel separated from the educational process and may be more likely to seek marginalized social contacts. (Teachman, Paasch and Carver, 1996, p. 782)

Controversy over the role of closure

One recent analysis has challenged the positive educational impact of Catholic schools, and in particular the positive impact of closure. Morgan and Sorensen (1999) analysed gains in mathematics between the 10th and 12th grades, using the NELS. They found that, once friendship density among the students themselves was controlled for, social closure among parents within public schools was *negatively* associated with achievements in mathematics. They argue instead that 'horizon-expanding' schools foster more learning than do 'norm-enforcing' schools, though they do still note a positive effect of closure within the Catholic school sector.

Morgan and Sorensen's research has caused something of a minor stir, and has itself attracted criticism. Some have argued that Morgan and Sorensen's research is conceptually confused and that this has affected both their analysis and their conclusions (Hallinan and Kubitschek, 1999). Others who have used exactly the same data have come to very different conclusions (Carbonaro, 1999).

How can we explain the apparently very different conclusions of Morgan and Sorensen to those of Teachman et al.? One major point to note is that Teachman et al. focus on school drop-out rates (as did Coleman), while Morgan and Sorensen are looking at school perfor-mance. An important aside is that more marginal students tend to perform significantly worse educationally than others. A school that is successful in retaining such students should therefore end up with sig-nificantly *worse* grades, all else being equal. In this sense, no difference between schools may in fact conceal an impressive performance. However, on the specific issue of closure – as measured by whether parents know the parents of their child's friends – perhaps there is not a conflict. Teachman et al. found that this particular variable was not sig-nificantly related to dropping out. Hence while they did strongly repli-cate Coleman's general finding that Catholic schools reduced drop-outs, and attributed the effect to social capital, they did not find much support for Coleman's specific notion of closure as mediating the effect.

Whether or not the detail of Morgan and Sorensen's analysis sur-vives closer inspection, the idea that they raise is certainly worth pur-suing. The distinction that they make is very reminiscent of that now made by social capital theorists between bonding and bridging social capital (see chapter 1). As has become clear through earlier chapters, both bridging and bonding have certain kinds of benefits, and a com-munity or social network based too exclusively on one or the other is likely to be at a disadvantage – both forms have uses. Hence it would be unsurprising to find that a community that was closed to the point of having few or no outside links – lacking any ability to expand hori-zons – might also limit the educational aspirations of its members. This would be especially so if the community concerned happened to gen-erally have low aspirations, as is the case in many disadvantaged urban communities (see also chapter 2 for a closely analogous finding in rela-tion to economic advancement). For example, for young women approaching the end of compulsory schooling, their educational choices are strongly shaped by their community's notions of 'success'. For those from disadvantaged or traditional communities, this may imply a notion of femininity that does not readily include staying on for high school or university (Thomson, Henderson and Holland, 2003).

We tested the potentially double-edged nature of closure in ongoing research on English 15–17-year-old young people. Following other research, we found that the educational qualification of parents' levels

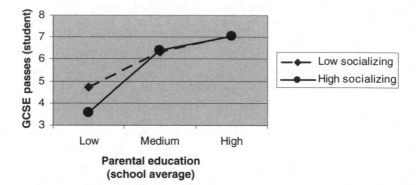

Figure 5.1 *Academic attainment by average parental education in school and network closure*
Note: Academic attainment = GCSE passes at age 16. Parental education = proportion of parents at the school with degrees. Closure = extent to which student's parents socialize with other parents at the school.

predicted students' educational attainments at both the individual and the school level. In other words, other factors being equal, going to a school where your classmates' parents had degrees was an advantage. However, we also asked students about the extent to which their parents socialized with their friends' parents. Students at schools where many parents were highly educated generally performed better whether or not their parents socialized together. But for those who attended schools where most parents did not have degrees, having parents who socialized with others at the school was actually a slight disadvantage (see figure 5.1).

Examples from other parts of the world help to illustrate why bonding without bridging social capital, while positive when the community concerned sets its sights high, might be negative under other circumstances. One such example comes from research conducted in Columbia, South America (Restrepo, 1998; see also chapter 4). In this context, with strong pockets of 'unproductive social capital', closure is most likely to lead to worse educational outcomes. Similarly, though less dramatically, attention has been drawn to how the relatively closed social strata and associated parental aspirations found in India reinforce one another to trap many young people in a cycle of low aspirations and low lifetime achievement (Dhesi, 2001). In short, the Indian school system seems to be a particularly clear example of how parents' aspirations affect which school a young person attends, and school-based aspirations and social networks then strongly affect the person's life-course.

Closure then, or tight bonding social capital in the absence of bridging social capital, does facilitate the ability of members of that community to pass on their values to the next generation. But if these values are anti-intellectual or presume low achievement, then high educational outcomes cannot be expected. It is clear that future educational research needs to attend to the impact of bonding and bridging aspects of community, *and* to the underlying values that such social capital is likely to facilitate in the particular context.

Do other aspects of community affect school performance?

The American evidence on the Catholic school effect indicated that much of its positive influence might lie in the community in which the school was embedded rather than in the school itself. Parent–school connectivity and the negative impact of high residential mobility have been strongly implicated.

As one leading researcher concludes, there is now 'unequivocal evidence that the average socioeconomic status of a child's class or school has an effect on his or her outcomes, even after taking account of (individual-level) ability and socioeconomic status' (Willms, 2000, p. 18). Similarly, research linking the American NELS to the 1990 census found not only that neighbourhood characteristics predict educational outcomes, but that the strength of these effects 'rivals that associated with more commonly cited family and school factors' (Ainsworth, 2002, p. 117). This study found that a large portion of these neighbourhood effects were explained by neighbourhood social capital, with 'collective socialization' having the strongest influence.

To show a community – or truly ecological – effect, ideally you should build a 'multi-level' statistical model. This does not only apply to education, but all outcome variables (see, for example, the impressive work of Robert Sampson on crime in chapter 4). If having only one biological parent in the household tends to lead to lower educational achievements in children, then a community with a high proportion of such single-parent and step-parent families will, on average, have a poorer educational record. This, by itself, does not imply a 'community' effect. It may be fully explained by the individual-level effects of the families. In other words, the lower average educational performance in a community with a high proportion of non-traditional families does not necessarily imply that a two-biological-parent family living in such a community will do any worse than such a family living elsewhere. Only if there is a true community or ecological effect will such a family be affected by the area it lives in.

Such a multi-level model has been constructed. Yongmin Sun has built a series of multi-level models examining the science, mathematics, reading and social studies test scores of American 8th-graders, again using the 1988 NELS (Y. Sun, 1998). Sun includes in the models 'control' variables, such as average family income, minority enrolment, urban location; and 'structural' variables, such as number of school changes, average siblings in families, and concentration of non-traditional families. Of great interest here, 'process' variables were also included, such as: proportion of students participating in religious activities; proportions participating in sports; parents belonging to organizations with other parents; numbers of other parents known; and extent to which parents report working together to support school policies.

At the individual level, Sun's models support most of the findings of the first section. Changing school, having more siblings, minority status and lower socioeconomic status were all associated with poorer academic performance. Similarly, higher parent–child communication, knowing other parents, parents' involvement in organizations and students' participation in religious activities were all positively associated with higher performance.

But the real added interest is in the community-level effects. Sun found highly significant community-level effects across the control, structural and process variables. Concerning the control variables, communities with lower family income and higher minority enrolment had lower performances across all four outcome measures. In other words, poor families living in poor areas suffered from a double disadvantage, first from being poor themselves, and second from the poverty of their neighbours. Similar community effects were seen as a result of the concentration of non-traditional families on science, mathematics and reading performance (but not social studies), and for average number of siblings (but not for mathematics).

All five of the community process variables were related to test scores. Statistical controls for the control and structural variables reduced the size of their impact, but still left significant effects. The percentage of students participating in religious activities, the proportion of parents who knew each other, and the extent to which parents reported working together to support school policies were all significantly related to test scores on at least three of the four test measures, even after both individual-level and community-level controls were taken into account.

These results strongly support Coleman's hypothesis that community characteristics affect educational performance. It is also striking that in this statistically superior model, Coleman's hypothesis that closure matters – measured here as parent-to-parent connectivity – is reinstated. The model also extends Teachman et al.'s finding that mobility, as measured by the average number of school changes, negatively affects educational performance. It would appear that such mobility affects not only the child concerned, but also the performance of classmates. But this effect is eliminated once community poverty, parent–parent and parent–school connectivity, and student participation in religious and other activities are controlled for. The results suggest that the negative effects of mobility on students' educational achievements at the community level lie mainly in the disruption that this mobility brings to community social capital.

There is an argument to be had about what is more important to educational achievement – family or community social capital. It would seem that both the structure and process of community social capital have an impact on high school students' educational achievements. Another recent analysis of the NELS confirmed both community and family effects on education, estimating that family social capital has the bigger impact overall (Israel, Beaulieu and Hartless, 2001). This said, the study also concluded that community social capital was particularly important in helping some students to excel. It seems a little like a relay race – families can take you so far, but wider social networks help to take you that extra mile. But the main point is that their effects are broadly additive. More of either will help children.

It is important to ask what factors might boost investments in such community social capital. The results imply that it is to the advantage of all students to live in areas with low residential mobility and high levels of parent connectivity, even if these factors do not apply to their own family. One careful study of Chicago neighbourhoods found that the best predictors of closure (parent–parent and parent–child connectivity) and neighbourly exchange were concentrated affluence, low population density and residential stability (Sampson, Morenoff and Earls, 1999). Concentrated disadvantage, in contrast, did not seem to inhibit such adult neighbourly exchange, but it did inhibit shared expectations for the informal control of children, even when perceived violence was controlled for. Historically, social homogeneity, wealth and low mobility have been found to be the key factors that fostered investment in public (state) secondary school education in the US from 1910–30, suggesting a virtuous circle of investment and stability (Goldin and Katz, 2001). Homeownership is also likely to be an important factor. Homeowners have been found to invest more in education and move less (DiPasquale and Glaeser, 1998; see also the discussion of causality in chapter 8).

The work of Sun and others indicates that strong community social capital is not entirely reducible to money, though it certainly appears to help. Put more positively, it has been found that the disadvantaged communities, such as schools with 50 per cent of students from single-parent families, can perform academically well when social relations and networks among parents are strong (Pong, 1998). Similarly, parental involvement within a school has been shown not just to increase educational attainment in general, but also to reduce social class differences in attainment (Willms, 2000).

As indicated in the section on micro-effects, immigrant status appears to be associated with higher educational aspirations for some groups, such as Chinese and Korean immigrants to the USA, but not others, such as Mexican immigrants to the USA (Hao and Bonstead-Bruns, 1998). This is partly the manifestation of a community- or group-level effect. Similarly, being able to speak the language of your own ethnic minority group is, all else being equal, generally advantageous to your educational achievement. For example, one study of Vietnamese immigrants found that literacy in Vietnamese was positively related to identification with ethnic group and to academic achievement (Bankston and Zhou, 1995). Retaining your ethnic minority language provides access to additional community social capital and therefore can contribute to mainstream education rather than compete with it.

In sum, the evidence indicates that there are clear effects of community-level social capital on educational performance, and these operate over and above the impact of family-level social capital. This is particularly problematic for low social capital, disadvantaged families who are in turn disproportionately concentrated in poor, low social capital communities – what Willms (2000) describes as 'Double Jeopardy'. However, the positive side to this story is that there is every reason to think that, armed with a clearer understanding of the importance of these factors, policymakers, communities and families have a good chance of focusing on these social capital deficits and doing something about them.

Social capital within the school

Recently, some education specialists have begun to think about the role that social capital fulfils within the school – in other words, the social networks between teachers, and between teachers and their principal.

David Hargreaves, formerly professor of education at Cambridge and adviser to the British government, wrote an interesting piece while head of the government body that sets the British school curriculum, in which he argued:

> many British teachers lack a culture of collaborative professional learning by which they might work smarter ... In a school rich in social capital, the high levels of trust generate a collaborative culture and strong networks among the organisation's members and stakeholders. High levels of social capital in a school strengthen its intellectual capital. (Hargreaves, 2001, pp. 5–6)

Hargreaves did not ignore the important educational role that can be played by strong parent–school and parent–parent links. But his main purpose was to emphasize that social capital within the school is also important. He points to cross-national comparisons of 'teacher effectiveness' to make his case. Comparative analysis of mathematics teaching in the USA, Japan and Germany implicates teacher-to-teacher social capital in the higher educational achievements of the Japanese (Stigler and Hiebert, 1999). In Japan, teachers participate in professional development groups that provide mentoring and also a collective forum within which teachers can develop and test new teaching techniques. Teachers develop 'research lessons' that they then share and implement collectively. They observe one another at work and develop a language in which to talk about what they are doing. And as the outcome is owned collectively, the teachers can constructively criticize one another without causing offence. In short, teachers actively and routinely collaborate collectively to innovate and share knowledge – social capital becomes a lubricant of knowledge transfer and development, and it pays considerable educational dividends.

Though Hargreaves did not refer to it, the evidence on failing schools strongly supports his hypothesis, not only in Britain but in other countries too. Failing schools are often characterized by high staff turnover, and this tends to undermine staff–staff social capital, just as high residential mobility undermines family and community social capital. Indeed, some have argued that reform initiatives in urban schools generally fail precisely because they deplete or prevent social capital from arising among teachers and administrators (Useem et al., 1997). High turnover rates and union rules that work against out-of-hours contacts between teachers further reinforce the solitary nature of teachers' work. In contrast, case studies of exemplary schools have identified, among the factors that enable such schools to excel, trust among school personnel, a collaborative stance towards learning, and an atmosphere of mutual support that enables personnel to take risks (S. A. Wolf et al., 2000).[7]

The parallel between these findings and the larger economic literature on what characterizes the successful firm are striking (see chapter
2). Stigler and Hiebert's description of what makes a Japanese school
so effective is very similar to the descriptions of management consul-
tants of successful and innovative companies. The comparison is made
even closer by the observation that Japanese schools are also unusual
in having close ties with employers (Brinton, 2000). This suggests that
not only do they have high internal bonding social capital, but they
also have good bridging social capital with other important players in
the economy and children's future lives. Similarly, there is a growing
recognition of the importance of collaboration not only within educational institutions, but between them too (Huotari and Livonen, 2001;
Herriot et al., 2002). For example, within the UK schools are being
encouraged to form 'federations' or clusters within which schools
actively co-operate with one another, in marked contrast to the straight
competition encouraged by previous policies and the emphasis on
league tables.

The macro-level

Tucked away in a footnote, Putnam (2000) reports a series of remarkable statistics, summarized in table 5.1. Essentially, US states with
higher levels of social capital at the aggregate level achieve consistently
better academic results.

Interestingly, a similar regional effect can be found tucked away in
the tables and regression models of Teachman, Paasch and Carver's
careful analyses of the NELS (1996). They found a consistent and powerful negative effect of living in the southern states of America on

Table 5.1 *Correlation across the US states between the Social Capital Index and the National Assessment of Educational Progress tests (1990s data)*

	4th grade (age 9)	8th grade (age 13)
Mathematics (1992)	.81	.91
Mathematics (1996)	.67	.88
Reading (1994)	.68	
Science (1996)		.85
SATs (1993)		.67
High school drop-outs (1990–5)		−.79

school drop-out rates. Residence in the south was associated with an increase in the odds of dropping out of school of 70–75 per cent. Furthermore, the effect of this variable hardly altered throughout all of the models they employed. Of course, it is the southern states that are consistently found to be lower on the Putnam index of social capital (see chapter 8).

The US is not alone in showing this remarkable relationship between social capital and educational attainment at the national level. Unpublished UK data show a similar very high correlation between educational attainment at 16 (e.g. percentage achieving 5 or more good GCSEs) and the social capital of the UK regions (using data from the British Social Attitudes surveys). Even more impressively, recent work has replicated this result on a finer scale by comparing the educational attainments of schools across more than a hundred British local authorities with social capital data from the UK's Citizens' Audit (Pattie, Seyd and Whiteley, 2002). The Citizens' Audit has a sample size of more than 10,000, providing an estimate of civic engagement and social trust within each local authority from more than 100 residents in each. The authors found that, having controlled for social, demographic and other characteristics, civic engagement was significantly related to areas' average level of educational attainment, and especially exam results at age 16, the key exams taken at the end of compulsory schooling.

This is an important replication of the US results. Educational spending in the UK is dominated by central government taxation and expenditure (unlike in the USA, where educational spending is strongly locally determined), and grades are nationally comparable in the UK. In other words, these British results cannot be explained away by differences in the financial resources available to schools, or by regional differences in exam marking.

These macro-level, or regional, differences are very substantial. For the US data, Putnam reports that the associations persist even when controls are added for a host of other factors, including racial composition, wealth, economic inequality, adult educational levels, poverty rates, educational spending, teachers' salaries, class size, family structure, religious affiliation and the size of the private-school sector. Indeed, while several of these other factors were statistically significant, social capital remained the single most important explanatory factor of state-level differences (Putnam, 2000, p. 300).

These striking findings are usefully juxtaposed with a long-standing puzzle in the American educational literature. A series of large-scale US studies have concluded, much to everyone's surprise, that there is little or no systematic relationship between school expenditures and measures of student achievement (Coleman, 1966; Hanushek, 1989, 1997, 1998, 2003; Burtless, 1996). On the other hand, an analysis by Card and Krueger found that there was a strong relationship between the rate of returns to schooling (i.e. wages) and average quality of schools in the individuals' home states (Card and Krueger, 1992, 1998). Bizarrely, this relationship is found strongly at the state level, but appears largely to vanish when examined at the school level. In other words, *states* that have better-resourced schools – smaller classes, higher teacher salaries etc. – perform better, but individual *schools* with better resources don't seem to do much better (Betts, 1995; Burtless, 1996).

Is it possible that state-level social capital is the missing link in this puzzle? For example, it could be that states with high social capital tend to achieve better educational outcomes (see above) *and* higher lifetime earnings (see chapter 2), while at the same time tending to have more social orientations and therefore investing more in public services. As noted elsewhere, higher public investment and a willingness to pay taxes may be one of the routes through which social capital impacts on socially desirable outcomes at the meso- and macro-levels (see, for example, Kawachi and Kennedy, 1999, in relation to health outcomes; see also chapter 6). However, it is worth noting that the same association has been found within the UK, where, as noted above, educational expenditure is largely determined by central government. In other words, high social capital regions within the UK don't receive any more money for their schools, yet still achieve higher results.

National differences

Can national differences in educational attainment also be explained by differences in social capital? It is slightly surprising that the authors of the OECD report on the role of human and social capital did not attempt to model this relationship, especially as the OECD gathers the relevant data on cross-national differences in educational performance (OECD, 2001a).

National differences in educational achievement are substantial. For example, the proportion of the adult population at the top two levels of prose literacy varies from less than 20 per cent in Chile to over 70 per cent in Sweden (OECD, 2001, p. 21). By inspection, national wealth cannot explain much of the pattern – the USA, for example, tends to hover a little below average despite its great wealth. If we look at the top three educational performers, time and again they are some combination of the Scandinavian countries: Sweden, Norway, Finland

and Denmark. A glance at the graph of national differences in social trust confirms the suspicion – these are also consistently among the highest-trust nations (see figure 2.1 and chapter 2). If we look at the industrialized nations with the lowest educational achievements, these tend to be South American and the former Soviet Union nations – the nations with the lowest levels of social trust. Clustered in the middle are North America and the Western European nations, just as they are for social trust.

We checked this relationship by calculating the correlation between national literacy levels and levels of social trust.[8] The correlation was a remarkable .82 (N = 18, p < .001). This is an exceptionally strong relationship, though very similar to that found across US states. But literacy rates do also significantly correlate with national wealth. Statistically controlling for GDP per capita reduced the strength of the association between literacy and social trust, but its partial correlation remained strong and significant at .63 (p < .01). On the other hand, controlling for social trust entirely eliminated the effect of GDP per capita, confirming that social trust was the dominant variable in explaining national educational attainment, not wealth.

Once again, the problem of interpreting causal direction arises. Do the Scandinavians have such outstanding educational achievements as a result of their high social capital, or do they trust each other more as a result of their universally high levels of education or equity more generally? This is an issue that we cannot resolve now. Indeed, we may not be able to do so for some time due to a lack of suitable time-series data to pick apart the causality. However, given the strength of the data at the micro- and meso-levels, a causal link from social capital to education must at least be a strong possibility.

Education as creator of social capital

In later chapters, we shall return in some detail to the question of how social capital may be created, sustained or destroyed (chapters 8 and 9). However, it is arguable that education has a particularly important role in this process. It is not just that social capital may foster educational achievement, but also that education may play a central role in the creation of social capital.

At the individual level, educational achievement is consistently found to predict social capital. Individuals with higher educational attainment have greater civic and voluntary engagement, larger and more diverse social networks, and higher trust in others. This relationship has been found across nations and measures. For example, in the USA, attendance at public meetings is over six times higher among the college educated than among those who only attended elementary school (18 per cent versus 3 per cent; Putnam, 2000, p. 46). Similar results have been found in Australia (F. E. Baum et al., 2000), Britain (Hall, 1997, 1999) and many other nations, with sharp increases in social and civic activities for each extra year of education.

Analyses of longitudinal data have confirmed that education seems to boost social capital, though it also suggests that the absolute size of this effect is probably exaggerated by cross-sectional analyses. For example, analysis of the British National Child Development Cohort has shown that going to university is associated with a particularly strong boost in social capital, in terms of both social trust and community engagement, even having controlled for a host of other variables (Bynner and Egerton, 2001). However, another analysis of the British Household Panel Survey has suggested that the social and civic engagement of young people who would go on to enter higher education was already higher in their late teens than of their peers who did not go on to enter university (Egerton, 2002a). The higher civic engagement of these children partly reflected patterns of family socialization and having parents in professional occupations (see also chapter 8). Nonetheless, even having controlled for this prior level of engagement and family background, the experience of higher education still provided a modest further boost to civic engagement, for both young and mature students.

Research is ongoing to identify what exactly it is that explains the relationship, but to date, no definitive explanation has been offered. The most immediate and obvious possibility is that young people who get to spend long periods of time growing up in the same institution build strong bonds with one another and the social skills to get along. Young people actively engage in experiences that enable them to develop social and co-operative skills, and educational environments as well as extra-curricular, peer- and community-based activities provide an opportunity to have these experiences (Dworkin, Larson and Hansen, 2003). Similarly, it is known that schools' policies have a big impact on student participation in extra-curricular activities, and these in turn have a big impact on young people's social networks and skills (McNeal, 1999; Langbein and Bess, 2002). When students leave school or university, these networks and skills prove to be a resilient and transferable form of social capital.

Another possible explanation, at least for certain forms of civic action, is that the general skills acquired through education, such as reading, writing and understanding complex civic institutions, help individuals to engage. A more cognitive slant on the same explanation is that education gives people the mental skills to foresee the consequences of their actions and to develop a more complex sense of enlightened self-interest. Well-educated people realize that it is in their own best interest, not to mention that of society, to engage with others in a constructive and trustworthy manner. A sociological explanation of the same effect might be that public education instils common norms that increase social cohesion and establish a common set of understandings that help people co-operate with one another (Gradstein and Justman, 2001).

One can even argue that the similarity of education, not only within nations but between them, is bringing with it new global norms and with them increasingly global forms of social capital. To take a specific example, the graduates who come from across the world to take western MBAs take back to their source countries shared understandings that facilitate international business (Mellahi, 2000; see also chapter 7). However, one puzzle is why social capital appears to be declining in some countries that have over the same period shown major expansions in education (see chapter 7).

An alternative causal account is also possible. It may be that those with better cognitive skills and lower discount rates – being prepared to forgo an immediate reward in favour of a larger, later one – invest in both their social and human capital because they can see the rationality of doing so. Hence, the link between educational attainment and social capital might be spurious, being explained by underlying differences in cognitive style. However, this doesn't seem a very plausible explanation of national or state differences.

Many of these hypotheses are currently being tested in a longitudinal study (Halpern, John and Morris, 2002). But most governments and societies are not waiting around for social scientists to tell them what they already suspect. Most people already believe that education plays a role in shaping the way young people behave, and can therefore play an important role in shaping the society of tomorrow. Virtually all industrialized nations now have some form of 'citizenship education', typically consisting of a combination of formal teaching about the structures of society together with some kind of practical or voluntary experience (Torney-Purta et al., 2001).

The evidence from both sides of the Atlantic is that the formal teaching of citizenship works a little, but not much (Niemi and Junn, 1998; Halpern, John and Morris, 2002). Teaching children facts and figures may drag up their knowledge slightly, but by itself it appears to do little to increase participation, feelings of efficacy or trust. The evidence on volunteering is rather more positive. Even when volunteering doesn't appear very voluntary, as it is done for course credit, something of the spirit of engagement seems to rub off (E. S. Smith, 1999). Indeed, longitudinal evidence indicates that this effect strengthens over time such that community service in school continues to boost social participation, volunteering and tolerance ten and even twenty years later in life (Janoski, Musick and Wilson, 1998).

At present, there is considerable interest in a hybrid form of civic education called 'service learning', at least within the USA (Sander and Putnam, 1999; CIRCLE, 2003; Drogosz, Litan and Dionne, 2003). This involves getting practical volunteering experience at the same time as closely related issues are taught and discussed in the classroom context. Hence children might take part in a community clean-up while at the same time having classes on the economics of recycling and taking part in discussions about the effects of global warming. The early indications are that service learning works well, fostering skills of participation and understanding, and encouraging a higher level of social engagement.

Nonetheless, the question remains as to how large the gains are from civic education *per se* as opposed to education in general. As Sen has famously noted in the health domain, education has been found to improve health more than *health education* improves health! The provisional evidence is that civic education does increase social capital more than education *per se*, and while these effects may appear modest among teenagers, they appear to strengthen through adult life.

The essence of the argument is simple. The values and behaviours that characterize a society do not come out of thin air, but are actively fashioned anew in each generation. Families, schools and the wider society socialize young people into citizens. In a modern society, whether we like it or not, education plays a big role in this process.

Summary and conclusion

The evidence suggests that social capital at the micro-, meso- and macro-levels has a significant impact on educational outcomes (see figure 5.2).

At the micro-level, higher levels of child–parent contact generally lead to higher educational aspirations and attainments, but it is the quality, not just quantity, of time spent that counts. A child's early interactions with attentive, responsive and consistent primary caregivers are critical to his or her mastering the basic social and cognitive skills

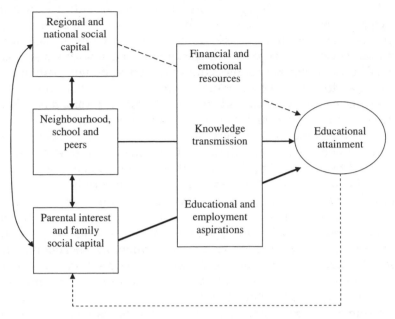

Figure 5.2 *The relationship between social capital and educational attainment*
Note: Strength of lines roughly indicates strength of direct relationship.

on which later learning is based. Parents' social capital – the support they receive from the rest of the family, their friendship networks and their relationship with the child's school – can also positively affect the child's educational outcome. These wider links appear to be particularly important in enabling high-ability children to reach their full potential. Differences in family social capital help to explain differences in educational achievements across family types, such as the lower attainment of children from single-parent and step-parent families; across social class; and across ethnic groups. Higher geographical mobility, and the disruption it causes to social networks, in turn helps to explain why single parents and other non-traditional families have more impoverished social capital.

At the meso-level, both school and community effects are found. Some school types, notably small and Catholic schools in the USA, appear to perform significantly better. Stronger parent–school relationships and parent–parent relationships appear to help explain the effect. The positive direction of the effect is conditional on the community's own outward-looking orientation and high aspirations. There is some evidence that social capital within the school – that is, teacher–teacher relationships – may also be important in explaining differences between schools. But many so-called school effects are really community effects. High concentrations of low social capital families in an area amplify disadvantage. The low average social capital of the community adds to the child's educational disadvantage, creating a 'double jeopardy' effect.

The macro-level reveals evidence of a startlingly strong relationship between social capital and educational attainment. Across US states, UK local authorities and nations, measures of social capital are highly correlated with educational attainment, and these relationships are not explained by statistical controls for other variables such as wealth.

Finally, we have seen that there is a strong relationship between past educational attainment, normally measured as years in education, and social capital. In other words, education appears to create social capital, as well as social capital helping to foster educational attainment. Many governments are active in seeking to strengthen this socializing effect through citizenship education and volunteering programmes, though it may be that education and the social experience of life at school and university itself explains much of the link.

In sum, social capital appears to have a very large impact on educational attainment. A key mediating variable across levels is educational aspiration. Social networks and high expectations can stretch, encourage and inspire a child; though equally, the anti-educational norms of some communities and peer groups can do the reverse. On the face of it, the impact of social capital on educational attainment dwarfs that of the factors that governments and educational professionals normally argue about, such as financial resources, class sizes and teacher salaries.

Finally, this chapter has emphasized the role that social capital plays in traditional educational attainment. As such, it has emphasized social capital within the school and home, the traditional learning contexts. However, we should recognize that much, and perhaps most, learning occurs outside these contexts. Much of what we know is tacit knowledge, and it is picked up in the workplace, from friends, and from everyday encounters. For example, medical staff don't just learn how to make people better from a textbook, but from a lifetime of informal learning that draws heavily on the experiences and shared knowledge of peers and elders (Gopee, 2002).

In this sense, the role that social capital plays in learning is far greater than the role it plays in education *per se*. As covered in earlier chapters, knowledge and knowledge transfer are the life-blood of the modern economy (chapter 2), health behaviours are learned primarily from our peers (chapter 3), and even the skills associated with crime must be acquired somewhere (chapter 4). In so far as social capital lowers the barriers to the transmission of knowledge in any setting, it boosts learning, and such learning should not be viewed through the lens of the school alone.

Further reading

For more on the importance of *early relationships* for child development, including academic attainment, try a good developmental textbook such as Shaffer (1994). A good recent general review specifically on the impact of parents on their children's educational attainment is Desforges and Abouchaar (2003).

There are a number of good academic papers examining the impact of social capital on *educational attainment*, such as Teachman, Paasch and Carver (1996) and Y. Sun (1999). There is also some interesting material and views on the relationship between education and social capital in the edited volume by S. Baron, Field and Schuller (2000).

For more information on cross-national differences in *citizenship education*, and how much children actually know, look to the papers being produced about the recent cross-national study, such as Torney-Purta et al. (2001). For a short, practical view dotted with examples of what schools can actually do to build social capital, try Sander and Putnam (1999). Another recent, though slightly partial, report is the fifty co-author CIRCLE (2003).

In terms of the role of social capital in *learning* more generally, a good start would be to look at the literature on firms and economic productivity. If you skipped chapter 2, it may be worth looking at it through this 'learning lens', and at the readings mentioned there too.

6

Government and the Effective State

Although many people now most closely associate Putnam with his work documenting the decline in social capital in the USA (Putnam, 2000), his interest in the topic was actually sparked by a relatively 'obscure' study of the effectiveness of regional governance in Italy (Putnam, 1993).

The core finding of Putnam's now classic study of regional differences in Italy was that regions with the most vibrant community life also had the most effective and trusted governments (Putnam, 1993). The constitutional arrangements for the regional governments were essentially the same, all having been created at the same time, and the regional governments remained highly constrained by a framework imposed by the central government. On the basis of a detailed empirical analysis, Putnam concluded that the differences in government effectiveness arose from the character of the associational life of the regions. The regional differences in patterns of trust (between non-family) and associational life were found to have been long-standing, and long preceded the development of Italy's regional government. The causal direction appeared clear – strong associational life and high levels of public trust led to more effective government.

This chapter looks at how far the evidence since Putnam's earlier study supports or contradicts the theory that the roots of government efficacy lie in its citizen's social capital, and what causal pathways might explain this relationship.

A distinction that may be useful in this chapter is that between primary, secondary and tertiary or 'abstract' democracy (Newton, 1997). Primary democracy refers to a group of people who mostly know each other, such as in a small community, all getting together to decide things themselves. Secondary democracy refers to political systems built on the principle of representation. It involves a division of labour – trusting someone else to vote for an issue on your behalf. Tertiary or abstract democracy refers to the way very large or 'imagined' communities organize themselves. These distinctions echo, in a governance context, the micro-, meso- and macro-levels – the difference between the way small collectives are governed and the way nation states and even larger units are governed.

Local and sub-local government: the micro-level

A group of people that cannot get on with one another will find it more difficult to organize and succeed than a group that does get on. Team sports and 'reality game shows' provide us with endless working examples. Such events and shows typically present competing teams with complex tasks that require co-operation between team members for success. Teams that fail to achieve a high level of internal co-operation, because of, say, a clash of powerful personalities, tend to lose, however able the individual team members.

Real world micro-case studies tell much the same story. For example, following the closure of military bases there are often a number of options for what happens to the land released. A case study by Burton and Williams contrasted the fate of the land from two airforce bases that were closed in the USA, both roughly equal in size and natural resource attributes. At one base, all the significant wildlife habitat was destroyed by real estate development, but at the other, nearly a fourth of the land was preserved as a wildlife refuge. The authors concluded that the most significant factor accounting for the radically different outcomes was not the strength of any objective case, but the social capital and political culture of the communities surrounding the bases, enabling one community to lobby and act much more effectively than the other (Burton and Williams, 2001).

Similarly, the effectiveness of work-based teams rests heavily on their ability to organize themselves – or 'self-govern' – which in turn rests on their internal cohesiveness. For example, a study of the relative performance of nursing teams in four midwestern metropolitan hospitals in the USA found that social integration and co-operation within teams was associated with significantly higher performance effectiveness (Barsness, 1997). Many of the examples presented in chapter 2 in relation to economic performance can also be seen as micro-examples of the importance of social capital to governance. It is difficult for a firm to be successful, or the management team within the firm to be effective, if the employees refuse to co-operate with one another.

An elegant micro-example of the importance of social capital for governance can be seen in the management of housing developments. As anyone knows who has had to deal with a condo or tenants' association, this can be nightmarishly complex if some of the residents don't get along. Put in more positive terms, if the tenants have ongoing positive social relationships with one another, the administration of the building is easy. This, essentially, was the key finding of a study evaluating the success of programmes in New York City in maintaining and revitalizing landlord-abandoned buildings – buildings taken back in lieu of taxes and handed over to the tenants to run themselves (Saegert and Winkel, 1998). Where the programmes were found to be successful, the authors concluded that 'the positive effects of tenant ownership were largely mediated by the higher levels of social capital found in these buildings' (p. 17).

Sometimes groups find it difficult to organize themselves at the micro-level because of clashes of personality or other personal differences, or sometimes simply because they do not know each other well. The physical environment, in as much as it shapes the patterns of social interaction, can have a big impact on whether, and in what form, a group organizes itself (see chapter 8). Essentially, physical spaces that make it easy for people to interact, but that do not force them to do so, help to create social capital that can then facilitate self-governance.

These processes are of interest in relation to the formation of social capital more generally, but also have a bearing on group formation and the conduct of politics in the more conventional spheres. It has been found that people who live in large apartment buildings, though more likely to know their immediate neighbours, are less involved in local politics than those who live in more traditional housing (Glaeser and Sacerdote, 2000). It would seem that the residents of large apartment blocks, while more connected to their own internal community, are less connected to the neighbourhood and public infrastructure around them. This disconnection also helps to explain the higher crime rate found in the space around such buildings (see also chapter 4).

The governance of an apartment block – raising revenue for the repair of the roof and the overhauling of the heating – is a simple affair compared with the running of even a small town. But similar lessons seem to apply. Small towns characterized by high social capital appear to have more effective local governments than those characterized by low social capital. A longitudinal study of rural American communities found that horizontal linkages of community leaders – their links with other important community figures – is particularly important for their communities' long-term viability (D. J. O'Brien, Raedeke and Hassinger, 1998).

The high social capital that facilitates coordination and effective political action by a small community is not without downsides. High social capital as manifested in high-trust, frequent meetings and freely flowing information among dense social networks can mean that the whole community is involved in decision-making, but it can also make the process time-consuming and extended. For example, a study of communities affected by the 1997 Red River Flood in Canada found that those with higher levels of social, as well as physical and human, capital were better prepared and more effective responders to the flood. But such higher levels of social capital also made decision-making more complex and brought with them the risk of delays (Buckland and Rahman, 1999). This is a major downside of primary democracy. Against this, it does seem that this involvement is generally experienced as positive. A study of life satisfaction across the cantons of Switzerland, arguably the world's largest direct or primary democracy, found that life satisfaction was significantly higher in those that held the largest numbers of referenda (Frey and Sutzer, 2000).

As we have often noted in earlier chapters, having a balance of different forms of social capital is important, and the same is true for successful micro-governance. Socially isolated communities often have high bonding social capital within them, yet may lack bridging social capital links to other communities. For example, small American rural communities located outside the commuter's reach of urban and suburban centres are typically rich in local organizations and democratic participation. But their isolation and disconnection from wider social and political networks leave them vulnerable to cuts in federal government budgets and being viewed as cheap labour by the corporate sector (Zacharakis-Jutz, 2001). Ironically, the strong ties that rural residents feel to family, farm and community and that make it difficult for them to move may sometimes put the community at a disadvantage in terms of the wider political context. Studies have found that small town councils are most effective when their leadership has well-developed social and political networks *outside* of the immediate community – in other words, bridging social capital. Similarly, a study of sixty-nine Indian village communities found that pre-existing social capital strongly influenced the level of active political participation. But the impact of this social capital was magnified when capable agents were present who could help individuals and communities connect with public decision-making processes – in other words, linking social capital (Krishna, 2002). For effective governance, as for many other outcomes, it seems that having a balance of different types of social capital is important.

Regional government: the meso-level

As mentioned at the start of the chapter, Putnam's early study of Italy that prompted his interest in social capital focused on regional governance (Putnam, 1993). He concluded that the substantial differences in the effectiveness of Italy's twenty regions were rooted in differences in the regions' social capital. Institutional performance was measured by a range of elements, including the timeliness of budgets, legislative innovation and bureaucratic responsiveness. Citizen satisfaction with the regional government was also measured, and correlated highly with the institutional performance measures. The vibrant and rich associations of the north seemed somehow to form a fertile soil in which effective government action could grow. The strong families and hierarchical structures of the south, including the strong Catholic church, appeared to be a much less fertile soil. The study suggested that the culture of trust, friendship and mutual respect between non-kin was important to government efficacy.

Putnam's work on Italy was truly a landmark study in our understanding of governance, social capital, and society more generally. However, in the reviews and discussions of Putnam's study that have emerged since, while many have found his evidence on the association between social capital and the effectiveness of government generally compelling, three key criticisms have been made against his interpretation of this association. First, there has been extensive discussion of the causal direction of the relationship between social capital and the effectiveness of government. Second, even if one accepts that at least some of the causality runs from social capital to government effectiveness, it can be argued that Putnam does not really explain how this linkage arises. Third, there are questions about the wider generality of the conclusions.

The first and second criticisms are taken up in a more general context at the end of this chapter, as they raise questions that apply not only to Putnam's description of the Italian case, but to the government–social capital relationship more widely. But on the specifics of the causal direction in the Italian case, an important supplementary analysis merits examination here. Helliwell and Putnam

(1995) built a time-series model seeking to relate the relative performance of the regions over time, and particularly in relation to economic
growth (see also chapter 2). They found strong evidence of pre-reform
catch-up effects – the poorer regions gradually catching up on the
economies of the richer regions – as found in cross-national econometric work on economic growth. But regional reforms appeared to
'disrupt' this closing of the gap, as the higher social capital regions of
the north surged ahead once again. This result suggests that the refor-
mation and strengthening of regional governance, though on the
surface the same across regions, were somehow used to much greater
positive effect in the high social capital north than in the south. This
careful longitudinal analysis leaves us significantly more confident that
the causal direction runs, at least partly, from the social capital of the
region – interacting with the reforms – to the effectiveness of the government, rather than the other way around.

Evidence beyond the Italian case

In terms of the third criticism – the extent to which the Italian case can
be generalized to other regional governments – there is now a whole
generation of researchers seeking to test Putnam's hypothesis in other
parts of the world. It should be said that none of these studies has yet
gathered the level of detailed data for other regions that Putnam did
for Italy. It is also worth noting that in those countries that have sought
to introduce regional governance since, this has often been done in a
regionally uneven manner, such as in Spain or Britain. Interestingly,
this unevenness generally reflects regional differences in identification
with the region – itself a potentially important form or indicator of
social capital. Hence in Britain, Scotland now has a parliament capable
of introducing primary legislation, Wales has a parliament that can
only modify the interpretation of legislation from Westminster, and
other regions, with the exception of London, merely have unelected
regional authorities with very limited powers.

Nonetheless, studies conducted in other countries have suggested
that the Italian case is not unique. Germany is a nation that has varied
and complex forms of regional and local government. Citizen surveys
show wide regional differences in satisfaction with local government
performance, ranging from around 30 per cent to nearly 70 per cent. In
a study of thirty small to medium-size municipalities in East and West
Germany, Cusack sought to explain this variation (Cusack, 1999). He
found that both institutional and social capital variables were important. In general, municipalities with greater institutional centralization
of power appeared to be more effective and were associated with

higher citizen satisfaction. He interpreted this as being the result of the smaller number of veto players in more centralized governments (such as with a powerful mayor), meaning that the government could act more decisively. But Cusack also found that the social characteristics of the area powerfully affected citizen ratings of local government performance. Smaller municipalities, by population size, had significantly higher performance ratings, with satisfaction levels falling by 1 per cent for every extra 10,000 residents. Areas where the leaders reported less conflict within the community were also associated with higher citizen ratings of government performance. Finally, higher levels of social trust, as reported by community leaders, were associated with higher citizen ratings of government performance. The model indicated that moving from a low- to a high-trust region was associated with a 13.5 per cent increase in satisfaction with local government performance.

Cusack's study is a useful replication in the German context of Putnam's study of Italy, albeit with rather more rudimentary measures. It also reassuringly indicates that both social capital *and* institutional structures matter for government performance, or at least citizen perceptions of such, suggesting that reform-oriented policymakers are not wasting their time.

Concerning the USA, while this was not a major theme in *Bowling Alone*, Putnam did review evidence indicating a relationship between government effectiveness and social capital. He noted a close parallel between Daniel Elazar's maps of American political cultures and his own maps of social capital – indeed the correlation between the two indexes was very strong ($r = .77$; Putnam, 2000, ch. 21, n. 48). The southern states, which are low in social capital, are described by Elazar as 'traditionalistic' and are dominated by elites resistant to innovation. In contrast, the high social capital midwest and northeast are described by Elazar as 'moralistic', and are characterized by issue-based campaigning, social and policy innovation, less corruption, and merit-based as opposed to patronage-based systems of government appointments – very much echoing the story of the north–south divide of Italy.

The economist Steve Knack has also looked at evidence from the USA, using ratings constructed by the Government Performance Project as his measure of government effectiveness. Knack found that states with higher social capital as measured by social trust, volunteering and census response (the proportion of people cooperating with the national survey) had significantly better governmental performance (Knack, 2002). In contrast, activity in associations and informal socializing were unrelated to government performance. He concluded that it was aspects of social capital relating to 'generalized reciprocity' that appeared to be important to performance, rather than 'social connectedness' – echoing the conclusions of his earlier work on economic growth (see chapter 2).

Other studies have shown similar patterns. For example, a study of local minority self-government in Hungary, using data from leaders within the regions, found that localities with higher institutional capacity were characterized by higher levels of social cohesion; majority social networks with norms of trust and co-operation; and local government with effective institutional linkages with extra-local organizations (Schafft and Brown, 2000). Similarly, the relative success of development finance schemes in various parts of the world has been found to rest on the local or regional endowments of social capital (Tufarelli and Fagotto, 1999).

Evidence comparing the performance and social development of India's fifteen largest states also provides some support for the role of social capital in facilitating development (Rossel, 2002). In the Indian case, institutional factors and a particular form of class mobilization have been argued to play an important role as well. Following Patrick Heller's influential study of the Indian state of Kerala, it has been argued that the successful formula for Indian development is a reconciliation of redistribution and economic growth, and labour movements tempering their militancy in exchange for progressive policies from the regional state (Heller, 1995, 1996). This blends a social capital account with a more traditional corporatist model of development.

Research contrasting that of the Russian regions appears to be telling a similar story. In particular, that of the Novgorod region has attracted attention. This region is characterized by high associational activity, high trust in government and, now, strong economic growth (Petro, 2001). The success of the 'Novgorod Model' again raises the important question of whether social capital led to more effective government or whether the policies of the regional government have created social capital, perhaps stimulating a virtuous circle of civic trust and growth (see also chapter 2). The author concludes that a virtuous circle has been created, and that 'even in the absence of a national consensus, local governments can do much to establish common social values and priorities for their communities' (p. 229).

National government: the macro-level

Studies of national differences in the performance of governments strongly echo the findings of Putnam and others at the regional level. La Porta et al. (1997), using data from the 1990 World Values Survey and controlling for GDP per capita, found that high social trust (trust between strangers) was strongly associated with:

- lower rates of government corruption at the national level, as measured by officials demanding bribes in connection with import and export licences, exchange controls, tax assessment, policy protection or loans;
- higher bureaucratic quality as measured by strength and expertise to govern, with autonomy from political pressure and without drastic changes in policy or government services;
- higher tax compliance;
- infrastructure quality; and
- higher efficiency and integrity of the legal environment.

La Porta et al.'s ratings of corruption and bureaucratic quality came from independently compiled data from the International Country Risk Guide, the Global Competitiveness Report, and the Business International Corporation (La Porta et al., 1997).

Additionally, La Porta et al. also found evidence to support the specific hypothesis of Putnam that it is horizontal rather than vertical forms of social association that lead to social trust. For each nation, they calculated the proportion of the population that belonged to a hierarchical religion (Catholic, Eastern Orthodox or Muslim). They found that the association between this proportion and social trust was high and statistically significant ($r = -.61$). The proportion of the population belonging to a hierarchical religion was strongly associated with greater corruption and lower government efficiency even having controlled for GDP per capita.

The La Porta et al. research is impressive, but it is again a cross-sectional study and the direction of causality is therefore ambiguous. Is it that high social capital, manifest through social trust, leads to more effective and trustworthy government? Or is it that corrupt and ineffective governments tend to undermine social capital more generally?

In a closely related cross-national study by Treisman, lower corruption at a national level was found to be associated with Protestant traditions, histories of British rule, more developed economies, and (probably) higher imports. Federal states were found to be generally more corrupt. Long exposure to democracy was also associated with lower corruption (Treisman, 2000). These results fit the view that historical events, such as the character of the interventions from external powers, can have lasting effects on a nation's social and political institutions generations later. But they may also be interpreted to suggest that the institutions themselves matter, such as the existence of democracy, and that these affect the character of the nation's social capital.

Evidence from the Former Soviet Union states

A string of studies examining the former Soviet states of central and eastern Europe have converged on the conclusion that the states' prior social capital is an important factor in their governments' post-transition performance. This transition is loosely comparable to the Italian case but at a national level. At approximately the same time, the citizens of these nations found themselves with new government structures and, like the Italian regions, the results were strikingly variable. One key study used the third annual New Democracies Barometer to compare the trajectories of eight former communist nations and to examine the hypothesis that support for the new democratic procedures would depend on the relative economic success of the nations post-transition (Kunioka and Woller, 1999). While some support was found for this hypothesis, the authors concluded that social capital was a more important factor in explaining citizen support for democratic procedures than were economic variables in these nations.

This result ties in closely with more detailed studies of individual post-Soviet nations. For example, one study compared the attitudes and behaviours of respondents living in Romania and the USA (in Indiana). It was found that the Romanians, compared with the Americans, discussed politics less, engaged in interactive forms of political participation at lower rates, knew less about their neighbours, and failed to link the interests of people in their community to broader political judgements (Mondak and Gearing, 1998). The authors saw this pattern of Romanian social and political disengagement as rooted in the numerous social and political constraints that limited civic engagement throughout central and eastern Europe during the Soviet era. They expressed grave concerns about the prospects for full democratization in a context such as Romania within which prior social interaction does not flourish.

In contrast, a detailed analysis of the situation in the Czech Republic was more positive about the prospects for the future precisely because of the underlying strength of the social fabric of Czech society (Blomberg, Maier and Yeisley, 1998). There was a rise of grey- and black-market activities in the period before the transition to a market economy in the Czech Republic, and these activities were linked to abuses of social capital – that is, corruption – at the highest levels of government. But Blomberg et al. remained upbeat about the prospects for the future because survey data showed low unemployment and

---

Box 6.1   What about 'political trust'?

Governments that are effective and competent are more likely to be trusted, but the relationship is far from perfect. Similarly, the relationship between social trust and political trust is modest. But political trust does matter. If we don't trust our government or political leaders, then we won't believe the advice they give us, we won't support their plans, and we'll kick them out of office, even if they do an objectively good job. Furthermore, if social trust – the trust between citizens – is low or falling, political trust matters even more, because we will need to rely even more on our formal political institutions to ensure that we all get along together (see chapter 7 for trends in social trust). The key factors for political trust seem to be:

- **Honesty and public-mindedness.** Politicians need to be open and honest, and the public are very sensitive to motives too. Institutionally, the same applies. For example, information and advice need to come from sources that are rigorously impartial and independent. Party finance arrangements often undermine this sense of honesty.
- **Competence.** If government or politicians are not seen as competent to deliver on their promises, then public support soon evaporates, though the relationship between objective delivery and trust is often modest. Rapid learning from mistakes is also critical. Public support for redistributive processes appears to be particularly sensitive to the perception that government will spend the money competently.
- **Institutional checks and balances.** Governments and parliaments tend to be trusted significantly more than politicians or government ministers (for example, in the UK the figures are 18 per cent against around 36 per cent). The institutional wrapping of checks and balances is important even for the most honest politician, but is absolutely vital in systems within which politicians are highly distrusted (e.g. Japan).
- **Respect for, and communication with, the public.** Even a government that is honest, competent and institutionally constrained can be viewed with suspicion and distrust if it fails to take the public with it. Providing information and 'treating people well' are consistent correlates of trusted public and private services (MORI, 2003). In general, services and professionals that deal with the public directly, such as doctors and schools, do better than politicians, who instead have to rely on indirect methods of communication and the media. Interestingly,

in hierarchical societies, those 'at the bottom of the pile' and whose self-esteem is already threatened are often the most likely to punish a government that fails to show that it is listening to and respecting them.

Political trust has fallen in many, but not all countries, suggesting that this is not inevitable. Denmark, the Netherlands and Norway seem to have bucked the trend (Dalton, 1998). Trust and interest in political parties have fallen particularly strongly and widely, but trust in many of the services provided by government has often remained strong – normally because they comply with the above.

stable trust in societal institutions, both indicative of a 'low anomic' transition. In short, it appeared that strong underlying social capital, despite some abuses by senior figures under the previous regime, provided a powerful platform for the new political and economic arrangements to build on.

As Kraft (1999) concludes, pre-existing institutional structures, social capital and the development of civil society have strongly affected the transition outcomes of the former Soviet nations. The experience has shown that it can be quite difficult to transplant effective democratic institutions to previously communist nations, but also that there are great dangers in failing to establish such institutions, especially in relation to controlling corruption and the unofficial economy. Where these effective institutions have not been established, vicious cycles are now apparent of growing political intervention, high tax rates, increasing unofficial economies and corruption, and further political intervention (Kraft, 1999).

Transnational governance

There is good reason to think that, in just the way that national-level social capital can facilitate the effectiveness of national governments, so too can transnational social capital facilitate transnational governance.

A study of Asia-Pacific sub-regionalism found that transnational ethnic social networks, based on ancestral and kinship ties, were of critical importance in 'glueing' citizens together on opposite sides of national borders (X. Chen, 2000). This social capital lubricated economic transactions across borders and induced more responsive and efficient policy initiatives and implementation across the sub-region. Chen raises the question of whether this cross-border social capital is actually a necessary condition for successful transnational sub-regionalism.

This is an issue that European politicians have become very familiar with as they struggle to match the rhetoric and logic of European Union with the resistance of popular opinion. Increasingly EU politicians have come to recognize that it is difficult to advance a political project of unification in advance of a fragmented base of social capital. Changing the character of this fragmented base, or building cross-national bridging social capital, is a slow process. The EU has funded extensive exchange programmes for many years for young people to spend time in other EU nations, and has funded networks to connect related academic and professional communities across the EU. These programmes are aimed at building up a fabric of personal relationships, shared languages and understandings – transnational bridging social capital, in short.

This build-up of transnational social capital is not limited to the EU. The advance of telecommunications, international mass media and lower-cost travel have made the world a psychologically smaller place. At the same time as capital and corporations have become international, so too have networks of activists in protest and social movements (Sklair, 1995). This growing connectivity is manifest in changing social attitudes as well as greater knowledge of distant nations. At the same time as the general publics of many affluent nations have become more resistant to supporting the unemployed within their own backyard, they have become significantly more willing to see their taxes used to support the poorer nations of the world (Halpern, 1995b). Similarly, tolerance for ethnic minorities within nations has increased sharply over recent decades.[1]

These changing attitudes have been reflected in changing institutional policies, practices and capabilities (Held and McGrew, 2000). After decades of inaction, wealthy nations are now helping their poorer neighbours through the cancelling of debts and the scaling up of aid programmes. Shared bills of rights, notably the Human Rights Convention, are being progressively incorporated into national laws. International courts of law have moved out of the textbook and into reality. Global bodies, such as the UN, have falteringly become real forums to coordinate supranational action and restrain rogue states. The nations of the EU have joined together to share a common currency and central bank. And, despite the cynicism of many, the scale and boldness of interventions by the international community to act in humanitarian disasters and violations of human rights across the world appear to be growing year by year.

One might attribute a part of this growing shared understanding and preparedness to act to the presence of extended kinship and ethnic networks across nations, as economic migration twinned with better communications has directly, and literally, related the citizens of distant nations to one another. Growing volumes of trade and economic interdependence are another powerful contributory factor. But important too – perhaps most important – is surely the gradually emerging, albeit sometimes faltering, shared normative framework that underpins this trade and the strengthening international institutions that surround us – the building of transnational normative social capital. This includes, but is by no means limited to, the networks of international leaders who now meet regularly and often know each other as part of a shared club. To paraphrase Clinton, the things that make us the same appear to be becoming more important than the things that make us different.[2]

Why is social capital associated with better government performance?

The nature of the causal pathway connecting social capital and government performance is taken up in some detail in a thoughtful review of Putnam's work by Boix and Posner (1995, 1998). They offer four possible causal pathways between associational life, social trust and more effective government. They suggest that social capital might:

- make citizens 'sophisticated consumers of politics' and offer channels through which their demands can be articulated;
- make bureaucrats better at co-operating with one another – in other words, bureaucrats would carry the same facilitating skills as other citizens in a high-associational, high-trust society;
- foster 'virtue among the citizenry' – in other words, shift tastes from the particularistic to the community-oriented, leading to citizens who are more law-abiding and therefore generally facilitating the implementation of policy; and
- make 'consociational democracy possible'.

Boix and Posner do not offer a view as to which of these channels may be most important. Rather they present them in the spirit of needing

further investigation, and as a way of plausibly plugging the explanatory gap. What these pathways have in common, with the possible
exception of the first, is that high-trust cultures facilitate co-operation.
Trust and shared norms make a whole range of new political solutions
possible.

J. L. Sullivan and Transue (1999) argue, from a social psychological
viewpoint, that effective democracies rest on two key foundations in
the attitudes and behaviours of citizens. First, democracies need citizens to be tolerant of others' efforts to participate in politics. This in
turn is influenced by commitment to democratic values, personality,
and the degree to which people view others as threatening. Second,
democracies need citizen participation. This is influenced by trust and
other features of culture that promote involvement in politics (J. L. Sullivan and Transue, 1999). Similarly, other researchers, using World
Values Survey data, have argued that social trust and other related
social psychological characteristics foster democratic government as
well as economic growth (Inkeles, 2000).

In Putnam's 1993 argument, egalitarian associational life is important because it provides a forum within which individuals learn the
skills and norms of co-operative endeavour and social trust. Hence
when people come together to make music, play sports or build model
railways, they discover how, by working together, they can collectively
achieve satisfactions that they cannot as individuals. They learn that if
they or someone else do not turn up, then this lets down the group.
They build up emotional and social bonds with one another; they
learn to trust each other; and more fundamentally, they become
trustworthy themselves. This social capital can then be used as a
resource to solve political problems, such as when the church
becomes an important force for political change and mobilization. This
account is roughly equivalent to Boix and Posner's first and last pathways. Individuals carry these traits and habits that make them trustworthy, and trusting, into other walks of life as responsible citizens
(obeying the law and paying taxes) and, for some, as policymakers
(cooperating in a constructive manner with political friends and oppo-
nents, and refraining from taking advantage of their political power
through corruption) – roughly equivalent to Boix and Posner's second
and third pathways.

There is now considerable evidence for at least the first and third
pathways proposed by Boix and Posner. On the first – the extent to
which social capital makes citizens more effective 'consumers' of
politics – various studies have shown how the existence of strong
community structures is associated with the passing of government
proposals that are more popular, and with higher support for govern-

ment itself (Berry, Portney and Thomson, 1993; Couto and Guthrie, 1999). Returning to the classic example of northern Italian cities, citizens' committees mobilize people to address local issues, though they are not necessarily continuously active. These committees have multiple channels of access to the institutions of local government, and government in turn perceives these committees as an important source of information (Della Porta and Andretta, 2002). It is also noteworthy that this is one of the causal channels flagged repeatedly by researchers looking at particular policy outcomes, such as how neighbourhood crime may be partly reduced through effective campaigns for better policing (Sampson, Raudenbush and Earls, 1997) or how population health may be improved through governments responding to pressures to invest in social goods (Kawachi and Kennedy, 1999).

There is also ample evidence that high social capital is associated with more 'virtuous citizenry'. For example, criminological work shows how some neighbourhoods hold down crime because residents take an interest in what is going on around them and intervene in the precursors of crime, and how prevalent social norms are strongly implicated in shaping or inhibiting crime (chapter 4). Another example is Putnam's documenting of the close relationship between tax paying in the USA and social capital – in high social capital states, tax compliance is significantly higher (Putnam, 2000). Indeed social capital variables are, to date, about the best known predictor of this very important variable. Similar results are found for co-operation with the US census and contributions to public broadcasting. As Putnam puts it: 'Democracy does not require that citizens be selfless saints, but in many modest ways it does assume that most of us much of the time will resist the temptation to cheat. Social capital, the evidence increasingly suggests, strengthens our better, more expansive selves' (Putnam, 2000, p. 349). And this virtue seems to be contagious. For example, it has been shown that the probability that an individual will vote is raised significantly if those around them are likely to vote, having controlled for all the usual factors associated with turnout (Knack and Kropf, 1998). The probability of voting is also correlated with the incidence of co-operative behaviours in other arenas, such as charitable giving or willingly serving on juries.

Evidence for Boix and Posner's second and fourth channels is more sparse, or at least has yet to connect to the social capital literature. La Porta et al.'s documentation of the relationship between corruption and social capital may be seen as offering some support for the proposition that social capital makes more co-operative and trustworthy bureaucrats. More work is needed to establish the relationship between co-operation between politicians and wider social capital. Since the level of co-operation between politicians and parties is also closely tied up with the nature of electoral and political systems, it may be difficult to test directly.

Some support for the importance of trust among policymakers might be gleaned from case studies where government practices were deliberately changed to rely more on formal contracts, and less on informal trust. In the case of New Zealand, a number of commentators have linked a dramatic shift to formal contracts to a deterioration in government performance, though this claim remains controversial (Gregory, 1999; Wallis and Dollery, 2001). Evidence might also be found from looking at the relative success of similar forms of government in different nations, such as proportionally elected assemblies, and testing whether the effectiveness of these governments varied with, and was mediated by, the co-operative skills and culture of the politicians. The paper by Cusack on Germany goes some way in this direction, as it shows that social trust among politicians is associated with citizen perceptions of better local government performance (Cusack, 1999). The Italian case is also suggestive of this channel being important, as is evidence from nations characterized by corporate politics such as Japan (Broadbent, 2000). But the analyses provided to date give us little clue as to the relative importance of these within-government channels compared with the alternative, citizen-based channels.

Might the causality run from government to social capital?

Some of the examples described above suggest that government action and the existence of effective and trustworthy institutions can create social capital, or at least an environment within which it can flourish. Of course, this form of reverse causality is of particular interest because, put another way, it implies that government can make policy interventions actively to create social capital, such as by opening their 'political opportunity structure' and engaging the community in trust-based partnership arrangements (Wallis and Dollery, 2002; see also chapter 8).

For example, the Novgorod region in Russia is described as actively fostering positive social relationships in the community, and studies of the relative success of the former Soviet nations point to the importance of securing legitimate and low-corruption institutions in rebuilding social capital (see above). Similarly, researchers seeking to understand the relatively poor performance of Russia in the post-communist era have highlighted how corruption has been sustained by ill-defined institutional boundaries between political and private business activity, and how in the Russian case, the state appears to facilitate rather than hinder corruption. For example, its complex tax laws leave too much room for 'interpretation' (Levin and Satarov, 2000). In general, an honest and efficient bureaucracy appears to play a vital role in the functioning of a market economy (Clague, 1997). African underperformance has also been 'to a substantial extent attributable to government behaviour', partly mediated, but not necessarily caused, by poor infrastructure and low social capital (Collier and Gunning, 1999). Knack and Keefer's (1997) study of cross-national differences between twenty-nine nations could also be interpreted in terms of reverse causality. They found that trust and norms of civic co-operation were significantly associated with the existence of formal institutions that effectively protected property and contractual rights – having well-defined legal rights might help underwrite social trust, rather than social trust helping to foster effective institutions. It is certainly the case that corrupt government leads to underperformance and poor outcomes on a number of fronts, not least being a significantly reduced subjective life satisfaction for the population who must endure such regimes (Helliwell, 2002a).

Some have therefore argued that vibrant social capital is better viewed as a *result* of good government than as a *cause* of it. More specifically, the view that social capital is a precondition for good government has been directly challenged by some researchers as 'almost certainly misconceived' (J. Harriss and DeRenzio, 1997, p. 919).

In reality, there is pretty good evidence, including that from panel design studies (Paxton, 2002), for the causal processes running in both directions. There can be little doubt that governments in nations, or regions, with high social capital – and especially bridging and linking social capital – have a major head-start over places that do not have this endowment. However, there is also ample evidence that the actions of governments can, to some extent, affect the character of a nation or region's social capital. These processes are generally self-reinforcing. Hence when government, business and the non-profit and informal sector co-operate to create systems of social accountability for the common good, markets behave in a self-regulating and 'civil' manner (Bruyn, 1999).

The specific view that effective governments 'crowd out' social capital is generally not supported (Woolcock, 1998). Rather, the character of government and the character of a nation's social capital seem loosely connected, like two climbers connected by a long and elastic rope. There are limits to how far one can travel without the other, and they generally pull each other up or, in some cases, down. They also act as an anchor to each other. Hence strong underlying social capital in the Czech Republic limited the damage done by a corrupt administration, while in other former Soviet states the weakness of this underlying social capital has acted as a brake on the development of effective democratic government. Similarly, a study in Bangladesh has shown how people have used local social capital, despite corruption within government, to implement policy (Mondal, 2000).

Active government and mobilized communities generally enhance each other's developmental efforts. Social and economic advancement is most easily fostered in societies characterized by egalitarian social structures and robust, coherent state bureaucracies. But such synergy is constructible even in the more adverse circumstances typical of third world countries (Evans, 1996).

Very importantly, government action and clear constitutional frameworks that promote and enforce a worldview based on equality of rights act as a bridge between disparate communities. This important role is illustrated by the consequences of ethnic diversity under different political structures. An analysis of ninety-four countries found that ethnic diversity is generally not a problem in democracies, but is very frequently a problem in the context of limited political rights (Collier, 2000). In this sense then, democratic government and constitutional frameworks of equal rights act as a form of bridging social capital or 'social capability', providing a shared normative framework that increases co-operation and reduces conflict across communities. In contrast, in democratic but ethnically diverse countries that lack a clear framework of equal rights, governments can become a potent channel for inter-racial conflict – normally of the majority over the minority – or a forum for narrow inter-racial alliances to the disadvantage of those excluded.

Does it matter? Are social capital and citizen participation essential for democracy?

The argument is widely made, particularly by politicians, that effective and legitimate democracy *requires* citizen participation. In this respect, falling voting rates in the USA and to a lesser extent elsewhere are seen as a grave concern (see also chapter 7). In Boix and Posner's model, one of the key channels through which social capital is seen as leading to more effective government is by making citizens more sophisticated consumers of politics and offering channels through which their demands can be articulated. Hence the argument goes something like this: well-connected citizens are well-informed citizens, who constructively debate issues, and who take the trouble to express their views so that government is directed to do what the well-informed citizenry want. Furthermore, it has been argued that non-political social networks can provide a resource that can be used for effective political action, such as the role that church-based networks played in the US civil rights movement.

It is certainly the case that voting is highly correlated with other measures of social capital. For example, the correlation between turnouts in US presidential elections and Putnam's social capital index across American states is a very high 0.84. However, other cross-national research has also shown that the relationship between social and political *trust* – having confidence in government and its institutions – is rather weak, though generally positive (Kaase, 1999). Indeed, Kaase highlights that across a sample of nine European nations, direct political action – participating in signing a petition, a boycott or a demonstration – is *negatively* associated with political trust. How are we to make sense of these findings?

The European political scientist Jan Van Deth has written a series of articles challenging the role that social capital plays in democratic politics. He has particularly challenged the conventional wisdom that the decline in active participation in politics, notably in the form of voting, implies a crisis of democracy.

Van Deth finds that there has been an unravelling of some of the traditional indicators of political engagement. While there is some evidence of falling voting and party membership, he finds that on average there has been no fall in 'political apathy', measured as the proportion of the population who never talk about politics. On the other hand, he notes that 'political salience' – how important politics is to people relative to other aspects of their lives – has fallen (Van Deth, 2000; see also chapter 7).

In terms of the relationship between political interest and social capital, as measured by associational membership, Van Deth confirms the finding that those who are involved in more organizations are somewhat more interested in politics than others in an absolute sense. But he finds that the saliency of politics – its importance relative to other aspects of their lives – is actually lower among most members of associations, with the obvious exception of members of political parties. This leads him to conclude that, for the most part, social capital and *political engagement* are largely unrelated. His interpretation is that citizens are keeping a watchful eye on politics, even if they are not getting so overtly involved.

Other, particularly American researchers have reached a different conclusion. In partial support of Van Deth, La Due Lake and Huckfeldt (1998) found that there was only a weak relationship between memberships in associations and political participation, and no relationship between memberships and reported frequency of political interactions and discussions. However, they did find that political engagement arose as a result of informal personal networks and discussions within these networks, and that the level of engagement was a function of the frequency of the political expertise, interaction and size of the network. La Due Lake and Huckfeldt concluded from their results that it is not so much the involvement in formal organizations that draws people into politics as having friends with whom they talk about political matters.

The study by La Due Lake and Huckfeldt (1998) is interesting, but is subject to the same criticism as so many studies: that the causality could run in the other direction. What is really needed to prove the case is an experimental intervention: would a group of randomly selected individuals who were engaged in a conversation about politics be more likely than a control group to engage in politics subsequently? Fortunately – and unusually – something very close to this has been conducted.

In a methodologically outstanding study, Alan Gerber conducted a randomized field experiment involving 30,000 registered voters in New Haven, Connecticut (Gerber and Green, 2000). Shortly before the November 1998 election, voters were randomly assigned into either a control group or one of several experimental groups. Each of the experimental groups was then subject to a different method of approach, but with the same non-partisan message reminding people about the coming election and encouraging them to vote. The methods used were: personal canvassing, which involved graduate students sent to contact randomly selected registered voters in their homes; direct mailings, up to three per selected voter; and telephone calls. In addition, three different forms of message were tried.

The results were clear cut. Personal canvassing greatly boosted the turnout rate, boosting voting by 14.6 percentage points (59.1 per cent voted compared with 44.5 per cent among controls). In contrast, direct mailing only modestly increased turnout. Telephone appeals, if anything, reduced turnout. Using multivariate modelling to control for other factors left the results essentially unchanged. Adjusting for other factors showed that personal canvassing boosted voting by 12.8 percentage points; three mailings boosted voting by 2.5 percentage points; and telephone appeals had no significant impact.[3]

In terms of the content of the communication, a message that highlighted a close election was slightly better than a general civic duty appeal, and substantially better than one emphasizing neighbourhood solidarity. Gerber also calculated cost effectiveness, estimating that the cost of each extra vote by direct mailing was around $40, versus around $8 for personal canvassing.

Gerber's is an important confirmation of the hypothesis that it is personal contact that draws people into political action, or at least voting. His results will come as a shock to the elites of many political parties, which have increasingly turned their backs on traditional canvassing to pursue slick, modern, mass-marketing techniques instead (see also chapter 7). Of course, the study does not purport to show the influence of personal social networks on politics, but if a personal appeal from a complete stranger can so dramatically impact on voting behaviour, it is difficult to believe that a similar request from a friend would not have at least the same impact.

In sum, the answer to the question of whether social capital and political participation are essential to democracy is complex, and ultimately rests heavily on your personal view of what democracy is. If the question is 'what makes people come out and vote?', then the answer appears to be that informal social contacts are critically important – but formal (non-political) organizational memberships do not appear to be particularly important.

If the question is a deeper one, such as 'does it *matter* whether people don't vote or politically engage?', then the answer is more difficult. Van Deth offers some comfort in his evidence that people are continuing to keep a watchful eye on politics, even if most of the time the saliency of the issues involved is not high enough to prompt direct engagement. This 'watchful eye' does not appear to rest on associational involvement. He interprets this positively as a sign that people are generally satisfied with the social and political outcomes they see around them. On the other hand, politicians might see it as a warning shot across their bows that political distrust channels itself into non-traditional political protest rather than mainstream activity, noting that while voting is falling, political protest remains resilient.

But arguably, what really matters is not so much whether everyone votes as what everyone votes for. A potential breakdown of social capital and common bonds across a nation has far deeper implications than just for voter turnout. A paradox of modern societies is that while in many ways we are becoming more diverse in our lifestyles and attitudes, we are also becoming ever more interdependent, albeit on strangers rather than kin. If falling voting and political interest are an indicator that we no longer identify with or care for those around us – and this is of course speculative – then we surely are in trouble. In a chilling paper, Alesina, Glaser and Sacerdote (2001) make the argument that the simple reason why the US lacks a European-style welfare state is that the white majority don't want to help the black minority. The problem is, the more we excuse ourselves from our common obligations, escaping into separate identities and a self-serving culture of blame and excuses to rid ourselves of the inconvenient needs of others, the more we weaken all kinds of subtle common goods on which we all rely. It's a dangerous game to play. If our sense of shared identity and common obligation erodes too far, then people will no longer pay their taxes, the public realm from health care to roads to common civic courtesies will decay, and all our lives will become impoverished.

If politics is to be more than a technical exercise with the electorate as watchful spectators, and even if it is merely to maintain a feeling of representativeness in a technical sense, then institutional arrangements need to change. Either we will need to find ways of allowing the public to engage in political discourse at low personal cost, such as through making voting easier, or we need to find ways of making the contributions made by individuals more salient or important. Such mechanisms might include increasingly small units of government so that individual contributions matter more; deliberative polls and citizens' juries, involving a randomly selected group of the public in detailed consideration of an issue; or referenda or elections that are triggered by popular petitions, thereby channelling non-traditional political action back into the mainstream (see also chapter 9).

So does everyone have to vote? No, though it may be wise for us to think about less onerous but more representative forms of democracy if current declines in voting continue (see chapter 7). But if not, voting is the tip of a deeper iceberg of decaying common identity and shared social norms – something we should neither assume nor ignore – then we should really be worried. For this won't just undermine the efficacy of government, it will undermine modern society itself and with it the efficiencies, justice and myriad of human satisfactions it brings.

Summary and conclusions

There is a considerable body of evidence showing that high social capital, and particularly social trust, are associated with more effective and less corrupt government.

At the micro-level, this can be seen in the relative success or failure of housing and condo associations, and in the relative effectiveness of small, local town councils. The effectiveness of the latter rests not only on the level of bonding social capital and trust within the community, but also on the extent of bridging social capital, and particularly that which connects the leadership of the community with communities elsewhere.

At the regional level, Putnam's study of Italy provides the classic example of the relationship between social capital and government effectiveness, and is noteworthy for its range of detailed measures of government efficacy. It particularly highlights the importance of 'horizontal' or egalitarian forms of social capital as being conducive to effective government, as opposed to the more hierarchical forms found in the south of Italy, such as the Catholic church. Though no other study of regional government yet comes close to matching Putnam's work for its comprehensiveness or detail, studies of regional government within Germany, Hungary, Russia and the USA have reported similar findings.

There are a growing number of studies at the national level, and their results strongly support Putnam's initial observations. Cross-national studies have shown that corruption within government is strongly and negatively associated with social capital, measured as trust between strangers. Putnam's observation that more hierarchical forms of social organization are less conducive to social trust and effective government is also borne out by cross-national analyses – having higher proportions of the population ascribing to hierarchically organized forms of religion (notably Catholisism) is strongly associated with lower social trust. More detailed research on the relative performance of the post-Soviet nations and on the failures of government within many African nations reveals a similar association between weak social capital and poorly performing government institutions.

Finally, there is evidence that even at the transnational level, the efficacy of government action and institutions relates closely to social capital. Successful cross-border co-operation and policy are strongly associated with cross-border kinship and ancestral links. More speculatively, links can be drawn more widely between the emergence of common cross-national attitudes, normative frameworks, and increasingly effective and empowered global institutions – even in the face of challenges such as the international disagreements over the war in Iraq, and tensions over world trade agreements and environmental treaties.

As we have seen throughout this book, it is not the case that all forms of social capital are associated with positive outcomes, and certainly not all of the time. At the micro-level, there is evidence that communities that bond together strongly and organize themselves well internally sometimes then neglect the people and spaces beyond their own community patch. At the macro-level, abuses of power are often born of tight-knit cliques among the empowered elite within a society, and many wars might be reasonably attributed to high levels of social capital within nations or particular ethnic groups. Bonding social capital appears to be a necessary but not sufficient condition for good government. Less hierarchical, more horizontal or egalitarian forms of social capital would seem to be particularly conducive to good government. Bridging and linking forms of social capital would seem to be particularly important to ensuring that the outcome of effective governance is directed to the benefit of all of society, rather than a particular group within it.

Across all these levels, there has been much speculation about both the direction of causality linking social capital and effective government, and about what might mediate this relationship. The emerging consensus is that the two have a loose, reciprocal causal relationship, each reinforcing or anchoring the other. It certainly does not appear to be the case that effective and legitimate government action 'crowds out' grass-roots social capital. Government actions and explicit constitutional arrangements that emphasize the common rights of citizens act as a form of bridging social capital, making it easier for disparate communities to live together in peace.

In sum, it would seem communities with high and egalitarian social capital foster more civic citizens who are easier to govern, a ready supply of co-operative political leaders, and a fertile soil in which effective government institutions can grow. These institutions in turn can act to reinforce those values and behaviours still further, raising the level of generality at which they are applied and rejuvenating the fertile civic soil from which they have grown (see also chapters 5 and 8). Indeed, some may view the institutions and egalitarian constitutions of governments as themselves being forms of social capital, especially as the common normative framework they embody gradually spreads into a shared global understanding of how people should treat and respect one another.

Further reading

The *classic study* on Italy is still well worth a read: Putnam (1993). Also worth looking at is the critique by Boix and Posner (1998). For another critical and differing view, try Van Deth (2000).

For a *cross-national comparison* of the health of our political systems try Norris (1999). Worth a look, both for its findings and its elegant experimental design, is Gerber and Green (2000). The 'chilling' paper mentioned at the end of the chapter is by Alesina, Glaser and Sacerdote (2001). It has been subject to some methodological criticisms but is well worth a provocative read, by Americans, Europeans and others.

Part II

Can Social Capital be Built?

7

Trends in Social Capital

In the mid-1990s, Putnam turned his attention from Italy to his home patch, the USA. He began to wonder how the USA stood in terms of the social capital that had turned out to be so important in explaining differences across Italy (see chapter 6). He found that the USA appeared fairly rich in terms of its associational and civic life, but – and here was the surprise – it appeared to be declining fast (Putnam, 1995).

As we shall see, subsequent work examining trends in other countries has revealed a complex and varied pattern of trends over time. Similarly, we should not assume that all aspects of social capital are moving in the same direction over time. With this in mind, this chapter looks at different countries, breaking down trends in each by associational participation, political participation, informal social connections, and giving and trusting. By necessity, the focus is on the national or macro-level, though some within-group trends are also noted.

The story in the USA: three decades of decline

Putnam published his initial results on the USA in a couple of academic papers in 1995. American social capital – the vibrant civic life that many saw as being as American as apple pie – had suffered a mysterious decline from the 1960s onwards. Putnam dramatically compared the mystery to an Agatha Christie murder, and 'Poirot'–Putnam proceeded to line up the suspects in the gradual death of American community.

Putnam's analysis immediately provoked widespread interest. Many academics criticized his analysis and methodology strongly. Numerous counterexamples were made of forms of social capital that were said to be on the rise, though generally without numbers to back up the claims. So what if fifty-year-old organizations were declining, since there was a proliferation of new forms of organization, such as environmental movements? Had Putnam counted right? Surely his measures were skewed towards older organizations that were more likely to be declining, rather than the newer ones that were growing? What about informal socializing? Maybe people were joining less, but meeting more informally instead? And what about the internet – wasn't this the greatest form of social capital yet?

The debate brought in more than academics. Policymakers and a more general audience were interested too.[1] Could it be that this decline lay at the roots of other aspects of American malaise, like the disenchantment with politicians and the rise in urban crime? One of Putnam's suspects, lurking suspiciously at the scene of the crime, was television. This link alone was enough to ensure a vigorous debate. It was an easy target for some politicians, and hit a vigorous existing fault-line of popular American debate.

To give Putnam credit, he is a focused and careful scholar. He took the criticisms made seriously, and recognized the validity of many of them. Joining him at his home in one of his regular sessions with his researchers and graduate students, one could not but be struck by how it was Putnam himself who was the most searching and demanding critic of his early 'Bowling Alone' hypothesis, always looking for the mistakes he might have made or the data that he might have missed. It seemed that there were times when Bob wanted to be proved wrong. He wanted to be able to come out and square the circle with the academic colleagues that he respected, and similarly, he didn't always feel especially comfortable with some of the non-academic audiences that he now found supporting his corner.

A major turning point and lucky break came when he was directed to the existence of a remarkable but little used data set. It turned out that a survey organization called DDB Needham had built up a commercial Life Style survey archive over two decades that included a rich variety of social capital data. After checking that the data were trustworthy by comparing them with other sources, Putnam and his team began analysing the trends. Much to their surprise, the data indicated that, if anything, they had underestimated the scale of the decline.

The data from the USA are now compelling. A large variety of indicators show a remarkably consistent pattern of declining social engagement from the 1960s to the present day.

Associational participation

As Putnam showed in 1995, the membership rates of a whole range of national local and national associations, from the Parent–Teacher Association to B'nai B'rith to the Scouts, have fallen over recent decades. Interestingly, this decline needs to be set against a longer-term history of rising membership rates from 1900 to around 1960 (see figure 7.1). Some organizations showed the decline earlier, such as the General Federation of Women's Clubs, which had peaked by the 1950s, while others showed it a little later, such as the Rotary Club, which remained strong until the 1980s.

There are, of course, some exceptions to this general trend. Environmental groups generally showed strong growth over recent decades, though it is noteworthy that even these seem to have lost much of their shine. Greenpeace, for example, which became the largest environmental organization in America and accounted for more than

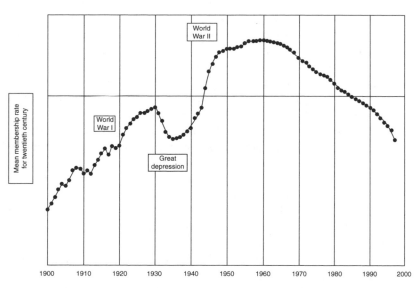

Figure 7.1 *Average membership rate in thirty-two National Chapter-based associations in the USA, 1900–97*
Source: Putnam (2000, p. 254).

one-third of members in national environmental groups at its peak in 1990, had lost 85 per cent of its former membership by 1998. There had also been a substantial growth in the number of non-profit organizations of national scope – the *Encyclopaedia of Associations* showed more than a doubling in numbers between 1968 and 1997 (Putnam, 2000).

But the pattern of relative growth and decline is very telling. In short, we find growth in associations that either have 'cheque-book' members only – in other words they do not actually meet or make any non-financial demands on members – or that have no members at all. The environmental organizations that have grown dramatically in the last two decades are a clear example – both leaders and members regard 'membership' more as support than as membership in the traditional sense. Membership rests very heavily on mass mailing drives; the commitment of members is weak; and for the vast majority, it never involves meetings or any form of direct action other than sending off a very occasional cheque.[2] In contrast, 'traditional' associations – that is, ones that actually involve the physical association of members – have almost universally declined, especially if they are locally based. Hence there are more organizations fighting over a smaller and smaller pool of members.

Perhaps a more important countertrend lies in the rise of encounter, reading and self-help groups. Some, like reading groups, have a long history, and the limited data indicate that they have managed to resist the decline of more formally organized groups. However, self-help groups, ranging from Alcoholics Anonymous to the Association for Retarded Citizens, tend to be a relatively recent and growing phenomenon. These groups represent an important, though modest-sized countertrend, though it should be noticed that, almost by definition, their scope and focus are relatively narrow.

Yet however many groups you look at, there is always the danger that the very groups that you have forgotten to ask about – not least because they are new – are the ones with rising membership. The 'killer' method therefore is to use survey data of a representative sample of the general population, asking this question about active membership in general: 'how many times over the last year did you attend a club meeting?' The results are startling. Average club attendance fell by 58 per cent from 1975 to 1999. In the mid-1970s, nearly two-thirds of Americans attended club meetings, but by the late 1990s nearly two-thirds *never* did (Putnam, 2000).

Other data also strongly support the trend. Time-use or diary-based studies show that time spent in organizational life fell by 38 per cent between 1965 and 1995 in the USA. Similarly, data from the US

Consumer Department shows that leisure expenditure on club and fraternal dues fell by 40 per cent from the late 1950s to the late 1990s.

Work-based and professional memberships have shown a similar decline. Union membership peaked in the 1950s with 32.5 per cent of the workforce unionized. Union membership has now declined to 14.1 per cent – a decline of 57 per cent. At a glance, memberships in professional associations seem to go against the trend, often with rising membership numbers over the period. But the rise in professional memberships has been driven by the sharp increase in the size of the professional groups concerned. When one looks at membership rates, the same pattern is found as elsewhere. Average membership rates peaked in the late 1950s and have, on average, fallen since, though perhaps at a more modest rate than those for union membership.[3]

Church memberships are very high in the USA compared with most OECD nations, and are analysed separately by Putnam (2000). The pattern of decline is fairly similar to that for other associational memberships. Church memberships have fallen on average by 10 per cent over the last three to four decades, but actual church attendance has fallen by 20 per cent or more[4] and involvement in related religious activities (such as Bible study groups and church socials) has fallen by 25–50 per cent. Time-budget studies show that Americans spent on average 31 per cent less time in worship or religiously related activities in 1995 than they did in 1965. Among religious groups, those that have most successfully resisted the pattern of decline are a cluster of Christian right, fundamentalist and other evangelical groups (see also Putnam and Feldstein, 2003). These groups have not shied away from political involvement either – see, for example, their prominent role in the US Republican party. They represent a striking exception to the general rule of decline, though controversy surrounds their actual membership levels.

Political participation

While there is little evidence to suggest that Americans are more ignorant (or less knowledgeable) about politics today than they were a few decades ago, there is widespread evidence that their interest and engagement in politics have fallen. Voting in American presidential elections rose in the first half of the twentieth century from a low in 1920 – when women first got the vote – up to 63.1 per cent in 1960 (Kennedy vs. Nixon).[5] It then fell, to 49.1 per cent in 1996 (Clinton vs. Dole), and still further in 2000 (Bush Junior vs. Gore) to 46.6 per cent – a fall of 26 per cent.[6] Local election turnout has fallen by about the same amount, though from lower starting points.

The proportion of Americans saying that they were 'interested in politics' fell from 52 to 42 per cent between 1975 and 1999 (DDB Needham data). Similarly, the proportion expressing 'a good deal of interest' in current events fell from 50 to 38 per cent between 1974 and 1996 (Roper data). These falls in political interest – 19 and 24 per cent respectively – are of a very similar scale to those found for voting.

Party financing grew dramatically over the same period. Between 1976 and 1986 alone, financial income more than doubled for the Democrats and quadrupled for the Republicans in real terms. The size of their party organization staff has also risen sharply. But despite this financial strength, voter commitment and citizen participation in the parties have slumped. Party identification fell from 75 per cent in the early 1960s to less than 65 per cent in the late 1990s – a fall of 15 per cent. Attendance at political meetings is down about 25 per cent; the proportion who have worked for a political party during the election campaigns has halved; and public attendance at political speeches has fallen by nearly 60 per cent. As Putnam puts it:

> Barely two decades ago, election campaigns were for millions of Americans an occasion for active participation in national deliberation. Campaigning was something we did, not something we merely witnessed. Now for almost all Americans, an election campaign is something that happens around us, a grating element in the background noise of everyday life, a fleeting image on a TV screen. (Putnam, 2000, p. 41)

The picture is not much better at the local or town affairs level. Between the mid-1970s and mid-1990s, attendance at town or school affairs meetings fell by 40 per cent, and serving on (any) local organization committee fell by 39 per cent. Political activities that are less dependent on physically meeting generally showed a more modest decline. Writing to a congressman or senator fell by 23 per cent; running for political office fell by 16 per cent; and writing a letter to the paper fell by 14 per cent.

The closest one can identify to a countertrend in the political domain is the rise of national social movements from the 1960s onwards. From the Mississippi civil rights movements to the Vietnam protests to the protest for and against abortion of the 1980s, these movements have had a substantial impact on American politics. However, rather like their environmental relatives, as the years have passed these movements have steadily gone 'professional', with small, full-time, paid staffs based in Washington. Marches still happen, and indeed the evidence indicates that there may even have been a slight increase in the proportion of Americans who have taken part in demonstrations and protests. But their character appears to have changed. Protests have become stage-managed events to capture the fleeting attention of the media rather than a marker of extended engagement.

One countertrend in the USA is found in state-wide ballots. These have increased by nearly four-fold since the late 1960s – though this development only applies to around five states and is dominated by California. But Putnam warns against an overly positive interpretation of this trend, quoting a recent study that concluded that a state-wide ballot is 'no longer so much a measure of general citizen interest as it is a test of fundraising ability' (Tolbert, Lowenstein and Donovan, 1998, p. 35). In essence, he interprets this trend as a variant of the story of American politics more widely – money and professional lobbyists have effectively displaced a politics based on real citizen involvement.

Until the recent spate of work on social capital, these declining levels of political participation were seen as rooted in, and explained by, a growing cynicism about and lack of interest in politics by the general public. Americans talk less about politics in their everyday lives – the proportion of Americans who reported discussing politics 'in the last week' fell from 51 per cent in 1980 to 28 per cent in 1996, a fall of 45 per cent in less than two decades. Even more dramatically, there has been a near collapse in trust in politics and politicians. In the mid-1960s, three-quarters of Americans said that you could 'trust the government in Washington to do what is right all or most of the time'. By the 1990s, only a quarter of Americans trusted the government in Washington (though see below for post-September 11 figures).

Political disengagement in the USA has been strong, and the growing financial resources of the political parties have done little to stem the tide. But in as much as the pattern is remarkably similar to the declines in other aspects of American social capital, it would seem wise to cast our causal net wider than just the political arena.

Informal social connections

One of the most powerful – and reasonable – criticisms levelled at Putman's 1995 analysis of the decline of social capital in the USA was that it rested almost entirely on measures of formal associational life. It was argued that while Americans might be joining clubs and formal associations in dwindling numbers, this was because they had instead developed rich social lives with friends, families and colleagues. Contemporary Americans no longer needed to rely on the clumsy institutions of their grandparents to organize their social lives – instead they could pick up the telephone and see their friends for dinner.

Time-budget studies confirm that Americans do indeed spend much more time engaged in informal than formal social activity. For example, they spend on average more than six times more time visiting friends than on formal, non-religious organizational activity. But the commercial survey data obtained by the Putnam team in the late 1990s have shown conclusively that those wishing to argue against the 'bowling alone' hypothesis will find no solace in the trends in informal socializing.

In the mid-1970s, Americans entertained friends at home about fourteen to fifteen times a year, but by the late 1990s this had nearly halved to just eight times per year – a fall of 55 per cent. Going to the home of friends, unsurprisingly, showed a similar fall. Going on picnics fell by 60 per cent. Going out to bars, night-clubs, discos and taverns fell by 40–50 per cent. Playing cards, which was three times more common than going to the movies even in 1980, has since halved. Sending greetings cards – even before the internet arrived – fell 15–20 per cent. And while the numbers of neighbourhood schemes are up (see also chapter 4), the numbers spending a social evening with a neighbour fell by 30 per cent.

Time-budget studies confirm the overall picture – from 1965 to 1995, the average time spent 'schmoozing' fell by 40 per cent. The trend shows little sign of slowing – another time budget showed that in the seven years from 1992 to 1999 alone, time spent socializing fell by 20 per cent.

Is it that Americans are instead retreating to a more intimate, family-based sociability? It does not appear so. The proportion of families reporting sitting down for family dinners has fallen 32 per cent, while the numbers of traditional families have also declined. The proportion of families with kids aged 8–17 who vacation as a family has fallen by 28 per cent. Even watching TV together is down 24 per cent, and just sitting and talking is down 19 per cent.

Is it that Americans have instead transferred their social focus to the work environment? It is certainly true that Americans spend a great deal of time at work, averaging about 2,000-plus hours a year worked, against a European average closer to 1,600 hours (OECD, 2001b). As Putnam admits, the data in this area are relatively thin, but you would have to be wearing pretty rose-tinted spectacles to think that Americans' workplaces had become revitalized loci of social life. In 1955, 44 per cent of American workers said they enjoyed time at work more than time not at work, but by 1999, this had fallen to 16 per cent – a fall of 64 per cent. Studies of personal networks have found that co-workers account for less than 10 per cent of Americans' friends, and when asked to whom they would turn to discuss 'important matters', less than half of workers listed even a single co-worker.

Going to sports clubs and exercising is up, as is attendance at major sporting events, which nearly doubled from 1960 to 1998. But participation rates in team sports are down, typically by 10–20 per cent. People are exercising more, but they do it alone, or at least in a room of other strangers. Similarly with music: while the music industry has boomed, the playing of musical instruments has halved. Bowling – now the motif of Putnam's work – is actually up, with more than a third of Americans bowling in a year. But league membership is down by a spectacular 70 per cent. Once again, it is not that Americans have stopped doing these activities, but that they are doing them, if not alone, in ever smaller social units. The difference in the character of these ways of engaging in sport is illustrated in the observation that league bowlers consume three times more beer and pizza per head than other bowlers; in other words, league bowling is – or was – a major social event.

In the area of informal socializing, there is one important exception to the general rule – the use of telecommunications to stay in touch. In 1998, two-thirds of adults had called a friend or relative on the telephone in the previous day 'just to talk' (Pew Research Center, 1998). As the proportion of households with telephones has doubled since 1940 – though it was close to its present level by the late 1960s – it is reasonable to argue that this has brought an important new form of social connection. This is particularly so for links to distant friends and relatives, as reflected in the growth of distant calls compared with local calls over the last three decades. Against this, it is clear that you do not meet new people by telephone, so the medium has mainly been important for maintaining rather than making social capital.

An important related question, which it is too early to answer either for the USA or more generally at present, is what role new forms of electronic communication will play in future trends. This latter question will be returned to in chapter 9 on policy implications.

Giving and trusting

Per capita giving nearly doubled between 1960 and 1995 in the USA, but as income rose even faster, giving as a proportion of GNP fell from 2.26 to 1.61 per cent – a 29 per cent fall. Involvement in community projects fell by 40 per cent; blood donations fell by 20 to 25 per cent; and there were falls in the number of volunteer fire-fighters.

Even quite low-level acts of giving of time appear to have suffered. Refusals to participate in surveys have doubled since the 1960s, and voluntary returns of public census forms have fallen by a quarter. It seems that America has become a meaner, more hostile and impatient place. Motorists no longer stop at stop signs – as one detailed study of a New York town found, the percentage of drivers running red lights rose from 29 per cent in 1979 to 97 per cent in 1996. Reported crime was up three-fold over the period, though murders – having doubled – plateaued by the late 1970s, and crime rates have fallen significantly since the early 1990s.

On the positive side, the proportion of Americans saying that they are 'involved in any charity or social service activities, such as helping the poor, the sick, or the elderly' *rose* from 26 to 46 per cent in the period 1977–91 – a 77 per cent increase. Other evidence indicates that volunteering has increased by around 25 per cent over the last few decades. This statistic stands out like an oasis in a desert of falling figures. However, most of the increase is concentrated in those aged 60 plus. As we shall see below, the pattern of decline in the USA is strongly generational, with the present older generation being consistently more civic. It would seem that as this 'civic generation' retires, it has thrown itself into volunteering, not least to assist its less able physical peers in their ailing years. However, there has also been a modest growth in volunteering among twenty-somethings, partly reflecting programmes for college credit.

Is there a way of bringing all these trends together? In chapter 1, it was suggested that the simplest general indicator of social capital, drawing on both empirical 'data reduction' and theoretical arguments, is social trust – the extent to which people regard others as trustworthy. We also saw in chapters 2–6 that social trust is a key predictor of many of the outcomes that the public, and policymakers, care about. So do Americans trust each other less? Sadly, yes.

In 1960, 55 per cent of Americans said that other people could generally be trusted. By 1998, this had fallen to 33 per cent – a 40 per cent fall. This fall lies around the middle to upper range of the percentages that we have seen for many indicators documented by Putnam et al. Surveys of high school students show an even greater fall in trust, from 46 per cent in 1976 to 23 per cent in 1995 – a fall of 50 per cent. The only positive glimmer in this headline statistic is that among high school students from 1995 to 1998, social trust crept back up a couple of percentage points, perhaps suggesting the first signs that the thirty-year decline in trust may be beginning to turn around (Rahn and Transue, 1998).

The final statistic of this bleak American story is that in the absence of informal, 'thick' trust, Americans seem to have come to rely on more formal methods and sanctions to establish trust of a sort. The numbers of police, guards and watchmen approximately doubled in the period 1960–96, while the numbers of lawyers and judges more than doubled. It would seem that expenditure on preventative law enforcement has soared, just as informal trust has fallen. In the private, but concerned, words of one senior American politician on a visit to Downing Street, 'who needs trust when you can sue the pants off each other'.

Post-September 11, 2001

It has sometimes been remarked that wars strengthen feelings of solidarity and community – bonding social capital – at least within the warring nations. Sadly, September 11 has allowed scholars to test the hypothesis. Early data indicate significant rises in a wide variety of social capital measures within the USA following the terrorist attack on New York on September 11, 2001.

Social capital surveys (Putnam, 2002) that had recently been completed were repeated in the months following the attack. These showed that net interest in public affairs grew, especially among younger people, many of whom had previously shown strong disengagement (27 percentage points up, compared with 8 per cent among the over 35s). The net change in trust in 'the people running your country' grew by 19 per cent in younger people and 4 per cent among older ones. And 51 per cent expressed greater confidence in the federal government than they had a year earlier, compared with just 7 per cent expressing less confidence – a net change of 44 per cent. This was the largest shift seen, and brought confidence in government up to levels not seen in decades.[7]

Net trust increased 19 per cent in local government, 14 per cent in the police, and 10 per cent in neighbours. Strikingly, trust in people of other races also increased by 11 per cent, though trust in Arabs lagged behind other groups and support for 'immigrant rights' showed a net fall of 11 per cent.

Changes in behaviour were more modest. There were net increases in the range of 5–7 percentage points in giving blood, volunteering, working on local community projects, and attending political meetings. There was little or no change in attending clubs or churches or in giving, and informal socializing – having friends to visit your home – was actually down 6 per cent. The last may have reflected the increase in television watching, which showed a net increase of 16 per cent, implying an increase of half an hour a day (to 3.4 hours on average).

In sum, the events of 9/11 appear to have sparked a sharp upturn in the trust Americans had in one another, but led to only modest changes in behaviour. The White House consulted Putnam extensively in this period, a fact reflected in President Bush's State of the Union Address in January 2002, which announced the creation of a large citizen corps and urged Americans 'to do something good for each other'. The impact of these policy programmes will be an important test case in our understanding of the creation and destruction of social capital.

Though clearly no American would have wished that it happen this way, September 11 made Americans reflect on what was important to them and strengthened their desire to connect with one another. However, the very latest data at the time of writing suggest that the boost in trust and engagement – and especially trust in government – has already largely dissipated. For example, in 2002, 50 per cent of Americans said they had a 'great deal of confidence' in the White House – an unprecedented level in forty years of Harris Polls – but by 2004 this had fallen back to a more historically typical level of 31 per cent. It looks as though even the terrible events of 9/11, or at least the way they have been responded to, have been unable to turn around the long-term trends in trust and engagement within the USA.

Summary: the US story

Putnam and his team present a remarkable and rather depressing array of data to suggest that, by almost all measures, social capital declined in the USA over the period from 1960 to 2000. This decline follows an earlier period of growth in US social capital stretching back to the beginning of the twentieth century. The scale of this decline varies by the measure employed, but is mostly in the range of 15–50 per cent.

There is a handful of indicators, or forms of social organization, that seem to have bucked the trend. Self-help groups, cheque-book-based social movements, and religious fundamentalist groups have managed to grow. In the political realm, political parties have grown in financial strength and have become increasingly professional, albeit with a withering of popular support, while the proportion of the population that has taken part in protests has risen slightly. In terms of informal socializing, almost all indicators are down, with the only possible exceptions being going to the gym, watching sports, and perhaps speaking to distant friends and relatives by telephone. Finally, in terms of giving and trusting, the only positive trends lie in an upturn in volunteering (though not in the middle-aged) and the suggestion that declining trust may have bottomed out in high school students. Falling crime rates in recent years might also be a good sign, though this may be due to factors other than social capital, such as rising private security.

Nearly all of the countertrends involve low-cost, minimal wider social contact activities. In contrast, the picture for cross-cutting, multi-faceted forms of social capital is almost universally of decline. Finally, data indicate that in the wake of the September 11 attacks, there was a rise in many forms of social capital. Trust in federal government showed the largest reversal, while behavioural changes were more modest. However, the early data indicate that these increases were not sustained.

Trends in other nations

Putnam and his team have in many ways led the way with their investigation of the decline of social capital in the USA, and their work provides an invaluable benchmark and challenge to researchers in other nations. At present, we do not have easily to hand the same comprehensive collation of data on social capital trends in other nations, but the data that we do have strongly suggest that the US story should not be taken as universally representative.

In this section, we examine the best available analyses on a nation-by-nation basis using a similar analytical framework to that used by Putnam in the American context. In the section following, general themes are identified, and consideration is given to whether other measures would tell a subtly different story.

Other nations show declining social capital: Australia and Britain

The pattern of more-or-less universally falling indicators of social capital is not unique to the USA. Though neither case is as clear cut as the US, both Australia and Britain show evidence of decline.

Australia

Of those nations on which we have a reasonable range of data, Australia is arguably the one that shows a pattern most similar to that of the USA.

Australia has seen falling membership in many long-established voluntary groups in recent decades, such as in trade union membership and the church. As in the USA, sports participation is up – but only in an individualized form, not in team sports. Many social movements, including the environmental movement, appear to have lost members too, as seems to have happened in the USA (Cox, 2002; OECD, 2001a).

As we shall see, the decline in traditional organizational member-ships is not especially unusual in an international context. But Australia has also seen declines in nearly all other measures of social capital as well. Volunteering has declined. Informal socializing has decreased. Trust in politicians has fallen, though the evidence for falling political activism is not clear cut: turnout in parliamentary elections remains at close to 100 per cent, but this reflects the Australian system of com-pulsory voting. Social trust, our key general indicator, has fallen – from 48 per cent in 1981 to 40 per cent in 1997. At the same time, there has been a substantial increase in litigation, including against local coun-cils and public bodies.

Britain

In earlier work, I argued that Britain was best characterized as 'mixed' in terms of its social capital trends (Halpern, 1997; Aldridge and Halpern, 2002). The gradual accumulation of data has led me to revise my assessment to one of decline, albeit a decline that has been uneven across the social classes and that may now be plateauing.

An extensive review by Hall (1999) covering the period up until around 1990 is relatively positive about the situation in the UK. More recent data suggest that he may have been too optimistic in some respects, with the overall picture for the UK increasingly looking like that for the USA (Grenier and Wright, 2001).

Overall, associational membership in the UK appears to have been stable, or even to have risen since the 1960s. The average number of associations belonged to rose falteringly from 0.73 to 1.43 from 1959 to 1999. This rise was strongly concentrated among women and higher social classes, further exaggerating the UK's marked class differentials in membership. In terms of associations, this rise was heavily concen-trated in environmental organizations, and to some extent in sports clubs. For example, the National Trust – which looks after Britain's stately homes – has seen more than a ten-fold increase in membership between 1971 and 2002 to more than three million members. The Royal Society for the Protection of Birds has seen a similar ten-fold rise to a membership over a million, as have a bundle of other environmental organizations. However, these large organizations that have grown strongly have done so on the back of 'cheque-book memberships'. The public register their support for an issue by sending in a cheque and joining the organization, and are in return sent information about the cause. Yet few members ever meet. Other organizational memberships are even thinner. For example, it is clear that the National Trust's impressive membership roll rests heavily on the discounts that 'members' get into the large number of heritage sites that they manage – if you are going to visit several sites in a year, it is more cost effective to join.

Other forms of associations have shown marked declines, at least since the early 1980s, including trade unions, traditional women's organizations, churches, youth organizations and service organizations. For example, membership of the National Federation of Women's Institutes fell by 46 per cent between 1972 and 2002 to 240,000, and membership in trade unions fell by 41 per cent from their peak in 1979 to 7.8 million in 2000 (Office of National Statistics, 2003). Similarly, church membership and attendance have dropped spectacularly over recent decades, such that, on current projections, the Church of England faces extinction within ten to twenty years. As recently as 1950, more than 70 per cent of British babies were baptized, just as they had been for the fifty years before. Since then, baptisms have been falling at a gently accelerating rate so that by 2000, they had fallen to around 23 per cent (Voas, 2003). By my projection, if the current trend continues, the last baby to be baptized in Britain will be born in 2016 – an incredible change for a custom that has been around for more than a millennium.[8]

Comparisons across cohort studies – that is, longitudinal studies of people born at a certain time – also show evidence of a marked decline in memberships in organizations from the 1960s to the 2000s (Ferri, Bynner and Wadsworth, 2003). When those born in 1946 were in their thirties, around 60 per cent of men and 50 per cent of women belonged to at least one organization. But for those born in 1958, when in their thirties, these percentages had fallen to around 15 and 25 per cent respectively. For those born in 1970, when in their thirties, only 10 and 15 per cent respectively belonged to at least one organization. Hence the evidence from the British cohort studies suggests that there was a dramatic drop in associational membership between those born immediately after World War II and those born just over a decade later.[9]

One of the most positive statistics, as in the USA, is for volunteering, with the proportion of people volunteering increasing during the 1980s, and then levelling off or falling modestly through the 1990s. Furthermore, among those who do volunteer, the amount of time spent volunteering increased from 2.7 hours per week in 1991 to 4 hours per week in 1997 (Grenier and Wright, 2001). As in the USA, the over-65s showed a marked increase in volunteering through the 1980s and 1990s, perhaps partly reflecting the increasing physical fitness of this group. UK data also suggest that the cohort currently in their fifties (i.e. those born immediately following World War II) are especially active volunteers. On the downside, the proportion of young people volunteering, and the amount of time young volunteers give, fell over the 1990s. Volunteering has also fallen among the unemployed. It would seem that young people would rather give money than time (Matheson and Summerfield, 2000).

The trends for charitable giving are not very positive either. Though Hall noted that giving had increased over the period up until 1993, the data since have shown falls. The percentage of people giving fell from 81 per cent in 1993 to 67 per cent in 2000 (Grenier and Wright, 2001). The total amounts given, in real terms, also fell over the 1990s, though with some evidence of this decline pausing in the most recent data. Response rates to surveys also provide a useful indirect measure of social capital – higher response rates have been found to be strongly associated with higher levels of social trust. Response rates to all of the UK's major public surveys have fallen markedly over the last decade. It seems that the giving of time has suffered much the same as the giving of money.

Data on perceptions of neighbourhood, from the British Crime Surveys, show a significant fall in helpfulness from the mid-1980s to the mid-1990s. For example, the proportion describing their neighbourhood as one in which 'people do things together and try and help each other' fell from 43 per cent in 1984 to 28 per cent in 1996. More encouragingly, perceptions of neighbourhoods improved from 1996 to 2000, the proportions rating their neighbours as helpful rising from 28 to 36 per cent. This turnaround appears to reflect the crime figures, which began to fall in the mid-1990s after decades of steady increases. However, the most recent data at the time of writing show that this trend in helpfulness has flat-lined for 2002–3, even though crime has continued to fall.

Until quite recently, it was widely felt that, despite steadily falling voter turnout in local and EU elections, the UK was resisting the US pattern of declining political engagement. In the mid-1990s Tony Blair's Labour Party even witnessed a marked expansion in membership – and one driven by young people – turning back a long-established trend of ageing and shrinking political parties. However, the 1997 and 2001 elections witnessed clear downward trends. The 2001 election saw the lowest turnout since 1918 and Labour Party membership has now been falling for several years once again. Turnout in local elections fell from a peak of around 50 per cent in 1987 to less than 30 per cent in 1998, a fall most marked in metropolitan areas.[10] Political trust and trust in parliament have fallen from the 1970s to the 2000s – though the trend is quite sensitive to the wording of the question. Questions that mention the political parties, such as whether politicians put the party first and the country second, show a marked deterioration – especially over the 1990s. More general questions, such as confidence in politicians or government ministers, show a fall through the 1980s and early 1990s, then a marked increase following the 1997 election. Confidence has since gradually fallen back, though not to the low levels of the early 1990s. In contrast, confidence in civil servants rose sharply from around 25 to 45 per cent between 1983 and 1997, where it has stayed fairly flat since (MORI data).[11] Radical constitutional reform, including the creation of a Scottish parliament following the 1997 election, has failed to dent these trends, with political trust continuing to fall on both sides of the border.

Alternative or protest activity, unlike in the USA, is up slightly in the UK. From 1986 to 2000, the proportion signing a petition rose from 34 to 42 per cent; contacting a Member of Parliament rose from 11 to 16 per cent; and going on a demonstration rose from 6 to 10 per cent.

The picture on informal sociability is best described as mixed. Visiting friends is down markedly across groups, and especially among men in full-time employment. But other forms of socializing, such as going to pubs and sports clubs, are up.

But perhaps the most dramatic and worrying trend for the UK is that social trust – a key headline indicator – has fallen sharply. In 1959, 56 per cent felt that most others could be trusted, but this had fallen to 44 per cent by the 1980s and to less than 30 per cent by 1996 – a fall of more than 50 per cent.[12] On a slightly more positive note, the most recent World Values Survey data at the time of writing suggest no further fall in social trust in 1999, and data from the British Social Attitudes surveys show a slight increase in social trust from 1997 to 2000.

But perhaps the most striking point about the UK data, brought out by both Hall (1999) and Grenier and Wright (2001), is the disparity in trends across social classes. While in the USA, Putnam has emphasized the large generational differences in social volunteering, membership and so on, in the UK it is the social class differences that leap out and appear to be growing over time – though recent evidence from the cohort studies suggests that marked generational shift may also have occurred (Ferri, Bynner and Wadsworth, 2003). To take one of any number of examples, levels of political interest in the UK look as though they have changed little overall between 1981 and 1999, falling marginally from 39 to 38 per cent of people describing themselves as 'interested' or 'very interested' in politics. But among professionals and managers (class AB), interest has risen from 56 to 66 per cent, while among the unskilled and semi-skilled (class DE), interest has fallen from 33 to 18 per cent. Hence we find that political protest activities, though rising, are dominated by the middle classes, while voting – which shows much less social skew – is falling. This pattern presents a serious challenge for democracy. Similarly, a recent review of trends in associational membership in England and Wales from 1972 to 1999 concluded that, despite a broad pattern of stability, there had been 'a class polarisation in membership in which working class men have been increasingly marginalised from associational memberships' (Li et al., 2002).

On balance, the overall pattern suggests that Britain has witnessed a significant decline in social capital over the last few decades, though not as universally or simply as the USA. There is some evidence that aspects of this decline have halted in very recent years. Perhaps more accurately we should place the UK's middle classes in a category of gently rising social capital, and the manual classes in a category of falling sharply.

Other nations

In terms of the headline indicator of social trust, most of the countries from the former Soviet Union can be provisionally placed in the category of declining social capital through the 1980s and 1990s, including Russia, Hungary, Poland, Lithuania, Estonia, Romania, Bulgaria and Latvia. This seems likely to reflect the destruction of the forms of social capital and network that allowed these societies to function under the previous regime. Marked declines in social trust also appear to have occurred in South Korea, Portugal and the South American countries of Argentina and Brazil, the latter three from levels that were already relatively low (see figure 7.2).

Nations showing stable or rising social capital: Sweden, the Netherlands and Japan

Perhaps the single most striking point from analyses of other nations is that the USA pattern of decline does not appear to be universal.

Sweden

Sweden, like its Scandinavian neighbours, is a strikingly high social trust nation (see figure 2.1), and has very high levels of organizational membership – 92 per cent of Swedes belong to a voluntary organiza-

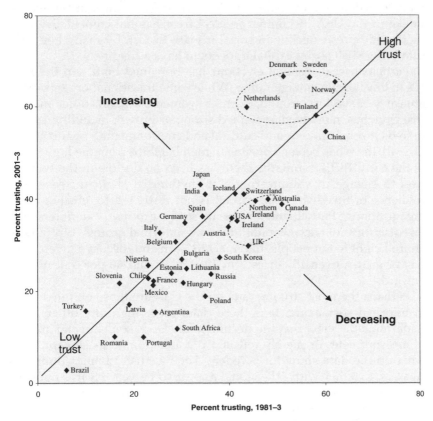

Figure 7.2 *Changes in levels of national trust from 1981–3 to 2001–3*
Source: World Values Surveys data and other sources.
Note: Nations above the diagonal line have shown increases in trust, while those below the line have shown decreases. Note the cluster of high- and rising-trust Scandinavian countries at the top right and the cluster of moderate- but falling-trust Anglo-Saxon countries in the centre right of the figure.

tion (Rothstein, 2001). One might therefore think that it would be a nation with the furthest to fall in terms of social capital. Trust in parliament and the government did indeed fall in the late 1980s, as Sweden's political institutions struggled to maintain the famed 'Swedish model' in the face of global economic pressures, scandals and tensions within the long-standing corporatist arrangements of the state. Political parties have become more professional, sidelining volunteer members. They have also seen a decline in youth membership levels, though overall membership levels have stayed constant. However, unlike in the USA, declining political trust has not coincided with a more widespread decline in social capital. In fact, by many key indicators, Swedish social capital appears to have strengthened.

Participation in general elections has remained high – in the high 80s to low 90s percentage range. While some traditional organizations appear to have lost ground, such as women's organizations and the free churches, most have remained strong or grown, including sports, retired citizens', unions, and cultural and environmental organizations. Overall, there has been no decline in memberships from the high levels of the early 1950s. Similarly, there has been no decline in the willingness to engage in volunteering – if anything, a slight increase. The resilience of Swedish social capital is not restricted to 'cheque-book' organizations. Participation rates in study groups – an interesting Swedish form of social capital involving informal groups, typically of around eight to ten people, that meet to learn and discuss a given topic – have grown from 15 per cent in 1960 to around 40 per cent in 1975 onwards.

Perhaps the most striking data on the USA are those on the decline in informal socializing. It is these data, more than any others, that undermine the view that the decline in the US is somehow an artefact of measurement, or merely reflect a privatization of social capital. So what do the data show for Sweden? The Swedish Living Conditions surveys, together with other data, appear to be very clear – informal socializing in Sweden has risen. For example, the percentage of people who get together with friends each week rose from 45 to 57 per cent between 1975 and 1995 – a rise of 21 per cent (contrast this with the fall of around 50 per cent in the USA over the same period). Similarly, a detailed study of the Swedish town of Katrineholm, with data from 1950 and 1988, concluded that residents had become more socially active, and now 'socialize more frequently with their fellow workers, neighbours and friends' (Perlinski, quoted in Rothstein, 2001, p. 224). The proportion of Swedes saying they have gone to a restaurant more than five times during the last five years increased from 25 to 41 per cent from 1982 to 1995 – a rise of 64 per cent. Reflecting this trend, the number of fully licensed restaurants increased seven-fold between 1967 and the late 1990s.

Finally, social trust, the headline indicator of social capital – despite already being among the highest of any nation – appears to have risen still higher. In 1981, 57 per cent of Swedes felt that most others could be trusted. By 1997, this had risen to 67 per cent. The same high level – 66 per cent – was found in the 2001–3 World Values Survey (see figure 7.2).

The Netherlands

The Netherlands shows a similar pattern to Sweden (De Hart and Dekker, 1999). Membership rates and intensity of engagement have increased for most types of organization, with the exception of traditional women's organizations and political parties. However, despite the relative fall in party memberships, voting has remained stable, and political activism has increased. Volunteering has also increased, though it declined among the younger age group. Unlike Germany, the proportion reporting that they would have someone to count on in times of difficulty rose across income groups from 1996 to 2001, from around 40 to more than 50 per cent (Eurobarometer data). Finally, social trust appears to have increased sharply, rising from 44 to 60 per cent between 1981 and 1999, a level maintained in the 2001–3 World Values Survey.

Japan

Japan is a relatively unusual nation in many respects, including in the character of its social capital. The data for Japan are not clear cut, but on balance appear to be fairly placed in the 'stable' or 'rising' social capital category. Fukuyama famously argued that Japan and the USA were alike in both being high-trust nations, unlike China, where he argued that trust tended not to extend outside of the family setting (Fukuyama, 1995a,b). But his analysis tended to ignore an important difference in that the Japanese have traditionally been very trusting of the people and institutions that they know personally (but which clearly extend to more than family), while being very wary of relative strangers (unlike the Americans, who show a more generalized trust).

Against this background, nearly all indicators of social capital appear to be rising in Japan (Inoguchi, 2000). The numbers of associations has expanded dramatically in Japan from the late 1950s – the number of non-profit associations increased approximately 400 per cent from 1957 to 1996. However, as we noted earlier, numbers of organizations are not a secure indicator of actual involvement – even in the USA, this indicator has risen (though by nothing like the same amount as in Japan). Time-budget studies show neighbourhood- and area-based civic involvement have remained approximately constant. More general civic 'social welfare' activities have been slowly rising, and volunteering to help children, the aged and the disadvantaged has risen dramatically, from 1.7 per cent in 1976 to 5.5 per cent in 1996 – a more than three-fold increase, though from a relatively modest starting point. However, these increases appear to be accounted for by an increasingly intense engagement by a fixed proportion of the population. Also, if the firm is accepted as a form of social capital – especially in the Japanese case – there must be a question mark over whether this form of social capital has declined, or at least significantly changed, as the traditional Japanese contract for life has weakened.

Trust in political institutions appears to have increased significantly in Japan from the 1960s to the late 1990s. For example, trust in elections rose from 67 to 77 per cent between 1976 and 1996, and the proportion rating democracy as 'good' rose from 38 to 59 per cent between 1963 and 1993. However, trust in politicians has fallen – the proportions agreeing that politicians should be entrusted to resolve problems fell from 43 to 24 per cent between 1953 and 1993. This disjunction between trusting the institutions of democracy, yet distrusting the politicians within it, is interpreted by Japanese scholars in terms of the long Japanese history of a trusted and powerful civil service, together with politicians, being viewed as very 'ordinary' people strongly entangled in local pork-barrel politics.

Trend data on informal socializing do not seem to be widely available. But Japanese data on social trust show a clear rise from 26 to 38 per cent between 1978 and 1993 – a rise of nearly 50 per cent. Separate data from the World Values Surveys show a similar rise in social trust, from 34 per cent in the early 1980s to 43 per cent by 2003. Japanese measures of distrust show a corresponding drop. The percentage agreeing that 'other people try to take advantage of you when you manifest a blind spot' fell from 39 to 25 per cent between 1978 and 1993.

Other nations

Other nations on which we have far fewer data, but which also appear to be in the 'stable' or 'rising' category on the basis of World Values Survey data, include Norway and Denmark at the high-trust end, and Mexico at the low-trust end.

Nations showing a mixed pattern: Germany and France

We saw earlier that Britain could arguably be placed in the 'mixed' category, at least in terms of the contradictory trends for those from different social classes. A number of other European nations do not appear to show the same declines as the Anglo-Saxon nations, but nor do they show the same resilience or even growth in social capital of nations such as Sweden.

Germany

Germany mostly shows a pattern of relative stability in social capital, though starting from relatively depressed post-war levels (Offe and Fuchs, 1998). Formal participation has generally increased, though some traditional organizations have shown a decline in memberships, notably the trade unions, political parties and churches. In 1953, 53 per cent were members of one or more associations and in 1996, the figure was almost unchanged at 55 per cent (West Germany only). Volunteering is, if anything, up slightly. As in Sweden, informal sociability has increased. Social trust increased modestly from 31 to 35 per cent from 1981 to 2001–3 (West German data, World Values Survey). However, there appear to be warning signs too, such as the fall in the proportion reporting that they would find someone to count on in times of difficulty. This fell sharply between 1996 and 2001, particularly among those in the lowest income quartile, falling from around 50 per cent to less than 25 per cent in West Germany and from around 40 to 30 per cent in East Germany – though possibly partly reflecting rising unemployment over the period (Eurobarometer data). There has also been a marked fall in associational activity among the youngest cohort, with the portion being a member in any organization falling from 55 to 46 per cent between 1984 and 1996, and in general memberships appear to be becoming more shallow and transient (Offe and Fuchs, 1998). As one recent review of trends in Germany concluded, 'there are instances of both declining and rising social capital' (Jungbauer-Gans, 2002, p. 189). Germany certainly doesn't seem to be characterized either by the general pattern of decline seen in the USA, or by the growth seen in Sweden and the Netherlands.

France

France starts from a base of relatively low social capital by most conventional measures (Worms, 2000). As in the UK and some other countries, there appears to be little overall change in levels of associational membership, but within this envelope many of the more traditional organizations have suffered falling membership, including trade unions, political parties and the church. Cultural and leisure organizations, together with special interest groups, have grown. In contrast to the UK, social class differences in associational membership appear to have reduced. Between 1983 and 1996, the percentage of the most educated who belonged to at least one association fell from 64 to 56 per cent, while amongst the least educated the percentage remained flat at around 35 per cent (Worms, 2000). Although Worms does not include the same range of data as is available for some other nations, data from the World Values Surveys suggest that social trust fell from an already low level of 24 to 22 per cent over the period 1981 to 2001–3, putting France in the 'mixed' category.

Summarizing the trends across countries

It is a fascinating picture that is beginning to emerge across countries. The simple hypothesis that social capital is falling in a uniform manner across nations is not borne out by the data. Some nations, such as Australia and the USA, appear to show a decline – or social disengagement – across most indicators. Other nations, such as Sweden, the Netherlands and Japan, show no such general decline and indeed appear to show an increase on many key measures. The UK increasingly looks like its Anglo-Saxon relatives, while France and Germany stand somewhere in between.

Yet even within this diversity, some near-universal trends can be made out. Across nearly all nations, traditional forms of organization such as the churches, women's organizations, trade unions and political parties tend to be on the decline. Where they are resisting the trend, this is generally linked to very particular national circumstances, such as the way unemployment benefits are paid via the unions in Sweden, making membership a virtual condition of such benefits.[13] In contrast, there has been a near-universal rise in the cheque-book-based memberships of environmental and other special interest groups. These organizations are generally less demanding of time, and increasingly look less like 'associations' – as members rarely meet or socially associate with one another – and more like a new way of expressing views in support of particular issues.

Political 'activism' too seems to be increasingly heading this way, with most mainstream political parties relying less on their membership base and more on a professional and media-oriented core. It is tempting to blame the widespread decline in voting on this professionalization of the parties. But it is equally likely that professionalization is what the parties have learnt that they have to do in order to succeed in the context of an electorate that is no longer prepared to dedicate itself to all-encompassing political parties and their worldviews.

Researchers studying value and attitude change have used the term 'moral entrepreneurs' to describe how people increasingly seem to be mixing and matching values and value systems to fashion their own particular viewpoints (Halpern, 1995b). So too we find that in most nations, citizens are just as willing as ever – if not more so – to sign specific petitions or join particular protests about specific issues, but they are not willing to sign up to an all-encompassing and inflexible package of beliefs.

Interestingly, the data suggest that across European nations, there has been little fall in either political knowledge or interest. Generally speaking, the people of most nations have only modest to low levels of political knowledge and interest, but this was always the case (Van Deth, 2000). This finding at first seems paradoxical in that it does not square with the widespread declines in voting. Van Deth's interpretation is that while interest in politics has not changed, as measured by how often people talk about it, the 'salience' of politics in people's everyday lives has declined (Van Deth, 2000; see also chapter 6). In other words, if you ask people how important various aspects of life are to them, politics is now very firmly at the bottom of the pile, with religion not that far behind. In contrast, the importance assigned to other areas of life, such as leisure time, friends and acquaintances, has risen sharply.

This widespread pattern of declining traditional organizations, voting and support for traditional political parties fits fairly well with Putnam's thesis, and also with the popular interpretation that across the world people are becoming more individualistic and even hedonistic. However, this simple story line does not then explain why other measures of social capital appear to be on such divergent trends across nations. Why is it that while Americans and Australians are seeing less of their friends, the Swedes and Germans are seeing more of them? Why is it that while Americans, Australians and the British have become less trusting of each other, the Swedes, Dutch and Japanese have become more so?

Rothstein describes the trends in Sweden as a shift 'from collective mass movements to organised individualism' (Rothstein, 2001, p. 15). Meanwhile, in a very different context, Inoguchi characterizes the shift in Japan as one from 'honorific collectivism' to 'co-operative individualism' (Inoguchi, 2000). Within the USA, in contrast, growing individualism seems to be manifested in a more privatized and materialist form.

It would seem that all nations are shifting towards a certain kind of individualism, but that the character of this individualism differs greatly between nations. In some places, such as Sweden, people seem to be finding a way of expressing their growing individuality within a lifestyle that maintains and enhances the connections between them – what Rothstein calls 'solidaristic individualism'. But in the USA it is manifested in a more fragmenting form of what we might call 'egoistic individualism'.

A concept such as 'solidaristic individualism' may seem a contradiction in terms, but the meaning of this concept is that solidarity does not necessarily imply collectivism, that is, that people have more or less the same values and share the same lifestyles and may be interested in and engaged in the same organisations. By 'solidaristic individualism' I mean that individuals are willing to give support to other individuals but also accept that they have other, different values and want to engage themselves for different causes. This support, however, is given under the condition that they can trust their fellow citizens to give the same support back for their own different lifestyles and organisational efforts. (Rothstein, 2001, p. 219)

It would seem that if we can explain this divergence in the nature and expression of individualism across nations, then we will have a better handle on the diverging patterns of social capital development across nations.

Other evidence: are there any important countertrends?

It may be that there are other aspects of social capital that have attracted less attention but that might tell a different story. For example, attention has been drawn to the potential importance of, but lack of systematic measurement of, childcare activities (Lowndes, 2000). Lowndes points out that regular, shared and reciprocal responsibilities are often involved in childcare arrangements. In fact, time-budget studies from several nations suggest that the amount of time devoted to childcare *has* increased significantly over recent decades.

Measures of household structure are another indicator that has been given little attention, except possibly as a control variable. In this case, the measure confirms the trends we have already seen. In many (perhaps most) nations, there has been a substantial growth in the number of single-person households across age groups. This trend probably reflects another aspect of rising individualism, with people choosing their own company over the 'compromises' involved in larger domestic arrangements.

Perhaps there are changes occurring in other kinds of institutional and cultural arrangements that compensate for the declines in certain types of social capital. For example, legal frameworks may be evolving to take on more of the burden of enforcing contracts (as Putnam indicates through his data on lawyers). This type of activity may not be termed social capital, but it may be taking on its functional role – you don't have to 'trust' others if you know you can 'sue their pants off' if they let you down.

Putnam notes that 'one potential yardstick for honesty and trust-worthiness is the crime rate' (Putnam, 2000, p. 144). He shows us a graph of both the total recorded crime rate and the murder rate for the USA from 1960 until the late 1990s, both of which show dramatic rises (and correlate very highly). Surely he is right about crime being an important yardstick, or indirect indicator of trust. Murder is a pretty dramatic indication of a break-down in trust and co-operation between people.

In fact, fascinating work has been done mapping the murder rate for various nations over much longer periods of time – not just over decades, but over hundreds of years (Eisner, 2001). This works relies on the painstaking compilation of court and other records, together with estimates of population sizes over the ages. Using these techniques, trends in murder rates have been calculated for ten different European nations stretching back more than 500 years. And the findings? All the nations studied show the same basic pattern. Murder rates have *fallen* dramatically over the last several hundred years, and the scale of these declines dwarfs the rises in many nations from the 1950s onwards. Typically, the murder rate has fallen approximately *one hundred-fold* since the Middle Ages!

It is easy to conjure a romantic image of a high social capital past: of cosy villages living in harmony and tranquillity. But Eisner's dramatic statistics remind us that people often did not get along. Minor slights of honour between individuals or families could lead to violent arguments, and such disagreements were surprisingly frequent. Over hundreds of years, and almost invariably starting in the cities and centres of learning, people have gradually and painfully learnt how to co-operate and get along better with each other. In particular, there has been a long-term growth in what we would call bridging social capital and explicit social norms (normative social capital).

To caricature, medieval villages were probably places that we would recognize as having very high bonding social capital. Though shared customs and practices might never be written down, people all knew each other well enough to work together bringing in the harvest or building a barn. However, contact with outsiders was relatively difficult and limited, and when a stranger did pass through the village, they would be the subject of great distrust. As trade and cities have grown, they have been premised on people developing codes of conduct – both formal and informal – that made living and trading together for mutual advantage possible. Small groups can achieve trust through direct knowledge and negotiation, but growing circles of acquaintances must instead rely on codifying the rules that govern their interaction as a way of achieving trust.[14]

Hence we see in the late Middle Ages not just the development of written laws, powerful judiciaries and state institutions, but also the development of manners and a host of other widely accepted codes of conduct. Not defecating at the dinner table or taking food off the plates of strangers are now so widely accepted that it would not occur to us that these behaviours are even options. Similarly, we have long since come to rely unthinkingly on a common and relatively abstract system of credit – money. When you reflect on this, as sociologists such as Simmel have done in the past, it is a remarkable phenomenon that we will part with objects of great practical value, like food or tools, for a handful of useless marked paper. Indeed today, most of the time we don't even get any paper, but simply trust some invisible electronic transaction overseen by distant machines and people. From this perspective, something truly remarkable has happened over modern history – there has been an immense transformation and growth in common understanding and trust, and this has greatly facilitated co-operative action between people.

There is a major 'spanner' in this great historical caricature. People may have been murdering each other less in an intimate, everyday sort of way, but what about wars and major conflicts? As everyone knows, the twentieth century was marred by wars and death on a scale never seen before. This must be part of our story too. As cities and nations have grown, formed on the back of wider and wider circles of shared understandings and perceived group memberships, this same growth has both facilitated co-operation within groups and, at the same time, aggravated the scale of conflicts between these groups. As pointed out right at the start of the book, social capital facilitates co-operative action but, just like other forms of capital, there is no guarantee that this capability will be used wisely. Conflicts are only reduced when social networks, shared understandings and systems of sanctions – the three components of social capital – expand, or converge across groups, to encompass the conflicting parties.[15]

Even in the USA, the same decades as have seen such marked declines in micro- and meso-forms of social capital have also witnessed the extension of civil rights, dramatic increases in tolerance in the personal and sexual domain, and substantial reductions in expressed racial, gender and other prejudices.

In my view, we cannot understand contemporary trends in social capital, and the rise of contemporary individualism, unless we see them against the background of this wider story of how societies have learnt to get along. When we drive on the road, we can only do so safely because we share a set of understandings with the countless other drivers whom we pass. When we stay in a strange village many miles from home, we do so without fear that our money will not be accepted or that we will be fleeced by distrustful villagers. And even when we go into a store in the USA and the sales person we have never met before, and will probably never meet again, says 'Have a nice day!', though they don't mean it in the same way as a friend we have known for life, it is nonetheless the tip of a huge iceberg of shared understanding that makes contemporary life liveable.

In short, I am arguing that the achievement of these mass common understandings is what make it possible for some forms of social capital to decay, but for society not to fall apart. This turns the account into a story primarily of *transformation* rather than decay. In terms of figure 1.4 (chapter 1), modern societies are witnessing an ongoing transformation of social capital to ever higher levels of generality – a steady growth of macro-level social capital, while in some nations at least, the micro-level is decaying as it becomes functionally no longer essential.[16]

Understanding the causes of changing social capital

Now that we have an overview of trends across nations, we can see that we have two quite different stories to explain. On the one hand, there are certain trends that appear to apply across nations, the most notable being the falling popularity of certain wide-ranging, fairly all-purpose organizations, such as the church, trade unions and women's organizations. On the other hand, we have to explain how it is that other forms of social capital, including informal socializing and social trust, have shown such divergent trends across nations.

Putnam's explanation of the decline in the USA

Putnam explores what might account for the decline in meso- and micro-level social capital in the USA through statistical modelling techniques (Putnam, 2000). He identifies four key variables, through the technique of multiple regression, that account for much of the change over time, these being (with rough percentages shown in brackets):

- generational change (50 per cent),
- television and electronic entertainment (25 per cent),
- work intensity (10 per cent) and
- urban sprawl (10 per cent).

There is no doubt that the pattern of change in the USA is strongly generational. In other words, each generation born since World War II has become somewhat less socially engaged, but each generation has more or less maintained a constant level of engagement over its life. Hence as older generations die off, the average level of engagement shifts towards that of the younger generations and therefore downwards.

While Putnam shows this pattern very convincingly, two big question marks hang over 'generational change' as an explanation. First, it is not really an explanation, as it replaces one question with another, albeit a more precise one: why is it that younger generations are less engaged? Putnam does offer a few pointers. He speculates that part of it may relate to the experience of the war, a plausible explanation that is boosted by the post-September 11 data. He also argues that some of it may be accounted for by a generationally specific effect of television watching – what statisticians call an interaction term. In essence, the social patterns of older generations were less affected by the development of mass electronic media, while those who were brought up watching TV did so at the cost of not picking up the social habits of their parents and grandparents. Second, it is important to note that the very marked generational differences seen in the USA appear very much less pronounced in other nations – though UK data hint at such an effect – raising the question of what it is about the USA in particular that gave rise to this pattern.

Electronic entertainment, and in particular television, looms large in Putnam's explanation of the US decline. This explanation is strongly supported by individual-level data showing that the more Americans watch TV, and the less they read newspapers, the less socially engaged they are.

Similarly, individual-level data support the view that the growing intensity of American working life has been a contributory factor. The rise of two-career families, and the intensification of work more generally in the US context, appear to have squeezed out many of the other activities that constituted traditional social capital building. This is not just a matter of women entering the labour market, but of the longer hours and more intense engagement in work of both men and women.

Urban sprawl, and the suburbanization and long commuting times that it has brought, are also supported as causal explanations by individual-level data. Americans have traded inner-city and small-town living and working for large sprawling houses in the suburbs, but the price has been a near total dependence on the car. While Europeans have generally clung to denser forms of urban living, for the average American every household purchase, visit to the gym, school or work, involves a car journey. In this petrol-based lifestyle, the fabric of informal social contacts built up around the neighbourhood store, the walk to school, or just strolling on the sidewalk is lost. Equally importantly, more and more time is used commuting; listening to one's favourite music in the privacy of your own automobile; leaving less time for other more social activities, while the network of freeways and busy roads divides neighbourhoods and reinforces the abandonment of the sidewalk.

Putnam and his team also helpfully eliminate some popular suspects from the explanation. Rising crime does not seem to add anything to the story, once these other variables are accounted for – it is a symptom rather than a cause. Immigration and differences across ethnic groups also don't make the cut. Some have argued that American pluralism has mutated into 'a society falling apart in group particularism', split along ethnic, gender and other lines (Munch, 2002, p. 455), but this may be as much cause as effect and is in any event not generally supported by the data. Finally, and very importantly in the US political context, big government displacing the social capital of ordinary citizens doesn't seem to be part of the explanation of decline. As mentioned in chapter 6, US states with bigger state governments (in terms of taxes and expenditure) are characterized by higher social capital. In addition, federal expenditure as a percentage of US GDP has actually fallen significantly since the 1950s.

Overall, Americans have developed highly individualized forms of consumption. Why go to a concert at which you will have to sit through a piece of Mozart which you dislike, when you could stay at home and listen to the Beethoven CD you just bought? Why make do with the communal parks of the big city when you could buy yourself a big house and garden in the suburbs? In whatever it is you want to do, why deal with the inconvenience of other people when you don't have to? What it is difficult to tell from the US data is what drives what. Is it that the supply of individualized consumer goods has caused social disengagement, or is that increasingly disengaged Americans have demanded and sought a lifestyle of individualized consumption?

How does the US explanation square with what is happening elsewhere?

While Putnam's analysis is careful and considered, it is almost completely US-based. This leaves it subject to various important criticisms. First, counterfactual cases are not considered. Second, more or less by definition, it cannot capture the potential importance of any US-specific but uniform variables. Third, by the time Putnam wrote *Bowling Alone,* he no longer had only academic audiences in his sights but was also concerned that the issues be taken up seriously by a wider audience. In the US political and ideological context, this may have led to the de-emphasis of parts of the story that are uncomfortable or difficult in the US. In particular, to a European eye at least, the limited discussion of economic inequality and the potentially positive causal role that might be played by the state is especially striking.

A wider international comparison does indeed throw up questions for Putnam's US account. First, the very pronounced generational differences in social engagement in the US are far less pronounced in other nations, and in some cases are even reversed (for example, in Germany).

The causal role of television and other electronic media is called into question by the straightforward observation that the same media are just as widespread in those nations that show little or no decline in social capital, such as Sweden and Japan. While it is true that TV became widespread in the US a few years earlier than in many other nations, a difference between the late 1950s and early 1960s cannot be very significant forty-plus years on. This suggests either that TV watching in the US is more a symptom than a cause, or that there is a TV–nation interaction, rather as Putnam suggests that there is a TV–generation interaction within the USA. Both explanations could draw support from the finding that, within the US, the small minority who watch public broadcasting TV are more engaged than those who don't. Similar results apply in the UK for those who watch the news. One plausible explanation for a TV–nation interaction is therefore that the content of TV matters. Commentators have long compared the character of US TV, with its multiple, attention-grabbing channels and high advertising content, with the more staid European style of TV, with fewer channels, state-funded channels, fewer adverts and more public information content. Over recent years, the advent of satellite and cable TV within Europe has brought TV content closer to the US style, and it will be interesting to see what impact this has.

Putnam's work-intensity and urban-sprawl explanations are the ones that, at a glance, stand up most convincingly to international comparison. Americans certainly do appear to be far more into work than their more relaxed European cousins, and the differences appear to be getting larger, not smaller. European states have developed far more extensive employment legislation – itself built on the back of popular sentiment – to ensure that workers do not work 'excessive' hours and that they get good long holidays. As any business traveller will tell you, the American work-life style of grabbing a sandwich for lunch continues to be regarded with disdain by the Italians, Spanish and French, all of whom consider that stopping for a decent extended meal is much more important than closing an extra deal. The French have even implemented the 'Aubrey rules', limiting the working week to 35 hours – and though they have subsequently softened their application, their very possibility is surely unthinkable in the US context.

Similarly, many European nations have strongly resisted urban sprawl, both in consumption patterns and through regulatory instruments. For example, some nations and regions place a limit on the maximum size of retail units in order to ensure that large retail shops do not displace small traders and the traditional urban city centre. European publics have also been far more willing to pay high petrol duties, and subsidize and invest in public transport.

Could it be that the differing nature of TV, employment legislation, and reduced urban spread helps to explain the relative lack of decline in social capital within mainland Europe? As ever with such trends, it is quite difficult to separate cause from effect, and demand from supply. In all likelihood, patterns of consumption and social capital trends are causally interlocked, feeding on and reinforcing each other, creating causal pathways that may radically diverge over time yet differ only slightly step by step (see also chapter 8). Mainland Europeans love their café culture, but who is to say which came first – the café or the culture?

In sum, the international comparisons only partly support the Putnam case. The causes that he identifies as implicated in the decline of social capital in the USA are less pronounced in mainland Europe, and so too is evidence of the decline in social capital. However, the causal direction of the interrelationship between these trends can be contested.

The role of government

One major difference that stands out in the international comparisons is the role of the state. In the US, the role of the state is popularly reviled in favour of the belief that the individual and community can sort things out for themselves. But in other nations, this popular antagonism over the role of government is far less pronounced. Most importantly, a number of social capital researchers looking at trends outside the US have been struck by how governments have often actively promoted social capital, even if they haven't used the term. Even in the UK, in many ways culturally similar to the USA, Hall (himself an American academic) notes in his review that: 'Since the turn of the century [i.e. the early 1900s], British governments have made great efforts to cultivate the voluntary sector, notably by involving it in the delivery of social services to a degree that seems striking in cross-national terms. This is an objective to which they have also devoted substantial resources' (Hall, 1999, p. 440). It is highly likely that the role of the state is part of the story. Even among the factors identified by Putnam in the USA, government action – or inaction – is always close at hand. Suburban sprawl relates closely to planning law, as well as to transport, education and urban policy. Work intensification relates to labour law and to a host of other variables affected by government action. Even television is greatly affected by the regulatory and funding structure set by government. As ever, the key question is whether government institutions and policy have effects over and above the effects of the values in the wider population that such policies reflect.

One tantalizing clue within the US data is provided by Brehm and Rahn (1997). In a statistical model to explain variations in social trust in high school children in the USA, they found that satisfaction with government significantly and positively predicts social trust. They found that confidence in government was extremely important in shaping social trust even when controlling for the potential reciprocal path from social trust to confidence in government. As we noted above, confidence in the US government has fallen dramatically over recent decades, in contrast say to Japan, and this may help to explain some of the trends in social capital. It will be interesting to see if the brief resurgence of more positive attitudes to the US government post 9/11 had any effect on high school children.

Economic inequality

Hall had in mind, in his quotation above, a relatively direct investment by governments in voluntary and charitable organizations. But perhaps equally, if not more important may be the actions of governments to create the conditions under which social engagement is facilitated and, in particular, containing the growth of inequality.

On this point, it is striking that while the UK – as Hall observes – maintained its long tradition of channelling funding through non-state bodies for the delivery of some front-line services, from at least 1979 to

1997 it failed to take serious action about widening economic and class inequality, and economic inequality rose sharply. Over the same period, class differentials in social capital in the UK also rose, and social trust fell (Grenier and Wright, 2001).

Other European nations have been much more successful in containing inequality. On the face of it therefore, changing levels of inequality are a good causal candidate to explain not just trends in social capital across nations, but absolute differences between nations too. This wider causal role is returned to in chapter 8.

Education

Virtually every piece of empirical research on social capital has concluded that education, and particularly university education, is associated with higher levels of social capital at the individual level. The more educated people are, the more clubs and associations they seem to join; the more politically engaged they are; and the more they trust other people (see chapter 5).

There is considerable uncertainty about why this may be. Being away from home and in contact with a wider circle of people; acquiring a core of shared cultural knowledge; and acquiring the basic human skills of team-working, trusting and understanding others are all plausible causal candidates. It could be that it is not the content of the education at all that matters, but that high-skills people end up in high-trust work environments, and that it is these environments that mediate the familiar education–social capital association. However, what is certainly true is that across OECD nations, levels of educational attainment and staying-on rates have increased greatly over the last few decades.

These increased staying-on rates in education – if the link is causal – should be driving *up* social capital across nations. Put another way, if we statistically control for rising educational levels, then the social capital story looks much more negative over time.

This observation raises two important points, one methodological and one substantive. On the methodological point, it implies that it is important to read the small print of the statistical analyses of social capital trends. Authors who statistically control for education will conclude that there has been a greater decline than those who do not. Second, it implies that the underlying trend in social capital in some nations may be more negative than current analyses imply. It may be that rising educational attendance – such as the massive expansion of higher education in the UK since the 1960s – is offsetting strong underlying downward pressures on social capital.

Summary of headline causes of change

Putnam concludes that a large portion of the decline in American social capital is generationally based, reflecting the dying off of older, more civic generations. This generational pattern does not seem to be seen across all nations, and itself requires further explanation. Work intensity and urban sprawl are plausible causes of decline that are supported by international patterns of evidence. TV watching *per se* is not supported by cross-national evidence as a cause of decline, though its content may matter. Rising economic inequality is also implicated as a possible negative factor. Rising education appears to be a positive factor, perhaps overshadowed by other rising negative factors.

A common thread is the emergence of individualized and privatized consumption patterns. The role of government is also implicated. But both factors are difficult to separate from other trends and from nations' underlying value base (see below and also chapter 8).

An 'ecology' of value and consumption change

As indicated above, some of the so-called causes – such as generational differences – are as much refined descriptions of the trends as true explanations. Even changing consumption patterns, government action and economic inequality are not entirely convincing explanations, as they in turn raise the question of why these patterns have changed. For example, the rise in economic inequality in the UK, compared with Germany, can partly be attributed to government policy, but it probably rests more with popular attitudes and values that made inequality more acceptable in the UK than in Germany. Tax regimes make a difference, but their impact is generally modest in comparison with that of the socioeconomic worldview that lies behind whether managers are paid ten times versus a hundred times more than their employees.

Value change

Hall notes that in as much as there has been a reduction in social trust, the causal factors 'may be rooted in a broader shift in moral values' (Hall, 1997, p. 25). There is clear evidence of changes in moral values having occurred in the industrialized nations since the late 1960s (Halpern, 1995b). However, the pattern of change is far more subtle and interesting than is indicated by most popular commentators. Here we shall focus on the specific issue of whether people have become more selfish and self-interested, and whether this undermines social capital.

Periodic moral panics occur as politicians, market researchers and others rediscover that young people tend to have very different values from older generations. A common finding in social surveys is that young people tend to have more tolerant – or permissive, depending on your standpoint – attitudes towards morally debatable acts. This means that if you project forward from a cross-sectional survey you are likely to come to the conclusion that a huge shift in values is taking place (e.g. Wilkinson, 1996). Yet this shift generally does not happen, and the reason is because people's values change as they age. In simple terms, we tend to become like our parents as we age. When we look longitudinally, the most common pattern is of only very modest or no change in values over time. But there are exceptions to this rule.

The post-materialism thesis

Perhaps the best-known exception to the rule of 'no change' is Ronald Inglehart's work on the shift towards what he calls 'post-materialism'. Inglehart (1990) measured post-materialism by asking people to choose between which of various objectives were more important. The choices included both material objectives (such as economic growth) and 'higher needs'[17] (such as freedom of speech). He used people's choices to categorize them as either 'materialists' or 'post-materialists', the latter identifying higher, less material needs as being more important.

Inglehart found that richer nations and younger generations were far more 'post-materialistic' than poorer nations and older generations, and that each generation had, more or less, kept its values over a period of more than two decades. This has meant that as older generations have died off, there has been a dramatic shift away from traditional, materialistic, economic-growth-oriented values towards post-materialist, 'higher-need' values. In short, Inglehart argues that in the world's wealthy nations, as their basic material needs have been met, they have become less concerned with material goals and more concerned with relatively esoteric objectives such as freedom of speech and the need to protect the environment.

The curious point about Inglehart's work is that, if anything, it would seem to imply that social capital ought to be going up, as economic self-interest is overtaken by wider social and liberal concerns.

The answer to this puzzle may lie in a methodological problem at the heart of Inglehart's work – his use of a forced-choice method. If I say that freedom of speech is more important than earning more money, it doesn't necessarily imply that I think earning money has become less important – it could be that I think that they are both more important! Inglehart's 'post-materialism' scale picks up not only 'materialism', but also a growing commitment to libertarian values – freedom of speech and democratic institutions. Hence his scale compounds two sets of values. Far from being opposites, both values seem be increasing at the same time – at least in the USA – though perhaps with the libertarian values growing slightly more strongly.

Individuals freed from tradition

Inglehart's work shows that some kind of widespread, generationally based value shift has occurred. As we have already seen, in virtually all nations, church attendance and party-political commitment are down. This connects us to a pre-existing debate about the break-down of traditional norms and customs (Halpern, 1995b).

Part of this value shift includes the erosion of the norm of obedience to authority itself. This is picked up not only in the widespread decline in respect for political leaders and institutions that we have already noted, but in the emphasis placed on the importance of alternative qualities by parents in their children. While stress on obedience in children has declined, more emphasis has instead been given to qualities such as independence of mind.

It would seem that the conditions of modernity expose individuals to many alternative worldviews and values. This exposure undermines the unthinking acceptance of established moral rules and social norms. For example, there has been a great increase in tolerance in the personal-sexual arena, such as attitudes towards divorce, homosexuality and prostitution. To a large extent, individuals can 'pick and mix' their values from those on offer, leading to the description of current younger generations as 'moral entrepreneurs' (D. G. Barker, 1991; Halpern, 1995b).

Such moral entrepreneurs no longer readily identify with the traditional communities of the past. For example, the proportion of people saying that they would be willing to fight for their country has fallen since the early 1970s in most industrialized nations. But national pride and identification are strongly associated (at the individual level) with higher social trust and social capital, even after having controlled for demographic variables (Whiteley, 1998). And declines in such national pride – or the 'imaginary communities' they indicate – are a

plausible contributor to falls in certain forms of associational membership and trust.

The role of technology and wealth

It is not only the undermining of monolithic value systems that
has loosened the bonds that helped to maintain more traditional
lifestyles. Economic growth, powered by the sheer efficiency and
productivity of modern economies, has also loosened the constraints
on people's lifestyles. Of course, this economic productivity is itself
partly premised on the shared understandings, or rules of trade
and habits of everyday engagement, that have become increasingly
universal.

Wealth means that people increasingly have the resources to escape
the web of immediate dependencies that have characterized most of
human history. Wealth means that families and communities no longer
need to share valuable resources, like housing. They no longer need to
come together to gather the harvest or build their barns. Instead we, in
the wealthy nations of the modern world, can all have our own homes,
our own TVs, fridges, cookers, cars or whatever. Our wealth enables
us to escape a myriad of minor inconveniences that beset our grandparents. We don't have to argue over who should fetch the water, which
tune should be played on the piano, or even which TV channel to
watch, as each person can have their own TV.

Many of these changes have been reflected in the physical design of
our houses and our neighbourhoods. Studies of housing design have
shown how, over the last two centuries and the last fifty or so years in
particular, there has been a gradual disappearance of 'semi-public'
space:

> Whereas the interior collective domain provides the prime example of a
> transition space during the nineteenth century, it has [today] been trans-
> formed into a cavernous, coercitive passage devoid of any potential use
> other than circulation. Moreover, it is more strongly demarcated
> from both the private and public realms of the residential areas than in
> the past. . . . This transformation has occurred in tandem with the
> localisation of an increasing number of activities inside the dwelling unit
> during this century. Just as the communal fountain in the street or
> courtyard, once used for laundering clothes, has been replaced by a
> washing machine for each household in the kitchen or laundry room,
> so the proliferation of private radios and televisions has reduced
> the social function of the neighbourhood café or cinema as a place of
> public information, communication and entertainment. (Lawrence, 1990,
> p. 89)

In general it would seem that the relative costs and benefits of suffering the inconveniences of our closest neighbours have shifted. Some of the costs are still recognizable enough – the imposition of unwanted judgements, obligations and preferences on us. But the benefits of physically close, ongoing relationships – or at least the sheer economic necessity of such close co-operation – have surely radically reduced. We don't need to work with our neighbours to ensure our economic survival. And we now have a vast array of sources of entertainment and pleasure that do not rest at all on our immediate neighbours or community. To adapt Hirsch's famous term, the 'economics of neighbouring' have fundamentally changed.

At the same time, the relative costs and benefits of contacts with those who are distant have shifted too. Telecommunications and travel have enormously reduced the costs of interaction with those physically distant from us. And the establishment of shared social norms (including legal and financial frameworks) has further reduced the costs of such interactions and pushed up the potential benefits.

It is no wonder, then, that the main story line of contemporary trends in social capital is one of ever-expanding weak social ties – ever broader and more diffuse bridging social capital, and capital that is based heavily on social norms rather than social networks and personal knowledge. We are moving into a world, powered by the efficient organization of our economies, that is more and more reliant on what some writers have called 'thin trust' – trust between relative strangers (Newton, 1999). This story holds for the USA just as it holds for Sweden. But it is a shift that places greater and greater emphasis on shared mechanisms at the most general level to solve collective action problems and maintain and develop the collective understandings on which it rests. In this latest phase of social development, it seems likely that those nations that start with a high level of distrust of high-level collective mechanisms – such as Americans' instinctive distrust of their federal government – will have most difficulty with this transition.

Individualistic values are not necessarily selfish values

Inglehart's work confirms the widespread rise in libertarian values, but his term 'post-materialism' is generally misleading. Other data show that people have not, in general, become less materialistic. For example, the importance attached to salary in surveys about work has actually increased (see Halpern, 1995b).

Surveys of US high school students from 1976 to 1995 show a marked increased in materialistic values (Rahn and Transue, 1998).

Materialism was measured by material expectations (will they own more possessions than their parents?); the minimal amount it would take to be satisfied (having 'much more than my parents'); and choosing 'having lots of money' as an important goal. These increases very closely match the declines in social trust in the same students. Rahn and Transue found that rising materialism was a much better predictor of declining trust than trends in TV viewing were. It is also striking that materialism appears to level off – perhaps even declining a little (especially the rated importance of money) – in the early 1990s, a year or two before the decline in trust levels off in the students.

If rising materialism in high school students is the source of their declining trust, then what is driving the materialism? A multiple regression provides some clues. As one might expect, disadvantaged background is also associated with greater materialism, identified by mother's lower education, absence of father, and black ethnicity. This could link back to trends in relative inequality, the rich getting richer and the poor being left behind. Rahn and Transue also find that commitment to religion is associated with lower materialism, and this commitment has been falling steadily.

More generally, cross-national data show that tolerance for acts of self-interest – as long as they do not have an obvious and direct 'victim' – has increased (Halpern, 1995b). Consider what happens if you are given too much change when shopping. If the mistake is made by a small shop, most people think that the mistake should be pointed out and the money returned. But if the shop is part of a large chain, people are far more likely to say that it is acceptable to keep the money (Johnston, 1988). Tolerance for such acts of 'self-interest' has shown an increase in recent decades. For example, across nations, people are now far more likely to adopt a 'finders keepers' mentality than they were in the late 1960s, and the scale of the change across time dwarfs national differences (Halpern, 2001).

On the face of it, it would seem that the logical corollary of self-interested values is low social trust. If I know that people are generally self-interested, then I should be wary about trusting others (and vice versa, as Hall points out), not least because we tend to assume that our own values are typical of those of the majority (L. Ross, Greene and House, 1977; Fiske and Taylor, 1991).

A quick analysis of the World Values Survey data confirms this strong negative relationship. However, a more careful analysis shows something very interesting – this strong negative association between self-interest and social trust seems to be unravelling. Even comparing the same group of nations between the 1981 and 1990 sweeps of the

World Values Survey, the strength of this negative association has fallen markedly. Hence widespread increases in self-interested values across nations were *not* generally associated with falls in social trust. This indicates that, contrary to doom-laden predictions, many modern societies are evolving to accommodate *both* the values of self-interest and those of social trust.

Furthermore, there is no sign of people becoming more tolerant of overtly illegal acts – like theft, or drink-driving – or acts of self-interest that have a clear victim. And while local and national loyalties may have weakened – though even this may be disputed – more distant bonds and responsibilities have grown. People have not simply become universally selfish. For example, they express more, not less, willingness to pay taxes to help the poorer nations of the world.

Summarizing value change:
the rise of enlightened self-interest?

The wider pattern of value and consumption change helps us understand the trends we have documented in social capital. On the one hand, we see that the widespread exposure of the population to alternative and competing worldviews and values has undermined traditional holistic and absolutist value systems, and particularly universal religious and political doctrines. Economic growth and technology have strongly underwritten this undermining of tradition and obligation, radically shifting the relative costs and benefits of social interaction away from favouring a reliance on immediate neighbours and in favour of distant, but chosen others. The bonds of ideology, obedience to authority, and reliance on our neighbours through economic necessity have been loosened, freeing people to pick and mix their own more individualistic values and lifestyles.

Yet it would be quite wrong to characterize the resultant values and societies as simply more selfish or just atomized. The individualism of many modern values is underwritten by a solid and widespread commitment to a core of shared understandings. These can be loosely summarized by the simple tenet of many religions, 'don't do unto others that which you wouldn't want done to yourself'. Hence, while across the world people are becoming much more relaxed about what consenting adults do to each other, especially in the privacy of their own homes, they remain steadfastly against dangerous or selfish behaviour that puts others at risk.

My own interpretation of this emerging pattern is that modern societies are learning to 'codify trust'. They do this generally with the help of government action, but also through the types of dialogue that occur in private interactions and through the mass media. This is how societies 'square the circle' between self-interest and social trust. This codifying does not only, or even primarily, result from the codification of appropriate behaviour in formal laws and regulations. Rather it results from the emergence of widely held understandings of what is moral and appropriate behaviour. These understandings, or emergent norms, are based in common culture rather than in traditional embedded communities. These understandings or norms range from the guarantees routinely offered by retailers; to the emergent habits of drivers, such as the now common habit flashing of hazard lights to warn of obstructions ahead (in some countries at least); through to the constant refinement of what constitutes acceptable behaviour in personal relationships.

This said, we still need to explain why it is that in some nations this individualism has taken a more materialistic and privatized turn, such as in the USA, while in other nations it has taken a more 'solidaristic' turn, such as in Sweden. To some extent, these differences may be explained by the economies, geography and internal diversity of different nations. In this sense, it may be that the sheer wealth, scale and diversity of the USA are part of the explanation of its social trajectory, with its particular pattern of consumption fuelling and reinforcing its privatized individualism. Levels of economic inequality, and perhaps social homogeneity more generally, are implicated. But part of the story must also lie in differences in attitudes towards, and power within, the mechanisms of collective action problem solving at the national level, notably government. Urbanization, work intensification, the character of the mass media and so on are not merely the result of individual action or 'exogenous' social and economic forces, but can be shaped by collectively made choices and government action – provided that mechanisms exist within which such choices can be made.

Summary and conclusion:
the contemporary transformation of social capital

Surveying the evidence on trends in social capital has revealed two key story lines. Across nations, certain forms of traditional social capital, such as attending churches and being active in political parties, have declined. At the same time, there has been a widespread increase in low-demand, more individualistic 'memberships' such as cheque-book-based environmental organizations and easy-exit self-help groups.

This trend in social capital is reflected in, and perhaps partly caused by, a rising tide of individualism across the world in terms of personal values and lifestyles. This individualism is itself framed by a growing core of shared values, tolerance of differences between people, and the codification of these values in both law and common practice. This background of shared and codified understanding explains how, across nations, the relationship between self-interested values and social trust is unravelling. Within this framework, it is possible for people to be self-interested, even hedonistic, and yet still trustworthy.

The trend towards the identification and codification of common social norms, and the ever greater extension of weak social ties or networks, stretches back way beyond the last few decades and into previous centuries. Within this wider historical scope, the story becomes less about the decline of social capital in one or two nations, and more about the long-term transformation of social relationships from the 'thick trust' of the traditional community to the 'thin' but powerful trust of the modern society.

Within this big and relatively uniform story, there is a second story line. In some nations, notably the Anglo-Saxon nations of the USA, Australia and perhaps the UK, trends towards individualism and social disengagement have become generalized over recent decades. It is this story that Putnam focuses on in *Bowling Alone*. People have been using their wealth and loosened social, economic and moral constraints to rid themselves of the potential 'inconveniences of others' in all walks of life, from family dinners, to sports clubs, to associations of almost every kind. Sometimes this has been obvious, such as with the growth of gated communities, but in general it has been a more subtle social and psychological withdrawal. In contrast, in nations such as Sweden, the Netherlands and Japan, there is little evidence of such general disengagement. On the contrary, many forms of informal socializing, volunteering and trust between people have increased.

We have identified a number of causal candidates to help explain this second story line of national differences. In the USA at least, suburbanization, work intensification and the mass media appear to help explain or mediate the disengagement from social life, and the shift is strongly generationally based. Looking cross-nationally, government action, backed by a public commitment to government as an appropriate way to solve certain kinds of problems, is strongly implicated as a way of squaring this circle and ensuring the emergence of a more 'solidaristic individualism'. So too is the extent of economic inequality, though it is difficult to say how far this precedes or follows government action, the structuring of social capital and popular values. And changing values and patterns of consumption, themselves partly driven by the choices made possible by contemporary technology and wealth, weave like a causal thread throughout the story.

In reality, these factors are woven together in a causal fabric that makes it difficult to separate them clearly, at least at present. With the passage of time, we will probably be able to document examples where each of these factors altered and the consequences rippled through the other aspects of society. Public values, economic inequality, government action and the structuring of a nation's social capital stand together in a dynamic equilibrium, a web of causality that is examined further in the next chapter. It may be that the shock of the September 11 attacks in New York will sufficiently impact on American stocks of social capital and values to alter government action dramatically and reshape significantly the structure of the American economy and society. The public reactions to the terrible shock of September 11 certainly created a range of opportunities that were there to be seized by the American administration. Similarly in Britain, it may be that the election of a Labour government in 1997, and the investment in public services that has followed, will reduce inequality and lead to more solidaristic values, and these in turn will redirect the character of British social capital away from the American and Australian trajectory and back towards that of its European neighbours. We shall see.

Further reading

If you wish to look at the trends in the *USA*, Putnam's (2000) massive volume is likely to be the Bible on this for some time (see especially chs 1–15).

Trend data for *other countries* are far less comprehensive. Perhaps the most striking contrast with the USA are the trend data for Sweden, usefully summarized in Rothstein (2001). For an example of a mixed story, look at trend data for the UK, such as in Hall (1999). A number of these articles have now been brought together in Putnam (2002).

For a much longer *historical perspective*, try looking at Putnam (2000), ch. 23, on the USA. For the intriguing work on trends in the murder rate over the last 500 years – surely the longest social-capital-relevant trend to be plotted to date – see Eisner (2001).

For those who are feeling adventurous, it is also possible to explore some of these trends for yourself. Most governments, and sometimes polling agencies, gather data that give useful clues to trends in social capital that can be accessed via the web. Also watch out for updated data and analysis from more recent surveys, such as the latest sweep of the World Values Surveys, which now contains survey data from over sixty countries (see WVS.isr.umich.edu). Coming years should also see the publication of time series from other sources, such as the International Social Survey Panels.

8

Causes

There are wide national, regional and local variations in social capital, and this requires an explanation. Why is it that some places are characterized by rich, interconnected social networks and a general atmosphere of trust, while others are characterized by closed, hostile networks and an atmosphere of distrust?

This variation is very large. The World Values Surveys show that the percentage of people agreeing that 'most people can be trusted' varies from over 65 per cent in Norway to less than 3 per cent in Brazil (World Values Survey, 1997; see also figures 2.1 and 7.2). Similarly, across US states, the percentage of people expressing distrust – agreeing that 'most people would try to take advantage of you if they got the chance' – ranges from over 40 per cent to less than 10 per cent. This scale of variation is one of the reasons why social capital is of such interest to policymakers and scholars, together with the policy outcomes that this variation in turn explains (see part I).

Previous chapters have touched on various factors that might cause or influence social capital. In this chapter, these factors are brought together using the same micro-, meso- and macro-framework as used in part I.

Micro-accounts: why are some people more connected and trustworthy than others?

Some people have larger social networks, are more engaged in the community and associational life, and are more inclined to be trusting than others.

There are some scholars who are uneasy about using the social capital concept at the individual level, arguing that it is really a community- or ecological-level phenomenon (see chapter 1). However, even if you wish to hold to this stricter definition, looking at what is happening at the individual level potentially offers vital clues about causality. For example, if you found that a community with exceptionally high levels of social capital had a very distinctive style of bringing up children, this might indicate that the child-rearing practices were part of the explanation or mediator of the community's high social capital. You would be even more confident of this conclusion if you found that outside of this community, those individuals who used the same child-rearing practices tended to have children who were more engaged and trusting.

Biology and personality

Neuroscientists – and most recently 'neuroeconomists' – have argued that humans may be hardwired to trust each other (Grimes, 2003). A repeated finding of game-theory experiments is that humans tend to trust each other, and to reciprocate acts of trusting, far more than appears to be rational in one-off encounters. The brain releases the feel-good hormone oxytocin when we reciprocate, and co-operation activates the pleasure centres of our cortex (McCabe et al., 2001; Rilling et al., 2001). Increasing amounts of evidence suggest that way back in our evolution, the role of oxytocin – the 'lust and trust' hormone – developed to suppress fear and aggression to enable mating to occur, to strengthen bonds between parents and offspring, and ultimately to promote co-operation through emotional attachment (Porges, 1998).

The role of biology, and of the hormone oxytocin, has led to some curious claims. One researcher, when asked how oxytocin might be boosted, responded, 'the easiest way for individuals to raise their own trust-and-transaction boosting oxytocin is, well, sex' (Paul Zak, quoted in Grimes, 2003, p. 37). As the author of the article could not resist commenting, 'not too onerous a civic duty, then'.[1]

That humans have a biologically based proclivity to co-operate is now widely accepted. However, the evidence that biology might explain *variations* across individuals, or even nations, is far more contentious. Psychologists have been studying patterns of individual differences for over a hundred years. They have sought to document and explain the consistencies in individual human behaviour that are seen over time and across situations. For example, some people tend to be reserved and quiet, preferring reading books to going to parties, while others tend to be more outgoing, talkative and 'fun-loving'. It has been found that this trait, known as extroversion, can be measured through a short questionnaire and is stable over a lifetime. It has also been found to relate to a host of other behaviour and to have a strong genetic component. Could it be that personality variables – and behind these our genetic composition – could help to explain the large and stable observed variations in social capital?

In recent years, psychologists have converged on a relatively simple model of personality traits known as the 'big five' (McRae and Costa, 1987). These five 'super-traits', or dimensions along which individuals differ, have been found in many studies and countries.

From a social capital perspective, the personality super-trait psychologists call 'agreeableness' immediately catches the eye. The agreeable person tends to be co-operative, trusting, sympathetic and interpersonally supportive. In its extreme form, agreeableness may be manifested in a dependent, self-effacing manner of dealing with others. The opposite pole of agreeableness is described as antagonism, or the tendency to set oneself against others. The antagonistic person is described as mistrustful, sceptical, unsympathetic, uncooperative, stubborn and rude (Liebert and Spiegler, 1990). Specific and closely related personality traits, such as the 'Machiavellianism' scale, have been found to be highly predictive of reciprocation (trustworthiness) and defection in one-shot bargaining games – though interestingly not necessarily predictive of trust (Gunnthorsdottir, McCabe and Smith, 2002).

However, unlike some of the other super-traits, such as extroversion and neuroticism, psychologists have found little evidence to suggest that variations in agreeableness lie in our genes. Instead they have concluded that agreeableness is mainly a product of learning and socialization rather than biology (Costa and McRae, 1988).

It therefore seems pretty clear that genetic differences are not going to explain the higher social capital of some people, or the exceptionally high social trust of the Scandinavians or low social trust of the Brazilians. However, the existence of the trait suggests that the skills and basic orientation of the high social capital individual are stable over time, and once fixed are relatively resistant to change. This may help to explain why there is a tendency for individuals who trust any one group or referent also to express high trust for another (Veenstra, 2002b).

Age

Different age groups show different patterns of social and civic engagement. Older people tend to show stronger ties to their neighbourhood while younger people tend to have larger networks of friends. For example, the British General Household Survey (2000) found that 33 per cent of those aged 16–29 saw friends daily compared with around 14 per cent of those aged 50 and over. In contrast, around 50 per cent of the over 50s spoke to their neighbours daily compared with only 17 per cent of those aged 16–29. In most countries, volunteering shows a U-shaped relationship with age, peaking in the late 30s to 40s.

These patterns suggest that demographic shifts, and the demographic profile of an area, may have some impact on social capital levels. However, the interpretation of ageing effects is complicated by the existence of 'cohort' effects – some generations appearing to be more civic than others (see chapter 7). For example, voting among young people has dropped in many countries, a finding of particular concern because it has also been found that those who do not vote initially tend not to vote in later life either.

Volunteering also tends to rise after retirement, though eventually drops again as ageing and frailty take their toll. Similarly, there is clear evidence that those with disabilities tend to be less engaged. It is noteworthy that physical disability reduces voting even when absentee ballots are available, suggesting that reduced contact, social capital and identification with mainstream society play a significant role.

The family: attachment theory, modelling and socialization

Families create norms and social ties. They are also the context within which the vast majority of people first learn to trust others. The psychologist John Bowlby famously documented how the infant and primary caregiver – typically the mother – gradually build up a strong bond between them (Bowlby, 1988). In Bowlby's observationally based theory, the young child becomes 'securely bonded' to the primary caregiver, and this bond becomes the secure emotional base from which the child can safely explore the world. Hence the young toddler holds onto the parent's coat-tails for comfort as he, or she, sits on the bench in the park. It is the existence of this strong, secure bond that eventually gives the child the confidence to let go and explore the world beyond the bench – examining the grass, picking up stones and chasing the ducks – albeit occasionally glancing back to ensure that the parent, and safe haven, remains.

There is now ample evidence that the character and strength of this early relationship have repercussions throughout later life. Though this is not deterministic, the securely bonded infant tends to grow into the secure and confident child and teenager. This in turn is predictive of the formation of stable and successful adult relationships, and of being a parent more likely to form a secure bond with their own children.

Bowlby's 'Attachment Theory' strongly suggests a positive domino effect of trusting relationships spreading out from the family and into wider circles of life. In contrast, disrupted, abusive or absent early relationships tend to lead to negative domino effects through later junctions in life – from the family context to teenage peer groups through to adult isolation and deviancy (Sampson and Laub, 1993). Most straightforwardly, people who remember being told by their parents not to trust other people – as well as those who are actually betrayed by their parents – end up not trusting other people as adults. But the positive side to this story is that this trajectory is not fully determined. If an individual manages to buck the trend at one of life's important junctions, normally because of an emotional commitment and bond from someone connected to mainstream society, the trajectory of their life can change dramatically (see chapter 4 on crime).

There is evidence that social capital tends to be lower for children in single-parent families. Single parents tend to have smaller social networks, partly as a result of residential mobility and family break-down, and the child tends to have less exposure to adult attention (see chapter 5 on educational attainment for further details). Much the same is true of teenage mothers, whose partners tend to be less reliable, less supportive and more abusive, and who tend to have smaller and more impoverished social networks (Moffitt, 2002). Divorce also seems to be associated with lower levels of generalized trust (Hall, 1999), while the loss or withdrawal of one of the parents – typically the father – deprives the child of access to that parent's social network as well as their emotional presence (Jonsson and Gahler, 1997). All these factors will tend to lower the social capital of a child brought up in such circumstances, as well as leading to higher rates of emotional and behavioural problems, lower educational attainment and higher rates of illnesses, accidents and injuries (Moffitt, 2002; see also chapters 3, 4 and 5). Family social capital affects the child both directly through the 'inheritance' of a smaller social network and indirectly through the individual psychological resources and traits that the child acquires, or does not acquire – feelings of security, the ability to trust, and the social skills to build relationships.

Ironically, while people tend to think of the family as the prime source of bonding social capital (because it is the most powerful form of such affiliation), they neglect the fact that it is also likely to be an important influence on bridging social capital. Feeling secure and confident in oneself is almost certainly a necessary prerequisite for interacting with others who seem different and unfamiliar, just as Bowlby suspected (Kraemer and Roberts, 1996). Children who see their parents and family interacting freely and respectfully with diverse other adults will tend to model their own behaviour on these interactions.

Children who see their parents volunteering, engaged in the community and so on are in turn more likely to engage in such behaviours themselves. Indeed, the influence and community engagement of parents appear to be one of the most robust routes through which social capital is formed or transmitted. In our work on 15–17-year-olds, having controlled for socioeconomic background, ability and other individual and school characteristics, we found that having parents who were more politically and socially engaged was associated with significantly higher voluntary engagement, community engagement, higher social trust, and higher civic and political knowledge (Halpern, John and Morris, 2002).

The influence of class

An alternative lens through which to view the influence of the family on social capital is through models of social class. It has long been known that individuals differ in their stocks of social capital and that these differences are divided along class lines, the middle classes having larger and more diverse social networks and reporting higher levels of social trust (Goldthorpe, Llewellyn and Payne, 1987). Similarly, the occupational composition helps to explain a significant proportion of neighbourhood-level variation in social capital and participation (M. Lindstrom, Merlo and Ostergren, 2002). Furthermore, these differences appear to be growing, at least within the UK (Hall, 1999; Grenier and Wright, 2001; see chapter 7). These differences are important not just for the adults concerned, but for their children too (see figure 8.1).

Researchers have documented how advantage and disadvantage often appear to be transmitted across generations (Goldthorpe, Llewellyn and Payne, 1987; Kiernan, 1996; Aldridge, 2001). This trans-

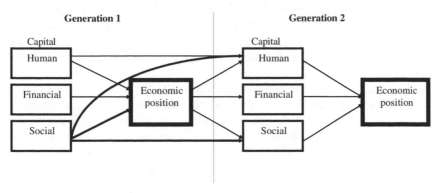

Figure 8.1 *The role of social capital in the transmission of advantage*

mission is not deterministic, but is nonetheless surprisingly resilient even in the face of persistent efforts by past governments to 'break the cycle' (Heath and Clifford, 1996; Oppenheim, 1998; Esping-Anderson, 2003). Such transmission does not seem to be simply or solely explicable in terms of the economic resources available to parents and children, but is mediated by a host of other subtler variables, including social, cultural and psychological factors (Quinon and Rutter, 1988; Feinstein and Symons, 1999; A. Sullivan, 2001).

Central to the cycle of disadvantage is educational failure – the failure to acquire human capital (see also below). But research has shown that although the human and financial capital of the parents helps to predict the educational success or failure of children, a significant amount of the remaining variance is explained by social capital (Teachman et al., 1996; Furstenberg and Hughes, 1995; see chapter 5 for more detail). In turn an individual's access to social capital depends to some extent on the total resources of the family that they grew up in. For example, a wealthy family can afford to send their child to a private school, thereby ensuring access to a peer group with strong middle-class aspirations and values, and with excellent 'contacts'.

Analysis of longitudinal panel surveys has shown that middle-class parents, and particularly professionals, were more likely to be involved in civic activities and this was in turn associated with higher civic engagement in their children. The children of managers were also involved in a wider range of social organizations. Statistical modelling of the family transmission of social capital, using the British Household Panel study, showed that parental education, and particularly the mother's education, has an especially strong association with civic activity among children (Egerton, 2002b). This effect was driven by those graduate mothers working in the public sector, suggesting that it was a particular configuration of high education and public sector work that was associated with higher civic activity in children, at least in Britain.

In sum, the family appears to be a critically important source of variation in social capital at the individual level. Early attachments have significant impacts on the psychological orientation, social skills and later relationships of the individual. The parents' endowment of social capital, in terms of their networks and expectations, also forms an important 'inheritance' for the child and young adult. Professional, highly educated parents – especially if working in the public sector – also tend to encourage more civic activity in their children. This partly class-based inheritance of social capital helps to explain the transmission of advantage, and disadvantage, across generations.

Education

Education has repeatedly been shown to be associated with higher levels of social capital at both the individual and aggregate levels (Hall, 1999; Putnam, 2000; Bynner and Egerton, 2001; see also chapter 5). The more years of education an individual has had, the larger and more diverse are their social networks, the more engaged they tend to be in the wider society around them, and more trusting they report their fellow citizens as being.

The exact causes of this relationship are not fully understood. Most straightforwardly, it may be that schools, like the family, play an important role in creating social norms, ties and the skills of reciprocity. It has certainly been argued that it is important even for very young children to experience the social environment of school and preschool in order to learn the skills needed for living in a social world (Cox, 1995).

Going to university appears to be associated with a particularly strong boost to social trust, tolerance and community and voluntary engagement. Careful analyses of longitudinal cohort data show that this effect is robust and cannot be explained by either background social variables, such as parents' social class or income, or individual attributes such as prior attainment or ability (Bynner and Egerton, 2001). The jury is still out on why this happens, but it seems likely that both the content and structure of the university experience are important. Western university education is traditionally liberal, and challenges and broadens the young person's beliefs about life and other people. This message is reinforced by the structure of university life, which typically involves living away from home for the first time in a young person's life; mixing with new people from all different walks of life; and an environment that is essentially safe, co-operative and supportive.

It seems likely that the social capital-boosting effects of education may have helped to offset declines in social capital in recent years (see also chapter 7). Hall (1999), writing about the UK, argues that the importance of increased educational participation and attainment is especially apparent in the case of women. In 1959, 1 per cent of women had some post-secondary education compared with 3–4 per cent of men. By 1990, 14 per cent of women had some post-secondary education, the same as men. While community involvement by men increased slightly (by 7 per cent) over the same period, community involvement by women more than doubled to converge with the rates of men.[2] A similar story can be told for voting in many countries, with the proportion of women voting increasing steadily over time. In short, social capital at the aggregate level may have been sustained largely by the increasing participation of better-educated men and (particularly) women in the community. This is arguably a one-off effect that may not be sustained in future, not only in Britain but in other countries too.

Work

Contrary to what might be expected on the basis of time available, people in full-time work are generally at least as involved in volunteering and in their communities as those who are unemployed or not in work. Indeed, on many measures, such as social trust, those in full-time work appear to report higher social capital. Of course, the social networks, and resources within them, tend to differ greatly between those in work and those outside. For example, the unemployed are typically about twice as likely as the whole population to have more than half of their friends in unemployment.

Interestingly, data from both sides of the Atlantic suggest that it is those in part-time employment who tend to show the highest levels of social engagement and many other measures of social capital (Putnam, 2000; Coulthard, Walker and Morgan, 2002). The key point appears to be that work *per se* has no simple causal relationship to social capital, though it may be that work intensity, and the extent to which it therefore displaces other activities, do have causal impacts (see below).

Religion

Surveys tend to find that those who are religious tend to volunteer more, trust others more, and go to more association meetings. However, many of these activities relate directly to their religious activities and communities of interest. The causal story is also complicated by the strong and near universal decline of religious organizations. On balance, it would seem that religious beliefs and activities are strong causal contributors to individual variations in social capital, but are themselves being powerfully undermined by other contemporary causal factors, leading to their being of diminishing importance overall in most societies (see chapter 7).

Television and individualized consumption

Television and other forms of electronic personal entertainment are convenient, low-cost and largely under our control. Whereas listening to music would once have involved the expense and effort of going out to a concert, today we can select a CD and listen to the music of our choice at any time, unaffected by the needs and preferences of anyone else. Television is arguably even more compelling, offering us a choice of dozens or even hundreds of channels at the flick of a switch. While individual programme content might be beyond our control – though it is so with video, DVDs, pay-per-view cable and so on – the medium is absorbing and easy. Entertainment no longer involves enduring the inconveniences of others, but can be had on tap from the convenience of our own sofas.

Putnam (2000) documents how, within the USA, people who watch more TV read newspapers less, are less trusting of others and are less engaged in their communities. Having controlled for demographics, those who describe TV as their primary form of entertainment were less than half as likely to have worked on a community project; attended fewer dinner parties and club meetings; spent less time visiting friends; entertained at home less; gave blood less; wrote or emailed less; and were less interested in politics. And when they did get out, their interactions with others were significantly less positive. For example, TV dependants were more than twice as likely as their demographically matched peers to have reported recently 'giving the finger' to another driver. As Putnam notes: 'Nothing – not low education, not full-time work, not long commutes in urban agglomerations, not poverty or financial distress – is more broadly associated with civic disengagement and social disconnection than is dependence on television for entertainment' (Putnam, 2000, p. 231).

Given the marked increase in television watching since the late 1950s in the USA, it is unsurprising that Putnam ascribes the decline in social capital over this period in large part to the increase in the amount of time people spend watching television at the expense of social engagement (see chapter 7). This impression is reinforced still further by the observation that the one type of television watching that is *not* negatively associated with civic engagement – news watching – has itself declined dramatically. The rise in television watching is also in part generationally based, with younger generations having increased their watching more than the markedly more civic US older generations. In the US context, therefore, there is strong circumstantial evidence to link increased television watching to lower social capital.

Alternative interpretations of the US data have been made. One analysis using data from the General Social Survey (GSS) argued that the key underlying variable was optimism for the future, this leading both to individuals being more trusting and to less watching of TV (Uslaner, 1998). Another analysis, also using the GSS, argued that people psychologically fail to distinguish between real friends and the imaginary ones they see on TV (Kanazawa, 2002). This provocative hypothesis was supported by the finding that 'people who watch certain types of TV are more satisfied with their friendships as if they had more friends and socialised with them more often' (p. 167). However, Kanazawa's claims were almost immediately countered by another analysis of the same data showing that when satisfaction with friends was measured relative to satisfaction with other areas of life – that is, controlling for overall life satisfaction – the positive associations between TV watching and satisfaction with friends largely disappear (Freese, 2003).

One recent study found that levels and types of TV watching interacted with residential mobility to affect civic engagement (Kang and Kwak, 2003). In residential areas with low mobility, or stable populations, the use of local public affairs news on TV led to significantly higher community participation. In contrast, in residential areas with higher mobility, time spent watching TV was associated with lower civic engagement.

We analysed the effects of TV in our own study on 15–17-year-olds in Britain (Halpern, John and Morris, 2002; forthcoming). We found that, even having controlled for a range of socioeconomic, ability and other variables, TV watching had an impact on levels of both voluntary engagement and social trust. Replicating the US findings, we found that the more hours a young adult watched TV, the less they volunteered or trusted others. On the other hand, watching the news on TV was associated with more engagement. Importantly, our research had a longitudinal component, allowing us to look at how TV watching at one point influenced engagement at another. We constructed 'change models' that controlled for level of trust and engagement at age 15, and then looked at what factors explained changed levels of trust and engagement a year later. Such models are generally thought to give a better grip on causality. Once again we found similar results. The more young people watched TV over the period, the less they volunteered or trusted others. In contrast, watching the news was associated with an increase in volunteering, though not in social trust.

A big puzzle is that while virtually all countries have seen an explosion in television watching, social capital does *not* appear to have declined universally. Indeed, in some countries, despite the spread of TV, social capital appears to have increased (chapter 7). At the same time, it *is* generally true across nations that those individuals who watch more television tend to be less socially engaged.

Several things are probably going on here. First, there is a basic problem with interpreting the causal direction of the TV–disengagement relationship at the individual level. While it is highly plausible that watching large amounts of television leads to disengagement, it is also possible that TV watching is itself a symptom of disengagement. In all likelihood, both are true.

Second, it would seem that the content and character of the television programmes watched matter. Those who watch more entertainment programmes and commercial channels, compared with those who watch news programmes and public broadcasting, show less civic-minded attitudes; a result that has been found on both sides of the Atlantic (Newton, 1999; Hooghe, 2002; Halpern, John and Morris, 2002). But again, it is difficult to be certain of the causal direction. It could just be that those who are more engaged choose to watch the news – though our own work suggests that at least some of the link is causal from TV to engagement.

Third, though the circumstantial evidence seems strong for television watching, and for personalized consumption more generally, helping to explain the decline in social capital in the USA, the absence of the same pattern elsewhere suggests that at the very least this relationship is conditional. It may be that where other forms of collective consumption are strong, the effects of television watching are cancelled out. Or it may be that American TV is especially problematic for social capital – perhaps because there is so much of it; or because having so many channels undermines its character as a collective experience; or because of the high volume of commercials.

Exposure to environments of distrust:
a negative effect from means-testing?

An interesting empirical observation has been made by the Scandinavian sociologist Bo Rothstein (2001). He conducted a study to try to understand why some individuals in Sweden, an otherwise exceptionally high social capital nation, didn't express high trust in others. One variable in particular showed up, and this was exposure to means-tested benefits.

Rothstein hypothesized that there was something about the experience of conflictual means-tested benefits that undermined trust. He has argued that the underlying dynamic of this means-testing is that the official is obliged to distrust the claimant. At the same time, the claimant is rationally incentivized to distort or inflate their claim. Rothstein argues that even if the claimant does not actually cheat, they come away from the process having been made aware that cheating is rational and that many others probably will do so.

A reverse example has been highlighted by Putnam (2000), who has pointed to the post-World War II GI Bill as one possible reason why the wartime generation may have shown such high civic engagement. He has argued that the GI Bill was an act of great (and heart-felt) generosity by the state to the veterans, and that this helped to create a cycle of trust and reciprocity between the veterans and the wider community that lasted a lifetime.

This is controversial and difficult evidence for policymakers, since most countries have welfare states that rely heavily on means-testing to target resources on the most needy in society. Nonetheless, it is a potentially important clue that echoes the literature on how trust and social engagement are perpetuated within the family. It may be that if we expect the worst of people, then this is sometimes what we get (see further below).

Meso-level causes and the role of associations

In the same way that some individuals appear to be markedly more engaged and trusting and have larger and more diverse social networks, so too some communities seem to exhibit more social capital than others. A classic illustration of this phenomenon was the Pennsylvanian town of Roseto, described by Bruhn and Wolf (1979), which had exceptionally strong social cohesion based on an egalitarian and close Italian community (see chapter 3). Sophisticated multi-level analyses show much the same – neighbourhood factors account for a significant amount of the total variation in social participation and engagement, even having controlled for individual-level variables (M. Lindstrom, Merlo and Ostergren, 2002). The question is: what kind of factors might lead to a community having more such social capital?

Civil society and associational involvement

Civil society consists of those groups and voluntary organizations that act independently of the state and the market. Putnam (1993, 2000) argues that such associations play a key role in the accumulation of bonding and bridging social capital. When individuals join a club or association, they come into regular contact with a wider group of people; they experience the group's collective achievements and satisfactions; and, it is argued, they learn the habits of reciprocity and mutual trust.

The group or association is itself a form of social capital that may be used by the individual or group to achieve objectives other than those it was originally formed to serve, such as when a church group becomes the agent of political action. The habits and trust learned within the group can also stimulate the creation of social capital more generally, such as when group members transfer their skills and networks to create new, additional groups.

Surveys show that individuals who belong to voluntary organizations are indeed very much more likely to be trusting of others and engaged in the wider community. For example, Putnam reports that those who belong to a non-religious club or association volunteer on average twelve times per year, compared with less than twice a year among those who belong to no associations or clubs (Putnam, 2000). Furthermore, it has been found that the more associations an individual belongs too, particularly if these are of diverse character, the higher their social trust and political tolerance (Cigler and Joslyn, 2002; Wollebaek and Selle, 2002). However, these associations could also be explained by positing that more trusting and engaged individuals are more likely to be joiners in the first place.

There is evidence that although individuals who join organizations do tend to become more trusting and community-engaged initially, this effect rapidly levels off (Stolle, 1998). Indeed, individuals who have been in organizations for more than five years tend to show *declining* social trust and engagement, perhaps reflecting their cumulative experiences of seeing others free-riding on them. Similarly, a careful analysis of panel data from the Michigan Socialization Studies from 1965 to

1982 found only limited evidence that belonging to groups makes individuals more trusting (Claibourn and Martin, 2000).

Stolle's data, mainly from Sweden and Germany, suggest that most of the differences between joiners and non-joiners were present *before* they joined the organization. It is likely that this individual-level finding is too negative, as it does not capture the externalities of the activities of these groups. But it should certainly serve as a warning against the simple hypothesis that creating more organizations will lead to a massive surge in generalized trust and community engagement.

One possible reason for the modesty of the relationship between the length of assocational membership and trust may be methodological. Studies tend to ask about current memberships, and to neglect past memberships. A recent study in Belgium found that previous memberships had strong effects on civic attitudes and feelings of empowerment (Hooghe, 2003). A failure to measure these past memberships is likely to lead to an underestimate of the impact of associational membership on trust.

Stolle's analysis also shows that some forms of voluntary organization stimulate more extensive forms of social capital than do others. For example, organizations that involve more diverse memberships, including contact with people of different nationalities or ethnicities, stimulate significantly higher levels of generalized trust and wider community engagement than those that consist of more homogeneous groups. In contrast, perhaps surprisingly, there appears to be relatively little evidence to date that active memberships boost social capital more than do passive ones (Wollebaek and Selle, 2002).

Our own study of 15–17-year-olds was fairly positive, at least about the impact of volunteering and community engagement on social trust. We found that changes in social trust over time were significantly predicted by the experience of volunteering and community engagement outside of school. In contrast, social trust – at least at the individual level – did not predict later volunteering. This suggests that the causality runs from engagement to trust, rather than the other way around. It may be that these results are clearer in teenagers than adults because it is not necessary to take account of decades of previous volunteering or organizational experience.[3]

School and community

There is some evidence that social capital is 'contagious'. The influence of parents has already been mentioned, but there is evidence that the same applies for schools and communities. There is evidence that the propensity to vote, trust or socially engage is to some extent a function of how much others around us are doing the same. Indeed, if you reflect on it, it is clear that some forms of social engagement necessarily rely on there being other people to engage with – if you've got no one to play with, then you'll just have to play alone (Jenkins and Osberg, 2003). This helps to explain why some forms of engagement can show a rate of decline that accelerates as it approaches extinction, such as playing bridge or even some forms of religion (see chapter 7).

Once again, our data on young people illustrate the point. We found that one of the most powerful predictors of an individual's social trust was simply the prevalent level of social trust in the school, even having controlled for social composition and individual factors. In other words, there was a powerful ecological effect. Clearly this makes some sense: it wouldn't seem to make much sense being the only trusting soul in your community. Other school factors were also important. For example, schools that encouraged more co-operation in the classroom seemed to boost levels of volunteering and community engagement outside of the school. Indeed, this kind of school ethos seemed to have a much bigger impact on engagement than did formal citizenship education, at least in the short term (see chapter 5).

Ethnic and social heterogeneity

There is considerable evidence that social and ethnic residential heterogeneity is associated with lower levels of social capital, not only between groups but within them. Social homogeneity makes social bonding easier. In contrast, the greater the social and cultural differences between people, the more difficult it tends to be for them to form social connections, and the higher the probability of direct exposure to prejudice, discrimination and conflict. This helps to explain why ethnic groups tend to have better health outcomes when clustered together, even if this is associated with higher socioeconomic disadvantage (Halpern and Nazroo, 2000; Franzini and Spears, forthcoming; chapter 3).

Largely unpublished US data suggest that social and ethnic heterogeneity may be one of the most powerful explanations of local and regional variations in social capital in the USA. The higher the level of ethnic mixing within an area, the lower the level of social trust, associational activity and informal sociability. The related argument has also been made that it is the reluctance of white Americans to help black Americans that lies at the root of the paucity of the US welfare state (Alesina, Glaser and Sacerdote, 2001). Comparable results have been found outside the USA. For example, it has been shown that across Africa, areas with the highest concentrations of different ethnic and religious groups tend to be the areas with a history of the highest conflict, this being one of the classic pieces of evidence for 'realistic group conflict theory' (Sherif and Sherif, 1953; Struch and Schwartz, 1989).

On the other hand, if social and ethnic groups do not come into contact at all, there is no possibility of the formation of bridging social capital across groups to break down these divides. The psychologist Gordon Allport (1954) influentially proposed the 'Contact Hypothesis', that 'prejudice may be reduced by equal status contact between majority and minority groups in the pursuit of common goals. The effect is greatly enhanced if this contact . . . is of a sort that leads to the perception of common interests and common humanity between members of the two groups' (Allport, 1954, p. 267). A recent meta-study of 203 studies concluded that face-to-face contact under such conditions does indeed significantly reduce prejudice (Pettigrew and Tropp, 2000). Unfortunately, of course, these conditions are often not met in the real-world circumstances under which groups live together.

One way of squaring this difficult circle may be through what have been termed 'protected enclaves' – places where particular social and ethnic groups socialize among their own (Charlesworth, 2000). In such environments, group members can feel safe from the put-downs and hostility of rival groups, and can feel at ease with themselves, and when contact does occur between groups it can be on more equal terms. It may be that, just as Bowlby describes within the family context, adults who feel they have a secure base from which to explore the world around them will be more likely to be able to form bridges with people very different from themselves.

There is evidence to support this important supposition. For example, group-density effects on health appear to show ceiling effects – a critical mass, not a majority, is necessary for the supportive effects of the group-density effect to show (Halpern, 1993). Similarly, a study comparing different immigrant groups in Amsterdam found that those groups with more associations of a bonding nature also had stronger bridging ties to the larger community, and were more – not less – well integrated into the social and political life of the Netherlands (Fennema and Tillie, 1999).

These results suggest that regions with marked ethnic and social divisions can build co-operation between groups, and avoid conflict, if a strong base of bonding social capital provides a platform of confidence within groups. An example from Putnam's original study of Italy is the region of Emilia-Romagna, where high levels of social capital appear to contain conflicts between very divided Catholic and com-munist communities (Putnam, 1993). Similarly, a recent analysis by Helliwell suggests that the children of immigrants in Canada – in con-trast to the USA – show similar levels of social trust to those of the national average (Helliwell, 2003; in contrast to the US results of Rice and Feldman, 1997). This is particularly striking in that scholars have generally characterized the Canadian pattern of immigration as one in which immigrants have maintained their ethnic distinctiveness. Ironi-cally, it suggests that bonds between different ethnic groups may grow more strongly when those groups also maintain a strong internal sense of identity and bonding social capital.

In sum, the general rule appears to be that social and ethnic hetero-geneity makes bonding social capital more difficult to form, both within and between groups. On the other hand, some degree of mixing is a prerequisite for the formation of bridging social capital between groups, though in order to reduce prejudice this contact needs to meet certain conditions, such as the perception of common humanity. Iron-ically, this may be more likely to occur if such groups have access to confidence-building, socially and ethnically homogeneous, 'protected enclaves' or internal bonding social capital.

Mobility

Residential mobility has consistently been found to be negatively cor-related with social capital at the neighbourhood level (Crutchfield, Geerken and Gove, 1982; Teachman et al., 1996; Sampson, Raudenbush and Earls, 1997; Sampson, Morenoff and Earls, 1999; M. Lindstrom, Merlo and Ostergren, 2002; Kang and Kwak, 2003). Similarly, residen-tial mobility helps to explain variations in social capital at the individ-ual level: people who move more, or who have lived in an area for a shorter length of time, tend to have weaker social capital. Such mobil-ity also helps to explain the impoverished social capital of single-parent families, especially following divorce, as family break-down is often associated with household mobility. Even the anticipation of mobility is associated with drops in individuals' civic and social engagement (Glaeser, Laibson and Sacerdote, 2002).

In communities with a high level of turnover, people tend not to get to know their neighbours or to put down roots. The pattern is self-reinforcing so tends to be stable over time. But sometimes a neigh-bourhood can be 'tipped' into a low social capital equilibrium by some third factor, such as crime, urban clearance, disruption by transport infrastructure, or strong inward migration.

The alienation and loneliness of large cities, particularly in the early stages of industrialization, is to a large extent a function of the disrupted and weak social networks of waves of inward migrants into the city. Similarly, it is striking that both upward and downward social mobility are often statistically associated with increased loneliness and psychiatric symptoms reflecting the disruption of supportive social networks.

However, radically improved telecommunications and cheaper travel may have to some extent changed the impact of mobility on social capital. These developments have enabled migrants to maintain bonding social capital to their distant source communities, while simultaneously connecting into the economic and social opportunities of the new context. While in many ways a benefit, this distant bonding social capital may act to slow the formation of new local bonding social capital.

Transport and commuting

Commuting is implicated in reducing social capital by reducing the time people have available to devote to the family, community engagement or informal socializing (Putnam, 2000). It has been estimated that every 10 minutes of commuting time cuts all forms of civic engagement by 10 per cent (Saguaro Seminar, 2000). Inasmuch as areas and countries differ markedly in the extent of their urban sprawl and consequent average journey times, this may help to explain some differences in social capital. It may also help to explain some differences in national trends in social capital (see chapter 7).

Commuting, and particularly a high reliance on the car, are also destructive of social capital by creating busy transport routes that divide and degrade communities. For example, the more cars that pass along a street, the less likely it is that residents will know their neighbours or describe them as friendly (Halpern, 1995a). Higher levels of commuting and travel also impact on the structure of retailing, tending to undermine local neighbourhood shops at the expense of superstores. This dynamic provides a clear example of path-dependent consumption. The more people get into the habit of driving to a superstore instead of walking to their local neighbourhood stores, the more likely it is that the neighbourhood stores will deteriorate and fail. Once this happens, then everyone has to drive to the superstore, even if previously they did not.

The physical environment and urban design

The physical environment impacts on social capital through the effects it has on the probability and controllability of informal social interaction. The power of the physical environment to influence patterns of social interaction was first conclusively demonstrated by a series of studies on housing for post-war college students. These studies found that the layout and design of housing – particularly the 'functional distance' between neighbours – had an almost deterministic impact on the formation of social groups. Researchers of a university village for veterans observed that 'interaction rises to an extremely high level and organises itself with almost molecular simplicity in terms of the spatial pattern of the community' (Caplow and Forman, 1950, p. 366). Once formed, these social networks became a powerful influence on many social attitudes. Hence it was found that within each court or cluster of houses, a uniform view would emerge towards the wider Residents' Association (Festinger, Schachter and Back, 1950). Festinger et al. also noticed that those who were 'deviants', holding views different from the rest of the court, were most likely to live in houses at the end of the court that faced in another direction. Because these houses oriented in a different direction, the randomly assigned residents were less likely to interact and become friends with the other courtyard residents and were therefore less likely to develop the same views.

Within the workplace, manipulations of the physical environment are a tried and tested method for forming effective work groups: partitions set up around the intended group increase their contact with one another, act as a symbol of their group identity, and help form an effective group (Sundstrom, 1986). Similarly, military studies have shown that the simple act of creating partitions (without doors) within barracks that divided the space into six-man cubicles served to increase the cohesiveness of the six, making penetration by outsiders more difficult. In terms of social capital, such an intervention increases bonding social capital but may reduce bridging social capital.

One criticism of the classic studies, such as Festinger et al.'s work on post-war veteran students, is that the populations studied were extremely socially homogeneous. Most environments involve far more socially and demographically mixed populations, and the physical environment is often designed deliberately to avoid social contact and maintain privacy. For example, a 'Beverly Hills' style residential layout, with large gated houses approached by car via long driveways, is designed to ensure that even immediate neighbours will never meet one another.

A design that forces residents to interact can produce very negative outcomes – neighbours who are withdrawn and hostile. Large-scale public housing projects, such as the infamous Pruitt-Igoe Project in St Louis, USA, illustrate this phenomenon (Yancy, 1971; Newman, 1980). The public spaces that architects imagined as places where residents would spontaneously meet and get to know one another instead became places to be feared and avoided.

What kind of physical environment leads to more positive relationships between residents or workers? In turns out that what matters is not whether an environment *makes* people interact, but rather whether it gives residents the *option* to interact.

This contrast was illustrated in an ingenious series of studies of student accommodation by A. Baum and Valins (1977). They studied the behaviour of first-year undergraduates randomly assigned to either a standard 'double-loaded corridor' design, with rooms on either side of a long corridor and a large common bathroom area, or a 'suite' design, with bedrooms clustered into groups of three with a bathroom shared between them.

In design terms, the corridor design is much more efficient – consider the probability of not finding an available toilet when all twenty are grouped together in one block versus when there is only one between every nine students. Yet residents in the suite design proved much happier and less withdrawn, got better grades, and at the end of the year were much more likely to stay together with their roommates. The authors of the study found that differences in the behaviour of the suite and corridor residents were not limited to the dormitory environment. In experiments and observations conducted in other locations, corridor residents were found to be more withdrawn, less likely to engage strangers in conversation, and more likely to engage in conflictual as opposed to co-operative strategies in games, and generally experienced social interactions with strangers as more uncomfortable and unpleasant.

In essence, residents living in the corridor design came to find the frequent and 'uncontrollable' social interactions of the dormitory aversive and unpleasant, and in response adopted a coping strategy of psychological withdrawal and hostility. People do not like the thought that every time they open their door they do not know who it is that they will bump into.

The same processes affect most environments. As an extensive study of neighbouring behaviour concluded: 'good fences make good neighbours' (Bulmer, 1986). In other words, positive social relationships rest on the ability to regulate your social interactions with others, so that you have some feeling of control over when, and how much, you interact with those concerned (see figure 8.2).

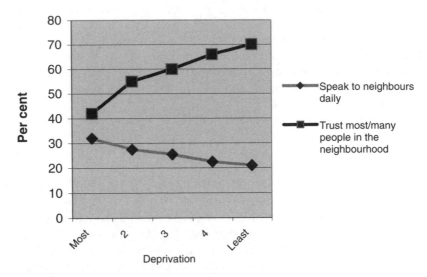

Figure 8.2   *Social contact and social trust*
Source: British General Household Survey, 2000.
Note: Social contact does not necessarily bring social trust: people who live in
more deprived areas are more likely to speak to their neighbours regularly, but
are less likely to trust them.

In a final confirmation of this theory, simple physical changes in such
problematic residential environments have been shown to have a dramatic positive impact on the quality of personal interactions between
residents. Baum et al. found that simply breaking up long corridors
with a series of internal doors was enough to eliminate their negative
effects (A. Baum and Davis, 1980). Newman noted that on the notorious Pruitt-Igoe project, the temporary construction of a fence around
one of the blocks transformed its character, leading to a dramatic drop
in its vacancy rate and to lobbying on the part of residents to keep the
fence (Newman, 1980). And Halpern found that closing off alleyways
that crossed a problem housing estate led to a dramatic increase in
positive neighbouring behaviour and mutual support, and a drop in
fear, anxiety and depression among residents (Halpern, 1995a).
    It is clear that the built environment, in terms of both transport and
the details of how the space affects residents' ability to regulate their
social interactions with one another, has a highly significant impact on
social capital. This is of particular interest both because the causality

can be particularly clearly shown and because it is a factor that is potentially relatively easy to change.

The importance of scale

The evidence on the impact of the physical environment on social capital hints at the importance of scale. A building in which 200 residents share one entrance is less likely to lead to positive social relationships between residents than one in which the entrance is shared by only ten.

Similar scale arguments have been made in many contexts. It has been found that civic engagement, volunteering and social trust tend to be higher in small than large towns (Putnam, 2000). Residents are rated as more friendly in short than long streets; smaller schools tend to feel much friendlier and may perform better than larger equivalent schools; and workplaces dramatically change in character once the workforce exceeds a threshold of around 200 (Willmott, 1963; Sundstrom, 1986).

However, smaller-scale communities and organizations may also lessen the opportunity for bridging and linking social capital, at least within the community or organization. It may also be that, even for bonding social capital, a critical ingredient is not so much scale as controllability, as illustrated above. Having 200 people share an entrance has very different consequences with doorman regulating who comes in, such as in an expensive apartment or office, than when there are no controls over who comes in, such as in public housing.

Macro-accounts: culture, economy and institutions

In the same way as there are micro- and community-level variations in social capital, there are marked national and regional variations. While these macro-differences may be manifest in micro- and macro-forms, such as national differences in 'personality', they are not explained at this level. British people may generally be 'reserved', Americans 'outgoing' and Scandinavians 'considerate'. But the fact that most Americans are outgoing and most Scandinavians are considerate requires a higher-level explanation than that their families brought them up to be that way. We have to be able to explain why it is that disproportionately more parents who live in Sweden raise their children in a particular way, or generally show high levels of civic engagement, trust and so on.

History and culture

Putnam's seminal study (1993) of regional differences in Italy found that large variations in the effectiveness of Italy's regional governments were explained not by their resources or structures, but by regional differences in social capital (see chapter 6). Putnam argued that the success of the northern Italian regions lay in the rich social fabric of vibrant associational life of those regions, in contrast to the 'amoral familism' – a distrust of strangers combined with strong family bonds – that typified the less successful southern regions.

Putnam's analysis linked these very longstanding cultural differences with historical events going back up to 1,000 years. He saw the vibrant civic life of the north having its roots in the northern city-states of centuries earlier. In contrast, he saw the culture of southern distrust as rooted in a history of invasion and oppression, and in the ancient traditions of patronage and the hierarchical nature of the Catholic church.

It is difficult to test such very long-term historical accounts. History tends to offer more of a narrative than a causal account. Perhaps even the climate is relevant. Could it be that, on balance, societies in harsh, cold climates could only survive if they developed cultures of co-operation, and that this helps to explain the stronger culture of co-operation and social capital within the northern European nations than the southern? Or is it instead something to do with historical accident and the emergence of the Protestant religion?

While it is difficult to be sure of the causal roots of any particular culture of social capital, the sense that a community's, region's or nation's social capital is stable over time has been clearly reinforced by subsequent work. An illustration of this stability over time is the finding that the large regional differences in social capital across the USA today correspond closely or exactly to the differences in social capital between the nations from which the ancestors of today's Americans came (Rice and Feldman, 1997). For example, the area around Minneapolis and St Paul's – the area of highest social capital in the USA on most measures – was populated with high-trust Scandinavians. Something has persisted over several generations, and separated by thousands of miles and different political structures, to explain why both the residents of Minnesota and the Scandinavian nations today remain so connected and trusting.

The implied stability of social capital over time, even though the population is continually changing, strongly points to the importance of culture. This stability suggests that a community's or nation's social fabric reaches a stable equilibrium, manifest in and reinforced by corresponding institutions, expectations and patterns of socialization (Rossteutscher, 2002). Theoretical modelling work confirms how systems tend to converge towards a stable equilibrium of co-operation or conflict (Axelrod, 1984; Good, 1988). Essentially, the models show how it is rational to trust and co-operate when at least a reasonable proportion of those around you are also trusting and co-operative. In such a context, co-operative strategies – such as reciprocity or 'tit-for-tat' – are found to predominate over time. But in a population where the vast majority is untrustworthy, co-operative strategies will be maladaptive and will disappear over time. Hence such emergent equilibria are robust and stable over time.

The apparent importance of long-standing and deep-rooted culture has been interpreted by many to mean that nothing can be done about social capital. However, the fact that a system tends to be stable over long periods of time does not preclude the possibility that change can happen, especially if the system is subject to some kind of external shock that kicks it into a new, equally stable equilibrium. Importantly, recent modelling work has also shown that co-operative strategies can emerge even when the networks have no geographical basis; in other words, when they are based on interactions between relative strangers. As the authors conclude, 'the surprising result is that if the pattern of interactions is selected at random, but is persistent over time, co-operation emerges just as strongly as it does when the interactions are geographically local' (Axelrod, Riolo and Cohen, 2002, p. 341). This gives grounds for optimism that as different cultures interact, high co-operation–high social capital equilibrium may win the day.

Social structures and hierarchy

Even if culture is stable over long periods, we can still seek to identify the key structures and institutions of the society that help to explain how its culture is propagated and maintained over time. In some cases these structures and institutions may even give us clues about how the stable equilibrium arose in the first place.

One of the characteristics of low social capital societies appears to be the preponderance of rigid and strongly hierarchical social structures. Such structures are typically highly patriarchal, where progress depends on loyalty to, and favours from, those on higher rungs of the ladder of power. These inegalitarian structures appear to form a poor soil from which to build mutual respect and trust between citizens, and the consequences of these settlements echo through the generations.

Once again, the classic example is the low social capital states of southern Italy, where the hierarchically organized Catholic church has remained dominant for centuries, alongside the equally hierarchical structures of the Mafia. Another example is the close correspondence between low social capital states in the USA and the areas within which slavery was most dominant, notably in the south where the plantations flourished.

In the Italian case, Putnam argues that these excluding hierarchies took root because of centuries of invasion by outside forces and warring factions, who systematically enforced ruthless hierarchies of control and suppressed more egalitarian social structures that could have become the focus for resistance. Similarly within the southern US states, powerful and cruel social practices reinforced the hierarchies of power on which the slave economy was built, including the ruthless and violent oppression of any who dared to challenge these institutionally embedded hierarchies. The corrupting and self-propagating nature of these hierarchies is illustrated in the writings of Fredrick Douglas (1855), a former slave. In one especially telling piece, he described how his new mistress, who was unfamiliar with these hierarchies of oppression, at first showed him kindness that he had never seen before. But within only a short time, the hierarchy of power and social expectancies changed her manner and behaviour until she became as cruel and harsh to her slaves as any other white mistress or master:

> Tommy, and I, and his mother, got on swimmingly together, for a time. I say for a time, because the fatal poison of irresponsible power, and the natural influence of slavery customs, were not long in making a suitable impression on the gentle and loving disposition of my excellent mistress. At first, Mrs. Auld evidently regarded me simply as a child, like any other child; she had not come to regard me as property. This latter thought was a thing of conventional growth. The first was natural and spontaneous. A noble nature, like hers, could not, instantly, be wholly perverted; and it took several years to change the natural sweetness of her temper into fretful bitterness. (Douglas, 1855, pp. 144–5)

The close match between patriarchal social hierarchies and low social capital is not limited to studies of Italy and the USA. Cross-national studies of variations in social trust have found such relationships to be widespread. For example, La Porta et al. found that national differences in levels of corruption and low trust were strongly correlated with the proportions of those from hierarchically organized religions in the population (La Porta et al., 1997, ch. 6). Similarly, psychological studies have shown that even where normal, well-adjusted individuals are randomly assigned to perform roles within a rigidly defined social hierarchy, such as guards and prisoners in the Stanford Prison Experiment, the subjects' behaviour rapidly takes on the roles. In the case of the Stanford Prison Experiment, this meant frightening brutality on one side and passive withdrawal on the other (Zimbardo, 1971). Indeed, so dramatic were the effects, in terms of the psychological disintegration of the prisoners and the escalating cruelty of the guards, that the experiment was stopped before the end of its planned two-week run.

In sum, the evidence is compelling that hierarchical social structures not only reflect low social capital, but actively undermine most positive forms of bonding, bridging and linking social capital.

Economic inequality

One can argue that economic inequality is simply another reflection of other forms of social hierarchy (see above). This is certainly the view that would have been taken by the sociologist Bourdieu (1986). But inasmuch as it may be determined by other exogenous factors, such as economic globalization, and has an important political profile of its own, it merits consideration in its own right.

Economic inequality has been found to be a close negative correlate of social capital across nations (Knack and Keefer, 1997), and across regions within states (e.g. the USA and Italy: Putnam, 1993; Kawachi et al., 1997). It has also been found to correlate negatively with social capital at the village level in developing nations (La Ferrara, 2002). It is difficult on the basis of the data available to date to establish the causal direction of this relationship, but it seems likely that the causality runs both ways. Beyond some threshold (which may vary from country to country), inequality stretches the social fabric, increasing the social distance between individuals and reducing the likelihood of shared interests, social associations, norms or mutual respect. At the same time, low social capital reduces the ability of a community to develop a shared social vision or build a commitment to public goods or a welfare state.

It may be that if the world is becoming a more meritocratic place (a point some may wish to contest), with ability and productivity replacing caste and social origin as the determinant of our position in society, then the causal role played by economically determined positional goods will loom larger. Either way, it seems clear that economic inequality should be somewhere in our line-up of likely causal candidates.

Labour market trends

Patterns of labour market participation may have impacts on social capital. One can argue that the more we work, the less time we have for other kinds of activities such as seeing our friends and taking part in civic associations. More subtly it can be argued that the worldview of the market is sometimes in tension with the worldview of the gift or 'civic economy'. The more we come to think that all that matters is money, then arguably the more we neglect non-monetary aspects of society such as love, care and affiliation.

Traditionally women have played a key role in voluntary organizations, and one might therefore expect that rising female labour force participation may have had adverse effects on societies' total stock of social capital. Both Hall (1999) and Putnam (2000) have examined this proposition. But they find little evidence for it.

In the USA, community participation appears to have declined amongst all women and men, whether or not in paid employment. In other words, women's entry into the labour market *per se* cannot account for this pattern of widespread decline. But the general increase in work intensity – for both men and women – *has* had a marked negative impact on social engagement due to pressure on time.

The evidence from the UK appears fairly similar. Hall argues that the growth of highly educated women, most of whom work, may actually have helped to offset a decline in social capital since education is strongly associated with increases in social capital (see above). In fact, labour market trends appear to include contradictory effects. Increasing levels of education and the dramatic expansion of the middle classes over the past century have led to a more widespread adoption of middle-class sociability. Since, on average, people in the middle class express higher trust and have twice as many organizational affiliations as the working class, this may have helped to sustain social capital notwithstanding any increase in economic inequalities. On the other hand, recent decades have also seen a marked increase in the intensification of work across classes, and this is likely to be depressing social capital through pressures on time (Burchell, 1999).

The size and nature of the welfare state

Another widely debated possible determinant of social capital is the size and nature of the role played by the state. Some have voiced the fear, especially within the Anglo-Saxon nations, that as the state has grown in size this may have weakened or displaced voluntary and informal ties. For example, in the days before the welfare state provided income support to the unemployed or disabled, many workers were involved in credit unions and 'Friendly Societies' to which they made contributions in exchange for protection in times of need. These societies were more than just private insurance schemes, as they functioned as mutuals and members were heavily involved in their administration as well as directly with one another.

However, there were always large numbers of people who were not covered by such Friendly Societies. The welfare state was designed to take on the social protection role of the Societies and extend this protection to the whole population. The question is, did the very efficiency of the rational bureaucratic welfare squeeze out a form of social capital of great value?

Although this displacement hypothesis feels intuitively plausible, the evidence does not generally support it. It is true that one can identify particular cases where a large state is implicated in the displacement, and even repression, of social capital – such as the low social capital found in parts of the former Soviet Union (Small, 2002). However, when we look cross-nationally we find that levels of social trust, volunteering, informal socializing and participation in community projects are generally significantly *higher* in countries with generous welfare states, such as the Netherlands, Norway and Sweden (OECD, 2001a; see also chapter 7). Similarly, US states with larger welfare and public programmes are those with significantly higher levels of social capital.

The causal interpretation of this association is inherently difficult. It is highly likely that high social capital nations and regions, by virtue of their values, low inequality and high capacity to solve collective action problems, find it easier and are more willing to organize generous welfare states. On the other hand, such generous welfare states are in turn more likely to foster the conditions under which social capital can flourish, such as by attenuating income inequality (see above).

It is also possible that the lesser reliance of generous welfare states on means-tested benefits helps to avoid the dynamics of mistrust described by Rothstein (see above). In this respect, it is interesting to note the observations of the British sociologist Julian Le Grand in the context of Anglo-American welfare state reform of the 1980s (Le Grand, 1997, 2003). He argues that the Reagan and Thatcher reforms involved a shift from viewing public servants as trusted and honourable 'knights', and users as trustworthy if passive 'pawns', to one in which all participants came to be viewed as 'knaves' – people who were not to be trusted and who would cheat the system wherever possible. Similarly, it has been argued that the situation of black Americans has been aggravated by the way the institutions of the welfare state have turned into 'instruments of surveillance, suspicion, and exclusion rather than vehicles of social integration and trust-building' and have accelerated the shrinking of the ghetto's own social capital (Wacquant, 1998, p. 25). In the meantime, non-profit organizations (NPOs) within the US are struggling with a lack of volunteers and funding, and are generally failing to fulfil the role of a 'shadow state'. As one recent survey of NPOs concluded, it means 'providing less assistance to the poor because the voluntary sector cannot match the capacity of the welfare state' (Merrett, 2001, p. 407).

The contrast in thinking on this issue between Anglo-Saxon and mainstream European models of welfare is sharp. American, British and Australian policymakers can barely comprehend how the generous welfare states of Germany or the Scandinavian nations can function. How can it be that the Germans and French bother to work at all since their welfare benefits are so generous that they would get almost the same if unemployed? Leaving aside the inherent satisfactions (and access to social capital) that work brings, the contrast illustrates a yawning divide that has opened up in our view of human nature and in our deeper assumptions. Most importantly, it may be that our expectancies have become self-fulfilling prophecies. If we communicate to one another that people are generally not to be trusted, then people take on this mantle and act in rational, self-interested ways, as Rothstein has noted at the individual level. But if we communicate our expectations that most people are trustworthy, honest and to be respected, then people seem to rise to the challenge and do not, for the most part, disappoint us.

Individual values and lifestyle choice

The issue of individual and societal values lies in the background of many of the causes discussed above. The populations of nations that are low in social trust also tend to report significantly higher levels of self-interested values, such as tolerance for 'keeping something you have found' or 'lying in your own interest' (Halpern, 2001). Similarly, it has been found that adults with a value-based commitment to benefit the collective are much more likely to participate in community affairs and efforts to solve collective problems (Funk, 1998), with similar results found in children (Crystal and DeBell, 2002).

Interestingly, this relationship is not especially strong at the individual level. If you reflect on it, this does make sense. If I happen to be a selfish person living in Sweden, at the same time as I report that I think it's OK to lie in my own interest, I will also be able to tell you that most people around me are trustworthy (perhaps making me a successful petty criminal). However, if lots of my acquaintances start following my lead and also start acting in self-interested ways, then at some point people more generally will start reporting that others cannot be trusted. Hence, while at the individual level self-interested values and social trust may be only weakly correlated, at the aggregate level they should be strongly related, which is exactly what we find.

These issues were discussed in some detail in chapter 7, so let us simply highlight a few key points here. The relationship between values and social capital is not a simple linear one. Some forms of value change have almost certainly impacted on certain forms of social capital. For example, there has been a widespread increase in the value placed on independence of thought and personal autonomy, while the value placed on obedience to authority has fallen. This growing ideological freedom has led to the characterization of younger generations as 'moral entrepreneurs', mixing and matching their values according to personal preference and thought. Such value changes may help to explain the widespread weakening in commitment to all-encompassing 'mass' traditional institutions such as the church, political parties and trade unions. Thus a recent OECD report (2001a) notes that confidence or trust in the state, the civil service, the police, churches, the education system and the media declined in most countries in the 1980s. These value changes may in turn reflect changes in our economy, technology and wealth – changes that have freed individuals from many of the immediate economic interdependencies of earlier periods.

On the other hand, value change has not led to a general collapse of social trust and the social order. For example, while people have generally become much more tolerant in the personal-sexual domain, they have not generally become more tolerant of acts of illegality and particularly of acts that have clear victims. Indeed in many areas, such as attitudes towards poorer nations, people have generally become more generous. Similarly, there has been a marked rise in the importance placed on freedom of speech and human rights. At the same time as these values have tended to erode support for many local and parochial forms of social capital, such as narrow nationalism, they have boosted support for other, more cross-cutting institutional forms and norms, such as human rights conventions, abhorrence of racial intolerance, and belief in democracy.

Of all the causes listed here, individual and societal values are arguably the one most difficult to separate from the social capital with which they are associated. As we saw in chapter 7, different nations appear to be on subtly different trajectories in terms of the social capital and nature of individualism that are evolving within them. Inasmuch as people can, and do, debate and adjust their values – both collectively and individually – values must be at least partly causally prior to the forms of social capital expressed in a society. At the same time, as we have seen repeatedly in this book, individuals' values are in turn shaped by the experiences and values of others that their social capital exposes them to. This is an old sociological and philosophical debate, but if we have any belief in the potential role played by personal agency and our ability to think, anticipate and choose our values, then this ability to choose our values and lifestyles should be in our causal line-up.

Putting it all together: towards a model of social capital formation and destruction

It is time to try to put these various causes together into a larger system model. This model will need to reflect the relative stability of social capital over time; the 'recursive' nature of the causality – wrapped around on itself with no clear beginning or end; and the different levels at which the causes are operating (micro-, meso- and macro-).

The 'Catherine wheel' model of social capital and its consequences

When I first had a go at putting this together a few years ago, I came up with a model called the 'Catherine wheel' of social capital formation (see figure 8.3; Halpern, 1998). Essentially it is a macro-level model. It illustrates how nations such as Sweden settle into a stable pattern of collective investments in public goods, such as education and the welfare state, that attenuate economic and social status differentials, and that in turn create an environment that stimulates social trust, community and associational life. As shown in earlier chapters, these conditions tend to throw off positive policy outcomes, such as better health, low crime, economic growth, low civil unrest and a 'virtuous' citizenry. These positive outcomes are the 'sparks' that fly off the Catherine wheel, and help to keep it spinning. Citizens in such a society are generally happy with this state of affairs, and are prepared to pay taxes and re-elect governments to keep the wheel spinning. And at the heart, or axle, of the wheel stand the society's common social values, such as mutual respect, trust and the consideration of others.

A vicious cycle is also possible that corresponds to an alternative equilibrium. A society characterized by low trust will generally fail to build trusted institutional structures. Its government and legal system

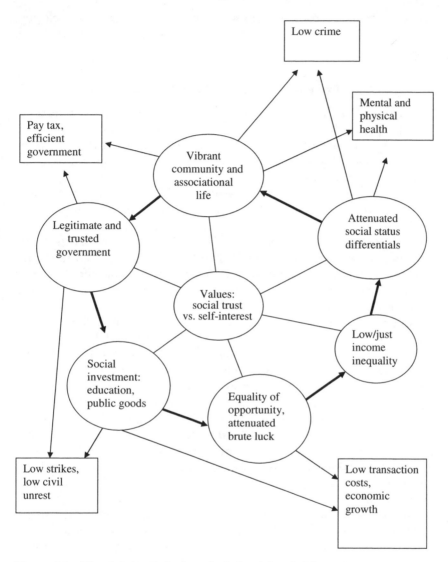

Figure 8.3 *The virtuous Catherine wheel of social capital formation*
Source: Halpern (1998).

will get infected by the same distrust as in the wider society and will
be characterized by corruption and failure to invest in public goods.
These institutions will fail to deliver the benefits of their high-trust
counterparts, reinforcing inequality and social status differentials
and undermining the trust on which civic life is based. This, sadly,

can be seen as a loose description of many nations in the developing world and, in recent years, some of the nations of the former Soviet Union.

Extending the Catherine wheel model

At the time, this Catherine wheel model was nicknamed by some other social capital scholars the 'Putnam-plus' model, because it borrowed many of his ideas but added to them the importance of the role of the state. The model was a useful development, but it nonetheless had a number of weaknesses.

First, the model's focus on the macro-level neglected the importance of micro- and meso-level factors. Second, it was unrealistic in the way each arrow led so tidily to the next causal box. The world was much messier than this, with many of the factors impacting more directly on one another and on social capital. Third, it probably placed too much emphasis on the importance of traditional associational life. Fourth, it implicitly neglected historical factors that might explain why a given equilibrium was achieved.

To be fair, many of these problems were apparent at the time, but there was something to be said for keeping the model as simple as possible. But after six years of seminars, conferences and scholarly discussions, it is time to attempt something a little more complex. For a start, we need to think about this Catherine wheel as more of a spiral, moving forward over time, so that at the end of the cycle the nature of the state and society it describes is slightly different, a turn of the cycle later. This should help us to visualize how the system's characteristics may change over time, such as when the whole system is subject to external or exogenous pressures such as labour mobility or tax competition, despite its general tendency to maintain a stable equilibrium.

But we also need to add to our system the micro- and meso-Catherine wheels of social capital formation and destruction that are simultaneously turning. These other cycles may be turning with very different time frames. Governments and their programmes stand and fall over periods of a few years, with policymakers often bemoaning how long it takes to turn major government policies around. Yet at the micro-level, the cycles operate primarily along generational lines – it typically takes thirty-odd years for an infant to be socialized through family, peers and the experiences of adulthood, and for that adult to start the cycle again with a child of their own. Of course, there is another key difference between these levels too. While at the macro- or national level, one can argue that there is a single identifiable cycle built around elections and the democratic process, at the micro-level there are literally millions of cycles turning, each family a cross-generational story of its own.

In this sense we need to picture not just the spiral of macro-causal processes, but also the multiplicity of micro- and meso-spirals that together form a thread of continuity over time. Perhaps the image to have in mind is rather like rope made of thousands of tiny causal threads entwined together into broader cords, which are then in turn bound together to form the rope itself.

Figure 8.4 shows a stylized representation of this multi-layered model. Inasmuch as these layers are interconnected, we would normally expect them all to be broadly driving towards the same equilibrium. However, it should be clear that this will not necessarily be the case, at least over the short to medium term. For example, it is possible, indeed common, to find pockets of low social capital communities and families even within relatively high social capital areas or regions. In the absence of active intervention, these pockets of 'social capital poverty' tend to persist over very long periods of time, and in particular can be passed from generation to generation along channels typically reinforced by social class divides.

In reality, the model should still have a lot more causal arrows, and more links between the levels of analysis. But at least it gives a sense of the complexity of the causality that we are dealing with, and provides a useful framework that we can use when considering policy options in the next chapter.

Summary

This chapter has identified the major causes that explain the large observed variations in social capital.

At the most basic level, humans appear to have a hard-wired tendency to reciprocate and co-operate – though this is not to say that this tendency cannot be overridden by other contradictory aspects of our nature, such as our proclivity to compete or form dominance hierarchies.

At the individual or micro-level, personality differences map onto variations in the propensity to engage in and stimulate social capital along a dimension labelled 'agreeableness' vs. 'antagonism'. The causes of these individual variations appear to lie in socialization and environmental factors rather than in our genes; hence they appear to

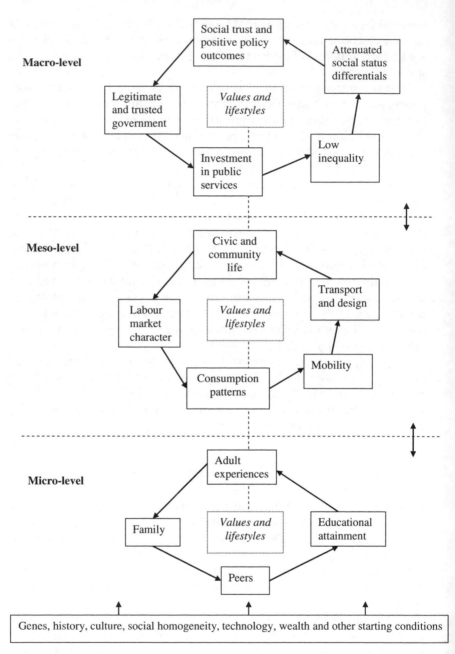

Figure 8.4 *Social capital formation and propagation*

mark rather than explain micro-variations in social capital. Socialization experiences in the family appear to have a major impact, as does the individual's social capital 'inheritance' from their parents and relatives. These early influences have domino effects through the child's peer groups and later relationships. Educational attainment, itself partly determined by family and social class origins, has powerful additional effects. Going to university appears to have a particularly strong effect on boosting the scale and diversity of an individual's social network and their propensity to trust others. In contrast, a lifestyle based on individualized leisure consumption, and particularly heavy commercial television watching, is strongly associated with social disengagement. Finally, there is some evidence that exposure to distrustful bureaucratic processes, notably conflictual means-tested benefits, is associated with lower trust and social disengagement.

At the meso- or community level, engagement with civic associations appears to lead to a modest boost to social engagement and trust, but the evidence is that much of this boost occurs in the first year of involvement in the organization, and perhaps more in the years of young adulthood. Engagement and trust are boosted more by involvement in associations with more diverse memberships. Ethnic and social heterogeneity has been found to act as an inhibitor of social capital, lowering trust and engagement not only between groups but within them too. That said, it is clear that without some mixing of groups, there will be no opportunity for the growth of valuable bridging social capital, implying a difficult balancing act for community development. Very importantly, there is some evidence that such bridging social capital is more likely to grow where ethnic groups also have strong internal bonding social capital – a safe base from which to reach out across any cultural divides. High levels of mobility, commuting, and physical environments that make it difficult for people to regulate their social interactions with others are all strongly implicated in causing lower social capital.

At the macro-, regional or national level, history and culture are strongly implicated in explaining the large and stable observed differences. Behind this broad backdrop, rigid hierarchical social and institutional structures appear to inhibit social capital formation by undermining mutual respect and equality, and in some cases by actively oppressing the formation of a more diverse and egalitarian civil society. More specifically, economic inequality has been found to be a close correlate of low social capital, indicating that a stretching of the socioeconomic fabric tends to undermine the common ground on which much social capital is built. Characteristics of the labour market have also been implicated. Higher work intensity appears to displace time otherwise spent in community and social involvement, and it may be associated with a wider devaluing of the gift economy or civic life. However, the increased entry of women into the labour market does not appear to explain variations in social capital over and above other factors. Finally, larger and more generous welfare states appear to boost social capital, rather than displace it, probably through their effects on lowering inequality and facilitating more fertile conditions for social capital growth.

Running through all levels we see a close relationship between values and the prevalent social capital. Inasmuch as individuals and societies can be said to choose their own values, these value choices in turn help to shape the kind of societies that we live in, and the kind of social capital that characterizes them. More individualistic lifestyles and values have been made possible by growing wealth and technology, from personalized entertainment through to the supply of affordable white goods, cars and homes. Even the transformation of social capital itself may have helped release the expression of more individualistic values, as trust between strangers and social norms of co-operation have released people from the bonds of family and immediate geographical community.

A macro-level 'Catherine wheel' model of social capital formation, sometimes known as the 'Putnam-plus' model, was described. It highlights the potentially critical role played by the state in supporting and stimulating social capital. This was expanded into a more general model that also captured the importance of processes operating at the micro- and meso-levels in the formation and propagation of social capital.

Further reading

This chapter has touched on a wide range of literatures, so readers will struggle to find sources that cover more than a narrow range of the issues covered. The following suggestions are therefore far from comprehensive, and rather offer a few particularly interesting leads.

The *developmental and social psychology* literature is rich in studies exploring how genes, early socialization and family dynamics affect the future relationships and relational style of the individual. Any general textbook will give a multiplicity of interesting leads, such as Shaffer (2005) or Fraser and Burchell (2001). The work of John Bowlby is perhaps of particular interest, and can be found in an accessible form in Bowlby (1988).

On the effects of *means-testing*, try Rothstein (2001). On the effects of *association group membership*, try Stolle (1998). And on the effects of the *built environment*, try Halpern (1995a).

For more *general* accounts of causality, as ever for the USA try Putnam (2000), chs 10–14, or ch. 15 for a summary. For a constructively critical review, try Szreter (2002). For an alternative attempt to compare different causal theories, see Delhey and Newton (2002). Another recent collection of essays on what causes social capital in different countries can be found in Stolle and Hooghe (2003).

9

Policy Implications

We have always said that human capital is at the core of the new economy. But increasingly it is also social capital that matters too – the capacity to get things done, to co-operate, the magic ingredient that makes all the difference.

Too often in the past government programmes damaged social capital – sending in the experts but ignoring community organizations, investing in bricks and mortar but not in people. In the future we need to invest in social capital as surely as we invest in skills and buildings.

Tony Blair's keynote speech, NCVO Annual Conference, 1999

The relationship between social capital and economic growth, health, crime, education and the efficacy of government, as documented in the preceding chapters, explains why policymakers across the world are becoming interested in social capital (Ahern, 2001; OECD, 2001a; Bush, 2002; Aldridge and Halpern, 2002; Brown, 2004). However, while these relationships are certainly strong enough to attract policymakers' attentions, they do not of themselves fully make the case for intervention or define a policy programme. For example, having children is a fairly essential activity for the long-term functioning of our economy and society, but most OECD governments leave this issue very much to individuals to decide. In fact, there are many areas of life that have big impacts on important policy outcomes that governments leave largely to individuals to decide and determine, such as the diet that we eat, individual investment decisions, and the beliefs that we hold. So we first need to understand why active intervention is likely to be necessary.

Before we do this, a caveat needs to be placed on this final chapter. The evidence is fairly compelling for the importance of social capital for society and policy. However, policy is something that needs to be fashioned in the particular context. My own familiarity is with the OECD nations, and really only with a minority of these – Britain and the US in particular. I hope that many of the policy proposals raised here will make sense in other national contexts, but I am sure that some of them will not. In particular, the way in which it is appropriate to operationalize social capital concepts and policies will differ enormously between the developed and developing nations (see the World Bank website; DeFilippis, 2002; Bebbington, 2002; Mayer and Rankin, 2002). This chapter is principally focused on the former – those with greater knowledge of other nations need to write suitable prescriptions for those contexts.

The case for active intervention

The case for active intervention in social capital is very strong. It rests on five key arguments.

First, social capital has now been shown to relate to nearly all the key policy objectives of modern societies and government, and even to the life satisfaction of the population (see part I; Donovan and Halpern, 2003).

Second, 'market failure' arguments apply. Social capital has strong public good characteristics (see chapter 1). As such, it is vulnerable to free-riding and systematic underinvestment by rational individual actors. In this sense, the case for state or collective intervention is very much like that for public infrastructure investment, skills training or the government sponsoring of research.

Third, equity arguments apply. It has been shown that in practice, social capital is not a pure public good, and may often be expressed as a 'club good' that provides advantages only to those who have access to it. The marked social class differentials in social capital are the most obvious manifestation of this issue (chapters 2, 7 and 8). This club-good character partly occurs as a natural response on the part of individuals and groups trying to create social capital in the absence of, and given the difficulty of, direct public investment in it. The equity argument for social capital investment is therefore much like that for some public funding or regulation of early education, health or welfare. In the absence of state intervention, social capital will be unevenly distributed across the population, and this distribution will substantially disadvantage certain groups.

Fourth, evidence that social capital is declining is a major source of concern for those nations affected, notably some of the Anglo-Saxon nations: the USA, Australia, Britain and probably Ireland (see chapter 7). These declines add urgency to the policymakers' concerns. The declines suggest that even if social capital once looked after itself, changing social and economic conditions may have undermined this delicate equilibrium.

Fifth, and perhaps most critical in practice, there is something that can be done. In my experience, whatever the brief, senior policymakers very rapidly move to the simple question – what can be done? If you don't have some pretty hard-nosed proposals, then you will rapidly lose their attention, and perhaps rightly so. In the world of policymaking, a problem without a solution isn't really a policy issue at all, it's just a fact of life. If healthy life expectancy was 700 years instead of 70, we could save a fortune on education and pensions; attitudes towards the environment would be transformed for the better; and crime might largely disappear. But until someone figures out how to stop us getting old, this is not something that policymakers are going to spend much time worrying about.

Arguably, it is this last argument that is the biggest stumbling block for policy at present. The academic arguments are relatively well advanced, and the concerns resonate with the instincts of many politicians. But the well-established importance of historical and cultural factors affecting social capital suggests to many that it may not be possible for policymakers to intervene effectively (see chapter 8). The primary objective of this final chapter must therefore be to overturn this largely unspoken assumption.

Intervene how?

Before examining specific policy proposals, it is worth reflecting at a higher level on the ways in which we might try to affect, and think about, social capital.

Understanding and measurement

It might seem a little dull, but good data built on good measurement are critical to successful intervention. There is still a great deal that we do not know about the various facets of social capital and their relative importance to policy outcomes. Effective intervention rests on a clear analysis of the problem, and having good information about what matters a lot and what matters only a little.

Good data are also essential to an assessment of 'what works'. An integral part of policy intervention is evaluation – did the intervention have the intended effect, and at what cost? This applies not only to policy interventions directly targeted at increasing social capital, but also to those that are targeted at very different issues but that might have unintended consequences for social capital (see next section).

It is worth noting that measuring social capital poses some challenges to conventional survey methods. Clustered sampling designs are needed to estimate ecological-level, or neighbourhood, effects. Similarly, direct behavioural measures, such as 'lost envelope studies' and blood donation, may prove more reliable estimates than conventional survey designs, which tend to be biased towards socially desirable answers and respondents who may be atypical of the general population. Indeed, the level of non-response to conventional surveys may itself prove to be an important indicator of social capital.

At the time of writing, extensive efforts are under way across the world to develop effective measurement tools for social capital and, in several cases, to incorporate them into national programmes of measurement and statistics. The World Bank has been active in this area for several years, and has made much progress in the measurement of social capital in the developing world.[1] Following the publication of the OECD's report on human and social capital (OECD, 2001a), the OECD held a follow-up meeting on measurement issues.[2]

National statistics agencies are also now getting involved in the effort. Within the UK, the measurement issue has been taken up by the Office of National Statistics (ONS), which has created a matrix of surveys relating to social capital and is looking at incorporating regular questions on social capital into its national surveys. These data will then be linked to a rich variety of other data sources down to small area level.[3] Within the USA, partly spurred by the success and influence of Putnam's 2000 'Benchmark Survey', the White House has moved to incorporate social capital measures within suitable national surveys.[4] Other nations too are moving forward with measurement programmes, notably the Canadians, Irish and Australians.[5]

There have also been several international gatherings to help coordinate measurement, notably a joint OECD–ONS gathering of over twenty nations and a UN Siena Group themed around social capital, and a joint US–EU meeting is also planned.[6]

To date it would seem that measurement activity has been greatest in the Anglo-Saxon nations. This may reflect measurement bias on my own part – and indeed my own limited social capital – or may reflect the fact that these are the nations that have been most affected by declines in social capital and are therefore most concerned about the issue.

Consider – and try not to destroy

One of the key policy conclusions is simply that policymakers need to consider social capital, along with many other factors, when drawing up and implementing policy. By way of comparison, there is now a large body of expertise and detailed protocols in most countries guiding policymakers in how to consider and weigh the potential environmental impacts of policy options (DoE, 1991; Halpern and Wood, 1996). We need to extend this logic to encompass other types of externality, including the likely impacts on social capital.

At least one government – the Irish – is actively considering a policy of social capital 'audits', checking the likely impact of future policies on social capital (National Economic and Social Forum, 2003). In the meantime, a group in New England has recently conducted such an audit of a proposed road-widening scheme. Such schemes are known to increase commuting distances and volumes, which in turn are known to have a detrimental impact on the community engagement and social capital of both commuters and the neighbourhoods that such routes bisect (chapter 8). The audit seeks to quantify these negative effects, and proposes the creation of compensatory community facilities and support to offset them.

Such audits or considerations are complicated by the existence of various forms of social capital, not all of which are associated with positive social outcomes. In particular, some forms of bonding social capital may be used for narrow sectional interests as well as for the public good. The most notorious example is organized crime, but more commonplace examples can include cartels, professional associations, and closed and inward-looking communities.

Since different forms of social capital have differential impacts on different policy outcomes, a social capital framework does not relieve us of decisions over what our relative policy priorities are. For example, economic growth appears to be particularly affected by macro-level, bridging, norm-based social capital, while health is particularly affected by micro-level, bonding, network-based social capital. Officials responsible for delivering a strong economy and those responsible for delivering public health will not necessarily agree on the same social capital policy programme. A more useful framework for the senior policymaker who must put these competing claims together is the 'vitamin model' sketched out in chapter 1. Healthy communities need a balanced range of social capital. Too little, or indeed too much, of certain forms of social capital 'vitamins' can prove socially and economically toxic. Policymakers – and communities themselves – need to ensure that they have achieved such a balance.

The most straightforward objective of social capital policy must be simply to avoid destroying it – unless the reasons for doing so are extremely strong. Examples of policies that have had unintended harmful effects on social capital include urban clearance programmes, concentrated public housing projects, some welfare programmes, and possibly even some community development programmes.

The slum clearance programmes of the 1950s, 1960s and 1970s typically made the mistake of focusing on the poor quality of the physical environment while failing to see the potential value and importance of the social capital of residents. On both sides of the Atlantic, classic sociological studies documented the enormous psychological and social toll these clearance programmes took on the residents who found their social networks and lifetime friendships broken apart by forced relocation (Young and Willmott, 1957; Gans, 1962). These studies revealed that many residents showed severe depression for up to three years after the clearance, reflecting the psychological damage of disrupted or destroyed social networks. In retrospect, had social capital been considered, renovation and refurbishment would often have been judged a better option. Sadly, thirty to forty years on, some of the same mistakes were still being made (Halpern, 1995a).

A related example is the large-scale concentration of social housing, and the planning policies that failed to tackle these concentrations, unintentionally creating enclaves of deprivation. Even where these areas consisted of good-quality housing stock, they often rapidly became 'sink estates' or ghettos, where those who could move out did so and only the desperate moved in. Such areas often become characterized by distrust and atomization, as the disadvantaged and desperate turn on one another. Even when some community spirit does grow, it is often inward-looking bonding social capital, with residents lacking bridging or linking social capital to the more advantaged – and employed – communities beyond their boundaries. The concentration of social housing might make it easier to deliver formal welfare services, but it tended to cut its residents off from the bridging social capital that might have allowed many to escape such dependence.

A similar critique can be levelled at many traditional welfare programmes. For example, the incentives to seek work built into many social security benefits generally encourage unemployed people to focus on formal labour market institutions, such as job centres in the UK, despite evidence that most people exit unemployment through informal networks and contacts.

Policies that involve excessive centralization of government, and the undermining of local government, might also be said to represent a regressive policy in social capital terms. Indeed, there is some cross-national evidence that fiscal decentralization boosts social capital, though the causal direction of this evidence may be contested (de Mello, 2000). However, it also should be noted that under a transformation account of changing social capital, certain forms of centralization – or at least communality across localities – may be seen as a positive development (see chapter 7).

Ironically, even many traditional regeneration and community development programmes fall foul of a social capital analysis. Traditional community development, as still widely practised, tends to emphasize self-help or capacity building to the exclusion of links to the wider community or economy. To the extent that such programmes create stronger bonding social capital rather than bridging social capital, members of the communities concerned may continue to be excluded from networks that could link them back into the wider society, boost the aspirations and attainments of their children, and link adults back into employment.

We should not be naïve. There will often be difficult trade-offs to be made between the destruction of one form of social capital and the creation of another – let alone the trade-offs between social capital and other outcomes. To take a highly specific, but illustrative example, state-level deregulation of the US trucking industry has led to significant loss of power and control by local communities, the trucking industry having previously rested heavily on tight social and familial networks (Gardner, 2002). But deregulation also opened up the industry to new ethnic, geographic and gender groups, effectively breaking community-based cartels and facilitating greater equality of opportunity.

In sum, while the role of the state is generally positive in relation to social capital (see chapter 8), poorly designed policy and governance – as well as markets – can crowd out important forms of social capital (Bowles and Gintis, 2002). Hall argues, in his review of social capital trends in the UK, that one of the reasons why the UK did not show the scale of decline in social capital seen in the USA over the 1950s to 1980s is that UK governments generally worked hard not to displace existing forms of social capital. British governments have tended to work with, and financially support, the voluntary sector rather than attempting to take over its activities directly. But sometimes the destruction of a particular form of social capital may be justified, either because of wider objectives or in order to facilitate the creation of new, more open or adaptive forms of social capital.

Getting the conditions right

The previous chapter implicated a number of general factors as being causally relevant to social capital. Such factors are often already the subject of policy interventions, and the social capital agenda simply reinforces the need to act effectively on them.

Inequality, and relative poverty in particular, is an example. The evidence is strong that the stretching of the socioeconomic distance between people tends to undermine the common ground on which social capital is built. Therefore initiatives to reduce poverty, as well as being defensible in their own terms, should have pay-offs in social capital. These pay-offs will ultimately benefit the whole of society and not just the poor, because of the way social capital impacts on economic growth, population health and well-being, crime, education and so on.

Policies aimed at stamping out corruption are another example. Zero tolerance of corruption, especially within government, is an important step in building trust in collective mechanisms, and in other people in general. Again, this is a policy that most people would sign up to regardless of any concerns over social capital, but the social capital agenda gives such drives added urgency.

Directly stimulating social capital

In principle, the most straightforward way of building up social capital is to go out and invest in it directly. It would seem that there is nothing to stop us as individuals going out and meeting our neighbours, joining and funding associations, engaging in volunteering, and generally being more considerate to one another – though the evidence on trends suggests that increasingly this is not happening in some countries.

Is it possible for the state, or communities, to invest in social capital directly? Well, it is clear that states already do. In most countries, governments heavily fund the voluntary sector, charities have tax-exempt status, volunteering is in some way supported, education is subsidized, citizenship education is taught in schools, and – perhaps most importantly of all – the state is heavily involved in codifying and ultimately enforcing codes of trustworthy behaviour between people, especially through the legal system. Much of the remainder of this chapter will examine how states and communities can do even more to invest directly in social capital.

Substituting for social capital

There are circumstances where there is little viable social capital to invest in, or where investing in existing stocks of social capital will be inequitable or otherwise problematic. Indeed, one can go further and argue that there are circumstances where it will be more efficient, equitable and generally desirable to invest in more formal institutions than in social capital.

For example, while the Friendly Societies of the nineteenth century may have had many positive social capital features, the publics of few OECD nations would wish to turn the clock back fifty years and dispense with the efficiency, equity and certainty of their welfare states. Indeed, when one looks at the desperate reliance of millions of people in the developing nations on their fragile social networks for day-to-day survival, it is clear that there are many circumstances under which the substitution of exclusive reliance on social capital is to be welcomed strongly (Dhanani and Islam, 2002). We should not be naïve about the shortcomings of a world reliant on informal social capital, just as we should be wary of a world reliant on state welfare alone.

Similarly at the micro-level, when considering the situation of a child who has been orphaned or subject to chronic abuse, a strategy of directly investing in the child's own family social capital may be out of the question. It may be that the best that the community or state can do under such circumstances is to seek to substitute for the absent or maladaptive social capital.

Where exactly the line between direct investment and substitution lies depends on your definition of social capital. For example, does government-sponsored foster-care count as direct investment or substitution? This takes us back to the definitional issues raised in chapter 1, though such issues are unlikely to be of much interest to policymakers. This earlier discussion suggested that any social structure – short of a fully formal institution – that facilitates co-operation and trust between people can be viewed as a form of social capital.

Implications for policy: lessons from America

Prompted by evidence of decline, American thinkers have arguably been 'ahead of the curve' in thinking explicitly about how social capital might be actively boosted. Putnam (2000) notes parallels to the social malaise that characterized the USA at the turn of the previous century. At that time, the response was an unprecedented period of association and society building, largely modelled on the associations created in Britain a few decades earlier, themselves created in response to similar social concerns.

Putnam concluded that it should not be assumed that simply reinvesting in the forms of social capital invented by the Victorians would be successful in the changed context of the twenty-first century. Instead he helped bring together a mixed group of policymakers and academics who met over three years to discuss practical new ways of rebuilding social capital. These meetings were called the 'Saguaro Seminars', named after the desert cacti that can grow underground for decades before bursting forth into flower, and their conclusions were summarized in their report, *Bettertogether* (Saguaro Seminar, 2000).

The six broad policy areas the Saguaro seminars identified are shown in table 9.1, together with short comments about the applicability of the proposals to other nations. Several general comments apply.

Many of the proposals inevitably reflect the US cultural and institutional context, such as the reference to campaign finance reform. More fundamentally, there are two glaring omissions, at least from a European political and cultural perspective – the role of inequality and the potential role for the state. These omissions have led to a string of articles, particularly by European academics, criticizing Putnam's 'apolitical analysis' (Navarro, 2002), highlighting the 'missing link' of 'the dramatically changing role the state has played in American life' (Szreter, 2002, p. 586), and declaring that 'the USA cannot play the role of a prototype' since 'it seems necessary not to forget the high value of European welfare state traditions for society and economy' (Lampert, 2002, p. 346).

On these issues we must see Putnam's scholarly instincts deferring to his political judgements. Make no mistake, Putnam – at least in private – is well aware of the potential importance of inequality in undermining social capital. But in the contemporary American political context, he knows this to be a difficult, if not impossible, story to sell. Indeed, he would argue that the only way of getting a policy programme directed at reducing inequality in America is by first building up the bridging social capital and empathy that could then form a platform of support for such a programme. In this sense, his judgement is that the virtuous Catherine wheel of social capital formation of the previous chapter has more or less ground to a halt in the USA. Instead it must be made to turn in the other direction – from social capital built from the ground up, to reduced social differentials, to support for state programmes to reduce poverty.

Table 9.1 *Proposals from the Saguaro Seminars for rebuilding social capital in the USA and applicability to other nations*

Area	Policy (example)	Comment
Education	Citizenship education and service learning in schools; volunteering for college credit.	There is much to be learnt here. Results from service learning are promising, and there is evidence that college volunteering programmes are having a significant impact on the youngest cohort.
Work	Legislation to enable workers to work flexibly and take time out for community activities.	Europe is arguably much further ahead in this area, and provides examples of such legislation and practice.
Urban design	Reducing urban sprawl and commuting times; pedestrian-friendly design; availability of public space.	US car dependence and commuting times are much higher than in most other nations', but nonetheless this is an important area for policy innovation.
Faith	A new 'great awakening' and engagement in 'one or another spiritual community of meaning'.	Putnam admits this 'would not be an unmixed blessing'. It relates closely to the very different role of religion in the US context.
Technology	Fostering new forms of electronic entertainment and communication that reinforce community engagement rather than forestalling it.	This has uncertain potential, to date based more on hope than on evidence.
Arts	Increasing participation in cultural activities, from group dancing to songfests to rap festivals.	This is seen as a slow, but potentially important focus for the building of bridging social capital, and less problematic than faith-based organizations.
Politics	Increasing participation; reforming campaign finance.	This reflects Putnam's long-held view that money has displaced activism and grass-roots involvement in US politics. The professionalization of politics is an issue cross-nationally, though many nations already have tight rules over finance.

The absence of a positive role for the state follows similarly. The almost instinctive distrust of central government runs deep in America. It seems likely that the American distrust of solving collective action problems through state mechanisms is part of the explanation for the difficulties that it is having in updating, or transforming, its social capital for the modern age (see chapter 7). However, it is no good simply protesting that what the USA needs is a Scandinavian welfare state – you need to offer a plausible pathway for the national context. Distrust of government is also a familiar, though less extreme, problem in Britain where two decades of right-wing government – including the influence of Thatcher – reduced the role of the state and popular belief in public services. It took the whole of Blair's first term to begin to turn this belief around, and would surely take a generation or more to do so in the USA.

Perhaps these comments help to explain why, although many of the Saguaro proposals are interesting, one cannot help but feel that they are like a thumb in a bursting dyke. They are simply too modest in scale to take on the powerful downward trends documented in the other twenty-three chapters and four hundred pages of Putnam's book. On this point, Putnam is reflective but sanguine. 'On Mondays and Tuesdays I am optimistic' he privately reflected, thinking of some of the positive examples of social capital building he had seen on a recent US tour. 'But on Wednesdays, Thursdays and Fridays, I am pessimistic, because it will take thirty years to replicate such social capital across the USA.' Perhaps it was a Friday when we had this discussion, but I must confess to feeling more optimism about the prospects for an active social capital policy outside the USA than within it, and this is mainly because of absence of a trusted state within the USA.

Stimulating social capital at the individual or micro-level

What more can be done by communities and governments to encourage individuals to volunteer, engage with their communities or socialize with their friends? In particular, what can be done to boost the social capital of individuals and families that start from a base of unusually impoverished social capital?

Greater support for families and parenting

The relationship between parents and their children is important for the development of both bonding and bridging social capital. Fortunately, in many ways modern families have become more, not less, responsive to the needs of children and adolescents – though the social versatility and skills demanded by modern societies have also grown (Larson et al., 2002).

The available evidence suggests that the ways in which parents and their children interact have major impacts on the social development of children. In particular, helping parents to bond and interact effectively with young infants is important for developing children's self-confidence and building their capacity to form trusting social relationships of their own in later life. Second, children whose parents are trusting and engaged tend to become trusting and engaged adults themselves. Third, parents' social networks, parent–parent connections, and parent–school interactions have significant impacts on children's educational attainment, delinquency, and later life chances. Parents who are connected with each other are able to coordinate and reinforce the values and behaviours that they wish to pass onto their children – parenting becomes a more collective and less individualistic act.

This approach underpins interventions such as the US Head Start and the UK Sure Start programmes, both of which are intended to help parents support their children. The evaluation of flagship early intervention studies, such as the US Perry Pre-school project, which tracked individuals up to age 27, has shown strikingly positive results. However, it should be noted that the larger-scale programmes now running tend to be much more modest interventions than the flagship studies. Furthermore, little is known about which aspects of these multi-faceted programmes account for their positive effects. Systematic evaluations of these programmes should play a crucial role in improving our understanding of precisely how these interventions work and thus how they might be better targeted and designed in future. Specific further measures that might be considered include:

- improving teenagers' understanding of the psychology of parenting, relationships and child development whilst they are still at school – not just to 'instruct', but to inform and engage young people before they become parents themselves;
- actively assisting parents – especially from disadvantaged backgrounds – to take part in parent–parent and parent–school interactions; building up confidence and facilitating social networks and mutual support;
- offering active guidance, counselling and support to parents in parenting skills, perhaps building on existing antenatal classes and, in

the UK, on the health visitor system. This might include training on how to help children focus their attention; how to 'mesh' or interact more effectively with the young child; and easy-to-understand information on effective or 'authoritative' parenting;

* stronger state support, such as through the tax system, for parents, and access to high quality childcare for all children over the age of 2.[7]

Many of these policies are already in place in some nations, and much can be learnt by examining successful practices.[8]

Mentoring

Mentoring schemes are a potentially powerful mechanism for giving people access to bridging social capital, and to some extent supplementing impoverished bonding social capital. The policy areas in which they can be used are many and varied, ranging from child development, to education, to business development. For example, researchers have concluded that effective guidance can be critical to helping young at-risk people avoid the damaging effects of extended periods not in education or employment and to help them make a successful transition to adult life (Bynner and Parsons, 2002). Provided the right mentors are involved, and the programme is suitably constructed, mentoring can have highly beneficial outcomes.

US studies suggest that early mentoring can have significant educational benefits. An evaluation of the Philadelphia 'sponsor-a-scholar' programme shows that mentoring by a caring adult, whether related or not, can significantly boost academic performance and reduce drop-out rates from school (Johnson, 1997). The evaluation found positive effects on academic performance for children in the 10th and 11th grades (aged 15 to 16) but not in the 12th grade (aged 17), and positive impacts on college (university) preparation and on college attendance during the first year after high school. It was found that disadvantaged children particularly benefited from the programme. Similarly, an evaluation (Kahne and Bailey, 1999) of the 'I have a dream' programme found even greater beneficial outcomes. This programme involved each mentor adopting an entire 6th grade class (11-year-olds) and, together with a project coordinator, provided students with long-term financial, academic and social support to help them graduate from high school and attend college. The evaluation found that the programme doubled high school graduation rates in inner-city areas from around 35 per cent to around 70 per cent (see chapter 5).

However, it is important to ensure that mentoring programmes do not stigmatize. This is especially a danger when they are part of an individually targeted programme, and therefore can become a label for failure or disadvantage, as was found in one UK-based educational intervention (Defty and Fitz-Gibbon, 2002). Young people who had the ability to stay on, but indicated that they were intending to leave school, were independently identified, then assigned either to an intervention group who received extra support and mentoring from the school, or to a control group who remained anonymous. It was found that the individuals who were identified and given extra support actually did significantly *worse* in their subsequent exams. The additional focus appeared to have acted as a self-fulfilling prophecy of underachievement. In contrast, the successful US programmes intervened on the entire class or peer group rather than trying to pick off individual underachievers.

This and other evidence suggest the potential importance of measures such as:

- the more extensive use of adult mentoring in educational settings, and especially for young people from disadvantaged backgrounds. The results suggest that early mentoring is more effective than late, and that it may be disproportionately more effective to mentor a whole class rather than an individual, not least because of the power of peer effects and culture;
- much wider application of child-to-child and child-to-young-adult mentoring. Importantly, such mentoring appears to benefit the mentor too: as one study concluded, 'students who volunteered to work with deprived children reported wide-ranging gains, most frequently in self-image – discovering new aspects of self and feeling improvement in self-image; in interpersonal relations ... and in improved flexibility of thought' (Osterweil and Feingold, 1981, quoted in Halpern, 1989);
- young-parent mentoring (see above);
- business 'angel' mentoring, whereby experienced, often retired business people offer their time and knowledge to help fledgling businesses and entrepreneurs get started.

The UK's 'Connexions' advisory service, aimed at 13–16-year-olds, represents one attempt to help mentor young people. Meanwhile in the USA, the president's January 2003 State of the Union Address announced a US$450 push to extend mentoring programmes: 'Government will support the training and recruiting of mentors; yet it is the men and women of America who will fill the need. One mentor, one person can change a life forever. And I urge you to be that one person' (President George Bush, 28 January 2003). Future research needs to clarify further our understanding of the circumstances under which mentoring works best – bad mentoring may have more negative than positive effects. Also, as we move towards a more extensive use of mentoring, particularly within the public services, work will be needed on how best to prepare and screen potential mentors.

New approaches to dealing with potential offenders

Committing a crime involves a break with mainstream social values and signals an absence of restraining personal and social relationships. At-risk young men (and increasingly women) who avoid offending usually do so because a mainstream relationship – typically with a girlfriend but sometimes with a peer or family member – binds them into the values, responsibilities and satisfactions of the wider community.

By contrast, when a young person is sent to prison, the few relationships that they have to family, nascent partners, teachers or workmates are disrupted and weakened (see chapter 4). At the same time, the young offender is connected into a network of 'criminal social capital', to gangs and other offenders. Strengthening potential young offenders' 'positive' social capital, and weakening – or at least not reinforcing – their 'negative' social capital, should therefore be an important part of strategies for reducing the incidence of crime. Possible measures include:

- providing extra-curricular or team-based volunteering activities that get children out of the home or away from their neighbourhood and peer group, so they can develop new personal and social relationships and 'positive' social capital;
- programmes to raise the ambitions of children; for example, by taking them to the workplaces of professions they are likely to be unfamiliar with, and by encouragement from trusted mentors (see also above);
- only using prison as a measure of absolutely last resort. It should certainly not be used as a response to minor, non-violent crime;[9]
- bringing young offenders face to face with their victims to establish a relationship, hear the effects of their actions on victims, and thereby to personify future potential victims in the potential reoffender's mind.

How best to target such measures on at-risk groups needs careful consideration. Within the USA and Britain, such policies are always difficult to get past the criticism of being 'soft on crime', despite the evidence of their effectiveness.

One possible model for extra-curricular and team-based activity is the Raleigh Youth Development Programme. Within Britain, the young people (17–25) on this modest-size programme are referred by community services, social services, the probation service and other local services. Of the 150 at-risk young people who took part in the programme in 2001, 40 per cent were long-term unemployed, 35 per cent had criminal convictions, and 50 per cent suffered from drug and alcohol abuse.

The programme involves a series of UK-based residential activities followed by a 10-week expedition and then a follow-up residential week to plan for the future. Each place costs £5,500 to provide. The young people involved have to raise enough money to cover the cost of kit and injections. All other costs are paid for by the Raleigh organization, including the cost of getting a passport. Funds are raised from the European Social Fund, the National Lottery, corporate sponsors and charities. Volunteers on 'ordinary' Raleigh programmes have to raise £3,300 to go, some of which subsidizes the trips for at-risk young people.

Among young people at risk, after they have completed the programme, 65 per cent access work or training; 95 per cent report improved levels of confidence and communication skills; 90 per cent report higher motivation, responsibility and ability to relate to others; and 70 per cent say their plans and ambitions have positively changed as a result.

Volunteering

Early experiences of volunteering and associational activity appear to be highly predictive of community engagement in later life. The data indicate that relatively short periods of associational involvement provide as much stimulus to trust and wider community engagement as longer periods. Involvement with associations with more diverse members stimulates somewhat higher levels of trust and wider community engagement than involvement with more homogeneous groups (see chapter 8).

This evidence suggests efforts could usefully be focused on ensuring that young people get some experience of volunteering, even if it is only for a limited period, and that this experience should involve working alongside people from different social and ethnic backgrounds. Efforts might perhaps be focused particularly on those young people who are unlikely to go to university, thus seeking to replicate some of the bridging social capital benefits that higher education appears to bring.

Interventions might therefore include:

- developing or sponsoring six-week to six-month away-from-home voluntary service programmes for all young people, and especially those from disadvantaged backgrounds. These might be developed not only for school leavers, but also for young people still at school who are finding school difficult and are at risk of dropping out;
- extending international exchange programmes for young people from all walks from life to enable them to volunteer and mix with others in very different contexts;
- offering financial rewards or college credits for volunteering. For example, a proposal was made by Bell and Chen (2002) for the wider application of an Experience Year for all, modelled on the US Americorps scheme. Americorps was set up by the Clinton administration to encourage volunteering among young people. After their term of service, Americorps members receive $4,725 a year to help finance college or pay back student loans.

One criticism is that such younger volunteers are increasingly concerned with volunteering opportunities as means to pragmatic ends, such as resumé building (Price, 2002). However, recent evidence from a two-year before-and-after analysis of Americorps volunteers found that members became more active in community groups and showed significant value shifts over the period, and that the programme helped solve unmet human and community needs (Simon and Wang, 2002). Other work shows that those who get experience of volunteering while young tend to persist with it later in life, and it has positive knock-on effects on social and political participation, and on pro-social attitudes (Janoski, Musick and Wilson, 1998; Halpern, John and Morris, 2002).

As announced in the 2002 State of the Union address, the Seniorcorps programme, which encourages over-55s to volunteer, was extended and new provisions introduced that enabled participants to earn scholarships that could be transferred to grandchildren or others.

Within the UK, the Millennium Volunteers programme, funded by the Department for Education and Skills, was launched to attract

100,000 new volunteers in the age range 16–24 by the end of 2003. It is now complemented by the Experience Corps, funded by the Home Office, which aims to attract 250,000 new volunteers aged over 50 by 2004, and began in November 2001, with a nation-wide roll-out in May 2002. Finally, at the time of writing, proposals are being consulted on to create a new 'matriculation diploma' for young people aged 14 to 19, one necessary condition of which will be the completion of a certain minimum period of voluntary service.

Other ideas for stimulating social capital at the individual level

With a little imagination, one can think of all kinds of ideas for stimulating social capital at the individual level – though most of these the government should probably stay well away from and leave for individuals and communities to organize for themselves.

For example, one of the characteristics of modern life seems to be later entry into lasting personal relationships, and a delaying – often indefinitely – of parenthood. One of the simplest indicators of this trend is the steady growth in single-person households (and the pressures on the housing market this is causing in many industrialized nations). In as much as these trends simply reflect lifestyle choices, these should be entirely a matter for the individuals concerned. However, there is some evidence – arguably including the spate of agonized TV shows about young and not-so-young singles wishing they were in relationships – that suggest that there might be some more systemic failure in relationship formation.

The answer is unlikely to lie in the creation of a government-sponsored dating agency (cf. the Japanese experience), or in the start of an advertisement campaign to 'get off your sofa and get a partner'. But maybe there is a problem here. For example, it is known that a large proportion of medical problems seen by general practitioners are psychosomatic or have psychosocial contributory causes. They are often manifested in patients who are overworked, lonely and emotionally unsupported. Given that this is the case, should medics keep doling out beta-blockers, sleeping pills and antibiotics for overstressed immune systems, or should they be introducing their isolated patients to one another and hoping a few might hit it off? In the housing market, should governments be changing the law to make it easier for un-related adults to buy and sell homes together?

Doctors prescribing dates probably isn't going to work. But then sometimes the best policy proposals start with just such a dumb idea.

Stimulating social capital at the community or meso-level

At the community or meso-level, there is already quite a lot of policy thought and development. For example, most nations have extensive and state-supported voluntary sectors. Similarly, the devolution of power to local and regional governments is also well advanced in many nations, and should contribute to social capital at local and regional levels. This section will therefore focus on some of the more innovative ideas for stimulating social capital at the community level.

It is important to remember that many of the communities that have most problems are also the ones with the least social capital, with residents or members atomized, distrusting and disconnected. Government or external agencies often have a key role to play in combating crime or providing basic services in order to create the ground conditions on which a community can flourish.

Neighbourhood and other very local governance

In some countries, Britain being a striking example, 'local' government isn't very local. Its scale is vastly above what most people identify as their neighbourhood. While certain functions may be more efficiently handled at larger scales – though the evidence for these scale effects is generally extremely modest – many functions could be delegated to the very local level. For example, two or three streets might easily be large enough to organize and support a small play area or park, and a neighbourhood warden to keep an eye on the park and the surrounding streets.

Similarly, while certain police functions need to be conducted at a regional, national or even international level, other functions could and should be directed by communities on the ground. If we are serious about reducing crime, we must intervene early, often and fast. Communities and their residents need the confidence and institutional framework to be able to act where they see teenagers starting to drift into trouble, graffiti starting to appear, or drugs starting to emerge. Perhaps neighbourhood councils should have the power not only to employ wardens and create facilities for young people, but to issue community punishments to be served in their midst. Such punishments might be very mild, but if they can divert a young person from crime at an early stage, as well as giving them an opportunity to 'put something back' and be rapidly forgiven by those around them, these punishments are likely to be far more effective than the more severe but uncertain, distant and delayed punishment of the formal criminal justice system.

- Countries lacking very local layers of government – areas with no more than a few thousand people within them, and perhaps less – should consider creating neighbourhood councils. Such councils would have their own budgets and would be responsible for local 'livability' issues, such as neighbourhood parks, litter, facilities for young people, and neighbourhood or park wardens.
- Such councils might also have some powers to issue mild community punishments, with clear channels to the police and other authorities to address more serious issues. They might also have the power to organize local referenda, perhaps to agree modest local tax surcharges to fund local facilities by community consent.
- Disadvantaged areas would need a more structured and supportive approach, at least over the short to medium term.

There is always the issue that the wider implementation of very local self-government will lead to greater inequalities between wealthy, high social capital areas and poor, low social capital areas. But localism does not mean that disadvantaged areas could or should not receive extra support from the wider community. This concern certainly should not be used as an excuse to do nothing.

Community-asset-based welfare

There may be links between social capital and *community* ownership of local public assets. For example, some local and national authorities are experimenting with, or considering piloting, proposals in which public assets (e.g. community centres) are transferred to 'community trusts', or the neighbourhood councils described above, over which neighbourhoods have greater control or even full ownership. Given appropriate governance arrangements and safeguards, community trusts of this type could be an important site of local civic engagement that contributes to the development of both bonding and bridging social capital.

Building networks between firms, employees and the community

As pointed out in chapter 1, firms are forms of social capital too. It has also been established that the social networks that exist between firms play an important role in prompting and spreading innovation. Consequently both private and state sectors are now active in trying to replicate the 'Silicon Valley' effect by seeking to cluster commercial and research activities, in order to maximize the chances that proximity and social networks will stimulate innovation and economic growth. However, what sometimes gets neglected is the essential role played by informal social interaction, rather than mere proximity.

- Firms need to ensure that they have the correct balance of within-firm bonding and between-firm bridging social capital. Trade organizations, universities and regional authorities can play an important role by helping potentially competitor firms to interact with one another on more informal terms.
- State-funded schemes to encourage networks between firms have proved themselves sufficiently valuable to firms for them to have become self-financing by the end of the scheme, suggesting a role for their wider seed funding (for example, see Cooke and Wills, 1999).
- Company-based 'champions' who act as facilitators and moderators between corporate interests and wider community interests have been found to foster effective community–industry dialogues (Scott and Sexton, 2002).
- Ethical codes within companies have been found to influence societal norms significantly and increase tolerance of diversity (Valentine and Fleischman, 2002).
- Firms may benefit greatly by allowing and funding staff to participate in challenging extra-firm activities that involve interaction with very different groups of people (see also box 9.1). For example, the London Theatre Festival, which organizes 'alternative' and challenging performances, has recently begun a highly successful programme of arranging access for rising corporate executives to see at least four alternative performances, followed by challenging discussion sessions with mixed groups from the audience. Executives find that the dynamics of the group combined with the challenging nature of the material helps them reassess their own assumptions and think more innovatively. The scheme has also raised substantial funds for the festival and has totally transformed the nature of corporate sponsorship and of the relationship between the corporate and performing arts sector, turning reluctant fund-givers into respectful clients and partners.

Many of these issues are already widely pursued in one form or another. However, they are often implicit and undervalued.

Box 9.1   Companies and community engagement:
three case studies

Yorkshire Water has set a target of 20 per cent of its workforce to be involved in company-based community programmes at any one time, a target which has been largely met. Community involvement is a mandatory part of the graduate training programme and is recognized within the performance management process for all staff. The company has also provided accommodation and other support for 'Reading Matters' – an initiative aimed at improving literacy standards by age 14. The company's strategy of community engagement is built into its business plan. It has led to the building of close links with the community and of strong staff and customer loyalty, and forms the basis of the personal development of staff.

Connex is a train operator. They agreed to give their employees 16 hours per month of work time to be special constables with the British Transport Police – volunteer policemen or women – and to reward employees with £1,000 in three monthly instalments to recognize their contribution and the extra skills they acquire. Connex also agreed to pay the British Transport Police for additional regular police constable hours to accompany their specials. The community, company and employees benefited in two key ways: through increased visibility of police in the transport system, and through the improved Connex staff skills in dealing with physical and verbal abuse to staff or customers.

The Royal Bank of Scotland decided to make an additional contribution of £2 for every £1 donated by staff from their monthly pay. Given further tax relief from the government, this means that, for a basic rate taxpayer, each pound that staff donate becomes nearly £4 received by the charity. Staff can also apply for community cashback awards of up to £1,000 for any organizations that they actively support as volunteers. Finally, the bank encourages employees to get directly involved in community organizations that are funded by the group's Community Investment Programme. Hence, individual giving, active volunteering and corporate giving and support are all mutually reinforcing and collectively recognized. (Examples all drawn from Her Majesty's Treasury, 2002)

Community information and communications technology (ICT) networks

Putnam has mused on the question of whether ICT, and the internet in particular, will turn out to be a 'fancy TV' that further isolates people or a 'fancy' telephone that helps reconnect them. Analysis of the DDB Life Style studies – the source used extensively by Putnam – suggests that use of the internet for information exchange encourages trust among young adult Americans (Shah, McLeod and Yoon, 2001). Around 63 per cent of Americans now regularly use email to keep in touch with friends and family, and interestingly people who use the internet more end up watching significantly less TV than non-internet users (UCLA, 2003). ICT has made it possible for new, large but diffuse communities of interest to come together, to develop new products and software, such as Linux, and to build up a common body of expertise and commentaries on particular issues, such as how to overcome bugs in programs (Pruijt, 2002).

On the other hand, some of the better-controlled studies have suggested that people who use the internet more tend to become more, rather than less socially isolated. Case studies indicate that the way in which ICT-based community networks develop depends heavily on the character of the community's pre-existing social capital (Sullivan et al., 2002). Most recently, Putnam has speculated that the internet, far from building social capital, may prove to be the ultimate form of narrow bonding social capital, allowing people to identify and connect only with others who share their interests in the most precise, narrow sense imaginable – not just other Chevy owners, but the owners of Chevy 1959s only![10]

Nonetheless, despite the mixed evidence to date, ICT appears to have significant potential to strengthen social capital (Davies, 2003). ICT can allow new, non-geographically based groups to form; can allow people to maintain ties despite separation by space and time zone; can facilitate 'just-in-time' social ties; and can extend the value of social networks through automated 'recommender' systems, where relevant information is automatically forwarded to friends of friends (Resnick, 2002).

For example, where networks of existing neighbours have spontaneously created shared email lists, they have proved powerful forces to strengthen the local community. The moral seems to be that the details matter. At the simplest level, ICT networks are most likely to boost social capital where they are overlaid on a more traditional potential, or actual, community. At a more sophisticated level, the potential of ICT for boosting social capital is likely to rest on the regulatory or structuring environment within which it operates. Policy conclusions include the following:

- When neighbours create a common email list, this can be a powerful resource to boost local or street-level social capital. With rapidly rising penetration rates, this should become more and more common. This doesn't have to be organized centrally, but can grow organically from just two or three neighbours at first sharing email addresses, then gradually adding others. One innovative programme involves facilitating the creation of a community-based photo-directory and email list, together with information gleaned from a local survey listing hobbies and interests (www.whothat.org). The idea is that the combination of detailed information about neighbours and the power of the technology makes it easy to identify neighbours with similar interests.
- There is a strong case for more comprehensive ICT pilot projects that connect up socially mixed, geographically dense areas. In particular, these networks should seek to connect work-rich and work-poor households, since this provides powerful opportunities for employment exchanges across the social divide. ICT training should be provided to those in need, and local intranet facilities should be provided to facilitate exchanges of information and trade between households, and collective community action. Information to be exchanged might include recommendations for trades, public and private services and so on. Trading might include childcare, gardening and school runs, as well as more formal work opportunities. And community action might include clubs, local campaigns, planning issues and so on.
- Consideration should be given to how the quality of information, and the build-up of electronic reputations online, should be regulated. In many countries, this may involve the revisiting of data-protection and privacy rules.

The vast majority of community ICT 'experiments' conducted to date have not met the conditions above. Often they involve little more than a basic website that provides information about traffic, weather and a smattering of community events, and do little to foster community dialogue (Tonn, Zambrano and Moore, 2001). The main lesson from these pilots, such as the London Street where 100 households were networked, is that the benefits have tended to come from the resulting incidental social interaction rather than from the ingenuity of the IT itself.[11] However, recent controlled studies have shown that the existence of a shared neighbourhood e-list among 150 to 200 family homes did not just boost email contact, but also doubled the number of neighbours talked to; trebled the numbers recognized; and led to a marked increase in the sense of neighbourhood community (Hampton, 2003).

In sum, ICT networks may have great potential to boost local social capital, provided they are geographically 'intelligent', that is, are smart enough to connect you selectively to your near neighbours; are built around natural communities; and facilitate the accumulation of collective knowledge, including of reputation (see box 9.2). They have particular potential to connect the work-poor and work-rich (given the proximity of these groups in the UK) and to increase the number of low-cost, but high-trust transactions that rest on reputation (such as childcare). Such exchanges would provide income for the less affluent – reducing the costs of benefits payments – and more leisure time for the wealthy.

Box 9.2   *The power of a local postcode: the example of upmystreet.com*

In many countries, a post- or zip-code is used to identify a small, geographically defined area. In the USA, zip-codes identify quite large areas – with up to tens of thousands of residents. Longer zip-codes exist that identify smaller groups of households, but these are not widely known. In contrast, UK postcodes identify much smaller areas, typically a single street or even less. As the codes also use letters, they tend to be short and memorable – everyone in the UK knows their own postcode.

This postcode may prove to be a powerful tool in the rebuilding of social capital at the local level. This potential was illustrated by upmystreet.com, where it was possible to enter your postcode and find out information about local schools and other facilities. It was also possible to take part in discussions which were automatically clustered both by geography – the closest people to where you live – and by interest. The power of this new local medium was illustrated by a series of exchanges between neighbours during an extended siege in a residential area of London, where near neighbours who did not previously know each other exchanged information about what was going on.

Upmystreet subsequently ran into financial difficulties, but other services have taken on its role, such as the BBC 'i Can!' in the UK.

New approaches to the planning and design of the built environment

Urban design is known to have very significant impacts on social networks and, through these, on outcomes such as crime and health. Quite simple and low-cost interventions can have extremely positive and dramatic results, particularly where these interventions give residents more of a sense of control over whom they are likely to meet in the immediate vicinity of their homes (see chapter 8). For example, the building of a fence around a notorious Pruitt-Igoe public housing block in the USA led to a drop in the vacancy rate from around 70 per cent to less than 5 per cent (Newman, 1980). Similarly, in the UK, an experimental intervention involving the closing of alley-ways on a problem estate led to marked increases in neighbourhood sociability and to more than a halving in clinical anxiety and depression among residents (Halpern, 1995a; see chapter 8).

Policy implications include:

- measures to change the character of residential streets from places that give priority to cars to places that give priority to pedestrians. Such street design has been successfully employed in the Netherlands since the 1970s but is now being tried out in many other countries. For example, the UK government has recently put £30 million (US$50 million) into piloting such 'Homezones'. Typically, such schemes involve resurfacing the road surface so that there is no distinction between road and pavement – instead it looks like a single giant pedestrianized area. Play spaces are created for kids, benches and tables for residents, and planting and bollards prevent motorists rat-running. Cars are generally parked diagonally in small groups, and can no longer park all along the street. In the UK, such zones have speed limits of 20 m.p.h., though the presumption is that cars will travel at walking pace. Such schemes make the street an attractive place to be, create opportunities for informal interaction, and thereby facilitate the development of social capital between neighbours;[12]
- building short roads and cul-de-sacs, not long through-roads. In fact this is a lesson now already familiar to most private developers. Shorter roads and cul-de-sacs create a more manageable, and recognizable, number of immediate neighbours;
- closing alley-ways that criss-cross residential areas, so that residents can be fairly confident that the people they see outside their homes are near neighbours. This particularly applies to large-scale public housing projects;

- making it easier for residents to hold street parties. Given that this may involve the closure of a public highway, it is often a complex and difficult procedure in many countries, but that could be simplified;
- upgrading local parks and play areas. The budgets that support such facilities are always easy targets for policymakers and administrators seeking to reduce expenditure, but they can play a key role in building a local community. The quality and variety of the facilities also vary hugely – a rusty swing and a patch of dirt aren't really enough to act as the focus of community play. Park caretakers, doubling as community facilitators, and subsidy schemes to support the viability of local shops and cafés are also worth thinking about (F. Baum and Palmer, 2002);
- making it easier for groups of residents to form or purchase areas of semi-public space (see figure 9.1 for a schematic example). The logic of such space is that it allows residents and their children to mix in a safe and closed environment if they so wish, but leaves them the option of sitting in their own private garden if they prefer to be undisturbed. Perhaps the closest model to such a design is the handful of residential blocks in Manhattan with a shared private garden within their cores (Drayton, 2000). Where they exist, such layouts are highly prized. This is reflected in the high values of properties with access to the garden, and in the commitment of residents, who join together at least once a year in a communal 'dig-day' to plant bulbs and tidy up the garden. Yet such semi-private gardens remain rare because of the sheer legal complexity of merging multiple ownerships, and the high probability that the scheme will be blocked by one or two objectors.

In some contexts, there may be a case for working actively with selected private developers to experiment with housing forms that facilitate stronger neighbourhoods. The rationale for this is that housebuilders tend to be conservative in their designs, and this can lead to homogeneous and atomized residential developments. Essentially, designs that make social interaction easy, but do not force it, lead to more positive and extensive social relationships between neighbours, impacting on both bonding and bridging social capital (A. Baum and Valins, 1977; Halpern, 1995a).

Dispersing social housing

Large physical agglomerations of social housing make it more difficult for disadvantaged communities to form and maintain bridging social

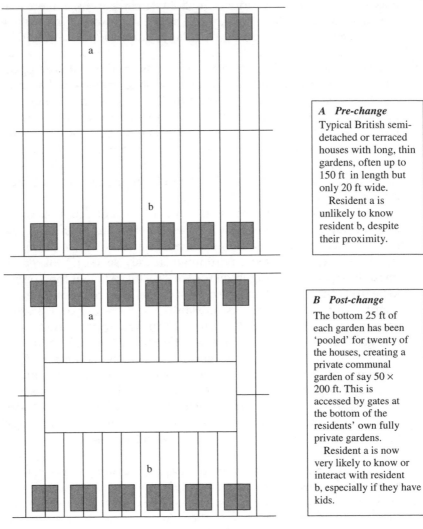

A Pre-change
Typical British semi-
detached or terraced
houses with long, thin
gardens, often up to
150 ft in length but
only 20 ft wide.
    Resident a is
unlikely to know
resident b, despite
their proximity.

B Post-change
The bottom 25 ft of
each garden has been
'pooled' for twenty of
the houses, creating a
private communal
garden of say 50 ×
200 ft. This is
accessed by gates at
the bottom of the
residents' own fully
private gardens.
    Resident a is now
very likely to know or
interact with resident
b, especially if they have
kids.

Figure 9.1 *The creation of a collective garden*

capital. More dispersed provision of social housing avoids this short-
coming. Policy options might include:

- widening the use of planning-gain contracts with private developers to reserve a portion of new housing for low-income renters.
  It is important to encourage the dispersal of single, low-rent

properties mixed in with more expensive properties rather than the normal ghettoization of such low-rent properties in large, separate blocks;
- more active purchasing, by housing associations or other providers of affordable housing, of properties in more affluent areas for letting or sale as social housing.[13]

The benefits of such dispersal policies would not be immediate and might take decades to realize. The scale of the benefits also depends on the characteristics of reciprocity and mutuality of pre-existing neighbourhood networks (Blokland, 2002). The benefits appear to be contingent on the dispersal of individual households rather than smaller estates or blocks of dwellings. Even then, social renters who get to live in more affluent areas do not immediately take on better jobs or see their incomes leap. The greatest beneficiaries are their children and teenagers, who grow up with the advantage of more diverse social networks, and of access to the aspirations and facilities of the middle classes around them. For example, fifteen years after the Chicago court-ordered Gautreaux public-housing desegregation, it was found that the children of suburban movers dropped out of school less, were more often placed in college tracks, were more often employed, had higher wages, and were more likely to have jobs with health and other benefits (Kleit, 2000).

Using personal networks to pull individuals and communities out of poverty

The life chances of disadvantaged individuals can be transformed by the presence in their personal networks of even a single employed individual. Policies to aid the development of personal and social networks may therefore help to reconnect disadvantaged individuals and communities to the social and economic mainstream. For example:

- firms should first be encouraged, probably by means including financial incentives, to recruit staff from disadvantaged areas;
- firms should then be encouraged to use successful recruits from disadvantaged areas to recruit further individuals from the same network and therefore area.

This was one of the ideas raised by the Saguaro seminars, but is equally relevant outside of the US context. Part of its attraction for firms is that individuals will be careful not to recommend someone to the firm who they feel will be unsuitable or untrustworthy, because of the knock-on effects on their own reputation.

Other ideas for stimulating social capital at the meso-level

Other, more speculative policy ideas worth thinking about for building social capital at the meso-level include the following:

- Regional differences in economic growth within countries may be partly explained by regional differences in the character and extent of social capital. Regions with strong bonding or club forms of social capital – such as chambers of commerce – but with relatively weak bridging and linking forms may need to pursue policies that actively help to rebalance their social capital. For example, policies might be pursued to change the rules of certain restricted members-only 'clubs' to force them to become associations that are accessible to the whole community.
- The state could support reading and informal study groups. Such schemes are considered extremely successful in Sweden, stimulating social networks in a way that does not arise from private reading and study.
- A street and café culture could be actively encouraged. Anglo-Saxon countries, such as the UK, tend to blame the absence of such 'Mediterranean' culture on the weather, but in fact a café culture thrives in much colder countries, such as Denmark, aided by street heaters and blankets on chairs. Café culture populates public spaces and creates opportunities for a wider range of spontaneous social interaction.
- Firms are forms of social capital too. Many firms have already taken steps to allow employees to take time off for volunteering, and more might be encouraged to do so, possibly with some forms of inducement such as tax credits. Many would also benefit from pursuing activities that would build up social capital within the firm, such as the increasingly common 'away-day' – especially if that day also involved a form of community engagement.
- Mobile telephones could have emergency help keys or codes that would activate the nearest three phones to indicate that the holder is in danger and needs assistance. Receivers of the distress signal would be expected to respond, at least to establish what the problem is and inform the emergency services. The scheme would break down the 'diffusion of responsibility' that inhibits strangers from helping each other in times of personal emergencies (Latane and Darley, 1976). It would be a way of using technology to

strengthen social norms of reciprocity and trust within the wider community, rather than weaken them.

Stimulating social capital at the macro-level

At the national and supranational level – the macro-level – social capital becomes less about specific social networks and more about shared norms, understandings, and everyday habits of co-operation and respect. This is reflected in the types of policy that might be pursued, most of which require a partnership between the public and the state.

Citizenship education and service learning

Traditional citizenship education involves teaching children the 'facts' about their rights, political system and constitution. The evidence shows that such programmes have some impacts on levels of political knowledge, but these impacts are modest and they do not appear to run very deep (Niemi and Junn, 1998). Service learning is a more dynamic, practice-based approach than traditional citizenship education, resting more on *doing* than formally learning about citizenship.

- Service learning is likely to offer a more effective approach to social capital building than traditional citizenship education. It involves a co-ordinated combination of doing (e.g. collecting rubbish for recycling), discussing (e.g. getting together as a group to talk about the experience), and learning (e.g. cross-references in the curriculum to the chemistry of recycling, ecology, global warming etc.). It is currently being evaluated by academic studies in both Europe and the US.[14]
- It is worth considering linking such learning programmes to course requirements to engage in community service or mentoring programmes (see above); to moves to give students more control over their school environments and the curriculum (at least in relation to citizenship studies); and to more formal recognition of young people in the wider society, such as lowering the voting age to 16 or below (see below).

Community service credit schemes

Community service credit schemes involve the giving of a non-monetary credit to volunteers, normally based on the number of hours of volunteering. These credits can then be exchanged, typically for some other service in kind. Such schemes first came to prominence in the USA in the mid-1980s, when the civil rights lawyer Edgar Cahn developed a community service dollar scheme in Washington.

It is important to realize that what makes these schemes of particular interest is not that they are simply rival monetary systems to enable people to avoid paying tax (as some LETS[15] may be argued to be). Rather, these schemes recognize the imperfect fungibility between acts of caring and monetary value – in everyday terms, 'you can't buy love'. The schemes seek to stretch the act of caring and reciprocity by applying the benefits of more abstract exchanges to the non-monetary or gift 'economy'. If a friend asks you round for a dinner at their house, it is clearly inappropriate to repay the favour by taking out your wallet at the end of the evening and paying for the meal that they've just cooked for you. Similarly, both paupers and millionaires get told off by their mothers if they don't come to visit often enough, however lavish the gifts they might send in lieu. The point is that there are some kinds of gift, or caring obligations, that cannot simply be discharged through a monetary repayment. Instead, we repay such acts in kind: by inviting friends back; by being there for them when they need us; and by a myriad other 'everyday' acts of affection and affiliation.[16]

Service credit schemes are gradually spreading across the world. They have been shown to be particularly useful in developing nations where governments and communities are cash short. For example, within Brazil one city began giving credits that could be exchanged for bus tickets for recycling rubbish, and within a few months children had picked the littered streets of the poor districts clean. The scheme worked so well that it became the only city of its size not to need expensive mechanical sorters for recycling materials. Such schemes can be a powerful tool for cash-poor administrations wishing to invest in public goods. In the same city, other tradable credit schemes – such as for open green space – helped to boost the city's growth rate above that of the region as well as making it an internationally recognized model green city.

The UK is fairly typical of OECD nations, with a modest but growing experimentation with such ideas. There are currently at least twenty-five 'Timebank' schemes in the UK loosely modelled on Kahn's idea, with at least another fourteen under development, often with some form of government support. These schemes involve volunteers being credited with hours that can then be 'spent' with other volunteers, or can be donated so that someone else can receive extra help. In some areas, these credits can also be used to gain access to local authority facilities, or for paying off library book fines and so on. However, at present these schemes are all very small scale and locally based, the largest involving no more than 120–30 people. Contrast this with some US schemes, such as that in St Louis, which now involves more than 12,000 people.

There is the potential for such schemes to operate on a much larger, even national scale. For example, the Japanese have introduced a successful scheme directed at the care of the elderly, a particular problem in the context of the ageing Japanese population. People who volunteer to care for the elderly gain credits related both to the time given and to the nature of the task (for example, helping with personal hygiene counts for more than doing shopping). These credits can be transferred to others, such as one's own elderly relatives living in another part of the country; donated on a needs basis; or used as credits for one's own future caring needs. The quality of care given through the scheme has been found to be higher than that of paid-for care, and is preferred by the elderly, who do not regard it as a form of charity.

Hence, specific policy ideas could be highly varied but might include:

- the expansion and spreading of local Timebank schemes, ideally linked to local ICT networks that match up volunteers to needs and demands at the local level (see also the section on ICT above);
- within the educational system, credits for children engaged in service learning, students in higher education offering to mentor school children, or volunteer classroom assistants. For example, within the UK it is proposed that children might have a magnetic 'Connexion card' to give them access to certain educational services, credit for turning up for classes, and to get free meals and so on. This card could also be used as a vehicle for storing non-monetary, volunteering credits. An alternative would be for the credits to be paid into a trust fund that could be used towards later education (Paxton, 2002);
- within health services, transferable credits for voluntary carers, translators and advocates, built loosely on the successful Japanese experience;
- within the benefits system, supplementing conventional financial benefits by additional non-monetary benefits in the form of community service credits. These could then be used to 'purchase' services offered by volunteers, such as parenting mentors, and to access other forms of social capital;
- creating nationally or even internationally recognized community service currencies.

A difficult question for community service credits is the extent to which they should be interchangeable for normal monetary currencies. In the US, President Bush's expanded volunteering schemes can provide benefits with clear monetary value, notably scholarships to college (see above). Some state-wide schemes, such as Minnesota Community Service Dollars, accrue in credit cards that also work as ordinary debit cards, and the Community Service Dollars are accepted by businesses as part-payment for goods. For example, a restaurant in the Mall of America might allow you to pay for half of the cost of your meal in Community Service Dollars, at least outside of peak hours. For businesses, this can be a low-cost form of giving, because of the low marginal cost to them of the additional service.

Such models could be generalized. For example, a volunteer at a hospital might accrue community service dollars, pounds or euros on a conventional credit card, and then be able to use these at a restaurant for an early lunch. Or they might perhaps use them to help pay off a young relative's university loan; provide mentoring in a local school; gain free access to a museum; or simply purchase additional care at the hospital.

The danger is that if the credits are too fully or easily interchangeable with normal money, there is a risk of corrupting the distinctive character of the caring and reciprocity that volunteering embodies. On the other hand, and especially for less affluent but time-rich volunteers, the ability to use the credits to purchase certain kinds of goods is an important feature of the schemes. What needs to be preserved is the caring nature of the exchanges. Hence when the state backs up the schemes, it needs to do so through acts that reinforce this logic of caring reciprocity. A grandparent using the credits to support their grandchild's university education seems an appropriate exchange. Being able to use credits to put a down-payment on a sports car does not.

Creating a contemporary shared 'moral' discourse

Shared understandings that facilitate co-operation between strangers, as well as friends, are what make society work and make it liveable. Such understandings range from 'Thou shall not murder' to standing on the right on escalators on the underground. But where do such norms arise from?

Occasionally, it is possible to witness the development of a new collective norm of pro-social behaviour, such as the emergence of using hazard lights to warn other motorists of danger ahead. An elegant micro-example of this phenomenon is provided in psychological studies of emergency situations (Latane and Darley, 1976). When a group of people are faced with an ambiguous situation where it is unclear how they should behave, they surreptitiously look to each other for clues. Psychologists have observed how a group of people will sit in a smoke-filled room, everyone acting as if nothing is wrong, nobody calling for help or shouting 'fire', and all because they are all noting that the others haven't panicked, so it can't be an emergency after all! Incredibly, it has been found that the more people that are involved – such as a group of eight instead of two or three – the less likely it is that anyone will intervene. Similarly, studies have shown that as soon as one person acts in a certain way, such as vandalizing a car, then others will much sooner follow suit.

One of the morals of this research is that social norms, understandings of what constitutes acceptable or appropriate behaviour, and even the very definition of what the situation is, are 'negotiated' between those present or from cues from other people. This particularly applies to new or unfamiliar situations. Social norms do not spring out of the ether; rather they evolve or are negotiated, generally over long periods of time.

Traditionally, religious communities were the sites of much of this discourse. Today it is increasingly conducted in the arenas of politics and the mass media. It is an activity around which there is considerable cultural ambivalence. The liberal and more individualistic traditions of western industrialized nations make us suspicious of politicians or other leaders telling us what they think our morals should be. Further thought must be given to how and where this type of debate or discourse should occur in contemporary societies and how it can be facilitated.

- Societies and communities need to consider what types of forum are appropriate in the twenty-first century for deliberating and agreeing their common moral and behavioural habits.
- One such form that merits much wider consideration is the use of random-sample deliberative forums in public policymaking, including at the highest levels of government. These forums involve bringing together a random sample of the population, normally of a hundred or more people, presenting to them both sides of an argument, then letting them vote to decide what the policy should be. Deliberative polls in both Europe and the USA (virtually all of which have been commissioned by the media) have been shown to be able to reach reasoned judgements about complex issues, including over government budgets.[17]
- Soap operas and other popular media play an important role in deliberating and exploring social and moral issues. Many govern-

ments and special interest groups already apply pressure in one
form or another to try to get their concern aired in such programmes, be it on drugs, abortion or whatever the issue. It may be
that this process needs to be made much more public, and programme makers should be obliged to allow air-time for public
debates following the exploration of difficult and important issues.
In exchange, there may be a case for some modest state protection
through the regulatory process of a small group of premier
channels. It may be that the sharing of the experience – having a
certain programme watched by large proportions of the population
– is as important as the content itself. It is much easier to have
a conversation if the conversants have access to the same
experiences.[18]

- Conventional methods, such as citizenship education – and education in general – have a major role in broadening people's conceptions of their group, stimulating bridging social capital, shared
understandings and reducing conflict (see above). But these
methods also need to be discursive. When we teach maths, science
and English at school, the curriculum and content are set
largely from above and with some fairly clear notions of what
the 'right answer is'. But this need not apply for citizenship.
Perhaps an important part of the citizenship curriculum in schools
should include feedback from what other pupils have thought
was right or wrong, and should include a clear sense of feeding
back into an ongoing debate through student-run surveys and
debates.

Facilitating mutual respect

Reciprocity, trust and most forms of social capital rest heavily on
mutual respect. From micro- to macro-levels, positive social relationships are unlikely to develop between individuals or groups without
this foundation of mutual respect. Status differentials can be destructive of social capital partly because they undermine this respect, a
lesson already learnt by many firms and some parts of our public
services, when they strip out excessive hierarchies of control and
instead create an atmosphere of team-working and equivalence (see
also chapter 8).

Possible policy implications include:

- breaking down barriers to mutual respect, sometimes literally – as
in the case of counter screens in benefit offices, hospitals and banks
– in order to build trust. The physical barrier often conveys a

message that those on the other side of the screen are dangerous and not to be trusted, and allows the server to remain distant and aloof. Often the need for physical security becomes the excuse, rather than the reason, for such screens.

- making more extensive use of mechanisms that bring political and corporate leaders directly into contact with the views of 'ordinary people', such as through the use of citizens' juries. A citizens' jury involves bringing together around a dozen ordinary people for a week to listen to the evidence on a particular issue and offer a view of what should be done. They normally have the power to call expert and senior witnesses to give evidence. Citizens' juries are thought to have been used by around one in five local councils in the UK with considerable success, though higher levels of government have employed them very little. Very importantly, citizens' juries and other similar mechanisms communicate to a wider population that government listens to, and cares about, 'people like me' – that is, 'ordinary' people. The same argument applies to deliberative polls (see above).

- listening to the young and entrusting them with more responsibility, including lowering the voting age (see also above). Young people have shown a sharp decline in political engagement at the same time as their expectations of personal autonomy have grown. This is of particular concern given the finding that once a young person has not voted at an election, they are unlikely to vote when older either. One response to this paradox could be to respect young people by listening to them and entrusting them with more responsibility, such as lowering the voting age to at least 16. Another possibility is to develop 'youth parliaments', such as has been done in the very ethnically mixed British town of Bradford.[19] If we want teenagers to learn about citizenship, what better way to get them (and politicians) engaged than to demonstrate respect by giving them the vote? Another interesting variant on this idea is to give the vote to much younger people, perhaps as young as 12, but for it to be held (and cast) in trust by the parent or guardian.[20] The presumption is that the parent will discuss the issues with the child and listen to their views, though not necessarily be bound by them. Again, mutual respect is a key part of the message.

- promoting human rights, democracy and the legal institutions to make them a reality. This cluster of values and institutions has been described as the development of 'cosmopolitan democracy' (Held, 1995), and perhaps foreshadows the evolution of an ultimate, global form of social capital.

An alternative to some of the above are ideas designed to make sure that we all get more involved in political and civic engagement. The most prominent example is the idea that there should be compulsory voting, as in Australia. A more radical idea is that countries should have 'deliberation days' that involve the entire population in a day of discussion (actually spread over two days so that workers in key services can take part too; Ackerman and Fishkin, 2004). These ideas are certainly worth thinking about, but one concern is that their relatively obligatory character fails on the count of mutual respect.

Other ideas for the promotion of social capital at the macro-level

Some might regard the ideas presented above as radical enough, but other ideas might include:

- the active creation of sports teams drawn from more 'rational' geographical or cultural areas, designed to bolster specific group identities. For example, the effectiveness and democratic accountability of regional governments are extremely variable, largely because only some regions have a meaningful regional identity. In Spain and Britain, for example, while some regional administrations have powerful elected parliaments, others have low-profile, unelected regional offices that simply administer central government policies. This also creates problems in the national parliament, where some regions are able to vote on issues that will affect other regions but will not directly affect themselves. In as much as sports teams create powerful affiliations, regional teams might accelerate the development of more even and widespread democratic accountability. Perhaps the same applies for supranational structures too. Would a European football team, formed to take on the Americas, help create a more fertile base for European democracy than a bureaucracy in Brussels ever could?
- deliberate and collective engagement in ambitious human endeavours, which has the potential to change how we think about ourselves and others. Wars are the classic, negative example. But positive examples abound too. When we see images of earth from space, rovers on Mars, distant galaxies through the Hubble telescope, or strange creatures from our planet's distant past, it tends to shift our focus away from our local identities and disputes towards that of a common identity of being human beings together. It is difficult to know just how many wars and conflicts might be

prevented by such positive shifts in identity. But in as much as such grand collective missions are one of the few mechanisms that we have for melding a more global identity, they surely represent money well spent.

Conclusion

The key question that this chapter has sought to answer is whether 'anything can be done to create social capital'. Even if one disputes some of the proposals made, the overall answer to this question must be a resounding 'yes'.

It is clear that there is a strong case for applying social capital thinking to a wide range of policy areas. Such applications have not been without critics. Social capital approaches have been criticized for faults ranging from attempting to develop a 'costless' approach to redistribution (Mohan and Mohan, 2002) through to being in tension with women's rights, particularly in the developing world (Molyneux, 2002). It is certainly true that not all forms of social capital building will lead to positive outcomes; rather, a 'vitamin model' should be applied. In particular, a narrow focus on increasing community bonding social capital may have significant negative externalities – such as conflict between groups, reinforcing social divisions, and sometimes entrapping individuals in poverty – if not balanced with other bridging and linking social capital building.

A final practical policy question is whether governments need an explicit 'social capital strategy'. While some policymakers see social capital building, or 'civil renewal', as an important goal in itself (Blunkett, 2001), most policymakers' interest in social capital is as a means to other policy ends, such as reduced crime and higher educational attainment. This widespread but moderate level of interest leads to many government departments all tinkering with the issue, sometimes with conflicting interests, and sometimes promoting contradictory policies. It tends not to reach the top of the agenda of any individual department, even though its total impact on policy is very large. It also tends to lead to duplicated efforts to promote traditional forms of social capital, such as through neighbourhood renewal programmes, while more innovative ideas tend to be neglected. These considerations suggest that governments organized around the classic policy divisions – health, crime, welfare, economic development and so on – may need to develop explicit social capital strategies with clear leadership at both local and national level.

Social capital should be seen as giving policymakers a useful handle on the character and importance of community and the social fabric, and as a useful source of insight into new policy levers, but it is not a simple or single magic bullet for solving all policy problems. Hopefully, future academic and policy development will improve on the ideas presented here. Perhaps some of the ideas will not work, while some of the 'wackier' ideas will prove to be the best. But what I do feel confident about is that this concept, and the ideas and issues that it prompts, will still be in play and debated for decades to come.

Social capital matters for our personal well-being, our economies and our society because we are deeply social beings. It's in our flesh and blood. Policy and debate that fail to address it are doomed to be shallow and unconvincing. Social capital is surely here to stay, both as a concept and as an everyday reality.

Further reading

For policy development in the *US* context, useful sources include publications from the Saguaro Seminars, which can be found at www.bettertogether.org or at the Kennedy School of Government website, www.ksg.harvard.edu/saguaro. A summary of the key conclusions of the Saguaro Seminars can also be found in the last chapter of Putnam (2000). For a source of interesting and encouraging case studies of successful social capital building, see Putnam and Feldstein (2003). Details on Bush's volunteering initiative can be found at www.usafreedomcorps.gov or www.americorps.org.

Follow-up papers should also be expected from the *OECD* in the wake of their report (2001a). It may take a little while, but the OECD normally produce interesting reports that compile policy developments across a number of nations, as well as more general lessons and analysis. Also well worth a look is a recent report drafted by Tom Healey, one of the authors of the OECD report, for the Irish government (National Economic and Social Reform, 2003). This is full of data and policy applied to the Irish context, but has many ideas that may work in other contexts, and a useful glossary of terms.

On the *UK*, readers may wish to look at Aldridge and Halpern (2002), though this document will overlap substantially with the discussion above. At the time of writing, both the Home Office and the Office of the Deputy Prime Minister were drafting policy position papers on civil renewal and community regeneration.

In terms of the *non-OECD* nations, readers would do well to start with the World Bank website, www.worldbank.org, and to key in the nations that you are most interested in on the social capital link.

Finally, and not just because he has been my editor, I recommend the work of David Held on the development of *'cosmopolitan democracy'*, such as Held (1995). Too often, the social capital agenda turns into a traditional community agenda. Thinking about the issues in a global sense prises us out of this mentality and gives a real, but positive sense of where we could be going.

Notes

Notes to preface

1 This case study is written up in Halpern (1995a, ch. 7).
2 See Halpern (1993); Halpern and Nazroo (2000).
3 See Halpern (1992).
4 Unpublished work conducted at Nuffield College in 1995–6, but see Donovan and Halpern (2003).
5 See Rutter and Smith (1995).
6 Commission on Citizenship (1990).
7 By the end of that year, I had written a paper on social exclusion and social capital, later updated into a think-piece entitled 'Social capital: the new golden goose?' But it is striking that, even though it was presented at a seminar at Westminster, the UK think-tanks were very ambivalent about publishing it, being worried about levels of interest. When an updated version of this paper was quietly put on to the UK Cabinet Office Performance and Innovation Unit in 2002, 10,000 people downloaded the paper in the first month alone (Aldridge and Halpern, 2002).

Notes to chapter 1

1 The parallel between bonding and strong ties, and bridging and weak ties, is not perfect (Tom Healy, pers. comm.). Some might argue, for example, that we are bonded to distant relatives even though the frequency of our

interactions and physical distance involved might suggest that the relationship is more of a 'weak' tie.

2 I am grateful to my ex-graduate student, Nir Tsuk, for bringing the relevance of Hegel to my attention.

3 See also Halpern (1999, section 5, 'The dark side of social capital: can it harm or exclude?') or Aldridge and Halpern (2002, section on 'The potential downsides of social capital').

4 This definition then leaves bridging social capital to refer to 'horizontal' links across groups and communities, while linking social capital refers to 'vertical' links through the power and resource strata of society.

5 The substantive issue raised here – that is, why the measure appeared so important in the Italian case, but was not necessarily important elsewhere – is discussed further in chapter 8.

6 See, for example, the extensive matrix of questions developed by the British Office of National Statistics.

7 As an interesting aside, it is worth noting the considerable difficulty the White House had in getting agreement to have social capital measures included in one of the big national surveys. The original plan was for a social capital module to be included in the Current Population Survey, which is best known for gathering unemployment statistics, in late 2001. After protracted discussions, at which the phrase 'over my dead body' was used, the module eventually found a home in another survey, and social capital data are now being gathered in the American Crime Victimization survey.

Notes to chapter 2

1 In an interesting exception to this general rule, a recent case study of the Dutch construction industry found little or no ethnic segmentation, even though this industry is generally considered to be the 'quintessential immigrant niche'. The author argues that social, economic and institutional processes in the Netherlands disrupt or render irrelevant the normal dynamics of this process (Rath, 2002).

2 A similar story applies at the national level. Econometric analyses conducted across two decades and sixteen countries by the OECD (Guellec and van Pottelsberghe de la Potterie, 2001) show clearly that the major economic benefit flowing from nationally based R&D is not the knowledge directly generated, but the ability to understand and gain value from the generally much larger volume of research being conducted in other countries.

3 The 1998–9 slowdowns among the eastern tiger economies do not appear to affect this model. First, inspection of figure 2.1 reveals that, despite the claims of Fukuyama, these nations are characterized by only moderate levels of social trust, so a slowdown in their growth may actually bring them back into line and improve the model. Second, national differences

in long-term growth rates are only modestly affected by short-term fluc-
tuations in the annual growth rates.

4   They note that higher levels of secondary education are also associated
    with higher levels of social trust. Much the same is found at the individ-
    ual level – people who are more highly educated report higher levels of
    trust. But, at the macro-level, this is difficult to interpret causally – perhaps
    nations with high levels of social trust and social capital invest more in
    education.

5   Florida has adopted a more conciliatory line in public lectures than in the
    book.

6   There are clearly examples going both ways on this issue. For example, a
    survey of eight African countries concluded that business associations in
    Africa conform better to the pluralist model of interest group behaviour
    rather than to Adam Smith's conspiring traders (Goldsmith, 2002). It may
    be that in the African case, a degree of conspiracy against potentially
    corrupt state institutions and across ethnic divides is on balance helpful.
    As ever, social capital can be used for good or bad, and this is often context
    dependent.

7   We might note from figure 2.1 that the WVS suggests that Fukuyama was
    mistaken in describing China as being low in generalized social trust,
    though there are concerns about the representativeness of the Chinese
    WVS sample.

Notes to chapter 3

1   Typical auditory hallucinations in schizophrenia are hearing voices talking
    critically about you in the third person. 'Inappropriate affect' refers to
    showing the wrong emotion at the wrong time, such as laughing when
    you hear tragic news.

2   These large sums of money are partly a function of the modest relation-
    ship between income and happiness.

3   Evidently the same pattern was found in the even more recent record heat-
    wave in France in summer 2003 (Tom Sander, Harvard, pers. comm.).

4   Even in a survey of many thousand people, only a handful may then suffer
    a heart attack in the year or two following.

5   An interesting exception is how young people brought up in the shadow
    of a previous generation of now ageing and unwell drug-users tend to
    avoid drug abuse, the negative consequences of it being all too plain to
    see (Lovell, 2002).

6   A partialling fallacy occurs when statistically controlling for a related vari-
    able artificially reduces the size of another statistical relationship, possibly
    leading one to conclude that the relationship was weaker than it actually
    was. For example, if you were trying to estimate the relationship between
    IQ and earnings, but then added shoe size to the equation (which happens
    to correlate with IQ), this addition would probably artificially weaken the
    IQ–income relationship.

7 Figures for 1993.
8 This finding is itself not without controversy. The strength of the relationship rests on certain corrections and adjustments in the data that not all
research groups follow, with particular controversy over studies using the
Luxembourg Income Surveys.
9 Relative inequality does have some effects on the absolute ability to buy
goods too, as certain low-cost goods may become difficult to obtain (e.g.
coal).

Notes to chapter 4

1 Of course there are some categories of crime that tend to occur later, notably
domestic violence and corporate fraud – not least because teenagers can't
normally get married and don't have senior positions in companies.
2 The actual measure is derived using factor analysis and is a composite
measure. 'Keeping money that you have found' is the strongest loading
item on the factor.

Notes to chapter 5

1 Also quoted in Putnam (2000, pp. 303–4).
2 This study has subsequently been criticized on methodological grounds.
Later and better-controlled studies have found more modest impacts on
IQ, but have confirmed that teachers' expectations significantly affect a
child's general performance at school (Snow, 1995; Mackintosh, 1998).
3 This supposition appears to have been supported by evidence from
welfare to work programmes. These have generally found that getting
mothers back into work boosts the educational attainment of children, at
least up to around age 12. Part of this effect is thought to lie in the mothers'
boosted self-esteem as well as their enlarged social networks and
resources.
4 If parental involvement is generally high (or low) inside a given ethic
group, then it cannot 'explain' much in a statistical sense simply because
it doesn't vary very much.
5 Contrast the positive effects of Catholic schools on social capital at the
micro-level with the negative effects of the Catholic religion on social
capital at the macro-level (La Porta et al., 1997; see also chapter 8).
6 One should note that school sizes in the USA are larger than in many other
countries. A careful analysis of UK schools found a U-shaped relationship
between school size and academic performance, having controlled for the
numbers of students on free school meals (an indicator of poverty), teaching inputs and type of school (Bradley and Taylor, 1998). These researchers
concluded that the optimum size of school was 1,200 for 11–16-year-olds
and 1,500 for 11–18-year-olds – sizes actually slightly above the average
sizes of schools in the UK. That said, since there is also good evidence to

support all-age schools, this may imply we should seek to have schools with fewer students per year or grade but with a fuller age range.

7 Other factors, as one might expect, include a consistently positive attitude towards learning, the principal's leadership, and reflection on the reform process itself.

8 The measure of educational achievement was an average of the percentage of the population attaining upper levels of prose and mathematics literacy. Social trust data were drawn from the World Values Survey. I am grateful to my research assistant, Zoe Morris, for pulling the data together for this analysis.

Notes to chapter 6

1 These trends were little affected by September 11, 2001, even within the USA. However, the worsening economic climate, and the issue of asylum seeking in some countries, tend to work against the positive, long-term, underlying trend.

2 At the time this draft was being prepared, the war with Iraq was raging. The tensions around this conflict across the international community clearly put a number of severe strains on the positive tone of this draft. Nonetheless, one must hope – and expect – that the more positive long-term trends described here will re-establish themselves in the post-conflict situation.

3 A later study with voters aged under 30 showed better results for telephone canvassing, boosting turnout by around 5 per cent. But face-to-face canvassing was still more effective, boosting canvassing by 8.5 per cent (Gerber and Green, 2000). Face-to-face canvassing also caused marked spill-over effects, increasing the voting of other household members, and helping to raise its cost effectiveness above that of telephone canvassing (i.e. to around $12 per extra vote). There was no evidence of either intervention having any long-lasting effects on political interest or engagement.

Notes to chapter 7

1 In fact, while Putnam's work on Italy had not attracted much attention outside of a relatively narrow academic circle, it was noticed by some policymakers. A colleague at No. 10 Downing Street recently told me of how, on a visit to Singapore in 1993 when serving in the Foreign Office, he found Singapore's political leader was reading, with great interest, an obscure book on Italian governance.

2 The rise and decline of Greenpeace illustrates the link to direct mailing – it was direct mailing that helped drive their spectacular growth in numbers. When they decided to stop using it as a technique, membership plummeted.

3 Calculating percentages from the figures mentioned by Putnam (2000), changes range from −50 per cent (nurses), −32 per cent (architects), −28 per cent (engineers) and −10 per cent anaesthetists to +3 per cent (surgeons).

4 There is some evidence that people overreport church attendance in the USA, and that this overreporting has grown in strength (Hadaway, Marler and Chaves, 1993).

5 The turnout in 1916 – the last male-only American national election – had been 62 per cent. It was pulled down in 1920 and for many years to follow by the lower turnout of women (Patterson, 1993; Hough, 2000).

6 Figures from the International Institute for Democracy and Electoral Assistance. The figures for 2000 were not available when *Bowling Alone* was written, but clearly reinforce the same downward trend.

7 The figures reported here are mainly net changes. In other words, if 20 per cent show more engagement and 5 per cent show less, the 'net change' is an increase of 15 per cent. A summary of the method and key results are available at www.ksg.harvard.edu/saguaro/press.html. See also updated figures by Putnam in Drogosz, Litan and Dionne (2003).

8 Many people just can't believe this projection. But it would seem that, at least in contemporary Britain, religiosity behaves like a recessive gene – the religiosity of the child follows that of the less religious parent. The trend line is also gently accelerating, which is what would be predicted given that the pool of potentially religious partners keeps shrinking, making it harder and harder to find another equally religious partner.

9 One puzzle in these data is why the massive cohort shift shown in these studies doesn't come through more clearly in the cross-sectional data. Do we have the generational pattern of decline as seen in the USA, or not?

10 Indeed, turnouts in British local elections are unusually low by international standards, particularly in comparison with our national turnout, an anomaly that may reflect our unusually large but not very powerful local government areas.

11 Contrary to popular opinion, confidence in politicians and government ministers has also marginally increased from 1983 to 2003, with a marked increase in confidence following the 1997 election of the New Labour government, but a modest decline since.

12 There is a slight puzzle as to why the World Values Survey data show a marked fall from the 1981 and 1990 sweeps to the 1995 and 2001 sweeps, while the British Social Attitudes surveys data show little to no change over the 1990s. A MORI question asking 'would you generally trust the ordinary man on the street to tell the truth?' shows a trend somewhere in between: the percentage agreeing rose slightly from 57 to 64 per cent between 1983 and 1993, but then fell to 52 per cent by 2000–1. It has since risen slightly to 55 per cent in 2004 (see www.mori.com/polls/trends).

13 Even in Sweden, there is evidence that union members, though stable in numbers, have become significantly less active.

14 Though I have not read it, I understand that a similar view is expressed in Diamond (1996).

15 There is some evidence that good socioeconomic performance – modern industrialized nations with strong welfare states and high social capital – helps to foster peaceful behaviour between states (Ohrn, 2002). That said, there is little evidence that social cohesion between members of the European Union has increased since the 1980s – though certainly there has been no war between member states (Berger-Schmitt, 2002).

16 Tom Sander has pointed out (pers. comm.) that, at least within the US, the increase in social tolerance is fairly independent of the decrease in social capital – it wasn't that individuals who were engaging less were also leading the way in terms of increased tolerance. But the key question is what is happening at the ecological level, that is, in terms of prevalent values and attitudes.

17 Based loosely on Abraham Maslow's theory of a hierarchy of needs.

Notes to chapter 8

1 Or as my colleague Stephen Aldridge put it, 'I wish we'd had that as a policy conclusion when we wrote our [2002] paper!'

2 This analysis has been subject to some criticism by Lowndes (2000), who argues that Hall and others tend to neglect the importance of more traditionally feminine types of social capital that may have been displaced (see also chapter 7).

3 The model described was a logistic regression predicting social trust at time 2, having controlled for social trust at time 1, as well as for a host of sociodemographic and other factors. But the basic pattern can be seen in the correlations between the times (see figure).

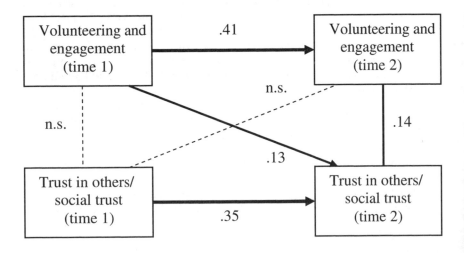

n.s. = Not significant

Notes to chapter 9

1 The World Bank programme is led internally by figures such as Deepa Narayan and Michael Woolcock.

2 Led within the OECD by one of the authors of the OECD report, Sylvain Cote, and more recently by Simon Field. However, not all elements of the OECD are as keen on social capital, and interest has tapered off following the departure of Tom Healy.

3 Alison Walker, director of the General Household Survey but at the Home Office, and Roz Harper have led this effort. Most of their material can be found on the ONS's excellent website.

4 Within the White House John Bridgeland has been a key figure, not least because of the need to have good information against which to assess the success of Bush-sponsored volunteering and faith-based programmes. The original plan was to incorporate measures into the 2002 Current Population Survey, but this ran into a number of 'over my dead body' problems and the focus shifted to the US crime survey. As with anything to do with social capital measurement in the US, Bob Putnam's team at the Kennedy School will know what is going on.

5 Within Canada, StatCan have fielded various surveys, and the economist John Helliwell has been an important figure; and within Ireland, the co-author of the 2001 OECD report, Tom Healy, now based in the Irish government's Department of Education and Science, has been influential, not least behind their National Economic and Social Forum Survey of social capital.

6 The initial date for the US–EU initiative happened to coincide with the start of the Iraq War, and was therefore cancelled.

7 The threshold of over 2 years old comes from both UK and US evidence on the impact of preschool provision across age groups.

8 Scandinavian countries have particularly good universal preschool provision, albeit at a high cost. However, the evidence indicates that this provision largely explains the high social mobility found in these countries (Esping-Anderson, 2003). It would seem that quality preschool provision is able to break the link between social class origins and class destination significantly better than conventional education, an observation that fits with the evidence from longitudinal studies showing large social class differentials in cognitive abilities by age 5. Such cognitive abilities relate closely to the child's social and emotional self-control. In essence, learning in humans is a social skill, and a child who lacks those skills finds it difficult ever to catch up.

9 In general, the certainty and rapidity of punishment are more important than its severity. Hence, for example, the major drive within the UK to halve the time between arrest and conviction is thought to have contributed to the UK's marked fall in crime over recent years.

10 Putnam made this provocative argument at a lecture at his Leverhulme Cambridge (England) lectures in May 2003.

11 One possibility for the UK is to build a pilot around emerging Timebank schemes sponsored by the Home Office Active Community Unit (and other government programmes such as Health Action Zones), though not precluding exchanges based on conventional monetary exchange.

12 As with all traffic schemes, attention must also be given to the displacement effects – more traffic being pushed through other streets and potentially destroying social capital elsewhere.

13 Such purchases already form part of policy in many nations, such as the Housing Corporation's programme for additional provision of social housing in England.

14 Teams working on the issue include Van Deth et al. in the Netherlands; John, Halpern and Morris in the UK; and Saunders and Putnam in the USA.

15 Local Exchange and Trading Systems. These have been viewed with particular suspicion by many tax officials as just another part of the black economy – people avoid paying tax by paying for things in goods and services instead of cash.

16 The movie *Pay it Forward* illustrates a simple scheme to stretch our habits of reciprocity. A child comes up with the idea for a school project of doing three good deeds; the beneficiary is asked to do the same, with the simple caveat that rather than 'pay the favour back' to the person that did it, they have to 'pay it forward' to someone else. Hence a pyramid of positive favours is created, and the world gets to be a slightly nicer place.

17 Similarly, an innovative exercise to develop a detailed, shared vision of a sustainable and desirable USA in the year 2100 concluded that it would embody a radically strengthened 'strong democracy' (Farley and Costanza, 2002).

18 For example, programmes such as *Big Brother*, which have replicated in many parts of the world, often attract not only a large numbers of viewers but also widespread media commentaries, as well as a myriad of heated conversations in workplaces, schools and homes across the nation. Although very mundane on one level, such commentaries – especially as they get revised in the light of wider reactions – become a forum within which society reaches a view on what is, or is not, acceptable behaviour. Often cheats become vilified, while the behaviour of others becomes quietly respected. Sometimes even the commentators themselves get slated and have to correct their positions when it becomes clear that others do not hold the same view. In the midst of all this chatter, society is negotiating with itself, and clarifying its own position, on what constitutes acceptable behaviour.

19 Similarly, see Wallerstein (2002) for reports of the positive results of a youth empowerment project in New Mexico.

20 This idea was brought to my attention by the Cambridge historian Simon Szreter.

Bibliography

Abbott, S. (2002) Prescribing welfare benefits advice in primary care: is it a health intervention, and if so, what sort? *Journal of Public Health Medicine*, 24(4): 307–12.

Ackerman, B. and Fishkin, J. (2004) *Deliberation Day*. New Haven, CT: Yale University Press.

Adams, D. (2002) Poverty: a precarious public policy idea. *Australian Journal of Public Administration*, 61(4): 89–98.

Ader, R. and Cohen, N. (1975) Behaviourally conditioned immunosuppression. *Psychosomatic Medicine*, 37: 333–40.

Aguilera, M. B. (2002) The impact of social capital on labour force participation: evidence from the 2000 Social Capital Benchmark Survey. *Social Science Quarterly*, 83(3): 853–74.

Aguilera, M. B. (2003) The impact of the worker: how social capital and human capital influence the job tenure of formerly undocumented Mexican immigrants. *Sociological Inquiry*, 3(1): 52–83.

Ahern, B. (2001) Social capital: lessons for public policy development. Speech by an Taoiseach, Mr Bertie Ahern TD, at a seminar on social capital, Dublin, 29 March. http://www.ex.ac.uk/shipss/politics/research/socialcapital/other/ahern.doc.

Ainsworth, J. W. (2002) Why does it take a village? The mediation of neighbourhood effects on educational achievement. *Social Forces*, 81(1): 117–52.

Aitchison, A. and Hodgkinson, J. (2003) Patterns of crime in England and Wales. In Simmons, J. and Dodd, T. (eds) *Crime in England and Wales 2002/2003*. London: Home Office.

Aldridge, S. (2001) Social mobility. Performance and Innovation Unit. www.number-10.gov.uk

Aldridge, S. and Halpern, D. S. (2002) Social capital: a discussion paper. Performance and Innovation Unit. www.strategy.gov.uk

Alesina, A., Glaser, E. and Sacerdote, B. (2001) *Why Doesn't the US have a European-Style Welfare State?* Harvard Institute of Economic Research, Discussion Paper No. 1933. post.economics.harvard.edu/hier/2001papers/HIER1933.pdf

Allport, G. W. (1954) *The Nature of Prejudice*. Cambridge, MA: Addison-Wesley.

Anand, V., Glick, W. H. and Manz, C. C. (2002) Thriving on the knowledge of outsiders: tapping organisational social capital. *Academy of Management Executive*, 16(1): 87–101.

Anderson, A. R. and Jack, S. L. (2002) The articulation of social capital in entrepreneurial networks: a glue or lubricant? *Entrepreneurship and Regional Development*, 14(3): 193–210.

Andrews, G. (1997) The inclusive society. Paper presented to the NEXUS stakeholder and social inclusion group.

Anheier, H. and Kendall, J. (2002) Interpersonal trust and voluntary associations: examining three approaches. *British Journal of Sociology*, 53(3): 343–63.

Annen, K. (2003) Social capital, inclusive networks, and economic performance. *Journal of Economic Behaviour and Organisation*, 50(4): 449–63.

Araujo, L., Bowey, J. and Eastern, G. (1998) Social capital, industrial networks and entrepreneurs. In Halinen-Kaila, A. and Nummela, N. (eds) Proceedings of the 14th IMP Annual Conference, *Interaction, Relationships and Networks: Visions for the Future*, Vol. 1: Competitive Papers: 55–83.

Argyle, M. (1987) *The Psychology of Happiness*. London: Methuen.

Ashford, S. and Timms, N. (1992) *What Europe Thinks: A Study of Western European Values*. Dartmouth: Aldershot.

Astone, N. M., Nathanson, C. A., Schoen, R. and Kim, Y. J. (1999) Family demography, social theory, and investment in social capital. *Population and Development Review*, 25(1): 1–31.

Au, K. Y. and Fukuda, J. (2002) Boundary spanning behaviours of expatriates. *Journal of World Business*, 37(4): 285–96.

Autiero, G. (2000) Market functioning and social rules. *Economic Analysis*, 3(1): 49–65.

Axelrod, R. (1984) *The Evolution of Co-operation*. New York: Basic Books.

Axelrod, R., Riolo, R. L. and Cohen, M. D. (2002) Beyond geography: cooperation with persistent links in the absence of clustered neighborhoods. *Personality and Social Psychology Review*, 6(4): 341–6.

Aye, M., Champagne, F. and Contandriopoulos, A. P. (2002) Economic role of solidarity and social capital in accessing modern health care services in the Ivory Coast. *Social Science and Medicine*, 55(11): 1929–46.

Azam, J. P., Fosu, A. and Ndung'u, N. S. (2002) Explaining slow growth in Africa. *African Development Review*, 14(2): 177–220.

Bankston, C. L. and Zhou, M. (1995) Effects of minority-language literacy on the academic achievement of Vietnamese youths in New Orleans. *Sociology of Education*, 68(1): 1–17.

Bankston, C. L. and Zhou, M. (2002) Social capital as a process: the meanings and problems of a theoretical metaphor. *Sociological Inquiry*, 72(2): 285–317.

Bard, M. and Sangrey, D. (1979) *The Crime Victim's Book*. New York: Basic Books.

Bard, M. and Sangrey, D. (1986) *The Crime Victim's Book* (2nd edition). New York: Brunner/Mazel.

Barker, D. G. (1991) Changing social values in Europe. Paper presented to International Symposium on the Unexpected Europe: Implications for the United States, 15 November, University of Maryland.

Barker, R. G. (1968) *Ecological Psychology: Concepts and Methods for Studying the Environment of Human Behaviour*. Stanford, CA: Stanford University Press.

Barnes, H. W. and Crawford, R. G. (1986) Relationships: the lubricant of Asian markets. Proceedings of the Academy of International Business, Southeast Asia, June.

Baron, S., Field, J. and Schuller, T. (2000) *Social Capital: Critical Perspectives*. Oxford: Oxford University Press.

Baron, R. A. and Markman, G. D. (2003) Beyond social capital: the role of entrepreneurs' social competence in their financial success. *Journal of Business Venturing*, 18(1): 41–60.

Barsness, Z. I. (1997) The impact of contingent workers on group effectiveness: a process model of the relationship between group composition and group effectiveness. *Dissertation Abstracts International Section A: Humanities and Social Sciences*, 57(11-A):4816.

Barton, A. (2000) A tale of two projects: the growth and development of two Neighborhood Watch schemes in South Wales. *Crime Prevention and Community Safety: An International Journal*, 2(3): 7–16.

Bassuk, S., Glass, T. and Berkman, L. (1999) Social disengagement and incident cognitive decline in community-dwelling elderly persons. *Annals of Internal Medicine*, 131: 165–73.

Baum, A. and Davis, G. E. (1980) Reducing the stress of high-density living: an architectural intervention. *Journal of Personality and Social Psychology*, 38(3): 471–81.

Baum, A. and Valins, S. (1977) *Architecture and Social Behaviour: Psychosocial Studies of Social Density*. Hillsdale NJ: Erlbaum Associates.

Baum, A., Revenson, T. A. and Singer, J. E. (2001) (eds) *Handbook of Health Psychology*. Mahurak, NJ: Erlbaum Associates.

Baum, A., Singer, J. E. and Baum, C. S. (1982) Stress and the environment. In Evans, G. W. (ed.) *Environmental Stress*. Cambridge: Cambridge University Press.

Baum, F. (1999) Social capital: is it good for your health? Issues for a public health agenda. *Journal of Epidemiology and Community Health*, 53(4): 195–6.

Baum, F. and Palmer, C. (2002) 'Opportunity structures': urban landscape, social capital and health promotion in Australia. *Health Promotion International*, 17(4): 351–61.

Baum, F. E., Bush, R. A., Modra, C. C., Murray, C. J., Cox, E. M., Alexander, K. M., and Potter, R. C., (2000) Epidemiology of participation: an Australian community study. *Journal of Epidemiology and Community Health*, 54(6): 414–23.

Baumrind, D. (1973) Will a day care center be a child development center? *Young Children*, 28(3): 154–69.

Baumrind, D. (1989) Rearing competent children. In Damon, W. (ed.) *Child Development Today and Tomorrow*. Jossey-Bass Social and Behavioral Science Series. San Francisco, CA: Jossey-Bass/Pfeiffer.

Beattie, J. M. (1984) Violence and society in early modern England. In Doobar, A. and Greenspan, E. (eds) *Perspectives in Criminal Law*. Amora: Canada Law Book.

Bebbington, A. (2002) Sharp knives and blunt instruments: social capital in development studies. *Antipode*, 34(4): 800–3.

Bell, K. and Chen, S. (2002) *An Experience Year for All*. London: Social Market Foundation.

Belle, D. (1982) *Lives in Stress: Women and Depression*. Beverly Hills: Sage.

Belle, D. (1987) Gender differences in the social moderators of stress. In Barnett, R. C., Biener, L. and Baruch, G. K. (eds) *Gender and Stress*. New York: Free Press.

Bennett, T. (1988) An assessment of the design, implementation and effectiveness of Neighbourhood Watch in London. *Howard Journal of Criminal Justice*, 27(4): 241–255.

Berger-Schmitt, R. (2002) Social cohesion between the member states of the European Union: past developments and prospects for an enlarged union. *Sociologicky Casopis*, 38(6): 721–48.

Berkman, L. F. and Glass, T. (2000) Social integration, social networks, social support, and health. In Berkman, L. F. and Kawachi, I. (eds) *Social Epidemiology*. Oxford: Oxford University Press.

Berkman, L. F. and Kawachi, I. (2000) (eds) *Social Epidemiology*. Oxford: Oxford University Press.

Berkman, L. F. and Syme, S. L. (1979) Social networks, host resistance and mortality: a nine-year follow-up study of Almeda County residents. *American Journal of Epidemiology*, 109: 186–204.

Berkman, L. F., Summers, L. and Horwotz, R. I. (1992). Emotional support and survival after myocardial infarction. *Annals of Internal Medicine*, 117: 1003–9.

Berry, J. M., Portney, K. E. and Thomson, K. (1993) *The Rebirth of Urban Democracy*. Washington, DC: Brookings Institution Press.

Betts, J. R. (1995) Does school quality matter? Evidence from the National Longitudinal Survey of Youth. *Review of Economics and Statistics*, 77(2): 231–50.

Bevis, C. and Nutter, J. B. (1977) Changing street layouts to reduce residential burglary. Presented at the American Society of Criminology. Cited in Mayo, J. M. (1979) Effects of street forms on suburban neighboring behavior. *Environment and Behaviour*, 11(3): 375–97.

Bianchi, S. M. and Robinson, J. (1997) What did you do today? Children's use of time, family composition, and the acquisition of social capital. *Journal of Marriage and the Family*, 59(2): 332–44.

Bjarnason, T. and Sigfusdottir, I. D. (2002) Nordic impact: article productivity and citation patterns in sixteen Nordic sociology departments. *Acta Sociologica*, 45(4): 253–67.

Blair, T. (1998) *The Third Way: New Politics for the New Century*. London: Fabian Society.

Blanchard, A. (1998) Virtual communities and social capital. *Social Science Computer Review*, 16(3): 293–307.

Blaney, P. H. and Ganellen, R. J. (1990) Hardiness and social support. In Sarason, B. R., Sarason, I. G. et al. (eds) *Social Support: An Interactional View*. Oxford: John Wiley.

Blazer, D. G. (1982) Social support and mortality in an elderly community population. *American Journal of Epidemiology*, 115: 684–94.

Blokland, T. (2002) Neighbourhood social capital: does an urban gentry help? Some stories of defining shared interests, collective action and mutual support. *Sociological Research Online*, 7(3): U29–U54.

Blomberg, T., Maier, K. D. and Yeisley, M. (1998) (eds) Democracy, crime and punishment in the Czech Republic. *Crime Law and Social Change*, 28(3–4): 189–327.

Blunkett, D. (2001) *Politics and Progress: Renewing Politics and Civil Society*. London: Politico's Publishing.

Boix, C. and Posner, D. N. (1995) Making social capital work: a review of Robert Putnam's *Making Democracy Work: Civic Traditions in Modern Italy*. Draft review.

Boix, C. and Posner, D. N. (1998) Social capital: explaining its origins and effects on government performance. *British Journal of Political Science*, 28: 686–93.

Bolino, M. C., Turnley, W. H. and Bloodgood, J. M. (2002) Citizenship behaviour and the creation of social capital in organisation. *Academy of Management Review*, 27(4): 505–22.

Borcherding, T. and Filson, D. (2002) Group consumption, free riding, and informal reciprocity agreements. *Journal of Economic Behavior and Organization*, 47(3): 237–57.

Borgida, E., Sullivan, J. L., Oxendine, A., Jackson, M. S., Riedel, E. and Gangl, A. (2002) Civic culture meets the digital divide: the role of community electronic networks. *Journal of Social Issues*, 58(1): 125–41.

Bornschier, V. (1989) Legitimacy and comparative economic success at the core of the world system: an exploratory study. *European Sociological Review*, 5: 215–30.

Bothwell, S. and Weissman, M. M. (1977) Social impairments four years after an acute depressive episode. *American Journal of Orthopsychiatry*, 47: 231–7.

Bourdieu, P. (1986) The forms of capital. In Richardson, J. (ed.) *Handbook of Theory and Research for the Sociology of Education*. New York: Greenwood Press.

Bourdieu, P. and Wacquant, L. J. D. (1992) *An Invitation to Reflexive Sociology*. Chicago: University of Chicago Press.

Bowlby, J. (1988) *A Secure Base: Clinical Applications of Attachment Theory*. London: Routledge.

Bowles, S. and Gintis, H. (2002) Social capital and community governance. *Economic Journal*, 112(483): F419–F436.

Bowling, A., Banister, D., Sutton, S., Evans, O. and Windsor, J. (2002) A multidimensional model of the quality of life in older age. *Aging and Mental Health*, 6(4): 355–71.

Boxman, E. A. W., de Graaf, P. M. and Flap, H. D. (1991) The impact of social and human capital on the income attainment of Dutch managers. *Social Networks*, 13: S.51–73.

Bradley, S. and Taylor, J. (1998) The effect of school size on exam performance in secondary schools. *Oxford Bulletin of Economics and Statistics*, 60(3): 291.

Braithwaite, J. (1989) *Crime, Shame and Reintegration*. Oxford: Oxford University Press.

Braithwaite, J. (1993) Shame and modernity. *British Journal of Criminology*, 33: 1–17.

Brannigan, A., Gemmell, W., Pevalin, D. J. and Wade, T. J. (2002) Self-control and social control in childhood misconduct and aggression: the role of family structure, hyperactivity, and hostile parenting. *Canadian Journal of Criminology*, 44(2): 119–42.

Brehm, J. and Rahn, W. (1997) Individual-level evidence for the causes and consequences of social capital. *American Journal of Political Science*, (3): 999–1023.

Brinton, M. (2000) Social capital in the Japanese youth labour market: labour market policy, schools, and norms. *Policy Sciences*, 33(3–4): 289–306.

Britten, J. R. (1977) *What is a Satisfactory House? A Report of Some Households' Views*. Watford: Building Research Establishment.

Broadbent, J. P. (2000) Social capital and labor politics in Japan: co-operation or cooptation? *Policy Sciences*, 33(3–4): 307–21.

Brown, D., Dickens, R., Gregg, P., Machin, S. and Manning, A. (2001) *Everything Under a Fiver: Recruitment and Retention in Lower Paying Labour Markets*. York: Joseph Rowntree Foundation.

Brown, D. W. and Konrad, A. M. (2001) Granovetter was right: the importance of weak ties to a contemporary job search. *Group and Organisation Management*, 26(4): 434–62.

Brown, G. (2004) Civic renewal in Britain. Speech by the chancellor of the Exchequer, Gordon Brown, at the NCVO Annual Conference. http://www.ncvo-vol.org.uk

Brown, G. and Harris, T. (1978) *Social Origins of Depression*. London: Tavistock.

Bruhn, J. G. and Wolf, S. (1979) *The Roseto Story*. Norman, OK: University of Oklahoma Press.

Bruni, L. and Sugden, R. (2000) Moral canals: trust and social capital in the work of Hume, Smith and Genovesi. *Economics and Philosophy*, 16(1): 21–45.

Bruyn, S. T. (1999) The moral economy. *Review of Social Economy*, 57(1): 25–46.

Bryk, A. S., Lee, V. E. and Holland, P. B. (1993) *Catholic Schools and the Common Good*. Cambridge, MA: Harvard University Press.

Buck, N. (2001) Identifying neighbourhood effects and cultural exclusion. *Urban Studies*, 39(S): 85–93.

Buckland, J. and Rahman, M. (1999) Community-based disaster management during the 1997 Red River Flood in Canada. *Disasters*, 23(2): 174–91.

Bulmer, M. (1986) *Neighbours: The Work of Philip Abrams*. Cambridge: Cambridge University Press.

Burchell, B. (1994) Who is affected by unemployment? Job insecurity and labour market influences on psychological health. In Gallie, D., Marsh, C.

and Vogler, C. (eds) *Social Change and the experience of Unemployment*. Oxford: Oxford University Press.

Burchell, B. (1999) The unequal distribution of job insecurity, 1966–86. *International Review of Applied Economics*, 13(3): 437–58.

Burrough, B. and Helyar, J. (1991) *Barbarians at the Gate: The Fall of RJR Nabisco*. New York: Harper.

Burt, R. S. (1999) The social capital of opinion leaders. *Annals of the American Academy of Political and Social Science*, 566: 37–54.

Burt, R. S. (2002) Bridge decay. *Social Networks*, 24(4): 333–63.

Burtless, G. (1996) *Does Money Matter? The Effect of School Resources on Student Achievement and Adult Success*. Washington, DC: Brookings Institution Press.

Burton, L. and Williams, T. (2001) This bird has flown: the uncertain fate of wildlife on closed military bases. *Natural Resources Journal*, 41(4): 885–917.

Busfield, J. (1996) *Men, Women and Madness: Understanding Gender and Mental Disorder*. Basingstoke: Macmillan.

Bush, G. W. (2002) State of the Union Address. www.whitehouse.gov

Bynner, J. and Egerton, M. (2001) *The Wider Benefits of Higher Education*. Institute of Education, London, Report 01/46.

Bynner, J. and Parsons, S. (2002) Social exclusion and the transition from school to work: the case of young people not in education, employment, or training (NEET). *Journal of Vocational Behaviour*, 60(2): 289–309.

Cabinet Office Strategy Unit (2002) Ethnic minorities and the labour market: interim analytical report. www.number-10.gov.uk/files/pdf/interim.pdf

Camerer, C. and Thaler, R. H. (1995) Anomalies: ultimatums, dictators, and manners. *Journal of Economic Perspectives*, 9(2): 209–20.

Campbell, A., Converse, P. and Rodgers, W. L. (1976) (eds) *The Quality of American Life: Perceptions, Evaluations, and Satisfactions*. New York: Russell Sage Foundation.

Caplow, T. and Forman, R. (1950) Neighborhood interaction in a homogeneous community. *American Sociological Review*, 15: 357–66.

Carbonaro, W. J. (1999) Opening the debate on closure and school outcomes: comment on Morgan and Sorensen. *American Sociological Review*, 64(5): 682–6.

Card, D. and Krueger, A. B. (1992) Does school quality matter? Returns to education and the characteristics of public schools in the United States. *Journal of Political Economy*, 100(1): 1–40.

Card, D. and Krueger, A. B. (1998) School resources and student outcomes. *Annals of the American Academy of Political and Social Science*, 559: 39–53.

Case, R. B., Moss, A. J., Case, N., McDermott, M. and Eberly, S. (1992) Living alone after myocardial infarction: impact on prognosis. *Journal of the American Medical Association*, 267(4): 515–19.

Casey, T. (2003) *The Social Context of Economic Change in Britain: Between Policy and Performance*. Manchester: Manchester University Press.

Caspi, A., Entner-Wright, B. R., Moffit, T. E. and Silva, P. A. (1998) Early failure in the labour market: childhood and adolescent predictors of unemployment in the transition to adulthood. *American Sociological Review*, 63(3): 424–51.

Chance, M. and Jolly, C. (1970) *Social Groups of Monkeys, Apes and Men*. London: Jonathan Cape.

Charlesworth, S. J. (2000) *A Phenomenology of Working Class Experience*. Cambridge: Cambridge University Press.

Chase, R. S. (2002) Supporting communities in transition: the impact of the Armenian Social Investment Fund. *World Bank Economic Review*, 16(2): 219–40.

Chen, N. (2004) Intra-national versus international trade in the European union: why do national borders matter? *Journal of International Economics*, 63(1): 93–118.

Chen, X. (2000) Both glue and lubricant: transnational ethnic social capital as a source of Asia-Pacific subregionalism. *Policy Sciences*, 33(3–4): 269–87.

Cigler, A. and Joslyn, M. R. (2002) The extensiveness of group membership and social capital: the impact on political tolerance attitudes. *Political Research Quarterly*, 55(1): 7–25.

CIRCLE (Center for Information and Research on Civic Learning and Engagement) (2003) *The Civic Mission of Schools*. New York: CIRCLE and Carnegie Corporation of New York. civicyouth.org/research/areas/civicmissionof schools.htm

Clague, C. (1997) The new institutional economics and economic development. In Clague, C. (ed.) *Institutions and Economic Development: Growth and Governance in Less-Developed and Post-Socialist Countries*. Baltimore, MD, and London: Johns Hopkins University Press.

Claibourn, M. P. and Martin, P. S. (2000) Trusting and joining? An empirical test of the reciprocal nature of social capital. *Political Behaviour*, 22(4): 267–91.

Clark, A. E. and Oswald, A. J. (2002) A simple statistical method for measuring how life events affect happiness. *International Journal of Epidemiology*, 31(6): 1139–44.

Clausen, C. and Olsen, P. (2000) Strategic management and the politics of production in the development of work: a case study in a Danish electronic manufacturing plant. *Technology Analysis and Strategic Management*, 12(1): 59–74.

Cohen, S. and Wills, T. A. (1985) Stress, social support, and the buffering hypothesis. *Psychological Bulletin*, 98: 310–57.

Cohen, S., Doyle, W. J., Soner, D. P., Rabin, B. S. and Gwaltney, J. M. (1997) Social ties and susceptibility to the common cold. *Journal of the American Medical Association*, 277: 1940–4.

Colby, A., James, J. B. and Hart, D. (1998) *The Development of Character and Competence through Life*. Chicago: University of Chicago Press.

Coleman, J. S. (1966). *Equality of Education Opportunity*. Washington, DC: Government Printing Office.

Coleman, J. S. (1988) Social capital in the creation of human capital. *American Journal of Sociology*, 94 Supplement: S95–S120.

Collier, P. (2000) Ethnicity, politics and economic performance. *Economics and Politics*, 12(4): 225–45.

Collier, P. and Gunning, J. W. (1999) *The Microeconomics of African Growth*. Washington, DC: World Bank.

Commission on Citizenship (1990) *Encouraging Citizenship*. London: HMSO.

Cooke, P. and Wills, D. (1999) Small firms, social capital and the enhancement of business performance through innovation programmes. *Small Business Economics*, 13: 219–34.

Costa, P. T. and McRae, R. R. (1988) Personality in adulthood: a six-year longitudinal study of self-reports and spouse ratings on the NEO Personality Inventory. *Journal of Personality and Social Psychology*, 54(5): 853–63.

Cottrell, J. S. (1976) The competent community. In Kaplan, B. H., Wilson, R. N. and Leigton, A. A. (eds) *Further Explorations in Social Psychiatry*. New York: Basic Books.

Coulthard, M., Walker, A. and Morgan, A. (2002) *People's Perceptions of their Neighbourhood and Community Involvement: Results from the Social Capital Module of the General Household Survey 2000*. London: Office of National Statistics, HMSO.

Coumarelos, C. and Allen, J. (1996) Predicting violence against women: the 1996 women's safety survey. *Crime and Justice Bulletin*, 42. Sydney: New South Wales Bureau of Crime Statistics and Research.

Couse, R. (1937) The nature of the firm. *Economica*, New Series, 16(4): 386–405.

Couto, R. A. and Guthrie, C. S. (1999) *Making Democracy Work Better*. Chapel Hill, NC: University of North Carolina Press.

Covey, H. C., Menard, S. W. and Franzese, R. J. (1997) *Juvenile Gangs* (2nd edn). Springfield, IL: Charles C. Thomas.

Cox, E. (1995) A truly civil society. Boyer Lectures 1995. Sydney: ABC Books.

Cox, E. (2002) Australia, making the lucky country. In Putnam, R. B. (ed.) *Democracies in Flux: The Evolution of Social Capital in Contemporary Society*. Oxford: Oxford University Press.

Crook, T., Raskin, A. and Elliot, J. (1981) Parent–child relationships and adult depression. *Child Development*, 52(3): 950–7.

Cross, R. and Prusak, L. (2002) The people who make organisations go-or-stop. *Harvard Business Review*, 80(6): 104.

Crutchfield, R. D., Geerken, M. R. and Gove, W. R. (1982) Crime rate and social integration: the impact of metropolitan mobility. *Criminology: An Interdisciplinary Journal*, 20(3sup4): 467–78.

Crystal, D. S. and DeBell, M. (2002) Sources of civic orientation among American youth: trust, religious valuation, and attributions of responsibility. *Political Psychology*, 23(1): 113–32.

Currie, D. (1996) Prospects and strategies for UK economic growth. In Halpern, D. S., Wood, S., White, S. and Cameron, G. (eds) *Options of Britain: A Strategic Policy Review*. Dartmouth: Aldershot.

Curry, G. D. and Decker, S. H. (2003) *Confronting Gangs: Crime and Community* (2nd edn). Los Angeles: Roxbury.

Cusack, T. R. (1999) Social capital, institutional structures, and democratic performance: a comparative study of German local governments. *European Journal of Political Research*, 35(1): 1–34.

Cuoto, R. A. (1999) *Making Democracy Work Better: Mediating Structures, Social Capital, and the Democratic Prospect*. Chapel Hill, NC, and London: University of North Carolina Press.

Dalgleish, T., Joseph, S., Thrasher, S., Tranah, T. and Yule, W. (1996) Crisis support following the 'Herald of Free Enterprise' disaster: a longitudinal perspective. *Journal of Traumatic Stress*, 9: 833–46.

Dalton, R. J. (1998) Support in advanced industrial democracies. In Norris, P. (ed.) *Critical Citizens: Global Support for Democratic Governance*. Oxford: Oxford University Press.

Daly, M. C., Duncan, G. J., Kaplan, G. A. and Lynch, J. W. (1998) Macro-to-micro links in the relation between income inequality and mortality. *Milbank Quarterly*, 76(3): 315–39.

Dasgupta, P. (1998) Economic development and the idea of social capital. Paper presented to the Faculty of Social and Political Sciences, Cambridge.

Dasgupta, P. and Serageldin, I. (2000) *Social Capital: A Multifaceted Perspective*. Washington, DC: World Bank.

Davies, W. (2003) *You Don't Know Me, but . . .: Social Capital and Social Software*. London: Work Foundation.

De Hart, J. and Dekker, P. (1999) Civic engagement and volunteering in the Netherlands: a Putnamian analysis. In Van Deth, J., Maraffi, M., Newton, K. and Whiteley, P. (eds) *Social Capital and European Democracy*. London: Routledge.

De Mello, L. (2000) Can fiscal decentralization strengthen social capital? International Monetary Fund Working Paper.

De Souza Briggs, X. (1998) Doing democracy up close: culture, power, and communication in community building, *Journal of Planning Education and Research*, 18: 1–13.

De Tocqueville, A. ([1840] 1969 trans.) *Democracy in America*. Ed. J. P. Mayer. New York: Doubleday.

De Ulzurrun, L. M. D. (2002) Associational membership and social capital in comparative perspective: a note on the problems of measurement. *Politics and Society*, 30(3): 497–523.

DeFilippis, J. (2001). The myth of social capital in community development. *Housing Policy Debate*, 12(4): 781–806.

DeFilippis, J. (2002) Symposium on social capital: an introduction. *Antipode*, 34(4): 790–5.

Defty, N. and Fitz-Gibbon, C. (2002) *Underaspirers: How Can We Help Them?* Curriculum, Evaluation and Management Centre Research Report, University of Durham.

Del Favero, M. (2003) Faculty–administrator relationships as integral to high-performing governance systems: new frameworks for study. *American Behavioural Scientist*, 46(7): 902–22.

Delhey, J. and Newton, K. (2002) *Who Trusts? The Origins of Social Capital in Seven Nations*. Berlin: Social Science Research Centre. http://skylla.wz-berlin.de/pdf/2002/iii02-402.pdf

Della Porta, D. and Andretta, M. (2002) Social movements and public administration: spontaneous citizens' committees in Florence. *International Journal of Urban and Regional Research*, 26(2): 244.

Department of Health (2000) *National Service Framework for Coronary Heart Disease*. London: Department of Health.

Desforges, C. and Abouchaar, A. (2003) *The Impact of Parental Involvement, Parental Support and Family Education on Pupil Achievement and Adjustment: A Literature Review.* DfES Research Report 433. London: Department for Education and Skills.

Desimone, L. (1997) Comparing the relationship of parent involvement and locus of control to adolescent school achievement: an analysis of racial/ethnic and income differences. *Dissertation Abstracts International Section A: Humanities and Social Sciences,* 57(12-A): 5109.

Desimone, L. (1999). Linking parent involvement with student achievement: do race and income matter? *Journal of Educational Research,* 93: 11–30.

Dhanani, S. and Islam, I. (2002) Poverty, vulnerability and social protection in a period of crisis: the case of Indonesia. *World Development,* 30(7): 1211–31.

Dhesi, A. S. (2001) Factors influencing post-school choice: some data from India. *International Review of Economics and Business,* 47(3): 451–72.

Diamond, J. (1996) *Guns, Germs and Steel: The Fates of Human Societies.* New York: Norton.

Diener, E., Sandvik, E., Seidlitz, L. and Diener, M. (1993) The relationship between income and subjective well-being: relative or absolute? *Social Indicators Research,* 28: 195–223.

Dika, S. L. and Singh, K. (2002) Applications of social capital in educational literature: a critical synthesis. *Review of Educational Research,* 72(1): 31–60.

DiPasquale, D. and Glaeser, E. L. (1998) *Incentives and Social Capital: Are Homeowners Better Citizens?* National Bureau of Economic Research Working Paper: 6363.

Dishion, T. J., McCord, J. and Poulin, F. (1999) When interventions harm: peer groups and problem behaviour. *American Psychologist,* 54(9): 755–94.

DoE (Department of the Environment) (1991) *Policy Appraisal and the Environment: A Guide for Government Departments.* London: HMSO.

Doebler, M. K. (1999) Successful outcomes for rural young women: a longitudinal investigation of social capital and adolescent development. *Dissertation Abstracts International Section A: Humanities and Social Sciences,* 59(8-A): 2867.

Donalson, T. and Dunfee, T. W. (1999) When ethics travel: the promise and the peril of global business ethics. *California Management Review,* 41(4): 45–63.

Donkin, R. and Lewis, C. (1998) Time to take account of the individual: winning back employees' trust should be a top management priority. *Financial Times,* 21 January.

Donovan, N. and Halpern, D. S. (2003) Life satisfaction: the state of knowledge and implications for government. Prime Minister's Strategy Unit. www.pm.gov.uk

Douglas, F. (1855) *My Bondage and My Freedom.* New York: Miller, Orton and Mulligan. http://docsouth.unc.edu/neh/douglass55/douglass55.html#p143

Drayton, W. (2000) Secret gardens. *Atlantic Monthly Company,* 285(6): 108–11. www.theatlantic.com/issues/2000/06/drayton.htm

Dressler, W. W. and Badger, L. W. (1985) Epidemiology of depressive symptoms in black communities. *Journal of Nervous and Mental Disorder,* 173: 212–20.

Drogosz, K. M., Litan, R. E. and Dionne, E. J. (2003) *United We Serve: National Service and the Future of Citizenship*. Washington, DC: Brookings Institution Press.

Durkheim, E. ([1893] 1964), *The Division of Labour in Society*. New York: Free Press.

Durkheim, E. ([1897] 1951) *Suicide*. Trans. J. A. Spalding. Toronto: Free Press/Collier-Macmillan.

Durlauf, S. N. (2002) Bowling alone: a review essay. *Journal of Economic Behaviour and Organisation*, 47(3): 259–73.

Dworkin, J. B., Larson, R. and Hansen, D. (2003) Adolescents' accounts of growth experiences in youth activities. *Journal of Youth and Adolescence*, 32(1): 17–26.

Eby, L. T. (2001) The boundaryless career experiences of mobile spouses in dual-earner marriages. *Group and Organisational Management*, 26(3): 343–68.

Edwards, B. and Foley, M. W. (1998) Civil society and social capital beyond Putnam. *American Behavioural Scientist*, 42(1): 124–39.

Egeland, J. A. and Hostetter, A. M. (1983) Amish study: 1. Affective disorders among the Amish, 1976–1980. *American Journal of Psychiatry*, 140: 56–61.

Egerton, M. (2002a) Higher education and civic engagement. *British Journal of Sociology*, 53(4): 603–20.

Egerton, M. (2002b) Family transmission of social capital: differences by social class, education and public sector employment. *Sociological Research Online*, 7(3): U133–U155.

Egolf, B., Lasker, J., Wolf, S. and Potvin, L. (1992) The Roseto effect: a 50-year comparison of mortality rates. *American Journal of Public Health*, 82: 1089–92.

Eisner, M. (2001) Modernization, self-control and lethal violence: the long-term dynamics of European homicide rates in theoretical perspective. *British Journal of Criminology*, 41(4): 618–38.

Eisner, M. (2002) Crime, problem drinking, and drug use: patterns of problem behavior in cross-national perspective. *Annals of the American Academy of Political and Social Science*, 580: 201–25.

Eitle, T. M., and Eitle, D. J. (2002) Race, cultural capital, and the educational effects of participation in sports. *Sociology of Education*, 75(2): 123–46.

Engels, F. ([c.1844] 1969) *The Condition of the Working Class in England*. Frogmore: Panther.

Engstrand, A. K. and Stam, E. (2002) Embeddedness and economic transformation of manufacturing: a comparative research of two regions. *Economic and Industrial Democracy*, 23(3): 357–88.

Esping-Anderson, G. (2003) Why no socialism anywhere? A reply to Alex Hicks and Lane Kenworth. *Socio-Economic Review*, 1(1): 63–70.

Evans, P. (1996) Government action, social capital and development: reviewing the evidence on synergy. *World Development*, 24(6): 1119–32.

Evans, M. and Fletcher, D. J. (1998) Residential burglary within an affluent housing area. *International Journal of Risk, Security and Crime Prevention*, 3(3): 181–91.

Fabrigoule, C., Letenneur, L., Dartigues, J., Zarrouk, M., Commenges, D. and Barberger-Gateau, P. (1995) Social and leisure activities and risk of dementia: a prospective longitudinal study. *Journal of American Geriatric Society*, 43: 485–90.

Fafchamps, M. and Minten, B. (2002) Returns to social network capital among traders. *Oxford Economic Papers*, New Series, 54(2): 173–206.

Fang, J., Mahavan, S., Bosworth, W. and Alderman, M. H. (1998) Residential segregation and mortality in New York city. *Social Science and Medicine*, 47: 469–76.

Faris, R. E. and Dunham, H. W. (1939) *Mental Disorders in Urban Areas*. Chicago: University of Chicago Press.

Farley, J. and Costanza, R. (2002) Envisioning shared goals for humanity: a detailed, shared vision of a sustainable and desirable USA in 2100. *Ecological Economics*, 43(2–3): 245–59.

Farrington, D. P. (1986) Age and crime. In Tonry, M. and Morris, N. (eds) *Crime and Justice: An Annual Review of Research, Vol. VII*. Chicago: University of Chicago Press.

Farrington, D. P. (1992) Criminal career research in the United Kingdom. *British Journal of Criminology*, 32(4): 521–36.

Farrington, D. P. (1994) Human development and criminal careers. In Maguire, M., Morgan, R. and Rieners, R. (eds) *The Oxford Handbook of Criminology*. Oxford: Oxford University Press.

Faulkner, D., Hough, M. and Halpern, D. S. (1996) Crime and criminal justice. In Halpern, D. S., Wood, S., White, S. and Cameron, G. (eds) *Options for Britain: A Strategic Policy Review*. Dartmouth: Aldershot.

Fawzy, F. I., Fawzy, N. W., Hyun, C. S. et al. (1993) Malignant melanoma: effects of an early structured psychiatric intervention, coping, and affective state on recurrence and survival six years later. *Archives of General Psychiatry*, 50: 681–9.

Fedderke, J. and Klitgaard, R. (1998) Economic growth and social indicators: an exploratory analysis. *Economic Development and Cultural Change*, 46(3): 455–89.

Fedderke, J., De Kadt, R. and Luiz, J. (1999) Economic growth and social capital: a critical reflection. *Theory and Society*, 28(5): 709–45.

Feinstein, L. and Symons, J. (1999) Attainment in secondary school. *Oxford Economic Papers*, 51(2): 300–21.

Feldstein, M. and Horioka, C. (1980) Domestic saving and international capital flows. *Economic Journal*, 90: 314–29.

Fennema, M. and Tillie, J. (1999) Political participation and political trust in Amsterdam: civic communities and ethnic networks. *Journal of Ethnic and Migration Studies*, 25(4): 703–26.

Ferrary, M. (2002) Regulating the structure of job qualifications according to the specificity of human capital: an analysis of the social capital of financial advisors in banks. *Sociologie du Travail*, 44(1): 119–30.

Ferrary, M. (2003) Managing the disruptive technologies life cycle by external-ising the research: social network and corporate venturing in the Silicon Valley. *International Journal of Technology Management*, 25(1–2): 165–80.

Ferri, E., Bynner, J. and Wadsworth, M. (2003) *Changing Britain, Changing Lives*. London: Institute of Education.

Festinger, L., Schachter S. S. and Back, K. W. (1950) *Social Pressures in Informal Groups*. Stanford, CA: Stanford University Press.

Fine, B. (2001) *Social Capital Theory Versus Social Theory: Political Economy and Social Science at the Turn of the Millennium*. London: Routledge.

Fisher, C. S. (1982) *To Dwell Among Friends: Personal Networks in Town and City*. Chicago: University of Chicago Press.

Fisher, I. (1906) *The Nature of Capital and Income*. New York: Macmillan. Repr. New York: A. M. Kelley, 1965.

Fiske, S. T. and Taylor, S. E. (1991) *Social Cognition* (2nd edn). New York: McGraw-Hill International.

Fletcher, G. and Allen, J. (2003) Perceptions of and concern about crime in England and Wales. In Simmons, J. and Dodd, T. (eds) *Crime in England and Wales 2002/2003*. London: Home Office.

Florida, R., Cushing, R. and Gates, G. (2002) *The Rise of the Creative Class*. New York: Basic Books.

Foley, M. W. and Edwards, B. (1999) Is it time to disinvest in social capital? *Journal of Public Policy*, 19(2): 141–73.

Forrester, D., Chatterton, M. and Pease, K. (1988) The Kirkholt burglary prevention project, Rochdale. Crime Prevention Unit: Paper 13. London: Home Office.

Fountain, J. E. (1997) Social capital: a key enabler of innovation in science and technology. In Branscomb, L. M. and Keller, J. (eds) *Investing in Innovation: Toward a Consensus Strategy for Federal Technology Politics*. Cambridge, MA: MIT Press.

Frank, R., Gilovich, T. and Regan, D. (1993) Does studying economics inhibit cooperation? *Journal of Economic Perspectives*, 7: 159–71.

Frank, R. H. (1987) If *Homo economicus* could choose his own utility function, would he want one with a conscience? *American Economic Review*, 77(4): 593–604.

Franzini, L. and Spears, W. (forthcoming) Contributions of social context to inequalities in years of life lost to heart disease in Texas.

Fraser, C. and Burchell, B. (2001) *Introducing Social Psychology*. Cambridge: Polity.

Fratiglioni, L., Wang, H., Ericsson, K., Maytan, M. and Winblad, B. (2000) The influence of social network on the occurrence of dementia: a community-based longitudinal study. *Lancet*, 355: 1315.

Freeman, H. F. (1986) Environmental stress and psychiatric disorder. *Stress Medicine*, 2: 291–9.

Freese, J. (2003) Imaginary imaginary friends? Television viewing and satisfaction with friendships. *Evolution and Human Behaviour*, 24(1): 65–9.

Frey, B. S. and Sutzer, A. (2000) Happiness prospers in democracy. *Journal of Happiness Studies*, 1(1): 79–102.

Friedman, M., Thoresen, C. E., Gill, J. J. et al. (1986) Alteration of type A behaviour and its effect on cardiac recurrences in post myocardial infarction patients: summary results of the recurrent coronary prevention project. *American Heart Journal*, 112(4): 653–65.

Fukuyama, F. (1995a) *Trust: The Social Virtues and the Creation of Prosperity*. New York: Free Press.

Fukuyama, F. (1995b) Social capital and the global economy. *Foreign Affairs*, 74(5): 89–103.

Funk, C. L. (1998) Practicing what we preach? The influence of societal interest value on civic engagement. *Political Psychology*, 193: 601–14.

Furniture Resource Centre (1997) *Directing Social Fund Expenditure*. Liverpool: FRC.

Furstenberg, F. F. and Hughes, M. E. (1995) Social capital and successful development among at-risk youth. *Journal of Marriage and the Family*, 57: 580–92.

Galbraith, J. K. (1992) *The Culture of Contentment*. London: Sinclair-Stevenson.

Galea, S., Karpati, A. and Kennedy, B. (2002) Social capital and violence in the United States, 1974–1993. *Social Science and Medicine*, 55(8): 1373–83.

Gambetta, D. (1988) (ed.) *Trust: Making and Breaking Co-operative Relations*. Oxford: Blackwell.

Gamm, G. and Putnam, R. D. (n.d.) Association-building in America, 1840–1940. Unpublished paper.

Gans, H. J. (1962) *The Urban Villagers: Group and Class in the Life of Italian-Americans*. Toronto: Macmillan.

Gant, J., Ichniowski, C. and Shaw, K. (2002) Social capital and organisational change in high-involvement and traditional work organisations. *Journal of Economics and Management Strategy*, 11(2): 289–328.

Gardner, A. M. (2002) The long haul from deregulation: truck drivers and social capital in the Louisiana oilpatch. *Human Organisation*, 61(4): 390–8.

Garland, D. (1985) *Punishment and Welfare*. Aldershot: Gower.

Geib, P. and Pfaff, L. (2000) (eds) Strategic management in central and eastern Europe. *Journal of East–West Business*, 5(4), special issue.

Gerber, A. S. and Green, D. P. (2000) The effects of canvassing, telephone calls, and direct mail on voter turnout: a field experiment. *American Political Science Review*, 94(3): 653–63.

Gilbert, L. and Walker, L. (2002) Treading the path of least resistance: HIV/AIDS and social inequalities – a South African case study. *Social Science and Medicine*, 54(7): 1093–110.

Gilligan, J. (1996) *Violence: Our Deadly Epidemic and its Causes*. New York: G. P. Putnam & Sons.

Gittell, R. and Vidal, A. (1998) *Community Organising: Building Social Capital as a Development Strategy*. Thousand Oaks, CA: Sage.

Glaeser, E. L. and Sacerdote, B. (2000) The social consequences of housing. *Journal of Housing Economics*, 9(1–2): 1–23.

Glaeser, E. L., Laibson, D. and Sacerdote, B. (2002) An economic approach to social capital. *Economic Journal*, 112(483): F437–F458.

Glass, D. C. and Singer, J. E. (1972) *Urban Stress: Experiments on Noise and Social Stressors*. New York: Academic Press.

Glennester, H. (1998) Tackling poverty at its roots? Education. In Oppenheim, C. (ed.) *An Inclusive Society: Strategies for Tackling Poverty*. London: IPPR.

Gold, R., Kennedy, B., Connell, F. and Kawachi, I. (2002) Teen births, income inequality, and social capital: developing an understanding of the causal pathway. *Health and Place*, 8(2): 77–83.

Goldin, C. and Katz, L. F. (1998) Human capital and social capital: the rise of secondary schooling in America, 1910–1940. National Bureau of Economic Research Working Paper, 6439.

Goldin, C. and Katz, L. F. (2001) The legacy of US educational leadership: notes on distribution and economic growth in the 20th century. *American Economic Review*, 91(2): 18–23.

Goldsmith, A. A. (2002) Business associations and better governance in Africa. *Public Administration and Development*, 22(1): 39–49.

Goldthorpe, J. H., Llewellyn, C. and Payne, C. (1987) *Social Mobility and Class Structure in Modern Britain* (2nd edn). Oxford: Clarendon Press.

Gomme, I. M. (1986) Fear of crime among Canadians: a multi-variate analysis. *Journal of Criminal Justice*, 14(3): 249–58.

Good, D. (1988) Individuals, interpersonal relations, and trust. In Gambetta, D. (ed.) *Trust: Making and Breaking Co-operative Relations*. Oxford: Blackwell.

Gopee, N. (2002) Human and social capital as facilitators of lifelong learning in nursing. *Nurse Education Today*, 22(8): 608–16.

Gotlib, I. H. and Macabe, S. B. (1990) Marriage and psychopathy: a critical examination. In Fincham, F. D. and Bradbury, T. M. (eds) *The Psychology of Marriage: Conceptual, Empirical and Applied Perspectives*. New York: Guilford Press.

Gottfredson, M. and Hirschi, T. (1990) *A General Theory of Crime*. Stanford, CA: Stanford University Press.

Gradstein, M. and Justman, M. (2001) Human capital, social capital, and public schooling. *European Economic Review*, 44(4–6): 879–90.

Granovetter, M. (1990) The old and new economic sociology: a history and an agenda. In Friedland, R. and Robertson, A. F. (eds) *Beyond the Marketplace: Rethinking Economy and Society*. New York: Aldine de Gruyter.

Granovetter, M. S. (1973) The strength of weak ties. *American Journal of Sociology*, 78: 1360–80.

Granovetter, M. S. (1985) Economic action and social structure: the problem of embeddedness. *American Journal of Sociology*, 91: 481–510.

Green, D. P. and Gerber, A. S. (2001) *Getting Out the Youth Vote: Results from Randomized Field Experiments*. Pew Charitable Trust. www.pewtrusts. com/pdf/pp_youth_vote.pdf

Greenberg, S. W. and Rohe, W. M. (1984) Neighbourhood design and crime: a test of two perspectives. *Journal of American Planning*, 50(1): 48–61.

Gregory, R. J. (1999) Social capital theory and administrative reform: maintaining ethical probity in public service. *Public Administration Review*, 59(1): 63–75.

Grenier, P. and Wright, K. (2001) Social capital in Britain: an update and critique of Hall's analysis. Presentation at ARNOVA's 30th Annual Conference, 29 November–1 December.

Grimes, K. (2003) To trust is human. *New Scientist*, 10 May: 32–7.

Grisham, V. (1999) *Tupelo: Evolution of a Community.* Dayton, OH: Kettering Foundation Press.

Grootaert, C., Oh, G. T. and Swamy, A. (2002) Social capital, household welfare and poverty in Burkina Faso. *Journal of African Economies,* 11(1): 4–38.

Grossman, G. M. (1997) Comment. In Frankell, J. A. (ed.) *The Regionalization of the World Economy.* Chicago: University of Chicago Press.

Guellec, D. and van Pottelsberghe de la Potterie, B. (2001) R&D and productivity growth: panel data analysis of 16 OECD countries. STI Working Papers 2001/3. Paris: OECD. www.oecd.org/dataoecd/26/32/1958639.pdf

Gunnar, M. R. and Nelson, C. A. (1994) Event-related potentials in year-old infants: relations with emotionality and cortisol. *Child Development,* 65(1): 80–94.

Gunnar, M. R., Tout, K., deHaan, M., Pierce, S. and Stansbury, K. (1997) Temperament, social competence and adreno cortical activity in preschoolers. *Developmental Psychobiology,* 31: 65–85.

Gunnthorsdottir, A., McCabe, K. and Smith, V. (2002) Using the Machiavellianism instrument to predict trustworthiness in a bargaining game. *Journal of Economic Psychology,* 23(1): 49–66.

Guttman, J. M. (2000) On the evolutionary stability of preferences for reciprocity. *European Journal of Political Economy,* 16(1): 31–50.

Hadaway, C. K., Marler, P. L. and Chaves, M. (1993) What the polls don't show: a closer look at U.S. church attendance. *American Sociological Review,* 58(6): 741–52.

Hagan, J. and Coleman, J. P. (2001) Returning captives of the American war on drugs: issues of community and family re-entry. *Crime and Delinquency,* 47(3): 352–67.

Hagan, J. and McCarthy, B. (1997) *Mean Streets: Youth Crime and Homelessness.* Cambridge: Cambridge University Press.

Hagan, J., Merkens, H. and Boehnke, K. (1995) Delinquency and disdain: social capital and the control of right-wing extremism among East and West Berlin youth. *American Journal of Sociology,* 100(4): 1028–52.

Hagell, A. and Newburn, T. (1994) *Persistent Young Offenders.* London: Policy Studies Institute.

Hall, P. A. (1997) Social capital in Britain. Paper for Bertelsmann Stiftung Workshop on social capital, Berlin, June.

Hall, P. A. (1999) Social capital in Britain. *British Journal of Political Science,* 29(3): 417–61.

Hallinan, M. T. and Kubitschek, W. N. (1999) Conceptualizing and measuring school social networks: comment of Morgan and Sorensen. *American Sociological Review,* 64(5): 687–93.

Halpern, D. S. (1989) Active citizenship and a healthy society. Paper prepared for the Commission on Citizenship.

Halpern, D. S. (1992) Entry into the legal professions. Research Study No. 15, Law Society, London.

Halpern, D. S. (1993) Minorities and mental health. *Social Science and Medicine,* 36(5): 597–607.

Halpern, D. S. (1995a) *Mental Health and the Built Environment: More than Bricks and Mortar?* London: Taylor and Francis.

Halpern, D. S. (1995b) Values, morals and modernity. In Rutter, M. and Smith, D. (eds) *Psychosocial Disorder in Young People: Time Trends and their Causes.* Chichester: John Wiley.

Halpern, D. S. (1996) Can moral values explain crime? Paper presented at the Royal Society of Edinburgh 'Causes of Crime' symposium, Edinburgh, 5 June.

Halpern, D. S. (1997) Social capital. Nexus discussion paper.

Halpern, D. S. (1998) Poverty, social exclusion and the policy-making process: the road from theory to practice. In Oppenheim, C. (ed.) *An Inclusive Society: Strategies for Tackling Poverty.* London: IPPR.

Halpern, D. S (1999) Social capital: the new golden egg? Nexus discussion paper.

Halpern, D. S. (2001) Moral values, social trust and inequality: can values explain crime? *British Journal of Criminology,* 41(2): 236–51.

Halpern, D. S. and Bates, C. (2004) Personal responsibility and changing behaviour. Prime Minister's Strategy Unit. www.strategy.gov.uk/files/pdf/pr.pdf

Halpern, D. S. and Nazroo, J. (2000) Mental health and ethnic group concentration: a confirmation of the ethnic density effect. *International Journal of Social Psychiatry,* 46(1): 34–46.

Halpern, D. S. and Reid, J. (1992) Effect of unexpected demolition announcement on health of residents. *British Medical Journal,* 304: 1229–30.

Halpern, D. S. and White, S. (1997) The principle of partitioned responsibility: a basis for a fair and efficient tax-benefit system. www.netnexus.org

Halpern, D. S. and Wood, S. (1996) The policy-making process. In Halpern, D. S., Wood, S., White, S. and Cameron, G. (eds) *Options for Britain: A Strategic Policy Review.* Dartmouth: Aldershot.

Halpern, D. S., John, P. and Morris, Z. (2002) Before the citizenship order: a survey of citizenship practice in England. *Journal of Education Policy,* 17(2): 217–28.

Hampton, K. N. (2003) Grieving for a lost network: collective action in a wired suburb. *Information Society,* 19(5): 1–13.

Hanifan, L. J. (1916) The rural school community center. *Annals of the American Academy of Political and Science,* 67: 130–8.

Hanifan, L. J. (1920) *The Community Centre.* Boston: Silver, Burdette.

Hannan, C. (1999) *Beyond Networks: 'Social Cohesion' and Unemployment Exit Rates.* Institute for Labour Research, discussion paper 99/28. Colchester: University of Essex.

Hanushek, E. A. (1989) Expenditures, efficiency, and equity in education: the federal government's role. *American Economic Review,* 79(2): 46–51.

Hanushek, E. A. (1997) Assessing the effects of school resources on students' performance: an update. *Educational Evaluation and Policy Analysis,* 19(2): 141–64.

Hanushek, E. A. (1998) Conclusions and controversies about the effectiveness of school resources. *Federal Reserve Bank of New York Economic Policy Review,* 4(1): 11–27.

Hanushek, E. A. (2003) The failure of input-based schooling policies. *Economic Journal*, 113(485): F64–F98.

Hao, L. and Bonstead-Bruns, M. (1998) Parent–child differences in educational expectations and the academic achievement of immigrant and native students. *Sociology of Education*, 71(3): 175–98.

Harding, S., Phillips, D. and Fogarty, M. (1986) *Contrasting Values in Western Europe: Unity, Diversity and Change*. Basingstoke: Macmillian.

Hargreaves, D. H. (2000) The Production, Mediation and Use of Professional Knowledge among Teachers and Doctors: a comparative analysis. In *Knowledge Management in the Learning Society*. Paris: OECD. 219–38.

Hargreaves, D. H. (2001) A capital theory of school effectiveness and improvement. *British Educational Research Journal*, 27(4): 487–503.

Harriss, J. and De Renzio, P. (1997) 'Missing link' or analytically missing? The concept of social capital: an introductory bibliographic essay. *Journal of International Development*, 9(7): 919–37.

Harris, T., Brown, G. W. and Robinson, R. (1999) Befriending as an intervention for chronic depression among women in an inner city. 1: Randomised controlled trial. *British Journal of Psychiatry*, 174: 219–24.

Hart, C., Ecob, R. and Smith, G. D. (1997) People, places and coronary heart disease risk factors: a multilevel analysis of the Scottish Heart Health Study archive. *Social Science and Medicine*, 45(6): 893–902.

Hawthorn, G. (1988) Three ironies in trust. In Gambetta, D. (ed.) *Trust: Making and Breaking Co-operative Relations*. Oxford: Blackwell.

Heath, A. and Clifford, P. (1996) Class inequalities and educational reform in 20th century Britain. In Lee, D. and Turner, B. S. (eds) *Conflicts about Class: Debating Inequality in Industrialism: A Selection of Readings*. London: Longman.

Held, D. (1995) *Democracy and the Global Order: From the Modern State to Cosmopolitan Governance*. Cambridge: Polity.

Held, D. and McGrew, A. (2000) The end of the old order? Globalization and the prospects for world order. In Higgott, R. and Payne, A. (eds) *The New Political Economy of Globalisation, Vol. 2*. Cheltenham and Northampton, MA: Elgar.

Heller, P. (1995) From class-struggle to class compromise: redistribution and growth in a South Indian State. *Journal of Development Studies*, 31(5): 645–72.

Heller, P. (1996) Social capital as a product of class mobilization and state intervention: industrial workers in Kerala, India. *World Development*, 24(6): 1055–71.

Helliwell, J. F. (2002a) How's life? Combining individual and national variables to explain subjective well-being. NBER Working Paper No. 9065. Cambridge: National Bureau of Economic Research. Pub. 2003 in *Economic Modelling*, 20(2): 331–60.

Helliwell, J. F. (2002b) Measuring the width of national borders. *Review of International Economics*, 10(3): 517–24.

Helliwell, J. F. (2003) Maintaining social ties: social capital in a global information age. Keynote address to the 75th Anniversary Conference of the University of Tilburg, 26–8 March, on Sustainable Ties in the Information Society.

Helliwell, J. F. (forthcoming) Well-being and social capital: does suicide pose a puzzle? Working paper.

Helliwell, J. F. and McKitrick, R. (1999) Comparing capital mobility across provincial and national borders. *Canadian Journal of Economics*, 32(5): 1164–73.

Helliwell, J. F. and Putnam, R. D. (1995) Social capital and economic growth in Italy. *Eastern Economic Journal*, 21: 295–307.

Henderson, A. T. and Berla, N. (1994) *A New Generation of Evidence: The Family is Critical to Student Achievement.* Washington, DC: National Committee for Citizens' Education.

Hendryx, M. S., Ahern, M. M., Lovrich, N. P. and McCurdy, A. H. (2002) Access to health care and community social capital. *Health Services Research*, 37(1): 87–103.

Her Majesty's Treasury (2002) Next steps on volunteering and giving in the UK: a discussion document. Stationery Office Ltd, or www.hm-treasury. gov.uk

Herriot, A., Crossley, M., Juma, M., Waudo, J., Mwirotsi, M. and Kamau, A. (2002) The development and operation of headteacher support groups in Kenya: a mechanism to create pockets of excellence, improve the provision of quality education and target positive changes in the community. *International Journal of Educational Development*, 22(5): 509–26.

Hillman, A. and Ursprung, H. (2000) Political culture and economic decline. *European Journal of Political Economy*, 16: 189–213.

Hills, J. (1995) *Income and Wealth, Vol. 2.* York: Joseph Rowntree Foundation.

Hinde, R. A. and Groebel, J. (1991) (eds) *Co-operation and Prosocial Behaviour.* Cambridge: Cambridge University Press.

Hirsch, F. (1977) *Social Limits to Growth.* London: Routledge.

Hirshleifer, J. (1994) The dark side of the force: Western Economic Association International 1993 Presidential Address. *Economic Inquiry*, 32(Jan.): 1–10.

Hodges, J. and Tizard, B. (1989) IQ and behavioural adjustment of ex-institutional adolescents. *Journal of Child Psychology and Psychiatry and Allied Disciplines*, 30(1): 53–75.

Hogarty, G. E., Anderson, C. M., Reiss, D. J. et al. (1991) Family psychoeducation, social skills training and maintenance chemotherapy in the aftercare treatment of schizophrenia. *Archives of General Psychiatry*, 48: 340–7.

Hogwood, B. (1987) *Trends in British Public Policy: Do Governments Make any Difference?* Buckingham: Open University Press.

Hokanson, J. E., Rubert, M. P., Welker, R. A., Hollander, G. R. and Hedeen, C. (1989) Interpersonal concomitants and antecedents of depression among college students. *Journal of Abnormal Psychology*, 98: 209–17.

Holmes, B. (1985) Victimization of the elderly: analysis of the level of social functioning in the community: an exploratory study. Dissertation, Ohio State University. Ann Arbor, MI: University Microfilms International.

Holmes, T. H. and Rahe, R. H. (1967) The social readjustment rating scale. *Journal of Psychosomatic Research*, 11: 213–18.

Holohan, C. J. and Moos, R. H. (1981) Social support and psychological distress: a longitudinal analysis. *Journal of Abnormal Psychology*, 90(4): 365–70.

Home Office (2003) Offender statistics. www.homeoffice.gov.uk/justice/ sentencing/rehabilitation/statistics.html

Hooghe, M. (2002) Watching television and civic engagement: disentangling the effects of time, programs, and stations. *Harvard International Journal of Press-Politics*, 7(2): 84–104.

Hooghe, M. (2003) Participation in voluntary associations and value indicators: the effect of current and previous participation experiences. *Non-Profit and Voluntary Sector Quarterly*, 32(1): 47–69.

Hough, L. (2000) The American voter. *Kennedy School of Government Bulletin Archives*, Spring. www.ksg.harvard.edu/ksgpress/ksgnews/publications/ theamericanvoter.html

Hourihan, K. (1987) Local community involvement and participation in Neigh-bourhood Watch: a case-study in Cork, Ireland. *Urban Studies*, 24: 129–36.

House, J. S., Robbins, C. and Metzner, H. L. (1982) The association of social relationships and activities with mortality: prospective evidence from the Tecumseh community health study. *American Journal of Epidemiology*, 116: 123–40.

Hunter, M. L. (2002) 'If you're light you're alright': light skin color as social capital for women of color. *Gender and Society*, 16(2): 175–93.

Huotari, M. L. and Livonen, M. (2001) University library: a strategic partner in knowledge and information related processes? *Proceedings of the 64th ASIST Annual Meeting*, 38: 399–410.

Husain, S. (1988) *Neighbourhood Watch in England and Wales: A Locational Analysis*. London: Crime Prevention Unit, Home Office.

Husain, S. (1990) *Neighbourhood Watch and Crime: An Assessment of Impact*. London: Police Foundation.

Hutton, W. (1995) *The State We're In*. London: Jonathan Cape.

Idler, E. L. and Benyamini, Y. (1997) Self-rated health and mortality: a review of twenty-seven community studies. *Journal of Health and Social Behaviour*, 38(1): 21–37.

Inglehart, R. (1990) *Culture Shift*. Princeton, NJ: Princeton University Press.

Inkeles, A. (2000) Measuring social capital and its consequences. *Policy Sciences*, 33(3–4): 245–68.

Inoguchi, T. (2000) Social capital in Japan. *Japanese Journal of Political Science*, 1(1): 73–112.

Ireland, R. D., Hitt, M. A. and Vaidyanath, D. (2002) Alliance management as a source of competitive advantage. *Journal of Management*, 28(3): 413–46.

Irwin, H. J. (1999) Violent and nonviolent revictimization of women abused in childhood. *Journal of Interpersonal Violence*, 14(10): 1095–110.

Isham, J. (2002) The effect of social capital on fertiliser adoption: evidence from rural Tanzania. *Journal of African Economies*, 11(1): 39–60.

Israel, G. D., Beaulieu, L. J. and Hartless, G. (2001) The influence of family and community social capital on educational achievement. *Rural Sociology*, 66: 43–68.

Jacobs, J. (1961) *The Death and Life of Great American cities*. New York: Random House.

356   Bibliography

Jahoda, M. (1972) *Marienthal: The Sociography of an Unemployed Community.* London: Tavistock.
Jahoda, M. (1982) *Employment and Unemployment: A Social Psychological Analysis.* Cambridge: Cambridge University Press.
Jahoda, M. (1995) Manifest and latent functions. In Nicholson, N. (ed.) *The Blackwell Dictionary of Organisational Behaviour.* Oxford: Blackwell.
Janoski, T., Musick, M. and Wilson, J. (1998) Being volunteered? The impact of social participation and pro-social attitudes on volunteering. *Sociological Forum,* 13(3): 495–519.
Jenkins, M. (2001) Technology clusters and knowledge architecture. *Cranfield School of Management Magazine,* 16: 21–3. www.drive.cranfield.ac.uk/cluster.pdf
Jenkins, S. P. and Osberg, L. (2003) Nobody to play with? The implications of leisure co-ordination. ISER Working Papers 2003-19. Institute for Social and Economic Research, University of Essex.
Johnson, A. W. (1999) *Sponsor-a-Scholar: Long-term Impacts of a Youth Mentoring Program on Student Performance.* London: Commonwealth Fund. www.cmwf.org/programs/youth/johnson_sp-a-sch_355.asp
Johnston, M. (1988) The price of honesty. In Jowell, R. et al. (eds) *British Social Attitudes: The 5th Report.* Aldershot: Gower.
Jonsson, J. O. and Gahler, M. (1997) Family dissolution, family reconstitution, and children's educational careers: recent evidence for Sweden. *Demography,* 34(2): 277–93.
Jordan, W. and Plank, S. B. (2000) Talent loss among high-achieving poor students. In Sanders, M. G. (ed.) *Schooling Students Placed at Risk: Research, Policy, and Practice in the Education of Poor and Minority Adolescents.* Mahwah, NJ: Erlbaum Associates.
Jungbauer-Gans, M. (2002) Is social capital on the decline? *Soziale Welt-Zeitschrift fur Sozial Wissenschaftliche Forschung und Praxis,* 53(2): 189–208.
Kaase, M. (1999) Interpersonal trust, political trust and non-institutionalised political participation in Western Europe. *West European Politics,* 22(3): 1–21.
Kahne, J. and Bailey, K. (1999) The role of social capital in youth development: the case of 'I have a dream' programs. *Educational Evaluation and Policy Analysis,* 21(3): 321–43.
Kamarck, R. L., Manuck, S. B. and Jennings, J. (1991) Social support reduces cardiovascular reactivity to psychological challenge: a laboratory model. *Psychosomatic Medicine,* 52: 42–58.
Kanazawa, S. (2002) Bowling with our imaginary friends. *Evolution and Human Behaviour,* 23(3): 167–71.
Kang, N. and Kwak, N. (2003) A multilevel approach to civic participation: individual length of residence, neighborhood residential stability, and their interactive effects with media use. *Communication Research,* 30(1): 80–106.
Kaplan, G. A., Pamuk, E., Lynch, J. W., Cohen, R. D. and Balfour, J. L. (1996) Income inequality and mortality in the United States: analysis of mortality and potential pathways. *British Medical Journal,* 312: 999–1003.
Kaplan, R. M., Sallis, J. F. and Patterson, T. L. (1993) *Health and Human Behaviour.* London: McGraw-Hill.

Kaplan, R. M., Salonen, J. T., Cohen, R. D., Brand, R. J., Syme, S. L. and Puska, P. (1988) Social connections and mortality from all causes and from cardiovascular disease: prospective evidence from eastern Finland. *American Journal of Epidemiology*, 128: 370–80.

Katz, E. G. (2000) Social capital and natural capital: a comparative analysis of land tenure and natural resource management in Guatemala. *Land Economy*, 76(1): 114–32.

Kawachi, I. and Berkman, L. F. (2000) Social cohesion, social capital and health. In Berkman, L. F. and Kawachi, I. (eds) *Social Epidemiology*. Oxford: Oxford University Press.

Kawachi, I. and Berkman, L. F. (2001) Social ties and mental health. Paper prepared for September special issue of *Journal of Urban Health*.

Kawachi, I. and Kennedy, B. P. (1999) Income inequality and health: pathways and mechanisms. *Health Services Research*, 34(1): 215–27.

Kawachi, I., Kennedy, B. P. and Glass, R. (1999) Social capital and self-rated health: a contextual analysis. *American Journal of Public Health*, 89(8): 1187–93.

Kawachi, I., Kennedy, B. P. and Wilkinson, R. G. (1998) Mortality, the social environment, crime and violence. *Sociology of Health and Illness*, special issue.

Kawachi, I., Kennedy, B. P., Lochner, K. and Prothrow-Stith, D. (1997) Social capital, income inequality and mortality. *American Journal of Public Health*, 89(9): 1491–8.

Kawachi, I., Colditz, G. A., Ascherio, A., Rimm, E. B., Giovannucci, E., Stampfer, M. J. and Willett, W. C. (1996) A prospective study of social networks in relation to total mortality and cardiovascular disease in men in the USA. *Journal Epidemiology Community Health*, 50: 245–51.

Keller, W. (2002) Geographic localization of international technology diffusion. *American Economic Review*, 92(1): 120–42.

Kennedy, B. P. and Kawachi, I. (1998) The role of social capital in the Russian mortality crisis. *World Development*, 26(11): 2029–43.

Kennedy, S., Kiecolt-Glaser, J. K. and Glaser, R. (1990) Social support, stress, and the immune system. In Sarason, B. R., Sarason, I. G. and Pierce, G. R. (eds) *Social Support: An Interactional View*. Chichester: John Wiley.

Kentworthy, L. (1997) Civic engagement, social capital, and economic co-operation. *American Behavioral Scientist*, 40(5): 646–57.

Kiecolt-Glaser, J. K., Malarkey, W. B., Caioppo, J. T. and Glaser, R. (1994) Stressful personal relationships: immune and endocrine function. In Glaser, R. and Kiecol-Glaser, J. K. (eds) *Handbook of Human Stress and Immunity*. San Diego, CA: Academic Press.

Kiecolt-Glaser, J. K., McGuire, L., Robles, T. F. and Glaser, R. (2002) Psychoneuroimmunology: psychological influences on immune function and health. *Journal of Consulting and Clinical Psychology*, 70(3): 537–47.

Kiernan, K. E. (1996) Family change: parenthood, partnership and policy. In Halpern, D. S., Wood, S., White, S. and Cameron, G. (eds) *Options for Britain: A Strategic Policy Review*. Dartmouth: Aldershot.

Kleit, R. G. (2000) Book review of *Segregation in Federally Subsidized Low Income Housing in the United States* by Modibo Coulibaly, Rodney D. Green and David M. James. *Journal of Urban Affairs*, 22(1): 103–4.

Klinenberg, Erik (2002) *Heat Wave*. Chicago: University of Chicago Press.

Knack, S. (2002) Social capital and the quality of government: evidence from the states. *American Journal of Political Science*, 46(4): 772–85.

Knack, S. and Keefer, P. (1997) Does social capital have an economic payoff? A cross-country investigation. *Quarterly Journal of Economics*, 112(4): 1251–88.

Knack, S. and Kropf, M. E. (1998) For shame! The effect of community co-operative context on the probability of voting. *Political Psychology*, 19(3): 585–99.

Koba, B. R. and Prescott, J. E. (2002) Strategic alliances as social capital: a multidimensional view. *Strategic Management Journal*, 23(9): 795–816.

Kobassa, S. C. (1979) Stressful life events, personality, and health: an inquiry into hardiness. *Journal Personality and Social Psychology*, 37: 1–11.

Kolankiewicz, G. (1996) Social capital and social change. *British Journal of Sociology*, 47(3): 427–42.

Kposowa, A., Singh, G. K. and Breault, K. D. (1994) The effects of marital status and social isolation on adult male homicides in the United States. *Journal of Quantitative Criminology*, 10(3): 277–89.

Kraemer, S. and Roberts, R. (1996) (eds) *The Politics of Attachment: Towards a Secure Society*. London: Free Association Books.

Kraft, E. (1999) Ten years of transition in Central and Eastern Europe: a somewhat opinionated survey. *Economic and Business Review*, 1(1–2): 7–52.

Krishna, A. (2002) Enhancing political participation in democracies: what is the role of social capital? *Comparative Political Studies*, 35(4): 437–60.

Krug, B. (1999) On custom in economics: the case of humanism and trade regimes. *Journal of Institutional and Theoretical Economics*, 155(3): 405–28.

Kunioka, T. and Woller, G. M. (1999) In (a) democracy we trust: social and economic determinants of support for democratic procedures in Central and Eastern Europe. *Journal of Socio-Economics*, 28(5): 577–96.

La Due Lake, R. and Huckfeldt, R. (1998) Social capital, social networks, and political participation. *Political Psychology*, 19(3): 567–84.

La Ferrara, E. (2002) Inequality and group participation: theory and evidence from rural Tanzania. *Journal of Public Economics*, 85(2): 235–73.

La Porta, R., Lopez-de-Silanes, F., Shleifer, A. and Vishny, R. W. (1997) Trust in large organisations. *American Economic Review*, 87(Papers and Proceedings): 333–8.

Laing, R. D. and Esterson, A. ([1964] 1970). *Sanity, Madness and the Family: Families of Schizophrenics*. Harmondsworth: Penguin.

Lampert, H. (2002) Zur Suche nach neuen sozialen Ordnungen im europäisch-nordamerikanischen Kulturkreis [The Search of New Social and Economic Orders in European and North-American Societies] Jahrbücher für Nationalökonomie und Statistik Bard, vol. 222/3, pp. 346–65.

Landry, R., Amara, N. and Lamari, M. (2002) Does social capital determine innovation? To what extent? *Technological Forecasting and Social Change*, 69(7): 681–701.

Lane, C. and Bachman, R. (1995) Risk, trust and power: the social constitution of supplier relations in Britain and Germany. Working Paper WP 5 2/95. University of Cambridge, ESRC Centre for Business Research.

Lane, C. and Bachman, R. (1998) *Trust Within and Between Organizations: Conceptual Issues and Empirical Applications*. Oxford: Oxford University Press.

Langbein, L. and Bess, R. (2002) Sports in school: source of amity or antipathy? *Social Science Quarterly*, 83(2): 436–54.

Larson, R. W., Wilson, S., Brown, B. B., Furstenberg, F. F. and Verma, S. (2002) Changes in adolescents' interpersonal experiences: are they being prepared for adult relationships in the twenty-first century? *Journal of Research on Adolescence*, 12(1): 31–68.

Latane, B. and Darley, J. M. (1976) *Help in a Crisis: Bystander Response to an Emergency.* Morristown, NJ: General Learning Press.

Latkin, C., Mandell, W., Oziemkowska, M., Celentano, D., Vlahov, D., Ensminger, M. and Knowlton, A. (1995) Using social network analysis to study patterns of drug use among urban drug users at high risk for HIV/AIDS. *Drug and Alcohol Dependence*, 38: 1–9.

Laub, J. H. and Sampson, R. J. (2001) Understanding desistance from crime. In Tonry, M. (ed.) *Crime and Justice: A Review of Research.* Chicago: University of Chicago Press.

Lavis, J. and Stoddart, G. (1999) Financing health care. In Hurley, J. et al., *Introduction to the Concepts and Analytical Tools of Health Economics.* Hamilton, On.: Centre for Health Economics and Policy Analysis, Special Report, May.

Lawrence, R. J. (1990) Public collective and private space: a study of urban housing in Switzerland. In Kent, S. (ed.) *Domestic Architecture and the Use of Space: An Interdisciplinary Cross-Cultural Study.* Cambridge: Cambridge University Press.

Laws, G. (1997) Globalization, immigration, and changing social relations in US cities. *Annals of the American Academy of Political and Social Science*, 551: 89–104.

Laycock, G. and Tilley, N. (1995) Policing and Neighbourhood Watch: strategic issues. Crime Detection and Prevention Series Paper, 60. London: Home Office Police Research Group.

Leadbeater, C. (1998) *The Rise of the Social Entrepreneur.* London: Demos.

Leadbeater, C. (1999) *Living on Thin Air.* London: Viking, Penguin.

Lee, G. R. (1985) Kinship and social support of the elderly: the case of the United States. *Aging and Society*, 5: 19–38.

Lee, L. J., Cheurprakobkit, S. and Denq, F. (1999) Neighbourhood Watch programs in Taiwan: police attitudes, crime rate and community support. *International Journal of Police Science and Management*, 2(1): 57–77.

Leffert, N. and Petersen, A. C. (1995) Patterns of development during adolescence. In Rutter, M. and Smith, D. (eds) *Psychosocial Disorder in Young People: Time Trends and their Causes.* Chichester: John Wiley.

Lefkowitz, M. M. and Tesiny, E. P. (1984) Rejection and depression: prospective and contemporaneous analyses. *Developmental Psychology*, 20(5): 776–85.

Le Grand, J. (1997) Knights, knaves and pawns: human behaviour and social policy. *Journal of Social Policy*, 26: 149–69.

Le Grand, J. (2003) *Motivation, Agency and Public Policy: Of Knights and Knaves, Pawns and Queens.* Oxford: Oxford University Press.

Lepper, M. R., Green, D. and Nisbett, R. E. (1973) Undermining children's intrinsic interest with extrinsic rewards: a test of the 'overjustification' hypothesis. *Journal of Personality and Social Psychology*, 28: 129–37.

Levin, M. and Satarov, G. (2000) Corruption and institutions in Russia. *European Journal of Political Economy*, 16(1): 113–32.

Levine, R. V., Miyake, K. and Lee, M. (1989) Places rated revisited: psychosocial pathology in metropolitan areas. *Environment and Behaviour*, 21(5): 531–53.

Levy, L. and Herzog, A. N. (1974) Effects of population density and crowding on health and social adaptation in the Netherlands. *Journal of Health and Social Behaviour*, 15: 228–40.

Lewis, D. A. (1981) *Reactions to Crime*. Criminal Justice Systems Annuals, 16. London: Sage.

Li, Y. J., Savage, M., Tampubolon, G., Warde, A. and Tomlinson, M. (2002) Dynamics of social capital: trends and turnover in associational membership in England and Wales, 1972–1999. *Sociological Research Online*, 7(3): U97–U132.

Liebert, R. M. and Spiegler, M. D. (1990) *Personality: Strategies and Issues* (6th edn). Belmont, CA: Brooks/Cole Publishing.

Lindstrom, M., Merlo, J. and Ostergren, P. O. (2002) Individual and neighbourhood determinants of social participation and social capital: a multilevel analysis of the city of Malmo, Sweden. *Social Science and Medicine*, 54(12): 1779–91.

Lindstrom, M., Moghaddassi, M. and Merlo, J. (2003) Social capital and leisure time physical activity: a population based multilevel analysis in Malmo, Sweden. *Journal of Epidemiology and Community Health*, 57(1): 23–8.

Lindstrom, P. (1993) *School and Delinquency in a Contextual Perspective*. Stockholm: National Council for Crime Prevention.

Liu, J. (1999) Social capital and covariates of reoffending risk in the Chinese context. *International Criminal Justice Review*, 9: 39–55.

Lochner, K., Kawachi, I. and Kennedy, B. P. (1999) Social capital: a guide to its measurement. *Health and Place*, 5(4): 259–70.

Loeber, R. and Farrington, D. P. (2000) Young children who commit crime: epidemiology, developmental origins, risk factors, early interventions, and policy implications. *Development and Psychopathology*, 12: 737–62.

Lohman, P. M. and van Dijk, A. G. (1988) *Neighbourhood Watch in the Netherlands*. The Hague: National Crime Prevention Bureau.

Lorcher, S. (1982) Japan's social capital in international comparison. *Internationales Asienforum*, 13(1–2): 103–35.

Loury, G. (1977) (ed.) *A Dynamic Theory of Racial Income Differences: Women, Minorities, and Employment Discrimination*. Lexington, MA: Lexington Books.

Loury, G. (1981) Intergenerational transfers and the distribution of earnings. *Econometrica*, 49: 843–67.

Loury, G. C. (1977) A dynamic theory of racial income differences. In Wallace, P. A. and LeMund, A. (eds) *Women, Minorities and Employment Discrimination*. Lexington, MA: Lexington Books.

Loury, G. C. (1987) Why should we care about group inequality? *Social Philosophy and Policy*, 5: 249–71.

Loury, G. C. (1992) The economics of discrimination: getting to the core of the problem. *Harvard Journal of African American Public Policy*, 1: 91–110.

Lovell, A. M. (2002) Risking risk: the influence of types of capital and social networks on the injection practices of drug users. *Social Science and Medicine*, 55(5): 803–21.

Lowndes, V. (2000) Women and social capital: a comment on Hall's 'social capital in Britain'. *British Journal of Political Science*, 30(3): 533–7.

Lowry, S. (1991) *Housing and Health*. London: British Medical Journal.

Lundberg, O. (1993) The impact of childhood living conditions on illness and mortality in adulthood. *Social Science and Medicine*, 36(8): 1047–52.

Luzzati, T. (2000) Norme sociali e sanzione: il ruolo del singolo individuo. (Social norms and individual sanctioning.) *Economia Politica*, 17(1): 53–67.

Lynch, J., Due, P., Muntaner, C. and Davey Smith, G. (2000b) Social capital: is it a good investment strategy for public health? *Journal of Epidemiology and Community Health*, 54: 404–8.

Lynch, J. W., Davey Smith, G., Kaplan, G. W. and House, J. S. (2000a) Income inequality and mortality: importance to health of individual income, psychological environment, or material conditions. *British Medical Journal*, 320: 1200–4.

Lynch, K. (1960) *The Image of the City*. Cambridge, MA: MIT Press.

Ma, Z. D. (2002) Social capital mobilization and income returns to entrepreneurship: the case of return migration in rural China. *Environment and Planning A*, 34(10): 1763–84.

Mackay, J. R. (1958) The interactance hypothesis and boundaries in Canada: a preliminary study. *Canadian Geographer*, 11: 1–8.

Mackintosh, N. J. (1998) *IQ and Human Intelligence*. London: Oxford University Press.

Madood, T., Berthoud, R. et al. (1997) *Ethnic Minorities in Britain: Diversity and Difference*. London: Policy Studies Institute.

Majoribanks, K. (1991) Ethnicity, family environment and social-status attainment: a follow-up analysis. *Journal of Comparative Family Studies*, 22(1): 15–23.

Majoribanks, K. and Kwok, Y. (1998) Family capital and Hong Kong adolescents' academic achievement. *Psychological Reports*, 83(1): 99–105.

Mann, W. (1995) *Building Social Capital: Self-Help in a Twenty-First Century State*. London: IPPR.

Marmot, M. G. (1986) Social inequalities in mortality: the social environment. In Wilkinson, R. G. (ed.) *Class and Health: Research and Longitudinal Data*. London: Tavistock.

Marmot, M. G., Davey Smith, G., Stansfield, S., Patel, C., North, F. and Head, J. (1991) Health inequalities among British civil servants: the Whitehall study II. *Lancet*, 337: 1387–93.

Marsh, A. and MacKay, S. (1994) *Poor Smokers*. Research Report, No. 771. London: Policy Studies Institute.

Martin, L. R. (1963) Research needed on the contribution of human, social and community capital to economic growth. *Journal of Farm Economics*, 45(1): 73–94.

Massey, D. S. and Espinosa, K. E. (1999) Undocumented migration and the quantity and quality of social capital. *Soziale Welt*, 12: 141–62.

Matheson, J. and Summerfield, C. (2000) (eds) *Social Focus on Young People*. London: Stationery Office.

Matthews, R. and Trickey, J. (1994) *The New Parks Crime Reduction Project*. Leicester: Centre for the Study of Public Order, University of Leicester.

Mayer, M. and Rankin, K. N. (2002) Social capital and (community) development: a North/South perspective. *Antipode*, 34(4): 804–8.

McCabe, K., Houser, D., Ryan, L., Smith, V. and Trouard, T. (2001) A functional imaging study of co-operation in two-person reciprocal exchange. *Proceedings of the National Academy of Sciences of the United States of America*, 98(20): 11832–5.

McCallum, J. (1995) National borders matter: Canada–US regional trade patterns. *American Economic Review*, 85: 615–23.

McCarthy, B., Hagan, J. and Martin, M. J. (2002) In and out of harm's way: violent victimization and the social capital of fictive street families. *Criminology*, 40(4): 831–65.

McConville, M. and Shepherd, D. (1992) *Watching Police, Watching Communities*. London and New York: Routledge.

McCord, J. (1978) A thirty-year follow-up of treatment effects. *American Psychologist*, 33: 284–9.

McCulloch, A. (2001) Social environments and health: a cross-sectional survey. *British Medical Journal*, 323: 208–9.

McKenzie, K. (2000) Neighbourhood safety and mental health outcomes. www.worldbank.org/poverty/scapital/sctalk/talk28.htm

McKenzie, K., Whitley, R. and Weich, S. (2002) Social capital and mental health. *British Journal of Psychiatry*, 181: 280–3.

McLanahan, S. and Sandefur, G. (1994) *Growing Up with a Single Parent: What Hurts, What Helps*. Cambridge, MA, and London: Harvard University Press.

McNeal, R. B. (1999) Participation in high school extracurricular activities: investigating school effects. *Social Science Quarterly*, 80(2): 291–309.

McRae, R. R. and Costa, P. T. (1987) Validation of the five-factor model of personality across instruments and observers. *Journal of Personality and Social Psychology*, 52(1): 81–90.

Mellahi, K. (2000) Western MBA education and effective leadership values in developing countries: a study of Asian, Arab and African MBA graduates. *Journal of Transnational Management Development*, 5(2): 59–73.

Merrett, C. D. (2001) Declining social capital and nonprofit organizations: consequences for small towns after welfare reform. *Urban Geography*, 22(5): 407–23.

Metz, I. and Tharenou, P. (2001) Women's career advancement: the relative contribution of human and social capital. *Group and Organisation Management*, 26(3): 312–42.

Miethe, T. D. and Meier, R. F. (1994) *Crime and its Social Context: Toward an Integrated Theory of Offenders, Victims, and Situations*. Albany, NY: State University of New York Press.

Milgram, S. (1977) *The Individual in a Social World: Essays and Experiments*. Reading, MA: Addison-Wesley.

Miller, R. (1996) *Measuring What People Know: Human Capital Accounting for the Knowledge Economy*. Paris: OECD.

Mittleman, M. S., Ferris, S. H., Shulman, E., Steinberg, G., Ambinder, A., Mackell, J. A. and Cohen, J. (1995) A comprehensive support program: effect on depression in spouse-caregivers of AD patients. *Gerontologist*, 35: 792–802.

Moerbeek, H. H. S. and Need, A. (2003) Enemies at work: can they hinder your career? *Social Networks*, 25(1): 67–82.

Moffitt, T. E. (2002) Teen-aged mothers in contemporary Britain. *Journal of Child Psychology and Psychiatry and Allied Disciplines*, 43(6): 727–42.

Mohan, G. and Mohan, J. (2002) Placing social capital. *Progress in Human Geography*, 26(2): 191–210.

Molina-Morales, F. X., Lopez-Navarro, M. A. and Guia-Julve, J. (2002) The role of local institutions as intermediary agents in the industrial district. *European Urban and Regional Studies*, 9(4): 315–29.

Molyneux, M. (2002) Gender and the silences of social capital: lessons from Latin America. *Development and Change*, 33(2): 167–88.

Mondak, J. J. and Gearing, A. F. (1998) Civic engagement in a post-communist state. *Political Psychology*, 19(3): 615–37.

Mondal, A. H. (2000) Social capital formation: the role of NGO rural development programs in Bangladesh. *Bangladesh Institute of Development Studies*, 33(3–4): 459–75.

Montgomery, J. D. (1991) Social networks and labor-market outcomes: toward an economic analysis. *American Economic Review*, 81(5): 1408–18.

Morenoff, J. D., Sampson, R. J. and Raudenbush, S. W. (2001) Neighbourhood inequality, collective efficacy and the spatial dynamics of urban violence. Population Studies Center, report No 00–451. University of Michigan.

Morgan, S. L. and Sorensen, A. B. (1999) Parental networks, social closure, and mathematics learning: a test of Coleman's social capital explanation of school effects. *American Sociological Review*, 64(5): 661–81.

MORI (2003) *Trust in Public Institutions: New Findings from a National Quantitative Survey*. London: MORI Social Research Institute.

Morris, M. (1995) Data driven network models for the spread of infectious disease. In Mollison, D. (ed.) *Epidemic Models: Their Structure and Relation to Data*. Cambridge: Cambridge University Press.

Mukherjee, S. and Wilson, P. (1987) *Neighbourhood Watch: Issues and Policy Implications*. Trends and Issues, 8. Canberra: Australian Institute of Criminology.

Mulgan, G. (1997) *Connexity: How to Live in a Connected World*. London: Chatto and Windus.

Muller, C. (1995) Maternal employment, parent involvement, and mathematics achievement. *Journal of Marriage and the Family*, 57(1): 85–100.

Munch, R. (2002) The limits of the self-organisation civil society: the American debate on multiculturalism, public spirit, and social capital from the point of view of modernisation theory. *Berliner Journal für Soziologie*, 12(4): 445–65.

Muntaner, C., Lynch, J. W., Hillemeier, M., Lee, J. H., David, R., Benach, J. and Borrell, C. (2002) Economic inequality, working-class power, social capital, and cause-specific mortality in wealthy countries. *International Journal of Health Services*, 32(4): 629–56.

Murphy, J. T. (2002) Networks, trust and innovation in Tanzania's manufacturing sector. *World Development*, 30(4): 591–619.

National Commission on Service Learning (2002) Learning in deed: the power of service learning for American schools. www.wkkf.org/Pubs/PhilVol/Pub3679.pdf

National Economic and Social Forum (2003) The policy implications of social capital. Forum Report No. 28, by Tom Healey. http://www.nesf.ie/documents/No28SocialCapital.pdf

Navarro, V. (2002). A critique of social capital. *International Journal of Health Services*, 32(3): 423–32.

Neace, M. B. (1999) Entrepreneurs in emerging economies: creating trust, social capital, and civil society. *Annals of the American Academy of Political and Social Science*, 65: 148–61.

Neaigus, A., Friedman, S. R., Curtis, R., Des Jarlais, D. C., Furst, R. T., Jose, B., Mora, P., Stepherson, B., Sufian, M., Ward, T. and Wright, J. W. (1994) The relevance of drug injectors' social and risk networks for understanding and preventing HIV infection. *Social Science and Medicine*, 38: 67–78.

Neeleman J., Halpern, D. S., Leon, D. et al. (1997) Tolerance of suicide, religion and suicide rates: an ecological and individual study in 19 Western countries. *Psychological Medicine*, 27(5): 1165–71.

Newcomb, M. D. and Bentler, P. M. (1988) Impact of adolescent drug use and social support on problems of young adults: a longitudinal study. *Journal of Abnormal Psychology*, 97: 64–75.

Newman, O. (1980) *Community of Interest*. New York: Anchor Books.

Newton, K. (1997) Social capital and democracy. *American Behavioural Scientist*, 40(5): 575–86.

Newton, K. (1999) Mass media effects: mobilization or mass media malaise? *British Journal of Political Science*, 29: 577–99.

Niemi, N. and Junn, J. (1998) *Civic Education*. New Haven, CT: Yale University Press.

Norris, P. (ed.) (1999) *Critical Citizens: Global Support for Democratic Governance*. Oxford: Oxford University Press.

Nova Institute (1977) *Reducing the Impact of Crime against the Elderly*. New York: Nova Institute.

Nuckolls, K. B., Cassel, J. and Kaplan, B. J. (1972) Psychological assets, life crisis and the prognosis of pregnancy. *American Journal of Epidemiology*, 95: 431–41.

Nuissl, H. (2002) Elements of trust: an analysis of trust-concepts. *Berliner Journal für Soziologie*, 12(1): 87–98.

O'Brien, D. J., Raedeke, A. and Hassinger, E. W. (1998) The social networks of leaders in more and less viable communities six years later: a research note. *Rural Sociology*, 62: 109–27.

O'Brien, M. and Jones, D. (1999) Children, parental employment and educational attainment: an English case study. *Cambridge Journal of Economics*, 23(5): 599–621.

Obstfeld, M. and Rogoff, K. (2000) The six major puzzles in international macroeconomics: is there a common cause? NBER Working Paper 7777. National Bureau of Economic Research, Cambridge.

OECD (2001a) *The Well-Being of Nations: The Role of Human and Social Capital*. Paris: OECD.

OECD (2001b) *Science, Technology and Industry Scoreboard 2001: Towards a Knowledge-Based Economy*. Paris: OECD. www.oecd.org/publications/e-book/92-2001-04-1-2987/index.htm

Offe, C. and Fuchs, S. (1998) A decline of social capital? The German case. *In Society and Civic Spirit (Gesellschaft und Gemeinsinn)*. Gütersloh: Bertelsmann Foundation. Pub. 2002 in Putnam, R. D. (ed.) *Democracies in Flux: The Evolution of Social Capital in Contemporary Society*. Oxford: Oxford University Press.

Offer, A. (1996) (ed.) *In Pursuit of the Quality of Life*. Oxford: Oxford University Press.

Office of National Statistics (2003) *Social Trends 33*. London: HMSO.

Ohrn, K. G. (2002) Democracy, trade and welfare: three theories of lasting peace. *Tidsskrift for Samfunnsforskning*, 43(3): 333–58.

Oigenblick, L. and Kirschenbaum, A. (2002) Tourism and immigration: comparing alternative approaches. *Annals of Tourism Research*, 29(4): 1086–100.

Oppenheim, C. (1998) *The Inclusive Society: Tackling Poverty*. London: Institute for Public Policy Research.

Orbanes, P. (2002) Everything I know about business I learned from Monopoly. *Harvard Business Review*, 80(3): 51.

Ornish, D. (1998) *Love and Survival: How Good Relationships Can Bring You Health and Well-Being*. London: Vermillion.

Orth-Gomer, K. and Johnson, J. (1987) Social network interaction and mortality: a six-year follow-up of a random sample of the Swedish population. *Journal of Chronic Disease*, 40: 949–57.

Orth-Gomer, K., Rosengren, A. and Wilhelmsen, L. (1993) Lack of social support and incidence of coronary heart disease in middle-aged Swedish men. *Psychosomatic Medicine*, 55(1): 37–43.

Paldam, M. and Svendsen, G. T. (2000) An essay on social capital: looking for the fire behind the smoke. *European Journal of Political Economy*, 16(2): 339–66.

Parcel, T. L. and Dufur, M. J. (2001) Capital at home and at school: effects on student achievement. *Social Forces*, 79(3): 881–912.

Parcel, T. L. and Geschwender, L. E. (1995) Explaining southern disadvantage in verbal facility among young children. *Social Forces*, 73(3): 841–74.

Parcel, T. L., Nickoll, R. A. and Dufur, M. J. (1996) The effects of parental work and maternal nonemployment on children's reading and math achievement. *Work and Occupations*, 23(4): 461–83.

Patterson, T. (1993) *Out of Order*. New York: Vintage Press.

Pattie, C., Seyd, P. and Whiteley, P. (2002) Does good citizenship make a difference? Paper presented to the EPOP Annual Conference, University of Salford, 13–15 September.

Pattie, C., Seyd, P. and Whiteley (2004) *Citizenship UK: Democracy and Participation in Contemporary Britain*. Cambridge: Cambridge University Press.

Paxton, P. (2002) Social capital and democracy: an interdependent relationship. *American Sociological Review*, 67(2): 254–77.

Pearce, N. and Smith, G. D. (2003) Is social capital the key to inequalities in health? *American Journal of Public Health*, 93(1): 122–9.

Perry, S., Difede, J., Musgni, G., Frances, A. J. and Jacobsberg, L. (1992) Predictors of post-traumatic stress disorder after burn injury. *American Journal of Psychiatry*, 149(7): 931–5.

Petersen, D. M. (2002) The potential of social capital measures in the evaluation of comprehensive community-based health initiatives. *American Journal of Evaluation*, 23(1): 55–64.

Petersen, T., Saporta, I. and Seidel, M. (2000) Offering a job: meritocracy and social networks. *American Journal of Sociology*, 106(3): 763–816.

Petro, N. (2001) Creating social capital in Russia: The Novgorod model. *World Development*, 29(2): 229–44.

Pettigrew, T. F. and Tropp, L. R. (2000) Does intergroup contact reduce prejudice? Recent meta-analytic findings. In Oskamp, S. (ed.) *Reducing Prejudice and Discrimination: The Claremont Symposium on Applied Social Psychology*. Mahwah, NJ: Erlbaum Associates.

Pew Research Center (1998) www.people-press.org

Piazza-Giorgi, B. (2002) The role of human and social capital in growth: extending our understanding. *Cambridge Journal of Economics*, 26(4): 461–79.

Pike, A. (2000) A complex responsibility: there are measurable benefits for companies in community involvement – even when the going gets tough. *Financial Times Guide to Business in the Community: Business in the Community Awards 2000*: 24–6.

Pilkington, P. (2002) Social capital and health: measuring and understanding social capital at a local level could help to tackle health inequalities more effectively. *Journal of Public Health Medicine*, 24(3): 156–9.

Plutzer, E. (1998) Family structure and the political participation of African American women. In Colby, A., James, J. B. and Hart, D. (eds) *The Development of Character and Competence through Life*. Chicago: University of Chicago Press.

Podolny, J. and Baron, J. (1997) Resources and relationships: social networks and mobility in the workplace. *American Sociological Review*, 62: 673–93.

Pong, S. L. (1998) The school compositional effect of single parenthood on 10th-grade achievement. *Sociology of Education*, 71(1): 23–42.

Porges, S. W. (1998) Love: an emergent property of the mammalian autonomic nervous system. *Psychoneuroendocrinology*, 23(8): 837–61.

Portes, A. (1995) *The Economic Sociology of Immigration: Essays on Networks, Ethnicity and Entrepreneurship*. New York: Russell Sage Foundation.

Portes, A. (1998) Social capital: its origins and applications in modern sociology. *Annual Review of Sociology*, 24: 1–24.

Portes, A. and Sensenbrenner, J. (1993) Embeddedness and immigration: notes on the determinants of economic action. *American Journal of Sociology*, 98(6): 1320–50.

Portes, A. and Zhou, M. (1992) Gaining the upper hand: economic mobility among immigrant and domestic minorities. *Racial and Ethnic Studies*, 15(4): 491–552.

Posner, R. A. and Rasmusen, E. B. (1999) Creating and enforcing norms, with special reference to sanctions. *International Review of Law and Economics*, 19(3): 369–82.

Potot, S. (2002) Transnational migrants: a new social figure in Romania. *Revue d'Etudes Comparatives Est–Ouest*, 33(1): 149–77.

Povey, D. and Allen, J. (2003) Violent crime. In Simmons, J. and Dodd, T. (eds) *Crime in England and Wales 2002/2003*. London: Home Office.

Poyner, B. (1983) *Design Against Crime: Beyond Defensible Space*. London: Butterworths.

Price, B. (2002) Social capital and factors affecting civic engagement as reported by leaders of voluntary associations. *Social Science Journal*, 39(1): 119–27.

Prime Minister's Strategy Unit (2003) Ethnic minorities and the labour market. www.pm.gov.uk

Pruijt, H (2002) Social capital and the equalizing potential of the internet. *Social Science Computer Review*, 20(2): 109–15.

Putnam, R. D. (1993) *Making Democracy Work: Civic Traditions in Modern Italy*. Princeton, NJ: Princeton University Press.

Putnam, R. D. (1995) Tuning in, tuning out: the strange disappearance of social capital in America. *Political Science and Politics*, 28: 1–20.

Putnam, R. D. (1996) The prosperous community: social capital and public life – the American prospect. www.prospect.org/print/V4/13/putnam-r.html

Putnam, R. D. (2000) *Bowling Alone: The Collapse and Revival of American Community*. New York: Simon and Schuster.

Putnam, R. D. (ed.) (2002) *Democracies in Flux: The Evolution of Social Capital in Contemporary Society*. Oxford: Oxford University Press.

Putnam, R. D. and Feldstein, L. M. (2003) *Better Together: Restoring the American Community*. New York: Simon and Schuster.

Putnam, R. D. and Yonish, S. (forthcoming) New evidence on trends in American social capital and civic engagement: are we really 'bowling alone'?

Qian, Z. and Blair, S. L. (1999) Racial/ethnic differences in educational aspirations of high school seniors. *Sociological Perspectives*, 42(4): 605–25.

Quinton, D. and Rutter, M. (1988) *Parenting Breakdown: The Making and Breaking of Inter-Generational Links*. Aldershot: Avebury.

Quinton, D., Pickles, A., Maughan, B. and Rutter, M. (1993) Partners, peers and pathways: assortative pairing and continuities in conduct disorder. *Development and Psychopathology*, 5: 763–83.

Rahn, W. M. and Transue, J. E. (1998) Social trust and value change: the decline of social capital in American youth, 1976–1995. *Political Psychology*, 19(3): 545–65.

Raiser, M., Haerpfer, C., Nowotny, T. and Wallace, C. (2002) Social capital in transition: a first look at the evidence. *Sociologicky Casopis*, 38(6): 693–720.

Rath, J. (2002) A quintessential immigrant niche? The non-case of immigrants in the Dutch construction industry. *Entrepreneurship and Regional Development*, 14(4): 355–72.

Reppetto, T. A. (1974) *Residential Crime*. Cambridge, MA: Ballinger.

Requena, F. (2003) Social capital, satisfaction and quality of life in the workplace. *Social Indicators Research*, 61(3): 331–60.

Resnick, P. (2002) Beyond bowling together: socio-technical capital. In Carroll, J. M. (ed.) *Human–Computer Interaction in the New Millennium*. New York: Addison-Wesley Professional.

Restrepo, P. P. (1998) Capital social, crecimiento económico y políticas públicas. *Lecturas de Economia*, 48: 33–65.

Rice, T. W. and Feldman, J. L. (1997) Civic culture and democracy from Europe to America. *Journal of Politics*, 59(4): 1143–72.

Rich, P. (1999) American voluntarism, social capital and political culture. *Annals of the American Academy of Political and Social Science*, 565: 15–34.

Rilling, J., Gutman, D., Zeh, T., Pagnomi, G., Berns, G. and Kilts, C. (2001) Imaging the neural correlates of social co-operation and non-co-operation in the Prisoner's Dilemma Game. *Neuroimage*, 13(6): S465.

Rob, R. and Zemsky, P. (2002) Social capital, corporate culture and incentive intensity. *Rand Journal of Economics*, 33(2): 243–57.

Roberts, E. (1997) Neighbourhood social environments and the distribution of low birthweight in Chicago. *American Journal of Public Health*, 87: 597–603.

Robey, J. S. (1999) Civil society and NAFTA: initial results. *Annals of the American Academy of Political and Social Science*, 565: 113–25.

Robinson, P. (1998) Employment and social exclusion. In Oppenheim, C. (ed.) *An Inclusive Society: Strategies for Tackling Poverty*. London: IPPR.

Rose, D. R. and Clear, T. R. (1998) Incarceration, social capital, and crime: implications for social disorganization theory. *Criminology*, 36(3): 441–80.

Rose, R. (2000) How much does social capital add to individual health? A survey study of Russians. *Social Science and Medicine*, 51: 1421–35.

Rosenthal, R. and Jacobson, L. (1968) *Pygmalion in the Classroom*. New York: Rinehart and Winston.

Ross, C. E. and Jang, S. J. (2000) Neighborhood disorder, fear, and mistrust: the buffering role of social ties with neighbors. *American Journal of Community Psychology*, 28(4): 401–20.

Ross, L., Greene, D. and House, P. (1977) The 'false consensus effect': an egocentric bias in social perception and attribution processes. *Journal of Experimental Psychology*, 35: 485–94.

Ross, N. A., Wolfson, M. C., Dunn, J. R., Berthelot, J. M., Kaplan, G. A. and Lynch, J. (2000) Relation between income inequality and mortality in Canada and the United States: cross sectional assessment using census data and vital statistics. *British Medical Journal*, 320: 898–902.

Rossel, J. (2002) The quality of democratic regimes: Robert Putnam's and Patrick Heller's explanation of political performance in Italy and India. *Politische Vierteljahresschrift*, 43(2): 302.

Rossteutscher, S. (2002) Advocate or reflection? Associations and political culture. *Political Studies*, 50(3): 514–28.

Rothstein, B. (2001) Social capital in the social democratic welfare state. *Politics and Society*, 29(2): 207–41.

Rowan, W. (1998) *Guaranteed Electronic Markets: The Backbone of a Twenty-First Century Economy*. London: Demos.

Ruberman, W., Weinblatt, E., Goldberg, J. D. and Chaudhary, B. S. (1984) Psychosocial influences on mortality after myocardial infarction. *New England Journal of Medicine*, 311: 552–9.

Rubio, M. (1996) *Social Capital, Education and Delinquency in Colombia. (Capital social, educacion y delincuencia juvenil en Columbia.)* Santa Fe de Bogota: Centro de Estudios sobre Desarrollo Economico Universidad.

Rupasingha, A., Goetz, S. J. and Freshwater, D. (2002) Social and institutional factors as determinants of economic growth: evidence from the United States counties. *Papers in Regional Science*, 81(2): 139–55.

Russek, L. G. and Schwartz, G. E. (1997) Perceptions of parental caring predict health status in midlife: a 35-year follow-up of the Harvard Mastery of Stress Study. *Psychosomatic Medicine*, 59(2): 144–9.

Rutter, M. and Smith, D. (1995) *Psychosocial Disorder in Young People: Time Trends and their Causes.* Chichester: John Wiley.

Rutter, M., Quinton, D. and Hill, J. (1990) Adult outcome of institution-reared children. In Robins, L. and Rutter, M. (eds) *Straight and Devious Pathways from Childhood to Adulthood.* Cambridge: Cambridge University Press.

Saegert, S. and Winkel, G. (1998) Social capital and the revitalization of New York City's distressed inner-city housing. *Housing Policy Debate*, (9)1: 17–60.

Saegert, S., Winkel, G. and Swartz, C. (2002) Social capital and crime in New York City's low-income housing. *Housing Policy Debate*, 13(1): 189–226.

Saguaro Seminar (2000) *Bettertogether: The Report of the Saguaro Seminar: Civic Engagement in America.* Cambridge, MA: John F. Kennedy School of Government, Harvard University. www.bettertogether.org/thereport.htm

Sampson, R. J. and Laub, J. H. (1993) *Crime in the Making: Pathways and Turning Points through Life.* Cambridge, MA: Harvard University Press.

Sampson, R. J., Morenoff, J. D. and Earls, F. (1999) Beyond social capital: spatial dynamics of collective efficacy for children. *American Sociological Review*, 64(5): 633–60.

Sampson, R. J., Raudenbush, S. W. and Earls, F. (1997) Neighborhoods and violent crime: a multilevel study of collective efficacy. *Science*, 277: 918–24.

Sander, T. H. and Putnam, R. D. (1999) Rebuilding the stock of social capital. *School Administrator Web Edition*, September.

Sanders, J., Nee, V. and Sernau, S. (2002) Asian immigrants' reliance on social ties in a multiethnic labor market. *Social Forces*, 81(1): 281–314.

Sarason, B. R., Sarason, I. G. and Pierce, G. R. (1990) *Social Support: An Interactional View.* Chichester: John Wiley.

Saunders, L. S., Hanbury-Tenison, R. and Swingland, I. R. (2002) Social capital from carbon property: creating equity for indigenous people. *Philosophical Transactions of the Royal Society of London, Series-A: Mathematical, Physical and Engineering Sciences*, 360(1797): 1763–75.

Saxenian, A. L. (1994) *Regional Advantage: Culture and Competition in Silicon Valley and Route 128.* Cambridge, MA: Harvard University Press.

Scantlebury, K. (2002) A snake in the nest or in a snake's nest: what counts as peer review for a female educator in a chemistry department? *Research in Science Education*, 32(2): 157–62.

Schafft, K. A. and Brown, D. L. (2000) Social capital and grassroots development: the case of Roma self-governance in Hungary. *Social Problems*, 47(2): 201–19.

Schoenbach, V. J., Kaplan, B. G., Freedman, L. and Kleinbaum, D. (1986) Social ties and mortality in Evans County, Georgia. *American Journal of Epidemiology*, 123: 577–91.

Schuller, T., Baron, S. and Field, J. (2000) Social capital: a review and critique. In Baron, S., Field, J. and Schuller, T. (eds) *Social Capital: Critical Perspectives*. Oxford: Oxford University Press.

Schur, L., Shields, T., Kruse, D. and Schriner, K. (2002) Enabling democracy: disability and voter turnout. *Political Research Quarterly*, 55(1): 167–90.

Schweitzer, J. H., Kim, J. W. and Mackin, J. R. (1999) The impact of the built environment on crime and fear of crime in urban neighborhoods. *Journal of Urban Technology*, 6(3): 59–73.

Scott, B. and Sexton, K. (2002) Promoting pollution prevention through community–industry dialogues: the good neighbor model in Minnesota. *Environmental Science and Technology*, 36(10): 2130–7.

Scott, K. (1993) *Monster: The Autobiography of an L.A. Gang Member*. New York: Atlantic Monthly Press.

Selye, H. (1956) *The Stress of Life*. 2nd edition 1978. New York: McGraw-Hill.

Servadio, G. (1976) *Mafioso: A History of the Mafia from its Origins to the Present Day*. New York: Stein and Day.

Shaffer, D. R. (2005) *Social and Personality Development* (5th edn). Belmont, CA: Brooks/Cole.

Shah, D. V., McLeod, J. M. and Yoon, S. H. (2001) Communication, context, and community: an exploration of print, broadcast, and internet influences. *Communication Research*, 28(4): 464–506.

Shane, S. and Cable, D. (2002) Network ties, reputation, and the financing of new ventures. *Management Science*, 48(3): 364–81.

Shane, S. and Stuart, T. (2002) Organisational endowments and the performance of university start-ups. *Management Science*, 48(1): 154–70.

Sharp, D., Hay, D., Pawlby, S., Schmucher, G., Allen, H. and Kumar, R. (1995) The impact of postnatal depression on boys' intellectual development. *Journal of Child Psychology and Psychiatry*, 36: 1315–37.

Sherbourne, C. D., Hayes, R. D. and Wells, K. B. (1995) Personal and psychological risk factors for physical and mental health outcomes and course of depression amongst depressed patients. *Journal of Consulting and Clinical Psychology*, 63(3): 345–55.

Sherif, M. (1956) Experiments in group conflict. *Scientific American*, 195(5): 54–8.

Sherif, M. and Sherif, C. W. (1953) *Groups in Harmony and Tension: An Integration of Studies on Intergroup Relations*. New York: Harper.

Shiverly, C. A., Clarkson, T. B. and Kalpan, J. R. (1989) Social deprivation and coronary artery atherosclerosis in female cynomolgus monkey. *Atherosclerosis*, 77: 69–76.

Sigelman, C. K. and Shaffer, D. R. (1995) *Life-Span Human Development* (2nd edn). Belmont, CA: Brooks/Cole.

Silver, H. (1993) National conceptions of the new urban poverty: social structural change in Britain, France and the United States. *International Journal of Urban and Regional Research*, 17(3): 336–54.

Silver, H. (1994) *Social Exclusion and Social Solidarity: Three Paradigms.* Geneva: International Institute for Labour Studies.

Simcha-Fagan, O. and Schwartz, J. E. (1986) Neighborhood and delinquency: an assessment of contextual effects. *Criminology,* 24(4): 667–703.

Simmons, J. and Dodd, T. (2003) (eds) *Crime in England and Wales 2002/2003.* London: Home Office.

Simon, C. A. and Wang, C. H. (2002) The impact of AmeriCorps service on volunteer participants: results from a 2-year study in four western states. *Administration and Society,* 34(5): 522–40.

Simpson, A. E. and Stevenson-Hinde, J. (1985) Temperamental characteristics of three- to four-year-old boys and girls and child–family interactions. *Journal of Child Psychology and Psychiatry and Allied Disciplines,* 26(1): 43–53.

Six, P. (1997a) *Escaping Poverty: From Safety Nets to Networks of Opportunity.* London: Demos.

Six, P. (1997b) Social exclusion: time to be optimistic. *Demos Collection,* 12: 3–9.

Sklair, L. (1995) *Sociology of the Global System* (2nd edn). Baltimore, MD: Johns Hopkins University Press.

Skogan, W. G. and Hartnett, S. M. (1997) *Community Policing, Chicago Style.* New York: Oxford University Press.

Skogan, W. G., Hartnett, S. M., DuBois, J. et al. (2000) *Public Involvement: Community Policing in Chicago.* Washington, DC: US National Institute of Justice, Office of Justice Programs.

Skrabski, A., Kopp, M. and Kawachi, I. (2003) Social capital in a changing society: cross-sectional associations with middle aged female and male mortality rates. *Journal of Epidemiology and Community Health,* 5(2): 114–19.

Small, L. A. (2002) Social capital for development: what does it mean if there isn't any? A case study of agricultural producers in Dmitrov Rayon, Russia. *Canadian Journal of Development Studies,* 23(1): 7–25.

Smith, A. ([1776] 1979) *The Wealth of Nations.* Oxford: Clarendon Press.

Smith, B. W., Novak, K. J. and Hurley, D. C. (1997) Neighborhood crime prevention: the influences of community-based organizations and neighborhood watch. *Journal of Crime and Justice,* 20(2): 69–86.

Smith, C. J. (1984) Geographical approaches to mental health. In Freeman, H. (ed.) *Mental Health and the Built Environment.* London: Churchill-Livingstone.

Smith, D. J. (1992) *Understanding the Underclass.* London: Policy Studies Institute.

Smith, D. J. (1995) Youth crime and conduct disorder: trends, patterns and causal explanations. In Rutter, M. and Smith, D. (1995) *Psychosocial Disorder in Young People: Time Trends and their Causes.* Chichester: John Wiley.

Smith, E. S. (1999) The effects of investments in the social capital of youth on political and civic behaviour in young adulthood: a longitudinal analysis. *Political Psychology,* 20(3): 553–80.

Smith, S. S. and Kulynych, J. (2002) It may be social, but why is it capital? The social construction of social capital and the politics of language. *Politics and Society,* 30(1): 149–86.

Snow, R. E. (1995) Pygmalion and intelligence? *Current Directions in Psychological Science,* 4(6): 169–71.

Social Exclusion Unit (1997) *Social Exclusion Unit: Purpose, Work Priorities and Working Methods*. London: Cabinet Office.

Soobader, M. J. and LeClerc, F. B. (1999) Aggregation and the measurement of income inequality: effects on morbidity. *Social Science and Medicine*, 48(6): 733–44.

Soskolne, V. and Shtarkshall, R. A. (2002) Migration and HIV prevention programmes: linking structural factors, culture, and individual behaviour – an Israeli experience. *Social Science and Medicine*, 55(8): 1297–307.

Soubeyran, A. and Weber, S. (2002) District formation and local social capital: a (tacit) co-opetition approach. *Journal of Urban Economics*, 52(1): 65–92.

Spangnolo, G. (1999) Social relations and co-operation in organizations. *Journal of Economic Behavior and Organization*, 38: 1–26.

Spiegel, D. (1993) *Living Beyond Limits: New Hope and Help for Facing Life-Threatening Illness*. New York: Times Books.

Spies-Butcher, B. (2002) Tracing the rational choice origins of social capital: is social capital a neo-liberal 'trojan horse'? *Australian Journal of Social Issues*, 37(2): 173–92.

Stansfled, F. (1997) Relating the concepts of organisational commitment and quality of life. Paper presented to the NEXUS Quality of Life Group.

Steinberg, L., Darling, N. E. and Fletcher, A. C. (1995) Authoritative parenting and adolescent adjustment: an ecological journey. In Moen, P., Elder, G. H. et al. (eds) *Examining Lives in Context: Perspectives on the Ecology of Human Development*. Washington, DC: American Psychological Association.

Stigler, J. W. and Hiebert, J. (1999) *The Teaching Gap: Best Ideas from the World's Teachers for Improving Education in the Classroom*. New York: Free Press.

Stolle, D. (1998) Bowling together, bowling alone: the development of generalized trust in voluntary associations. *Political Psychology*, 19(3): 49–525.

Stolle, D. and Hooghe, M. (2003) *Generating Social Capital: Civil Society and Institutions in Comparative Context*. Basingstoke: Palgrave.

Stone, L. (1977) *The Family, Sex and Marriage in England, 1500–1800*. London: Weidenfeld and Nicolson.

Strang, H. and Vernon, J. (1992) *International Trends in Crime: East meets West*. Canberra: Australian Institute of Criminology. Distributed in North America by Criminal Justice Press, Monsey, NY.

Struch, N. and Schwartz, S. H. (1989) Intergroup aggression: its predictors and distinctness from in-group bias. *Journal of Personality and Social Psychology*, 56(3): 364–73.

Sullivan, A. (2001) Cultural capital and educational attainment. *Sociology*, 35(4): 893–912.

Sullivan, J. L. and Transue, J. E. (1999) The psychological underpinnings of democracy: a selective review of research on political tolerance, interpersonal trust, and social capital. *Annual Review of Psychology*, 50: 625–50.

Sullivan, J. L., Borgida, E., Jackson, M. S., Riedel, E. and Oxendine, A. R. (2002) A tale of two towns: assessing the role of political resources in a community electronic network. *Political Behavior*, 24(1): 55–84.

Sun, L. and Jiang, Q. (2000) Community values according to the I-Ching. *International Journal of Social Economics*, 27(1–2): 99–113.

Sun, Y. (1998) The academic success of East-Asian American students: an investment model. *Social Science Research*, 27(4): 432–56.

Sun, Y. (1999) The contextual effects of community social capital on academic performance. *Social Science Research*, 28: 403–26.

Sundstrom, E. D. (1986) *Work Places: The Psychology of the Physical Environment in Offices and Factories*. Cambridge: Cambridge University Press.

Suomi, S. J. (1997) Early determinants of behaviour: evidence from primate studies. *British Medical Bulletin*, 53: 170–84.

Szreter, S. (1999) *A New Political Economy for New Labour: The Importance of Social Capital*. Policy paper 15. Political Economy Research Centre, University of Sheffield.

Szreter, S. (2002) The state of social capital: bringing back in power, politics, and history. *Theory and Society*, 31(5): 573–621.

Tajfel, H. (1970) Experiments in intergroup discrimination. *Scientific American*, 223: 96–102.

Tajfel, H. (1981) *Human Groups and Social Categories: Studies in Social Psychology*. Cambridge: Cambridge University Press.

Taylor, M. (2002) Enterprise, embeddedness and exclusion: business and development in Fiji. *Tijdschrift voor Economische en Sociale Geografie*, 93(3): 302–15.

Taylor, S. and Taylor, B. (1996) Transport and the environment. In Halpern, D. S., Wood, S., White, S. and Cameron G. (eds) *Options for Britain: A Strategic Policy Review*. Dartmouth: Aldershot.

Taylor-Gooby, P. (forthcoming) Markets and motives: trust and egoism in welfare markets.

Teachman, J. D., Paasch, K. and Carver, K. (1996) Social capital and dropping out of school early. *Journal of Marriage and the Family*, 58: 773–83.

Teachman, J. D., Paasch, K. and Carver, K. (1997) Social capital and the generation of human capital. *Social Forces*, 75(4): 1343–59.

Temple, J. (1998) Initial conditions, social capital and growth in Africa. *Journal of African Economics*, 7(3): 309–47.

Temple, J. and Johnson, P. A. (1998) Social capability and economic growth. *Quarterly Journal of Economics*, 113(3): 965–90.

Therell, T., Blomkvist, V., Jonsson, H., Schulman, S., Berntorp, E. and Stegendal, L. (1995) Social support and the development of immune function in human immunodeficiency virus infection. *Psychosomatic Medicine*, 57: 32–6.

Thomas, C. B. and Duszynski, K. R. (1974) Closeness to parents and the family constellation in a prospective study of five disease states: suicide, mental illness, malignant tumor, hypertension, and coronary heart disease. *John Hopkins Medical Journal*, 134: 251.

Thompson, B. and Aikens, S. (1998) If only Jefferson had email. *New Statesman*, 20 February.

Thomson, R., Henderson, S. and Holland, J. (2003) Making the most of what you've got? Resources, values and inequalities in young women's transitions to adulthood. *Educational Review*, 55(1): 33–46.

Titmuss, R. M. (1970) *The Gift Relationship*. London: Allen and Unwin.

Tolbert, C. J., Lowenstein, D. and Donovan, T. (1998) Election law and rules for using initiatives. In Bowler, S., Donovan, T. and Tolbert, L. (eds) *Citizens as Legislators: Direct Democracy in the United States*. Columbus, OH: Ohio State University Press.

Tonn, B. E., Zambrano, P. and Moore, S. (2001) Community networks or networked communities? *Social Science Computer Review*, 19(2): 201–12.

Torney-Purta, J. (2002) The school's role in developing civic engagement: a study of adolescents in twenty-eight countries. *Applied Developmental Science*, 6(4): 203–12.

Torney-Purta, J., Lehmann, R., Oswald, H. and Schulz, W. (2001) *Citizenship and Education in Twenty-Eight Countries: Civic Knowledge and Engagement at Age Fourteen*. Amsterdam: International Association for the Evaluation of Educational Achievement (IEA).

Trasler, G. B. (1980) Aspects of causality, culture and crime. Paper presented at the 4th International Seminar at the International Center of Sociological, Penal and Penitentiary Research and Studies, Messina.

Treisman, D. (2000) The causes of corruption: a cross-national study. *Journal of Public Economics*, 76(3): 399–457.

Trower, P., Gilbert, P. and Sherling, G. (1990) Social anxiety, evolution and self-presentation. In Leitenberg, H. (ed.) *Handbook of Social and Evaluation Anxiety*. New York: Plenum Press.

Tufarelli, C. and Fagotto, E. (1999) Operationalising the social capital hypothesis for development finance. *Economic Analysis*, 2(3): 223–44.

Tyler, K. A., Hoyt, D. R. and Whitbeck, L. B. (2000) The effects of early sexual abuse on later sexual victimization among female homeless and runaway adolescents. *Journal of Interpersonal Violence*, 15(3): 235–50.

UCLA (2003) *The UCLA Internet Report: Surveying the Digital Future*. http://ccp.ucla.edu/pdf/UCLA-Internet-Report-Year-Three.pdf

Urry, J. (2002) Mobility and proximity. *Sociology: The Journal of the British Sociological Association*, 36(2): 255–74.

US Senate Special Committee on Aging (1993) *Consumer Fraud and the Elderly: Easy Prey?* Washington, DC: US Government Printing Office.

Useem, E. L., Christman, J. B., Gold, E. and Simon, E. (1997) Reforming alone: barriers to organisational learning in urban school change initiatives. *Journal of Education for Students Placed at Risk*, 2(1): 55–78.

Uslaner, E. M. (1998) Social capital, television, and the 'mean world': trust, optimism, and civic participation. *Political Psychology*, 19(3): 441–67.

Uzzi, B. (1997) Social structure and competition in interfirm networks: the paradox of embeddedness. *Administrative Science Quarterly*, 42: 35–67.

Uzzi, B. (1999) Embeddedness in the making of financial capital: how social relations and networks benefit firms seeking financing. *American Sociological Review*, 64(4): 481–505.

Valadez, J. R. (2002) The influence of social capital on mathematics course selection by Latino high school students. *Hispanic Journal of Behavioural Sciences*, 24(3): 319–39.

Valentine, S. and Fleischman, G. (2002) Ethics codes and professionals' tolerance of societal diversity. *Journal of Business Ethics*, 40(4): 301–12.

Valenzuela, A. and Dornbusch, S. M. (1994) Familism and social capital in the academic achievement of Mexican origin and Anglo adolescents. *Social Science Quarterly*, 15(1): 18–36.

Van Deth, J. W. (2000) Interesting but irrelevant: social capital and the saliency of politics in Western Europe. *European Journal of Political Research*, 37: 115–47.

Van-de-Klundert, T. (1999) Economic efficiency and ethics. *De Economist*, 147(2): 127–49.

Vaughn, C. E. and Leff, J. P. (1976) The influence of family and social factors on the course of psychiatric illness: a comparison of schizophrenic and depressed neurotic patients. *British Journal of Psychiatry*, 129: 125–37.

Veenhoven, R. (1991) Is happiness relative? *Social Indicators Research*, 24: 1–34.

Veenstra, G. (2000) Social capital, SES and health: an individual level analysis. *Social Science and Medicine*, 50(5): 619–29.

Veenstra, G. (2002a) Social capital and health (plus wealth, income inequality and regional health governance). *Social Science and Medicine*, 54(6): 849–68.

Veenstra, G. (2002b) Explicating social capital: trust and participation in the civil space. *Canadian Journal of Sociology*, 27(4): 547–72.

Veiga, J. F. et al. (2000) Using neural network analysis to uncover the trace effects of national culture. *Journal of International Business Studies*, 31(2): 223–38.

Voas, D. (2003) Intermarriage and the demography of secularization. *British Journal of Sociology*, 54(1): 83–108.

Vogt, T. M., Mullooly, J. P., Ernst, D., Pope, C. R. and Hollis, J. F. (1992) Social networks as predictors of ischemic heart disease, cancer, stroke and hypertension: incidence, survival and mortality. *Journal of Clinical Epidemiology*, 45: 659–66.

Vuille, J. C. and Schenkel, M. (2002) Psychosocial determinants of smoking in Swiss adolescents with special reference to school stress and social capital in schools. *Sozial und Praventivmedizin*, 47(4): 240–50.

Wacquant, L. J. D. (1998) Negative social capital: state breakdown and social destitution in America's urban core. *Netherlands Journal of Housing and the Built Environment*, 13(1): 25–40.

Waldinger, R., Aldrich, H. and Ward, R. (1990) *Ethnic Entrepreneurs*. London: Sage.

Walker, R. (1998) Unpicking poverty. In Oppenheim, C. (ed.) *An Inclusive Society: Strategies for Tackling Poverty*. London: IPPR.

Wallace, R. and Wallace, D. (1997) Community marginalisation and the diffusion of disease and disorder in the United States. *British Medical Journal*, 314: 1341–5.

Wallerstein, N. (2002) Empowerment to reduce health disparities. *Scandinavian Journal of Public Health*, 30(3): 72–7.

Wallis, J. and Dollery, B. (2001) Government failure, social capital and the appropriateness of the New Zealand model for public sector reform in developing countries. *World Development*, 29(2): 245–63.

Wallis, J. and Dollery, B. (2002) Social capital and local government capacity. *Australian Journal of Public Administration*, 61(3): 76–85.

Walmsley, D. J. (1988) *Urban Living*. Harlow: Longman.

Wang, H. Z. and Hsiao, H. H. M. (2002) Social capital or human capital? Professionals in overseas Taiwanese firms. *Journal of Contemporary Asia*, 32(3), 346–62.

Warr, P. (1987) *Work, Unemployment and Mental Health*. Oxford: Clarendon Press.

Watson, G. W. and Papamarcos, S. D. (2002) Social capital and organisational commitment. *Journal of Business and Psychology*, 16(4): 537–52.

Watt, R. G. (2002) Emerging theories into the social determinants of health: implications for oral health promotion. *Community Dentistry and Oral Epidemiology*, 30(4): 241–7.

Watts, F. and Morant, N. (2001) Health and illness. In Fraser, C. and Burchell, B. (eds) *Introducing Social Psychology*. Cambridge: Polity.

Webb, J. (1996) *Direct Line Homesafe*. Nottingham: Janice Webb Research. Unpublished report for Crime Concern.

Webb, V. J. and Katz, C. M. (1997) Citizen ratings of the importance of community policing activities. *Policing: An International Journal of Police Strategies and Management*, 20(1): 7–23.

Wedmore, K. and Freeman, H. (1984) Social pathology and urban overgrowth. In Freeman, H. (ed.) *Mental Illness and the Built Environment*. London: Churchill Livingstone.

Weijland, H. (1999) Microenterprise clusters in rural Indonesia: industrial seedbed and policy target. *World Development*, 27(9): 1515–30.

Weiner, B. (1979) A theory of motivation for some classroom experiences. *Journal of Educational Psychology*, 71: 3–25.

Welin, L., Tibblin, G., Svardsudd, K., Tibblin, B., Ander-Peciva, S., Larsson, B. and Wilhelmsen, L. (1985) Prospective study of social influences on mortality: the study of men born in 1913 and 1923. *Lancet*, 1: 915–18.

Wenger, G. C. (1997) Nurturing networks. *Demos Collection*, 12: 28–9.

West, A. and McCormick, J. (1998) Citizens' involvement in combating poverty at local level. In Oppenheim, C. (ed.) *An Inclusive Society: Strategies for Tackling Poverty*. London: IPPR.

West, M. D. (2002) The resolution of karaoke disputes: the calculus of institutions and social capital. *Journal of Japanese Studies*, 28(2): 301–37.

Whitbeck, L. B. and Hoyt, D. R. (1999) *Nowhere to Grow: Homeless and Runaway Adolescents and their Families*. Hawthorne, NY: Aldine de Gruyter.

White, M. (1991) *Against Unemployment*. London: Policy Studies Institute.

Whitehead, A. (forthcoming) Recovering communitarianism. Paper circulated to NEXUS Quality of Life group.

Whiteley, P. (1997) *Economic Growth and Social Capital*. Sheffield: Political Economy Research Centre.

Whiteley, P. (1998) The origins of social capital. Paper presented to Political Studies Association workshop on 'Social Capital Theory and its Implications for Policy and for Comparative Research'. Bath University, 6 November.

Whyley, C., McCormick, J. and Kempson, E. (1998) *Paying for Peace of Mind: Access to Home Contents Insurance for Low-Income Households*. London: Policy Studies Institute.

Wilkinson, R. G. (1996) *Unhealthy Societies: The Afflictions of Inequality*. London: Routledge.

Wilkinson, R. G. (1997) Income, inequality, and social cohesion. *American Journal of Public Health*, 87: 104–6.

Wilkinson, R. G. (2000) Social capital, economic capital and power: further issues for a public health agenda. *Journal of Epidemiology and Community Health*, 54: 409–13.

Williams, A. W., Ware, J. E. and Donald, C. A. (1981) A model of mental health, life events, and social supports applicable to general populations. *Journal of Health and Social Behaviour*, 22: 324–36.

Williams, J. (1997) On the dynamic decision to participate in crime. Dissertation, Rice University. Ann Arbor, MI: University Microfilms International.

Williams, J. and Sickles, R. C. (2002) An analysis of the crime as work model: evidence from the 1958 Philadelphia birth cohort study. *Journal of Human Resources*, 37(3): 479–509.

Willmott, P. (1963) *The Evolution of a Community*. London: Routledge and Kegan Paul.

Willms, J. D. (2000) Three hypotheses about community effects relevant to the contribution of human and social capital to sustaining economic growth and well-being. Paper prepared for the OECD International Symposium on 'The Contribution of Human and Social Capital to Sustained Economic Growth and Well-Being', March.

Wilson, P. N. (2000) Social capital, trust, and the agribusiness of economics. *Journal of Agricultural and Resource Economics*, 25(1): 1–13.

Wilson, W. J. (1987) *The Truly Disadvantaged: The Inner City, the Underclass, and Public Policy*. Chicago: University of Chicago Press.

Wilson, W. J. (1997) *When Work Disappears: The World of the New Urban Poor*. New York: Alfred A. Knopf.

Wolf, S. and Bruhn, J. G. (1993) *The Power of Clan: The Influence of Human Relationship on Heart Disease*. New Brunswick, NJ: Transaction Publishers.

Wolf, S. A., Borko, H., Elliott, R. L. and McIver, M. C. (2000) 'That dog won't hunt!': exemplary school change efforts within the Kentucky reform. *American Educational Research Journal*, 37(2): 349–93.

Wollebaek, D. and Selle, P. (2002) Does participation in voluntary associations contribute to social capital? The impact of intensity, scope, and type. *Nonprofit and Voluntary Sector Quarterly*, 31(1): 32–61.

Woolcock, M. (1998) Social capital and economic development: towards a theoretical synthesis and policy framework. *Theory and Society*, 27: 151–208.

Woolcock, M. and Narayan, D. (2000) Social capital: implications for development theory, research and policy. *World Bank Research Observer*, 15(2): 225–49.

World Bank (1999) www.worldbank.org/poverty/scapital

World Values Survey www.worldvaluessurvey.org

Worms, J. P. (2000) Old and new civic and social ties in France. In *Society and Civic Spirit (Gesellschaft und Gemeinsinn)*. Gütersloh: Bertelsmann Foundation. Pub. 2002 in Putnam, R. D. (ed.) *Democracies in Flux: The Evolution of Social Capital in Contemporary Society*. Oxford: Oxford University Press.

Yan, W. (1999) Successful African American students: the role of parental involvement. *Journal of Negro Education*, 68(1): 5–22.

Yanay, U. (1994) The 'big brother' function of block watch. *International Journal of Sociology and Social Policy*, 14(9): 44–58.

Yancy, W. (1971) Architecture, interaction, and social control: the case of a large-scale public housing project. *Environment and Behaviour*, 3: 361–70.

Yarwood, R. and Edwards, B. (1995) Voluntary action in rural areas: the case of Neighbourhood Watch. *Journal of Rural Studies*, 11(4): 447–59.

Yin, P. (1982) Fear of crime as a problem for the elderly. *Social Problems*, 30(2): 240–5.

Young, M. and Willmott, P. (1957) *Family and Kinship in East London*. London: Routledge and Kegan Paul.

Zacharakis-Jutz, J. (2001) Strategic planning in rural town meetings: issues related to citizen participation and democratic decision making. In Campbell, P. and Burnaby, B. (eds) *Participatory Practices in Adult Education*. Mahwah, NJ: Erlbaum Associates.

Zajonc, R. B. and Markus, G. B. (1975) Birth order and intellectual development. *Psychological Review*, 82(1): 74–88.

Zimbardo, P. G. (1971) *The Psychological Power and Pathology of Imprisonment*. Statement prepared for the US House of Representatives Committee on the Judiciary. Ceremonial Courtroom, San Francisco.

Zoccolillo, M., Pickles, A., Quinton, D. and Rutter, M. (1992) The outcome of childhood conduct disorder: implications for defining adult personality disorder and conduct disorder. *Psychological Medicine*, 22: 971–86.

Zweigenhaft, R. L. (1993) Prep school and public school graduates of Harvard: a longitudinal study of the accumulation of social and cultural capital. *Journal of Higher Education*, 64(2): 211–25.

Index